Young Adult Fiction by African American Writers, 1968–1993

GARLAND REFERENCE LIBRARY OF THE HUMANITIES
VOLUME 1606

Young Adult Fiction by African American Writers, 1968–1993

A Critical and Annotated Guide

Deborah Kutenplon
Ellen Olmstead

Garland Publishing, Inc.
New York and London
1996

96-466

Library of Congress Cataloging-in-Publication Data

Kutenplon, Deborah.
  Young adult fiction by African American writers, 1968–1993 : a critical
and annotated guide / by Deborah Kutenplon and Ellen Olmstead.
      p.   cm. — (Garland reference library of the humanities ; vol.
1606)
    Includes indexes.
    ISBN 0-8153-0873-6 (alk. paper)
    1. Young adult fiction, American—Afro-American authors—Bibliogra-
phy. 2. Young adult fiction, American—Afro-American authors—Book reviews. 3. Young adults—United States—Books and reading. 4. American
fiction—20th century—Bibliography. 5. Afro-Americans in literature—Bibliography. 6. Afro-American youth—Books and reading. 7. Best books—
Bibliography. I. Olmstead, Ellen. II. Title. III. Series.
PS153.N5K88   1996
813'.540809283—dc20   95-20051
                                                                      CIP

Cover Design: Lawrence Wolfson Design, NY

Cover photo of Walter Dean Myers (top) provided by HarperCollins Publishers, Inc.
Cover photo of Candy Dawson Boyd (middle) reprinted with the permission
    of Simon & Schuster Books for Young Readers.
Cover photo of Harriette Gillem Robinet (bottom) reprinted with the permission
    of Atheneum Books for Young Readers. Photo by McLouis Robinet.

Printed on acid-free, 250-year-life paper
Manufactured in the United States of America

To the students at Martin Luther King, Jr.,
High School in New York and
Charles H. Hickey, Jr., School in Baltimore

and

To Amy Richlin and Rhonda Cobham-Sander for your teaching,
mentoring, and friendship

Contents

Preface

Young Adult Fiction by African American Writers, 1968-1993: A Critical and Annotated Guide is as comprehensive and current as possible, including all fiction titles published between 1968 and 1993 by African American authors and targeted toward young adult readers—166 titles by 57 authors. Only works of fiction—historical fiction, modern realistic fiction, fantasy and science fiction, and mystery and suspense— by African American authors and centering on African American protagonists are included. We chose 1968 as a cutoff year because earlier works tend to be out of print or dated. Several factors precipitated by 1968 a momentous, albeit short-lived, boom in the publishing of African American children's and young adult literature. Every effort has been made to locate and evaluate books published by large and small presses. If we missed a book, please let us know!

While some of the world's most celebrated African American authors have written novels and stories featuring African American young adult protagonists that are of interest to young adult readers, young adult literature is a special genre, and only books written specifically for, and marketed to, young adults are included in this bibliography. The protagonists of these books are between twelve and nineteen years old, in sixth through twelfth grade, if they are in school. Books without illustrations and at least 100 pages long that feature nine- to eleven-year-old protagonists are also included.

This bibliography follows a traditional format— alphabetical by author, with all titles by each author arranged in order of publication date. The brief Introduction places contemporary young adult fiction by African American

writers in an historical and political context. The annotation
for each title is much longer than annotations found in usual
bibliographies: it reads more like a full-length book review,
presenting the salient themes and plot twists, drawing
attention to minor themes or plot points if they are unique or
problematic. Plus it offers an in-depth critical appraisal of the
novel or story, judging the quality of writing, the appeal and
development of characters, problems, and themes, and its
handling of complex and sensitive cultural, historical, and
sociopolitical issues, where applicable. Each annotation also
includes recommended reader age and gender, based on the
developmental, emotional, and intellectual level of the
intended audience.

　　Scholars in the field of African American literature for
young people are pioneers. Only a handful of critical articles
and books on the subject have been published, most within the
past twenty years. The articles are scattered and the selection
of titles included in them is often random and incomplete.
Previous book-length discussions are dated, since they include
only books published through the mid-1980s. Typically the
critical materials look at African American young adult fiction
in general, examining broad themes and trends within the
whole field of publishing, rather than examining specific
authors and texts closely. The scholarship also tends to focus on
the better known, award-winning authors and their best-selling
titles. Comprehensiveness, currency, and extensive criticism of
individual titles differentiate this bibliography from superb
forerunners of its field: Diane Johnson's *Telling Tales: The
Pedagogy and Promise of African American Literature for
Youth*, Donnarae MacCann and Gloria Woodard's *The Black
American in Books for Children: Readings in Racism*, Barbara
Rollock's *The Black Experience in Children's Books* and *Black
Authors and Illustrators of Children's Books*, Barbara Dodds
Stanford's *Black Literature for High School Students*, Rudine
Sims' *Shadow and Substance: Afro-American Experience in
Children's Fiction*, and Helen E. Williams' *Books by African
American Authors and Illustrators for Children and Young
Adults*.[1]

While it's wonderful that an ever-increasing number of books by African American authors about African American protagonists are being published, it's disturbing that some people promote a book simply because it is "multicultural." We evaluated each book on its literary merits as well as in terms of its direct and indirect treatment of developmental or psychological issues and issues of race, gender, class, ability, age, sexuality, and sexual orientation. Books have the potential to socialize young readers and transmit values to them; books have the potential to affect young readers' self-image, attitudes, and emotional and intellectual development. Our bias is in favor of ambiguity and complexity over preachy propaganda. Pace, character, and a plot focusing on a real life problem are important ingredients of popular young adult fiction:

> Overwhelmingly, . . . students liked books with teen protagonists and stories that might be termed realistic fiction or 'problem' novels. . . . [T]hey liked books that seemed real to them or that involved teens with problems that they themselves had or thought those around them had. They selected books because they liked a writer's style, especially the ability to create an exciting, fast paced story and to make them feel involved in the action through the development of a character. . . . And they selected books because they were interested in a particular subject and wanted to read about it.[2]

An author is an individual, in perspective and voice, and shouldn't be expected to represent a people. Furthermore, one writer or one story can't take on the whole group experience. We don't expect only African American authors to create African American characters; nor do we expect African American authors to write only about African American characters. Being European American doesn't inherently result in writing that's racist, that objectifies or misrepresents African Americans, but, statistically, that's been the trend. A good writer can speak to anyone and write about anyone. And a writer's ethnic or racial identity doesn't guarantee that accuracy or authenticity will come across in her/his storytelling, and, as some of the writers reviewed here prove, it's no insurance against unintentionally expressing internalized racism! However, being an insider automatically certifies that the authorial perspective— popular, palatable, or not—is indeed an indigenous African American one. There's a lot to be said for people speaking for themselves.

In addition, this bibliography focuses on books featuring African American protagonists only by African American authors because their works are underpublished, underpromoted, and largely unrecognized, particularly when compared to the number and commercial success of books about African American characters written by European American authors. Even African American authors who have already published critically and financially successful books recount horror stories of how they do not enjoy equal access to the publishing industry and of the creative limitations publishers attempt to impose upon them. Publishing has mirrored the changes in racial awareness in broader society. In the mid-1960s, only 7% of all children's books published included African American characters; that number increased to 14% in the mid-1970s, following the Civil Rights Movement, but has since dropped again to only 2% today.[3] Currently, on average only 1% of all children's and young adult books published are *written* by an African American, and 20% of these books are published by small presses.[4] Meanwhile, the number of picture books is increasing and the number of novels is decreasing.[5]

This bibliography includes only books which feature African American protagonists, because somewhere in this body of literature African American young adults will recognize themselves and gain a window on the extraordinary diversity and immensity of the African American experience. African American youth, marginalized, miseducated, and villainized by American society, need this validation and education. "Adolescence is a time of very serious work in terms of self-identity and self-worth," and good literature can provide "opportunities and models for learning . . . positive messages about [oneself]," aiding the developmental process and the building of self-esteem.[6]

Not only African American young adults should read the books included in this bibliography, just as African American young adults do not read books only by and about African Americans. The African American experience is a strand inextricably entwined with the American experience, so all young people need to read the best of these books. A Eurocentric curriculum gives young people a misleading conception of the world and their relationship within and to it. Wherever there is an issue of difference, there is a connection to be made, a stereotype to dispel, or a notion of homogeneity to shatter, and the best of these books do it irresistibly and masterfully with grace and passion. The best books simultaneously tackle universal adolescent dilemmas while introducing the reader to an individual protagonist in all her/his particularity and conflict, as a person possessing strengths and weaknesses. Our intention in focusing exclusively on young adult African American fiction is not to further isolate or segregate but to identify and make accessible, to provide a unique resource for the connoisseur and the curious.

The need for these young adult books is obvious. But why this bibliography? We hope that parents, teachers, librarians, bookstore owners, and young people will use this bibliography. Armed with *Young Adult Fiction by African American Writers, 1968-1993: A Critical and Annotated Guide*, visit your school library or local library or your favorite bookstore and take an inventory to see how many of the titles included in this bibliography are available for you to borrow or to buy. Or, survey the curriculum in your school to see how many of these titles are included in the reading list for your classes. The need for this bibliography, whose purpose is to bring your attention to many outstanding but virtually unknown writers, will be painfully clear after this exercise. Ignorance is no longer an excuse! Seek out, borrow or purchase, and promote authentic multicultural literature.

Notes

1. Dianne Johnson, *Telling Tales: The Pedagogy and Promise of African American Literature for Youth* (Westport, CT: Greenwood Press, 1990). Donnarae MacCann and Gloria Woodard, eds., *The Black American in Books for Children: Readings in Racism* (Metuchen, NJ: Scarecrow Press, 1985). Barbara Rollock, ed., *The Black Experience in Children's Books* (New York: New York Public Library, 1984). Barbara Rollock, *Black Authors and Illustrators of Children's Books* (New York: Garland Publishing, 1988). Rudine Sims, *Shadow and Substance: Afro-American Experience in Children's Fiction* (Urbana, IL: National Council of Teachers of English, 1982). Barbara Dodds Stanford, ed., *Black Literature for High School Students* (Urbana, IL: National Council of Teachers of English, 1978). Helen E. Williams, *Black Authors and Illustrators for Children and Young Adults* (Chicago: American Library Association, 1991).

2. Barbara G. Samuels, "Young Adults' Choices: Why Do Students 'Really Like' Particular Books?," *Journal of Reading* 32.8 (May 1989), p. 717.

3. Barbara Dodds Stanford, ed., "Introduction," *Black Literature for High School Students* (Urbana, IL: National Council of Teachers of English, 1978), p. 3.

4. Elizabeth Fitzgerald Howard, "Authentic Multicultural Literature for Children: An Author's Perspective," *The Multicolored Mirror: Cultural Substance in Literature for Children and Young Adults*, Merri V. Lindgren, ed. (Fort Atkinson, WI: Highsmith Press, 1991), p. 93.

5. Rudine Sims Bishop, "Evaluating Books by and about African-Americans," *The Multicolored Mirror: Cultural Substance in Literature for Children and Young Adults*, Merri V. Lindgren, ed. (Fort Atkinson, WI: Highsmith Press, 1991), p. 34.

6. Virginia M. Henderson, "The Development of Self-Esteem in Children of Color," *The Multicolored Mirror: Cultural Substance in Literature for Children and Young Adults,* Merri V. Lindgren, ed. (Fort Atkinson, WI: Highsmith Press, 1991), p. 20-24.

Acknowledgments

We are grateful to Suellen and Albert Kutenplon for your generous support, and to Charles Olmstead and Bob Mansfield for bailing us out of a desperate computer crisis. Thank you also to our editors, Marie Ellen Larcada and Phyllis Korper.

Introduction

What is the history of young adult fiction featuring African American protagonists written by African American authors? American children's literature, which emerged as a distinct genre last century, "has a long, sorry history" of "cultural substance, authenticity, and accuracy" where books about African Americans are concerned. Over one hundred years of children's literature, created predominantly by and for European Americans, usually grossly misrepresented the personal and collective realities of African Americans, and "offered inaccurate and hurtful images."[1] The prevalent stereotypes included: "'the contented slave,' 'the wretched freeman,' 'the comic Negro,' 'the brute Negro,' 'the tragic mulatto,' 'the local-color Negro,' and 'the exotic primitive.'"[2]

The tradition of literature created by African Americans for children of all races likewise spans more than a century. Its "tumultuous past" included: "limited awareness among readers; circumscribed publication and distribution; omission from libraries, schools, and bookstores; and uninformed criticism."[3] Pinpointing the exact starting date and a complete list of titles for the African American tradition of children's literature is difficult, for few texts survived of those produced by African American economic, fraternal and sororal, religious, and social organizations, reputedly the principal producers of curriculum materials targeted toward African American children.

In light of the pivotal role that the church played in promoting education and literacy, the publication of children's literature by African American religious organizations takes on greater significance; the dearth of relics greater sadness. From 1887-1889, Mrs. A.E. Johnson edited and marketed a magazine for African American children, *The Joy*, that delivered a message of "racial uplift"; published by the European American-administered Baptist Publication Society, *The Joy* featured African American characters in church-oriented stories. In 1896, its first year of operation, The National Baptist Publishing Board, headed by Richard Henry Boyd, published 700,000 church school materials geared toward African American youth, centered around Bible stories and religious moral teachings.[4]

The oldest extant children's literature created by African Americans does not qualify for consideration in this bibliography: Mrs. A.E. Johnson's novel, *Clarence and Corinne, or, God's Way*, published in 1889, features European American protagonists; Paul Laurence Dunbar's *Little Brown Baby*, published in 1896, is a collection of dialect poems. In the 1800s, few African American children were literate, and "few could have encountered the texts in their schooling because major strictures were placed on funding, curricula, and type of schooling provided for African Americans."[5]

But in the 1900s, an emerging formally educated, literate, African American middle class "demanded culturally authentic literature" for their children, fueling the expansion of that tradition. "Enhancement of the new tradition also necessitated the emergence of an educated group of persons interested in writing as a vocation or avocation. It also depended on the further development of African American publishers and changes in attitudes among White publishers."[6] These necessary preconditions were met by 1920, when W.E.B. DuBois and Augustus G. Dill formed the DuBois and Dill Publishing Company, which produced Elizabeth Ross Haynes' twenty-two volume biography series of African Americans called *Unsung Heroes*, and *The Brownies' Book*, a multidisciplinary, multigenre, African diaspora-centered newsmagazine "designed to inform, educate, and politicize children and their parents and to showcase the achievements of people of color" and edited by Jessie R. Fauset.[7] *The Brownies' Book*, set within an African American cultural context, but accessible to children of all races, was the premier periodical for African American children until *Ebony Jr.!* ,

edited by Constance Johnson, appeared in 1973. *The Brownies'*
Book sought to inculcate race and class consciousness, pride in
African roots and African American heritage, African
American unity, family loyalty, and respect for basic values
and education. It provided role models, entertainment, and
inspired readers toward activism, "racial uplift and
sacrifice."[8] *The Brownies' Book* struggled financially and
folded after two years, in 1922, with a circulation of 4,000.[9] In
the tradition of *The Brownies' Book*, the less classist, but also
less feminist and internationalist *Ebony Jr!* accentuated the
positive and praised "moderation." It likewise succumbed to
financial constraints and folded after ten years, in 1985,
peaking at a circulation of 100,000.[10] Although a different
genre, these children's magazines best represent the beginning
of an African American tradition of children's and young adult
fiction, for they provided a forum and support for artists of the
Harlem Renaissance of the 1920s and 1930s and the Black Arts
Movement of the 1960s and the 1970s to write fiction
specifically for African American young people.

Carter G. Woodson, whose legacy includes establishing
Negro History Week, which became Black History Month, and
the Association for the Study of Negro Life and History,
founded the Associated Publishers in 1920 to produce literature
"explicitly designed to educate, entertain, and emancipate,"
and he authored groundbreaking textbooks, beginning with *The
Negro in Our History*, in 1922.[11] Woodson's project specialized
in non-fiction, however.

Arna Bontemps and Langston Hughes published
children's books, beginning in 1932 with their joint juvenile
picture book venture, *Popo and Fifina: Children of Haiti*.
Critics characterize Bontemps, with his sixteen books for
children, as "the contemporary 'father' of African American
children's literature."[12] However, "father" seems a misnomer
within the context of the African American tradition of
literature for young people, for, as the aforementioned firsts
indicate, women pioneered as authors and editors. Bontemps
geared his fiction toward young children, his non-fiction and
poetry toward young adults. His only publication that might

qualify as an early work of young adult fiction is *We Have Tomorrow*, true stories of twelve barrier-breaking African Americans, published in 1945, with its style resembling historical fiction. Hughes concentrated first on poetry for young adults, then on non-fiction Afrocentric geography, history, and music, with his *First Books of...* series, beginning in 1952. Backed by major European American publishers and addressing children of all races as their audience, Bontemps and Hughes enjoyed unrivalledly successful readership and book sales. Not coincidentally, their work signals a "shift from an emphasis on explicit racial themes and consciousness . . . to a more assimilationist posture utilizing only subtle racial undertones."[13]

The assimilationist bent of the literature of the 1940s and 1950s corresponds with the thrust for integration that occurred during that era. Lorenz Graham and Jesse Jackson established the foundation for African American young adult fiction with their first assimilationist yet pioneering novels, *South Town* and *Call Me Charley*, published in 1945 and 1958, respectively. At the same time, Shirley Graham wrote a quasi-historical fiction biography series, beginning with *There Once Was a Slave: The Heroic Story of Frederick Douglass*, in 1947, as did Ann Petry, beginning with *Harriet Tubman, Conductor on the Underground Railroad*, in 1955.

In carefully choosing themes and characters to contradict stereotypes in their own writing, African American publishers and authors of the 1910s and 1920s implicitly critiqued European American children's literature by creating "oppositional texts," i.e., "works that contradict a theme, motif, or stereotype."[14] In the early 1940's, Augusta Baker and Charlemae Rollins ushered in the formal critical movement in African American children's literature. Coordinators of Children's Services at the New York Public Library, Baker and her successor Barbara Rollock influenced the movement for critical analysis of African American children's books for forty years, starting in 1944, producing annotated bibliographies, essays, reports, and studies on images of African Americans in children's literature and publishing trends. Their work spurred the publishing of African American children's authors. Under their direction, the New York Public Library published *The Black Experience in Children's Books* beginning in 1950. Charlemae Rollins, Children's Librarian for the Chicago Public Library, under the auspices of the National Council of Teachers of English, published annotated recommendation lists entitled *We Build Together: A Reader's Guide to Negro Life and Literature for Elementary and High School Use*, beginning in 1941. In 1965, the *Saturday Review* published a landmark study conducted by educator Nancy Larrick; Larrick's article, "The All-White World of Children's Books," shamed publishers into producing more multicultural books and spurred buyers and readers to demand more multicultural books from publishers.

In 1967, Bradford Chambers founded the Council on Interracial Books for Children, "a powerful force for change," in New York City.[15] The *Bulletin of the Council on Interracial Books for Children* "provided a forum for socially conscious criticism of children's books" through articles and reviews— often deservedly harsh and confrontational—by content specialists, which played an instrumental role in improving images of African Americans in children's books. In addition, the bulletin sponsored contests for unpublished African American writers and illustrators, which sparked the careers of the core of best-known authors included in this bibliography.[16] In 1969, African American librarians "seeking to formally acknowledge excellence in published writing by Black authors of books for children and young adults" established the Coretta Scott King Award, administered through the Social Responsibilities Round Table of the American Library Association.

Surging Civil Rights and Black Nationalist activism, urban riots in response to injustice and violence, heightened awareness within the educational and publishing establishments of racial crisis and racism, and African American librarians' assault on European American publishers and authors' distortions and omissions of African Americans in young people's literature brought the ongoing struggle between "cultural imperialism" and "self-affirmation" to a productive head.[17] The majority of books featuring African American characters published through the 1960s were written by European American authors, from a Eurocentric perspective and geared toward a European American audience: they wrote about African American children for European American children. Publishers, committed to selling books, not to creating images or influencing attitudes, operated on the assumption of a white primary audience or market, which influenced the authorship, theme, and content of their projects. European American authors wrote about active, central white characters who befriend or "help" sketchy, passive African American characters in a setting where benevolent European Americans are colorblind or pitying.

The best-intended of books written by European American authors in the 1960s and 1970s and featuring African American young people as protagonists leave much to be desired. Categorizable as "social conscience" books, "which are mainly those characterized . . . as being about Blacks and written to help whites to know the condition of their fellow humans," and "melting pot" books, "which . . . were written for both Black and white readers on the assumption that both need to be informed that nonwhite children are exactly like other American children, except for the color of their skins," are products of an era that prescribed integration as the panacea to widespread social problems.[18] Some black writers, miraculously oblivious to racism or eager to get published, obliged, creating characters who met "white middle-class standards" of manners, dress, and speech in order to be acceptable and accepted. The "social conscience" books served a purpose: they increased visibility of African Americans in young adult literature. "Their topics were timely, highlighting prominent social issues of concern to everyone," but the literary quality of the bulk of these books "is poor enough to suggest that had they not been timely, they might not have been published at all."[19] "Melting pot" books, which "make a point of recognizing our universality . . . [and] make a point of ignoring our differences, . . . do not concern themselves with racial prejudice, discrimination, or conflict."[20] The "melting pot" books:

> ... create that imaginary, racially integrated social order in which ... [blacks and whites] live and work together harmoniously, and in which [blacks] have assimilated and have been assimilated into the larger white cultural milieu. ... On one level, to project such a social order is a positive act. It permits one to assume a primary audience of both Black and white readers. ... It also allows for the integration of the all-white world of children's books. ... On some other level, however, ... the ignoring of differences becomes a signal that the recognition of them makes people uncomfortable or unhappy. ... [T]he implication is that ... differences ... signify something undesirable. To ignore ... [specific characteristics or differences of a] group of children may be another means of conferring a kind of invisibility on them. They are permitted to exist in books only so long as they conform to the norm of middle-class Euro-American social and cultural values and life experiences.[21]

In other words, "a story that could have been about anybody is probably a story that could have been about precisely nobody at all."[22] Most African American literature for young adults published contemporaneously with the "social conscience" and "melting pot" books by their European American counterparts clearly are written on some level in response to them.

Cultural and political events of the 1960s forced nurturers and publishers to evaluate how African Americans and racial relations were portrayed in children's books and the significance of these depictions or lack thereof. Educators stepped up their critiquing of children's books. Increased government funding for educational, literary, and social programs starting in the 1960s made more money available for agencies to buy books, fueling business opportunities for publishers: in the early 1970s, approximately 14% of children's books featured African Americans as the central characters, and 60% "demonstrated a positive sensitivity" toward African Americans.[23] Within ten years, publishers could point to change: in 1965, African American characters appeared in 6.7% of all children's literature, 14.4% in 1975; in 1965, 60% of black characters appeared in settings outside of the United States, 20% in 1975; in 1965, African American characters appeared in a contemporary setting in 14% of all children's literature, 28% in 1975.[24] However, "the number of books published . . . [featuring] African Americans . . . hovered around two hundred books per year."[25] European American-authored fiction of 1971-1982 compared to that of 1958-1970 exhibited less blatantly racist content but continued to feature inauthentic African American characters and experiences.[26]

Not surprisingly, African American writers primarily have produced what critics regard as the best books featuring African American protagonists, the "culturally conscious" books, "written primarily, though not exclusively, for Afro-American readers . . . [and which] attempt to reflect and illuminate both the uniqueness and the universal humanness of the Afro-American experience from the perspective of an Afro-American child or family."[27] Between 1965 and 1979, African American authors produced approximately two thirds of all "culturally conscious" young people's books, and just five African American authors—four of whose books are included in this bibliography, Eloise Greenfield, Virginia Hamilton, Sharon Bell Mathis, and Walter Dean Myers—produced approximately a third of the total books.[28] Where European American authors promoted "racial harmony and American cultural homogeneity," African American authors promoted "self-affirmation for Afro-American children" by creating literature that:

> . . . clearly reflects Afro-American cultural traditions, sensibilities, and world views. It presents an image of Afro-Americans as courageous

survivors with a strong sense of community and cultural affinity and with positive feelings about being Black. It presents Afro-American children as strong, resilient, capable, and confident . . . [able to achieve their self-identified goals despite oppression and violence]. . . . Its focus is on the human relationships and inner resources that provide support and comfort and strength.[29]

The "culturally conscious" books, predominantly of the contemporary realistic fiction or historical fiction genre:

. . . recognize, sometimes even celebrate, the distinctiveness of the experience of growing up simultaneously Black and American. . . . [T]he major characters are Afro-Americans, the story is told from their perspective, the setting is an Afro-American community or home, and the text includes some means of identifying the characters as Black.[30]

African American writers assumed the task of providing authentic representations of African American characters and situations and countered the insidious, covert, and subtle racism of their European American counterparts' writings.

African American writers concentrated on writing books about African American youth for African American youth. The milestones in this tradition for young people are: John Steptoe's *Stevie*, the first picture book by an African American about an African American child for an African American child, published in 1969, and Virginia Hamilton's *Zeely*, a novel created by an African American author for and about an African American young adult, published in 1967.

The core writers whose books are included in this bibliography broke into print during the late 1960s and 1970s, critically regarded as an exciting breakthrough time of "quality . . . literature . . . peopled with black characters growing into a positive sense of black-self—rediscovering and redefining their past, looking into themselves, and exercising some degree of self-determination as they look to the future."[31] The vanguard of this movement had to be "substantially superior in order to be published," as evidenced by "the disproportionately high percentage of books by [these] authors that went on to receive prestigious prizes and distinctions" in the 1970s.[32] For example, Virginia Hamilton's *M.C. Higgins, the Great*, published in 1974, is the only children's book ever to win three of the most coveted children's literature prizes: the Boston Globe-Horn Book Magazine Award, the National Book Award, and the John Newbery Medal Award. More than half of the writers included in this bibliography have earned at least one major award or distinction. Virginia Hamilton, Julius Lester, Walter Dean Myers, and Mildred Taylor are big award winners in the field of children's literature. Yet these writers, regardless of their track record, felt constrained thematically and stylistically by their publishers. Into the 1980s, when a novel featuring an African American protagonist received critical recognition or an award, more often it was written by a European American author than by an African American author.

Furthermore, a number of major awards with themes particularly relevant to African American young adult literature have never been awarded to African American authors. For instance, no African American author has ever won the Scott O'Dell Award for historical fiction. Very few have won the Jane Addams Book Award—for a children's book that stresses themes of togetherness and peace, equality of the races and sexes, and social justice—or the John Newbery Medal Award—for a distinguished children's book. Only one African American writer, Walter Dean Myers, has won the Margaret A. Edwards Award, and one, Virginia Hamilton, has won the Laura Ingalls Wilder Award, both given to an author for young people for a book or books that contribute to illuminating their experiences. Finally, in 1995, one writer received the long overdue recognition that several African American writers for young adults deserve: Virginia Hamilton received the MacArthur Foundation (Genius) Grant, the ultimate award.

While the Civil Rights Movement, the Black Power Movement, and the ongoing tradition of black consciousness and militancy deeply impacted the psyches of African Americans, it seemed to make no deep and permanent inroads in the European American power structure of the book trade. "Retrenchment" in the publishing of books by and about African Americans marked the 1980s. Declining political activism, an upsurge in conservatism, a backlash to progressive movements, government spending cuts, and a lack of commitment on the part of publishers—the majority of whom indicated that they felt the market for African American writers had decreased in recent years—contributed to the reversal in publishing of African American young people's literature. During the 1970s, most alternative presses that cyclically "emerged or expanded to fill the void" created by "mainstream presses . . . pulling back" from their commitment to multicultural publishing, folded within the decade.[33] The need for analysis and publishing continued, but "progressive" publishing and criticism in the 1980s swung toward other issues, particularly sexism, ableism, and general multicultural representation in children's literature.[34] New writers struggled to break into print. Established writers watched their award-winning books go out of print while they suffered multi-year gaps in getting their latest books published.[35] In 1980, librarians nationwide expressed a willingness or urgency to spend from 5% to 25% of their budgets on books by and about blacks, who represented 12.2% of the national population, if such books were available; "yet Black authors participate[d] at a market rate of only 1.3%." In 1985, less than 5% of children's and young adult books featured African Americans.[36] Only 18 children's books written or illustrated by African Americans were published in 1985.[37]

Content Trends in the Literature

Until the turn of this decade, there were many more African American male-centered than female-centered novels: not only was the narrator or central character male, but almost all of the characters in the story were male. Females were incidental at best or hateful at worst, particularly mother figures. This literary state of affairs perpetuated, if not intensified, a contradictory condition of invisibility and targeting for African American girls and women. Ironically, there were nearly four times as many women writers on the market. Presumably, the phenomenon of girls reading books about boys and girls, but boys reading only books about boys, accounted for the preponderance of male-focused novels. The dominant issues of the male-centered novels suggested that African American experience was monolithic and grim, with its unrelenting focus on drugs, police violence and/or arbitrary arrest, and violence and death.

Taken as a group, African American young adult fiction now offers a relatively healthy balance of positive male and female characters. It portrays an essential, full picture of young people's lives that are about a lot more than just their oppression—about their surviving, struggling, and living with beauty, grace, joy, love, and power. The current body of literature also realistically represents hard problems and oppression along with suggestions for or descriptions of young people working through and strategizing to change problems in their lives and in society at large.

Until recently, images of family were another major shortcoming of this literature: too many absent fathers; too many sick, dysfunctionally neurotic or addicted mothers, too many children parenting themselves. Rare was the novel featuring a female-headed household where the mother was present and positive—a "good" parent, healthy, hard-working, or even ordinary. Typically, the novels set up a dichotomy of two kinds of mother figures: the sick mother—abandoning, abusive, or alcoholic—versus the neurotic mother with middle-class aspirations. Only within two-parent families were there positive female role models, i.e., women could be "good" if there was a man by their side, and kids needed a father regardless. Married women were commonly portrayed as entirely passive. If the father was present, he was almost always the most important figure in the young adult's life. The other common scenario was even more depressing: parentlessness or abandonment, with the young adult protagonist trying to grow up alone or trying to take care of a parent or family.

The last decade's novels balance out the representation of family life. While continuing to tackle issues of family dysfunction, the literature is starting to show at least some portraits of strong families and mature parental presence, as well as rare positive representations of female-headed households. These positive images, too, reflect an important reality of African American life, particularly the incredible work of many African American mothers. In addition, there is a growing number of novels featuring strong grandmothers, supportive kinship networks, and engaged communities.

Today, we are, fortunately, on the crest of a dramatic expansion in the publishing of fiction by African American authors about and for African American young adults. "The success of small presses and their authors . . . [and] major demographic changes during the [1980s]" contributed to a "revitalization that went beyond even the gains of the 1970s."[38] African American-owned "ventures that published African-American authors frozen out of the mainstream," emerged and stabilized in the 1980s.[39] "A new wave of . . . authors emerged . . . being given a chance to grow and develop rather than having to prove perfection with their first manuscript. . . . A greater diversity of statements is being made, and readers are learning about [a] multiplicity of life-styles, communities, and experiences."[40]

Nevertheless, several factors can make or break this dynamic development. The struggle within the educational system for genuine multicultural education will continue to play a central part. The existence of traditional literary canons limits students' potential exposure to the books included in this bibliography:

> Canons . . . constitute the literature many students read. . . . Unfortunately, literary canons tend to include a preponderance of [Anglocentric]

> books. . . . Few texts written by African Americans
> . . . are designated classics, even though many
> exhibit extraordinary literary merit, expand or
> reinterpret literary forms, or provide a forum for
> voices silenced or ignored in mainstream
> literature.[41]

Because publishing is an industry that responds to profit, the law of supply and demand ultimately determines its future. Children's books divisions of publishing conglomerates rarely score large profits and are, in fact, often subsidized by the gargantuanly profitable adult divisions. Publishers regularly veto projects because they assume that the targeted audience cannot sustain the product—and they often assume that only African Americans will support African American children's literature. This creates a double-bind for African American young adult fiction; the demand is low in part because access to the product is limited. Even an African American young adult book that makes it to publication may commonly be difficult to find because bookstores, libraries and schools seldom carry them, and don't display them prominently when they do. Advertising is often inadequate or inappropriate, and mainstream publications may choose not to review the book. Then, because the book is not widely purchased, the publisher assumes that it's not needed or wanted. The economy and political climate, which determine the resources available to schools and libraries—the major consumers of trade books for young adults—to purchase and publicize multicultural materials, show signs of ever-waning support. Nevertheless, the emergence of new writers "suggests that African American children's literature will remain a viable, vibrant tradition, albeit one that remains unfairly neglected."[42]

Twenty-five years ago, the entry of African American authors into the European American-dominated children's book field assured a focus on diverse themes and plots, particularly a focus on conflicts and issues within African American communities, on African and African American heritage and identity, on culturally specific developmental and political issues. The ever-increasing diversification of personalities, locales, and issues in African American-authored young adult fiction is a trend that grows more robust by the decades. Yet the dominance of a few authors—shaped largely by publishers and awards committees—inherently limits the diversity of concepts and perspectives. A number of vital issues relevant to African American young adults today are glaringly lacking in the literature that has been created for them thus far. Topics demanding further exploration include class issues; the world of work; critical analyses of materialism; biracial identity; sexual decision making and the spectrum of sexual expression; pregnancy, abortion, and teen parenting; foster care and adoption from the child's and the mother's perspective; HIV and AIDS; Black Muslims; relations between African Americans and other individuals and communities of color; sexism; sexual abuse and rape; experience with the police, courts, prison or reform school; gangs from an insider's perspective, articulating the needs met by belonging as well as the dangers; lesbian, gay and bisexual identities; and developmental, emotional and physical disabilities.

More works of historical fiction also need to be written, focusing on figures and events in African Americans' four hundred years of history besides slavery and the Civil Rights Movement. The historical fiction also needs to include more women as fictional protagonists and actual historical figures. Furthermore, many popular genres of fiction are underrepresented, including suspense thrillers, fantasy and science fiction, mystery, romance, and multi-volume series featuring the same characters.

Notes

1. Kathleen T. Horning and Ginny Moore Kruse, "Looking into the Mirror: Considerations Behind the Reflections," *The Multicolored Mirror: Cultural Substance in Literature for Children and Young Adults*, Merri V. Lindgren, ed. (Fort Atkinson, WI: Highsmith Press, 1991), p. 1.

2. Violet J. Harris, "African American Children's Literature: The First One Hundred Years," *Freedom's Plow: Teaching in the Multicultural Classroom*, Theresa Perry and James W. Fraser, eds. (New York: Routledge, 1993), p. 167.

3. *Ibid.*, p. 167-168.

4. James Fraser, "Black Publishing for Black Children: The Experience of the Sixties and Seventies," *School Library Journal* 20.3 (November 1973), p. 19.

5. Violet J. Harris, *op. cit.*, p. 171.

6. *Ibid.*, p. 171-172.

7. *Ibid.*, p. 173.

8. Courtney Vaughn-Robertson and Brenda Hill, "*The Brownies' Book* and *Ebony Jr.!*: Literature as a Mirror of the Afro-American Experience," *Journal of Negro Education* 58.4 (Fall 1989), p. 497.

9. *Ibid.*, p. 495.

10. *Ibid.*, p. 496.

11. Violet J. Harris, *op. cit.*, p. 175.

12. *Ibid.*

13. *Ibid.*, p. 176.

14. *Ibid.*, p. 175.

15. Kathleen T. Horning and Ginny Moore Kruse, *op. cit.*, p. 4.

16. Kathleen T. Horning and Ginny Moore Kruse, *op. cit.*, p. 3.

17. Rudine Sims, *Shadow and Substance: Afro-American Experience in Children's Fiction* (Urbana, IL: National Council of Teachers of English, 1982), p. 11.

18. *Ibid.*, p. 14-15.

19. *Ibid.*, p. 29-30.

20. *Ibid.*, p. 33-34.

21. *Ibid.*, p. 45-46.

22. *Ibid.*, p. 46.

23. Evelyn Graves Gibson, "The Black Image in Children's Fiction: A Content Analysis of Racist Content, Black Experience and Primary Audience in Children's Books Published Between 1958-1970 and 1971-1982," *University Microfilms International* #8521083 (1985), p. 4-5.

24. Jeanne S. Chall, Eugene Radwin, Valerie W. French, and Cynthia R. Hall, "Blacks in the World of Children's Books," *The Black American in Books for Children: Readings in Racism*, Donnarae MacCann and Gloria Woodard, eds. (Metuchen, NJ: Scarecrow Press, 1985), p. 218-219.

25. Violet J. Harris, *op. cit.*, p. 179.

26. Evelyn Graves Gibson, *op. cit.*, p. 117.

27. Rudine Sims, *op. cit.*, p. 15.

28. *Ibid.*, p. 77.

29. *Ibid.*, p. 103-105.

30. *Ibid.*, p. 49.

31. Karima Amin, "Adolescent Literature by and about Black People," *Black Literature for High School Students*, Barbara Dodds Stanford, ed. (Urbana, IL: National Council of Teachers of English, 1978), p. 98-99.

32. Lyn Miller-Lachmann, ed., "Introduction," *Our Family, Our Friends, Our World: An Annotated Guide to Significant Multicultural Books for Children and Teenagers*, (New Providence, NJ: R.R. Bowker, 1992), p. 7.

33. *Ibid.*, p. 8.

34. Evelyn Graves Gibson, *op. cit.*, p. 6.

35. Lyn Miller-Lachmann, ed., *op. cit.*, p. 7.

36. Evelyn Graves Gibson, *op. cit.*, p. 52.

37. Lyn Miller-Lachmann, ed., *op. cit.*, p. 8.

38. *Ibid.*

39. *Ibid.*

40. *Ibid.*, p. 8-9.

41. Violet J. Harris, *op. cit.*, p. 171.

42. *Ibid.*, p. 179.

Guidelines for Evaluating the Books

It is much harder to create something new than to critique what someone else has created. Therefore, before we go any further, we would like to honor all of the African American authors who've put their hearts and sweat and vision into creating these stories to help the next generation grow up strong and proud. This bibliography recognizes and celebrates the accomplishments and promise of a body of literature whose very existence is in itself an achievement. Reading can be a powerful vehicle for learning about new ways of life, for learning about African American history or envisioning a better future, and for developing a sense of self. African American children, in particular, are bombarded with so many negative messages about themselves and their people that reading affirming books can be a lifesaver. So to all these authors we owe a debt.

Children and teens have to be seduced by reading if it is to hold their interest in the face of competition from television, action movies, and the street. If books don't interest them, if they don't see themselves reflected in the characters and the situations portrayed, they're not going to like reading and they're not going to do it. Reading requires more energy than most other forms of entertainment, but ultimately it delivers more as well. It holds within it the possibility of opening new worlds, teaching kids to think for themselves, and facilitating educational success. We have been exacting in our criticism of these young adult books because African American children deserve the best. They deserve multilayered characters, interesting plots, and beautiful language. They deserve realistic dialogue. They deserve a complex wrestling with the issues of their lives, and empowering but unsentimental portrayals of black history. The best books in this collection deliver these qualities. Many more of these books offer strengths and weaknesses, but are still well worth reading. A few are best passed over entirely; we do young people a serious disservice by offering them books that they are not going to like, which may discourage them from reading altogether. We hope that young readers, teachers, librarians and parents will use this bibliography to select books that not only inform but are also most likely to draw young adults into reading more.

The good news is that the spectrum of issues tackled by African American young adult books is constantly broadening. Young adult readers can now choose from fictionalized slave narratives and accounts of the Civil Rights Movement, from romances, sports stories, mysteries and science fiction, from stories about surviving the ghetto to tales about life on the South Carolina sea islands, and just about everything in between! On these pages, readers can meet orphans and teen mothers, activists and addicts, brilliant students and dropouts, gay and lesbian teens and disabled kids, musicians, athletes, and ordinary friends. There truly are books for every taste, and the beauty is that all of them feature African American characters. We invite you to explore these cultural riches.

Like any critique, these book reviews are subjective, informed by our personal perspectives and experiences. Although reviewers sometimes feign objectivity to give their opinions more authority, ultimately all critiques are simply opinion. To balance this, we have tried to give extensive details both about the novel's content and about how we arrived at our opinions of its quality. We encourage readers to use these details—and not simply our conclusions—to decide whether to read a particular book themselves. If a book interests you, but we've rated it poorly, don't let that stop you from reading it and forming your own opinion of it. In some cases, books which we've rated poorly have won major literary awards—so clearly other reviewers had higher opinions of them! For this reason, we have included both our own list of "best books" and a list of titles which have won major literary awards. Never let a negative review keep you from reading a book which interests you, but *do* check out the books which we rated highly. There are a number of little-known gems in this category which deserve a much broader audience.

We've tried to be very specific in both our criticism and our praise, to enable you to filter and adjust our critiques to your own values. Since any review is value laden, we believe that the most honest and helpful approach is to verbalize our values as explicitly as we can, to allow you to identify those with which you agree or disagree. These values are set out in the next section, in the guidelines on how to critique books on your own. Obviously, if some of your values differ from ours, you will have to adapt the relevant guidelines. Although we've tried to find and review every young adult book written between 1968 and 1993 by an African American author featuring African American protagonists, new books are always coming out. Therefore, these guidelines on how to critique a young adult book yourself may prove a useful tool for the future, as well as describing explicitly what we looked for in critiquing the books in this collection.

Literary Guidelines

Are the characters multifaceted, with strengths and weaknesses, and well developed through their appearance, words, thoughts, and actions, and other characters' responses to them? Are the characters flat or full, static or dynamic?[1] Is character development inextricably woven into the plot?

Are there a limited number of characters so that they can be fully fleshed out? Are the relationships between key characters well developed and realistic? Are the characters individuals, not mere representatives of a group or point of view? Is the antagonist merely a foil or stereotype? Are there stock characters? Does the story make a character or a group of people more understandable? Does the reader grow to care what happens to the characters?

Is the story told from a young adult's perspective? If told from an adult or omniscient perspective, is the voice didactic or dogmatic? If the writer uses a first-person voice, is the narrator's understanding of people and events, use of language, focus, and attitude appropriate for and consistent with that character's personality, maturity, and experience? "Does the writer stay within the limitations of the chosen point of view?"[2] Do the characters experience conflicts and concerns that are realistic for their age and life situation? Can readers identify with them?

Does the protagonist reach an understanding or achieve something by the end of the story? If the character grows or undergoes change in the story, is the process of change clear, realistic, and convincing?[3] Does the book demonstrate how characters become aware of their inner strength and resources, and leave the reader with a sense of hope and direction? Do the characters, by example, teach the reader skills necessary for survival and success? Does the book inculcate positive values?

Is the dialogue age-appropriate? Is it current or dated? If it relies heavily on Black English or a local slang, does this limit the story's accessibility to weaker readers? Is the dialogue understandable to African American readers from a variety of local cultures?

Is the theme relevant to young people today? Does the theme challenge the reader to question and think? Is it explicit or implicit? Does it seem that the theme was the author's "first motive for writing"? Or is it easy to "believe in the character, . . . believe in the experience, and . . . accept the theme"?[4] Does the author preach? Is the theme dealt with in full complexity or oversimplified? Is the author's approach biased, and if so, in what direction?

Is the plot realistic, believable, and unpatronizing? Is it relatively uncomplicated and fast paced? Whether information and events are related chronologically or through flashbacks, is it easy for the reader to follow? Is the plot too formulaic or predictable? Is characterization and plot exaggerated or sensational?

Does the story's conflict or resolution rely on coincidence or sentimentality?[5] If the story takes an honest look at a painful or seemingly futile situation, is it pessimistic or ultimately positive, without being solved too simply?[6] If the story leaves the reader feeling frustrated, confused, or angry, are these responses appropriate to the seriousness of the theme and the age of the intended audience?

Is the setting accurately described? Does the character "live in the setting . . . or move over it? Are action and character superimposed upon time and place?"[7] "Does the historical information seem more important to the writer than understanding of human beings? Are the historical details seen as important to our understanding of the story, or are they the purpose of the story?"[8] Or does context illuminate character, establish mood, or symbolically support theme? Does the character seem to be a product of a particular time and place? Is the setting historically accurate? Is it situated within the overall context of American and African American experience/history?

If the writer uses figurative language, allusion, imagery, symbolism, or wordplay, is it accessible and integrated into the pace and purpose of the story? Is the writing tight and lively?

General Guidelines
Does the author perpetuate misconceptions, myths, or stereotypes about:

      —African Americans, Asian and Pacific Islander
      Americans, European Americans, Latinas/Latinos, or
      Native Americans?
      —men or women?
      —young people or old people?
      —poor, working-class, or owning-class people?

—people with developmental, emotional, intellectual, or physical disabilities?
—Jews or Muslims?
—lesbians, gays, or bisexual people?

Is negative characterization or negative action attributed or linked to a character's group identity? Is there a blanket statement about a group of people that begins with, "All . . . "? If an individual character espouses oppressive opinions, is the character's opinion clearly differentiated from the author's? Are all characters of a particular racial or religious background negative, or all strictly positive? If a single character is especially villainous, are there other positive or neutral characters of the same background to balance the portrayal?

Does the book celebrate differences and cultural pluralism, counter stereotypes, and encourage critical thinking? Does it reflect respect for personal and cultural differences and affirm the worth and importance of individuals and peoples?

How many female characters are there? In what roles? Are the female characters passive? What values are reinforced for male versus female characters? Are girls applauded only for beauty or cooperativeness? Are they portrayed as interested only in clothes and boyfriends? Are boys applauded just for external accomplishments, never for the quality of their character? Are they portrayed as interested only in sports and girlfriends? Are they permitted to feel?

To what extent are different characters defined by their gender? Do they experience universal adolescent feelings, dilemmas and exploits, or only gender-specific ones? Will their lives interest readers of the other sex?

Is sex and sexual decision-making part of the story? If so, are the descriptions age-appropriate for both the characters and the intended audience? Does the author offer a balanced portrait of the attractions and risks of sex? Is the author overly judgmental? Is there a double standard for female and male characters? Do the characters make active decisions about sex or fall into it? Do they protect themselves from pregnancy and disease? What is the take-home message about teenage sex and sexuality?

In general, are the young adult characters active participants and decision makers in their own lives, or do events carry them passively along? Does the author suggest that teenagers can make a difference, both in their own lives and in the world?

African American Guidelines

Does the book employ oversimplifications or stereotypes of African Americans? Are African American characters defined according to European Americans as the norm? Are strong African American characters treated as exceptional or extraordinary?

Is the story presented from an Afrocentric or a Eurocentric perspective?

Recognizing that there exists a diversity of African American cultures, geographies and histories, lifestyles and traditions, religious practices, speech patterns, and perspectives, does the author write with accuracy, authenticity, and stress individuality and specificity? Does the book provide insight into the experience of a distinct African American individual or culture? "Are there a variety of class backgrounds, settings, and family situations portrayed?"[9] When differences are mentioned, are they mentioned respectfully?

In what ways are the characters portrayed as African American? "To what extent are the conflicts, issues, and specific details unique to African Americans, and to what extent are they universal? Could non-African American characters have been substituted, with little or no change in the content of the work?"[10] Does the author stress that there is no difference between African Americans and others? Does s/he deny the uniqueness of African American identity to do so?

Are the characters' race and culture central to their identity, either implicitly or explicitly, without being the sum total of their identity? Does the book depict personal struggles as well as societal struggles? Is there a sense of balance and multidimensionality to the issues presented?

"Are the characters ... presented as 'model victims,' or are they allowed to be human beings capable of the full range of human emotions? ... Are problems solved by African Americans themselves or by benevolent whites?"[11] Are African Americans portrayed as active and assertive or passive and subservient? Is the character's being African American represented as a "problem" or are the joys as well as the challenges of being African American in racist American society depicted? Does the book portray African Americans' relationships with each other as equally or more important than their relationships with European Americans? If the book focuses on the interactions between African Americans and the dominant culture, is this focus justified by the book's theme? Are African American characters defined primarily in relation to European Americans?

Is pride in educational and occupational advancement presented? How many of the characters exhibit a sense of identity and pride? Does the narrative refer to or incorporate elements of African or African American history and heritage? Is the character's culture a significant part of her/his life? Is cultural information "presented in a manner consistent with the flow of the story"? Does the author "halt ... the story to explain cultural details ... [or present it] as exotica [and not as a normal part]—whether major or minor—of an individual's life[?]"[12] Does the author make African American culture palpable in the details?

Does the book authentically depict and interpret African Americans' lives and histories, expanding the reader's knowledge of the past and/or present? Is slavery the only past African American experience presented? Is the Civil Rights Movement presented as the only African American resistance movement? Does the book provide insight into individual or institutional racism, if racism is depicted in the story? Are racist incidents presented without comment? If the African American protagonist is angry, jaded, or distrustful of European Americans, does the narrative on some level legitimate those feelings and explain their genesis? Is there a suggestion in the book that solutions to oppression require more than an individual response, that structures must change? Is the present depicted as a utopia of equality, with racism eradicated, or more realistically, as a time of co-existing progress and powerlessness? Does the character respond to injustice through resistance or struggle, or does s/he passively accept it? Does the story tend to "blame the victim"?

Is dialect used? How? Does everyone speak the same, regardless of place of origin, region, age, class, education, and audience? Does the story feature nicknames, proverbs, colloquial/figurative expressions, rhymes, and verbal contests? Are demeaning epithets and profanity used? To what effect? Is color symbolism used baldly, wherein black or darkness is negative and white or lightness is positive? What terminology is used to define the character's identity—Colored, Negro, black, Afro-American, African American, or African?

"To what extent do the characters in a novel have a 'history' as African Americans, communicated by family members, other adult role models, and their own discovery of their heritage? How is the past portrayed?"[13]

How is family represented? Are loving relationships emphasized? Are adults shown as positive role models? "Are personal and family problems in African-American communities treated realistically, or are they either downplayed or sensationalized?"[14] Are any adults acting as responsible parents, or are all the children parenting themselves? How are male and female roles in the family portrayed? Are all the families fatherless? Are all the family's troubles ultimately blamed on the mother figure (who is too strong/not strong enough, overinvolved/selfish, "just a housewife"/never home—or simply female)? Does the story suggest that every family needs a man to be healthy?

Is there an extended family or a sense of community? Does some adult in the child's life offer support and guidance? What role does religion play in the story? How is the black church portrayed? Where do characters find strength and community?

Notes

1. Rebecca J. Lukens, *A Critical Handbook of Children's Literature* (Boston: Scott, Foresman and Company, 1986), p. 59.

2. *Ibid.*, p. 144.

3. *Ibid.*, p. 60.

4. *Ibid.*, p. 123.

5. *Ibid.*, p. 87.

6. *Ibid.*, p. 182.

7. *Ibid.*, p. 108.

8. *Ibid.*, p. 124.

9. April Hoffman, Sandra Payne, and Reeves Smith, "United States: African Americans," *Our Family, Our Friends, Our World: An Annotated Guide to Significant Multicultural Books for Children and Teenagers*, Lyn Miller-Lachmann, ed. (New Providence, NJ: R.R. Bowker, 1992), p. 27.

10. *Ibid.*, p. 26.

11. *Ibid.*, p. 27.

12. Lyn Miller-Lachmann, *Our Family, Our Friends, Our World: An Annotated Guide to Significant Multicultural Books for Children and Teenagers* (New Providence, NJ: R.R. Bowker, 1992), p. 19.

13. April Hoffman et al., *op. cit.*, p. 27.

14. *Ibid.*

Our Best Book Choices

Bright Shadow. Joyce Carol Thomas.
Chevrolet Saturdays. Candy Dawson Boyd.
Circle of Gold. Candy Dawson Boyd.
Conjure Tales. Ray Anthony Shepard.
The Dark Thirty: Southern Tales of the Supernatural. Patricia
    McKissack.
Don't Explain: A Song of Billie Holiday. Alexis DeVeaux.
Edith Jackson. Rosa Guy.
Fallen Angels. Walter Dean Myers.
Fast Talk on a Slow Track. Rita Williams-Garcia.
The Friends. Rosa Guy.
The Future and Other Stories. Ralph Cheo Thurmon.
The Gift-Giver. Joyce Hansen.
Guests in the Promised Land. Kristin Hunter.
A Hero Ain't Nothin' but a Sandwich. Alice Childress.
If Beale Street Could Talk. James Baldwin.
Last Summer with Maizon. Jacqueline Woodson.
Let the Circle Be Unbroken. Mildred Taylor.
Maizon at Blue Hill. Jacqueline Woodson.
Marked by Fire. Joyce Carol Thomas.
Marvin and Tige. Frankcina Glass.
Motown and Didi. Walter Dean Myers.
The Road to Memphis. Mildred Taylor.
Roll of Thunder, Hear My Cry. Mildred Taylor.
Scorpions. Walter Dean Myers.
Song of the Trees. Mildred Taylor.
The Soul Brothers and Sister Lou. Kristin Hunter.
Sweet Illusions. Walter Dean Myers.
Sweet Whispers, Brother Rush. Virginia Hamilton.
The Sweetest Berry on the Bush. Nubia Kai.

Young Adult Fiction by African American Writers, 1968–1993

The Book Reviews

Key To Ratings

*****Outstanding, a must-read
****Highly recommended
***Good
**Has some problems, but may still be worth reading
*Not worth the time

1. Baldwin, James. *If Beale Street Could Talk.* New York: Dell Publishing Co., 1974. 213 pages. *****

American Library Association Notable Books for Children and Young Adults, 1974

If Beale Street Could Talk is a moving book about the survival of a black family in New York City in the late 1960s. Tish is eighteen years old, pregnant, and very much in love with Fonny. Fonny is twenty-one, a sculptor, in jail awaiting trial for a rape he didn't commit. Tish and her entire family are working very hard to free Fonny, while Fonny tries hard to survive his time in jail and to get back to Tish before the baby is born. Through this struggle and a series of flashbacks, the beauty of Tish and Fonny's love for each other and Tish's family's love is pitted against the devastating power of a racist criminal justice system.

The most accessible for young readers of all Baldwin's novels, *If Beale Street Could Talk* carries the same strength of vision and poetry of language that one expects from Baldwin. Love and despair are the most tangible elements in the story, and neither is oversimplified. Baldwin has a rare talent for exploring and attacking racism without ever sacrificing the complexity of his characters to his moral message. The characters are entirely human and the plot, without clear resolution, is only too believable.

This is an excellent book to introduce teenagers to Baldwin—the relatively short length, the elegant simplicity of voice, and the age and issues of the protagonists invite high-school readership. The explicit, and loving, sex scenes will undoubtedly keep teenagers' attention. There are strong black role models, both male and female, and the young people are powerful actors in their own lives, making decisions and coping together with the oppression that contracts their lives. Although the lack of plot resolution is frustrating, everything else about this novel is beautiful, and I highly recommend it.

2. Boyd, Candy Dawson. *Circle of Gold.* New York: Scholastic, Inc., 1984. 124 pages. ****

Coretta Scott King Honor Book, 1985

Eleven-year-old Mattie Mae Benson and her twin brother Matt miss their father, who was killed by a drunk driver six months earlier. The loss of her father is especially devastating for Mattie because she was his "princess," whereas her mother favored Matt. Regardless of this favoritism, the twins love and support each other through their mother's episodes of crying and yelling. Their mother juggles two jobs— managing the apartment building in which they live on the south side of Chicago and working in a factory. Mattie baby-sits and Matt delivers newspapers to supplement the family's meager income and they clean the house, make the meals, and perform many of the chores around the apartment building.

With Mother's Day fast approaching and her mother's heart and mind a million miles away, Mattie agonizes over what "miracle gift" to get her mother and how to afford it. She sets her sights on an unusual pin, a "circle of gold," a symbol of the family's wholeness and connection, which costs fifty-five dollars. To get the money together, she enters a writing contest about "what your mother means to you," sponsored by a Chicago newspaper. First prize means fifty dollars and dinner for the winner's family in a choice restaurant. After several rounds of unsatisfactory drafts, Mattie begs her best friend, Toni Douglas, to write the essay for her.

In the end, Mattie submits her own raw and unfinished essay. She puts twenty dollars down as a deposit on the pin, but is forced to admit defeat at the end of the thirty-day limit to pay the balance—besides, someone else wants to purchase the pin. Ironically, after this blow she wins the writing contest. The newspaper editor awards her the prize, plus—to everyone's surprise—the pin, which he tracked down because it figured largely in Mattie's essay. Mattie's essay touches her mother deeply.

Toni helps Mattie ride out every crisis with Mattie's archenemy in the fifth grade, her misnamed classmate Angel. Angel is the "Queen Bee" of the class because everyone envies her gray eyes and long, wavy hair, her expensive clothing and jewelry. When Angel accuses Mattie of stealing a special bracelet, Toni helps Mattie prove her innocence. It turns out that Angel's "best friend," Charlene, who envies Angel as much as she admires her, stole the bracelet.

Mattie turns to her elderly neighbor and church member, Mrs. Elvira Staples, for parenting. Mrs. Staples helps Mattie to keep her mother's behavior in perspective and encourages her to seek professional help for her mother. Although her mother becomes infuriated when Mattie asks Reverend Harris for help, Mattie's desperation in seeking outside help eventually pushes her mother to enter therapy. Therapy enables Mattie's mother to begin to pull the family's life together as the story ends with the family together in church.

The loving and supportive relationships between Mattie and her brother, Toni, and Mrs. Staples are precious and provide readers with hope. However, Candy Dawson Boyd creates a disturbing portrait of a family nearly destroyed by the loss of a parent. She presents the mother, in denial and despair, struggling as a working-class single parent, keeping her problems private for pride's sake. This portrayal, from Mattie's perspective, contains such candor and depth that readers will be upset with and yet understand Mattie's mother.

Whether readers share Mattie's circumstances, they will be compelled by the intensity of the drama. The author empowers young readers with the message that parents, like children, are people who have problems, fears, and worries, some of which children can understand, some of which children can help fix, and none of which children are to blame for.

Mrs. Staples, in brief conversations, teaches Mattie that tough times and tough decisions can be "skin-stretching," even though fraught with risks: "If you live your life based only on what you think you can do well, you won't achieve very much. [H]ow do you know what you can do until you try?" As Mattie's relationship with her mother deteriorates, Mrs. Staples helps Mattie to not take her mother's behavior personally but to see it as a response to pain and pressure, and to understand that "[t]his is when loving your mother really counts." Mrs. Staples teaches Mattie that there is no miracle cure for complex emotional and financial problems. Through Mattie's relationship with Mrs. Staples, Candy Dawson Boyd simultaneously provides the reader with comforting reassurance and instruction as well as a testament to cross-generational friendships.

Upper-elementary and middle-school students, particularly girls, will identify strongly with at least some of the emotions and experiences portrayed nearly perfectly in *Circle of Gold*.

3. Boyd, Candy Dawson. *Breadsticks and Blessing Places*. New York: Macmillan Publishing Co., 1985. 210 pages. ****

Twelve-year-old Toni lives a middle-class Chicago life, worrying about math tests, menstruation, and squabbles between her two best friends. Her parents want more for her, though, and are pushing her to pass the entrance exams for King High School, Chicago's elite college-preparatory public high school. Toni's not sure she wants to go to King and is even less sure that she can pass the math section of the exam anyway. Her best friend Mattie, a serious student and choir soloist, plans to attend King for its music program. Her other best friend, Susan, favors parties and shopping—including shoplifting—over schoolwork, and insists that she will be leaving to live with her musician father in New York any day now. Toni is caught in the middle, confused.

Then Susan is killed by a drunk driver, and nothing else matters. Devastated, Toni sinks into a depression that lasts for many months. Unable to concentrate on her schoolwork or anything else, Toni lashes out at everyone who goes on with their lives. Mattie understands what she's going through because her own father died only a year before. Finally, Mattie and Mrs. Stamps, Toni's surrogate grandmother, help Toni construct a ceremony to say good-bye to Susan. Afterward, she can pick up her own life again, despite her sadness.

Breadsticks and Blessing Places does a very good job of exploring the difficult, bewildering feelings that accompany a young person's death. Young readers who have experienced the death of a close friend or relative will find this book affirming, particularly in its description of how long Toni's pervasive sadness and anger continued and how unhelpfully most people responded to it. The story suggests that everyone, including children, can and must find within themselves the strength to go on after a terrible loss.

The novel is reassuring for young readers in that, despite Susan's death, it returns Toni to the more mundane concerns of twelve-year-old life. It also tries to be reassuring in providing a plethora of understanding, helpful adults to guide Toni, but this is one of the book's weaknesses as well—none of the characters has major faults. It's hard to believe that any teenager is surrounded by so many patient, wise parents, teachers, neighbors, and friends' parents. Similarly, Toni's friends are all too good to be true, except perhaps Susan, who dies anyway. These characters ring false in what is otherwise an unsentimental and moving depiction of a teenager's response to her friend's death.

Although *Breadsticks and Blessing Places* is long, its protagonist's age and concerns are most relevant for younger teens, ages ten to fourteen. The young characters are not yet into adolescent rebellion, so older teens may have trouble identifying with them. They may also find it hard to relate to King High School with its unrealistically enthusiastic students, complete racial harmony, and spirited class discussions. This is not like any public high school I've ever seen!

On the other hand, *Breadsticks and Blessing Places* is an excellent book to use with teens of any age who have experienced a friend's or relative's death, both to stimulate discussion and to affirm their experience. It is one of very few young adult books which deal so sensitively and honestly with death. This novel was also issued as *Forever Friends* in 1985.

4.   Boyd, Candy Dawson. *Charlie Pippin.* New York: Macmillan Publishing Co., 1987. 182 pages. ****

Eleven-year-old Chartreuse "Charlie" Pippin lives in a middle-class, Afrocentric home in a comfortably multiracial neighborhood in Berkeley, California. Charlie suffers the sometimes arbitrary and excessive rules and reprimands of her sixth-grade teacher, Mrs. Hayamoto, and her principal, Mr. Rockers, at Hayden Elementary School. The staff at Hayden are bent on molding the students into clone-like "responsible learners."

Mostly, Charlie gets in trouble for the entrepreneurial enterprises she sets up in the school yard at recess; since second grade, she's been making origami animals and plants to sell along with carrying convenience items such as school supplies. It's in her blood. Her grandmother is an artist who reminds Charlie that turning art into objects of everyday use and hawking them is part of her West African heritage. Likewise, her grandfather runs a convenience store.

The events in *Charlie Pippin* are structured around Charlie's work on a social studies project about war and peace, focusing on the Vietnam War. It is the tenth anniversary of the end of a war in which Charlie's father survived two tours of duty on the front lines. Through the assignment she hopes to gain a better understanding of him. She yearns to get around the strained superficiality of his commanding and criticizing tone with her, to break through his mysterious silence about Vietnam in order to gain insight into his anger and his relationship with her. However, Charlie's father refuses to talk about Vietnam; any mention of the war sends him into a violent fit.

In the process of interviewing and research, Charlie learns that her father lost his youth and his innocence in the war. He had to fight a triple war—as a black man in America, as a soldier, and as a black soldier in Vietnam. Partially penetrating her father's silence, Charlie learns that he risked his life to save two friends, irreparably damaging his leg; the friends died. Nevertheless, he expresses support for the war. Although to Charlie he seems a man of rules and responsibilities who makes her home life one long series of punishments, he had dreams of owning land, starting an inn, raising four children on the Oregon coast, and, primarily, painting. He returned from Vietnam unable to dare or to dream.

Charlie's investigation culminates in sneaking off to visit the Vietnam War Memorial in Washington, D.C., with her Aunt Jessie and Uncle Ben. This requires an elaborate alibi and careful planning. The experience is indescribably powerful. While there, she gets a rubbing of her father's two friends' names on the Memorial, places origami cranes—symbols of peace—near their names, and takes pictures of the panels. When Charlie returns, after she lets her parents vent their anger and worry, she presents her father with her "souvenirs" of the trip. The rubbings and photographs catch Oscar by surprise, and the resulting moment of vulnerability opens up the possibility of a truce and a whole new relationship between father and daughter.

Charlie Pippin is a sweet and sassy story, its star a wholly likable character—independent, artistic, resourceful, a critical thinker. Although she is only eleven and the school routine of line partners, Halloween parties, and after school detentions draws attention to the elementary school setting, the issues and actions presented in *Charlie Pippin* will engage readers of all ages and reading abilities, especially middle-school readers. This book, paired with Walter Dean Myers' *Fallen Angels*, provides an outstanding entry into the Vietnam war experience, or the theme of war and peace in general.

Author Candy Dawson Boyd explores substantial issues with ease, packaging her prose in crisp, immediate writing. In the course of documenting Charlie's research project, Boyd manages to present an easy-to-digest but far from simplistic analysis of big issues including war and peace, racism and colonialism, communism and freedom. The book never sounds didactic and never settles for facile explanations. And the author never forgets that *Charlie Pippin* is a novel, not a history text.

In addition, Boyd subtly critiques Charlie's school's demands for conformity and cowardice of conscience and its accent on discipline and standardized testing. In its focus on Charlie's growthful experience with her war and peace project, *Charlie Pippin* implicitly pleads the case for a relevant, student-centered curriculum and for cooperative learning methods.

The other related positive element is Charlie's empowerment; at a peace march, another young African American girl, Akina, sparks Charlie's political consciousness and inspires her to become an activist, to take her research a step beyond reporting what happened in the past to educating for world peace for future generations. At the end of the novel, Charlie applies her entrepreneurial and artistic skills to help another social studies group organize a fund-raiser for an African hunger relief agency.

When Charlie works with her team on the war and peace project, she makes a few moves that are totally appropriate and true to her wonderful character. When Chris assumes that she will take the notes for the project because she's female, Charlie tells him that she's not his secretary. When he starts taking up all the meeting time just to hear himself talk, she tells him to get to the point and to quit being condescending. When he rolls his eyes at Charlie's ideas, dismissing them as unimportant, she cuts through his arrogance with rapid-fire questions that reveal his ignorance and insensitivity.

The narrative effectively builds up to the very real sense of dread that Charlie feels when she know she must face her angry father and dramatizes well Mama's regular refereeing between Oscar and Charlie. However, the reader comes away with an uncompromisingly positive impression of the Pippin family. The are a loving extended family. Mom and Dad are readily available; Dad's parents are nearly neighbors; and Mom's siblings call and visit frequently. It is refreshing to see a household where parents are parents and kids are kids. Eleanor, a billing clerk, and Oscar, an insurance claims manager, provide emotional and material security, and spend quality time with their daughter, offering affection and dialogue. Charlie shares in household chores, but her domestic responsibilities leave her plenty of time for secret boyfriends and business adventures. She never worries about death, homelessness, and hunger—the unfortunately too-familiar problems depicted in many black YA books. And no character is all good or all bad. There are few easy alliances or polarizations, few predictable reactions. Rather, each character comes across as three dimensional and each relationship is described as a process, with a long history rooted in complicated familial and social contexts.

Feisty and funny female role models abound in *Charlie Pippin*, so it's little wonder where Charlie got her spunk. Her grandmother, Mama Bliss, encourages her entrepreneurship and her aggressive inquisitiveness into family secrets. She takes Charlie to craft fairs and peace marches, affectionately calling her "rebel." Charlie's mother likewise validates her daughter's burgeoning peace activism by making a connection between it and the Civil Rights Movement. The strong female characters who dominate the story make it most appealing to girls.

In the end, the author leaves key threads of her story unresolved, which is realistic and satisfying. Charlie's parents refuse to divulge some memories and emotions which are too private, leaving Charlie to ponder whether or not it works for a family "to keep secrets to keep from hurting each other." At the same time, her defiant prying enables her first real conversation with her father, and they reach a starting point for a depth of appreciation and understanding of each other. Oscar cries in front of Charlie for the first time, and answers her most daring questions. Charlie recognizes that Oscar's reactions to her have a deeper source than her recent "peace nut" phase, and they agree to disagree. And Oscar promises to share more one day.

5.   Boyd, Candy Dawson. *Chevrolet Saturdays*. New York: Macmillan Publishing Co., 1993. 176 pages. *****

Eleven-year-old Joey Davis lives in Berkeley, California, with his mother, Ernestine, and his stepfather, Franklin, whom he calls Mr. Johnson. Although his father, who moved out two years ago, moves to Chicago for promotion to an insurance management position, Joey holds onto the hope that his parents will reconcile and his father will come home again.

At Joey's multiracial school, Mrs. Hamlin terrorizes the entire fifth-grade class with her criticism and yelling. Mrs. Hamlin singles Joey out for special negative attention, treating him as if he were stupid and lazy. Whereas Joey hopes to be referred for testing for a gifted and talented program, Mrs. Hamlin refers him for special education classes for attention deficit disorder. Mrs. Hamlin avoids teaching science, which is Joey's favorite subject, and she believes class bully Clark Miller when he frames Joey for assorted mischievous pranks. Fortunately, Joey's affirming fourth-grade teacher, Mrs. Alder, and the principal, Mrs. Mack, who is "tougher than a tank" but fair, intervene. Mrs. Mack monitors Mrs. Hamlin's class and allows Joey to test for the gifted program. Joey qualifies for a special program in science at the University of California at Berkeley.

Franklin makes a supreme effort to reach out to Joey. For him, an orphan never officially adopted and without any family until he married Ernestine, forming a family with Joey is especially important. Franklin installs security systems for a corporation all week and works all weekend independently, building up clientele and business for the contracting business he's trying to start so that he can be his own boss. After he buys a 1953 Chevrolet pickup truck for his business—and paints "Johnson and Family, Contractors" on it as a sign of his desire to make Joey part of the family—he invites Joey to work with him on Saturdays. Joey reluctantly accompanies Franklin, only to find that he relishes Franklin's treating him like a manly assistant-apprentice while sharing confidences about moral and emotional dilemmas he experienced as a young man.

Even after Franklin advocates aggressively and effectively on Joey's behalf to rectify problems at school, Joey continues to call Franklin "Mr. Johnson," keeping him at a distance. However, an incident with Franklin's Airedale terrier, Josie, becomes the turning point in their relationship: Joey forgets to lock the gate one day, and Josie runs off, gets hit by a car, and is badly injured. Joey now feels compelled to prove himself to his stepfather. In caring for the injured dog, Joey bonds with her and, by extension, his stepfather. In the end,

Joey forgives Franklin for displacing his father, and Franklin forgives Joey for treating him like an outsider and nearly killing his dog. Joey starts calling Franklin "Mr. J."

Surrogate father figure, Doc, who runs a soda fountain and pharmacy, cheers Joey up after every rough day at school. He tries to redirect Joey's perspective on problems; consoles him with stories of how he misses his deceased wife; and employs Joey part time, which makes Joey feel competent and enables him to contribute toward Josie's costly veterinary bills. Joey's best friend, D.J. Tyler, also provides camaraderie and consolation, refusing to assume that he is smarter than Joey simply because he is in the gifted program and nudging Joey to regard Franklin as an extra father—a distinct advantage from his perspective, as an only son with six sisters.

Chevrolet Saturdays is a substantive, thoughtful, and wise work. Candy Dawson Boyd celebrates ordinary people as role models—hardworking, moral, honest, sensitive, and devoted to family and kin. No elitism in the narrative privileges Joey's highly educated middle-class father over his worldly-wise, working-class stepfather. All readers will find themselves caring deeply about every member of this gentle family, and readers agonizing over divorce and/or a stepparent will find themselves totally absorbed in Joey, Ernestine, and Franklin's growing pains. Ernestine's anger and despair about her son's troubles are not extreme, only all too human. The very "together" Franklin, with the remarkable presence of mind to declare his anger without inflicting it on others, never raises his voice or hand to Joey. He only loses his composure when Joey's well-being is threatened or Josie's safety is endangered. Particularly moving is the evolving relationship between Joey and Franklin.

The age of the protagonist suggests a fourth- to sixth-grade audience, though middle-school students will not feel far more mature than Joey. High-school readers may feel overly aware of the protagonist's eleven years while finding the sentiments and solutions cathartic. Selective readers will enjoy the science riddles and trivia which Joey spouts, which to the most disinterested readers will, at worst, seem funny.

Although Joey is suffering from the divorce, he is blessed with loving and highly involved parents. *Chevrolet Saturdays* presents a realistic yet refreshing portrait of changing families. Ernestine and Franklin are always there for Joey, firm but tender; his father spoils him. While the relationship between Joey's divorced parents is amicable, it is not idealized: when Joey's father disappoints him, his mother flares up righteously and critically about her ex-husband. Generally, however, she facilitates Joey's close relationship with his father, demonstrating that parents' splitting up doesn't mean that parents and children must split up, too.

Candy Dawson Boyd allows adult characters to teach without being didactic. For instance, in counseling Joey on how to cope with being African American in racist American society, Doc frames Joey's problems in a larger context. Family and school are Joey's first tests and work will be the next test. But Doc urges Joey not to wait passively for "fate" but to make choices and to take action to influence his destiny. Mr. Johnson extends Doc's message: as an African American man, Joey will face a particular and trying constellation of challenges, but he must be proud and persistent in striving for his goals. Joey's father filed a discrimination complaint against his employer for passing him over for advancement opportunities even though it jeopardized his job and, by extension, his marriage; he never gives up pursuing his dream of becoming a manager although it requires him to leave his son. The author takes the potentially negative aspect of racism and turns it on its head. The adults, acting as agents instead of victims—without denying the realities of racism—see the oppression as a unique challenge which demands the best of them.

While the author emphasizes that boys need men in their lives, that sons need fathers or father figures, she does not negate the importance of mothers. Ernestine, who runs her own beauty shop, begs Joey to accept Franklin. When Joey actively hurts Franklin by neglecting his dog, Ernestine challenges her son with: "Sorry and love are just words. They don't mean a thing unless your actions back them up."

Through every adult example in the novel, Candy Dawson Boyd affirms the industry and determination of African Americans. Doc explains that through work he prevails: "Work gives me a great deal of solace and joy."

The author evokes the tense struggle between Mrs. Hamlin and Joey without portraying Mrs. Hamlin as wholly evil or foolish. Nevertheless, through examples rather than statements, the author dramatizes the power that teachers and schools have over young people, shaping esteem and determining not only an individual's future but a family's and a people's future. The African American adults in *Chevrolet Saturdays* invest heavily in the power of education to provide opportunities for their children. Special education, particularly because African American males are disproportionately tracked and trapped into it, is a prime target for the narrative's attack. Ironically, the story seems to plug gifted programs, when the reader would expect it to oppose such programs as a form of tracking.

6. Brown, Kay. *Willy's Summer Dream.* San Diego: Harcourt Brace Jovanovich, Publishers, 1989. 132 pages. **

Fourteen-year-old Willy Palmer lives with his mother in a Brooklyn brownstone. Although he looks more adult everyday, most things in his life confuse him. Like why the neighborhood kids make fun of him and call him a retard. Or why he is being moved to a special class in school, even though he tries to pay attention and doesn't laugh uncontrollably in the middle of class the way he used to. His mother tells him he'll outgrow all his troubles, but at the same time, she transfers him to a new school every time he is placed in special education.

Willy's life starts to improve when Kathleen moves in next door from the West Indies. The beautiful Kathleen goes out with Willy almost every day. She doesn't think anything is wrong with him, but when he confesses his frustration and loneliness to her, she begins tutoring him. He is less interested in the tutoring than in his feelings of sexual awakening. Soon, though, she must return to the West Indies, leaving Willy as devastated and depressed as when his father left him.

In the meantime, Willy is confused about whether he is actually mentally retarded or not. He makes friends on vacation with an eleven-year-old boy, whom he saves from an abusive baby-sitter; he tells himself that a retarded person could not have done that. When Willy returns home, he starts practicing basketball every day, hoping to win the acceptance and friendship of the neighborhood boys. The story ends with them inviting him to join a game.

I wanted to like *Willy's Summer Dream* because of what author Kay Brown is trying to do—to bring the reader inside the experience of someone labeled retarded—but the story just never grabbed me. Brown's depiction of Willy's reality is powerful, including the confusion, disappointment, and frustration that he feels about his learning disabilities and his social isolation. However, the story never moves beyond that. Despite Willy's experiences in various relationships and a well-paced plot, Willy has changed little when the story closes, giving the entire book a static tone. Perhaps this was Brown's intention, to emphasize the limits of Willy's life. In any case, I think YA readers may be frustrated by it.

Although written in the third person, *Willy's Summer Dream* is nonetheless written from Willy's perspective. This is both a strength and a weakness, making his experience very vivid but not offering the reader any distance to gain insight into what's actually happening to him and why. For instance, Kathleen's motives for spending so much time with Willy are never clarified. Is she interested in him as a boyfriend? Does she see herself solely in a helping role? Is she just lonely? Or, coming from a more accepting culture, does she simply value him as a friend despite his disability? This ambiguity accurately mirrors Willy's confusion about her motives, but I'm not sure it offers the reader much insight. In contrast, Willy's mother's character is nicely drawn, alternating between exasperation over her teenager's rebellion, concern over his future, and an attempt to deny his disabilities. Willy's relationship with his self-centered father also rings true, as he moves from idolizing him, to disillusionment, to anger.

Despite a little optimism in the last chapter, *Willy's Summer Dream* offers a bleak picture of his life and his future. There is no exploration of any formal supports or programs for him, and the people in his life are sadly unable to bridge his isolation. Ultimately, this leaves the reader acutely aware of his despair but unable to picture a way out.

This novel's reading level and subject matter are appropriate for eighth- to eleventh-grade readers. It may appeal to boys more than girls since the primary female character, Kathleen, is poorly developed, serving mainly as a foil for Willy's feelings. Readers with a particular interest in learning disabilities may connect more with this story than most teenage readers, who will simply find it depressing.

7. Brown, Margery W. *That Ruby*. Chicago: Reilly and Lee, 1969. 154 pages. *

That Ruby describes the sixth-grade year of Bonnie Jean Walker, her friend Kathy, and Ruby Johnson, a sullen twelve-year-old girl in their class who already flunked sixth grade once. The story follows the girls through their excitement about Girl Scout barbecues, school book fairs, and a math competition.

Ruby is an outsider, suspected of stealing Bonnie's clown pencil and another classmate's train book. However, when Ruby's apartment burns following a gas leak explosion, she goes to stay with Kathy's family and the girls get to know her better. They learn that Ruby's father died last year, her mother works long hours, and she has major responsibility for taking care of her younger brother. They realize that she's a good cook and a good cooking teacher. Ruby warms up to the girls as they become friendlier to her, and eventually they even invite her to join their Girl Scout troop.

That Ruby is "Father Knows Best" meets "The Cosby Show." The sixth graders of Room 412 love their teacher, each other, and their studies. Bonnie's storybook nuclear family never fights. Even Ruby, who provides the only small conflict to propel the plot, comes around quickly with minimal effort. In other words, *That Ruby* is boring, unrealistic, and inane. The characters use expressions like, "Golly!," ensuring that no reader over the age of nine will want to identify with them. In addition, none of the characters ever becomes real to the reader; rather, they skate from event to event without ever delving below the surface. The characters could be of any racial or cultural background—no details of locale, dialogue, or identity ground them in African American culture.

With illustrations, an easy reading level, and the preadolescent concerns of its characters, *That Ruby* is appropriate for fourth- or fifth-grade readers. Boys will find little to interest them in the all-female cast, but girls are unlikely to be engaged by the insipid plot. Although *That Ruby* has a worthwhile theme of extending friendship to a defensive outcast, the lack of plot and character development makes it a poor choice for young readers.

8. Brown, Margery W. *The Second Stone.* New York: G.P. Putnam's Sons, 1974. 124 pages.**

Fifteen-year-old Henry Wilson lives with his older brother Dan's family in an unnamed inner city. A good student and athlete, he works as a counselor at the Boys Club. His best friend Ric Martinez is more troubled, coping with a drunken, unemployed father. Ric is in danger of dropping out of school and joining a local teenage gang which Dan, a cop, believes to be responsible for a recent series of muggings and robberies in the neighborhood.

When a shopkeeper is shot during one of the robberies and Henry's niece Patty disappears at the same time, he goes in search of her. He finally tracks her down to the old Andrews' place, the only private estate left in the neighborhood. Unable to flee before the police cordoned off the neighborhood, the teen gang hides out at the Andrews' house, holding Patty and the two elderly Andrews sisters hostage. After Henry sends for the police, he overhears Ric offering the gang an escape car if they'll let Patty and the women go. Then the police burst in, fatally wounding Ric in the ensuing struggle and arresting the rest of the gang. Tormented by his friend's death, Henry briefly joins in the rioting that follows but repents after accidentally hurting a woman with flying glass. Thereafter, he vows to stay away from gangs.

The Second Stone is only a moderately interesting book. In jumping back and forth from Henry to Ric to the child-artist Jay, Margery Brown dissipates much of the book's focus, decreasing the reader's emotional connection with any of the characters. The themes are important, particularly the choice of male adolescents deciding whether to pursue the straight and narrow path with potentially slow rewards versus dropping out and joining get-rich-quick, illegal schemes. However, the somewhat unfocused plot, the dated language, and the "goody two shoes" tone limit this novel's appeal to contemporary young adult readers. In addition, the story unnecessarily kills off Ric to prove how dangerous gangs are instead of using Henry's more moderate experience of following the crowd against his better judgment and then feeling regret over hurting someone.

Despite these faults, *The Second Stone* offers easy reading and a plot that keeps moving. Henry's home life is a fine example of caring extended family, with both surrogate father and mother very involved in his life and maturation. Henry's brother Dan is an African American man committed to his community and his family, working hard to make a living and to protect the people in his neighborhood.

Sixth through eighth graders will find *The Second Stone*'s reading level accessible, though they may be insulted by the fact that it contains many illustrations. Because the plot focuses entirely on boys, female readers will find little to interest them. Even male readers may have trouble identifying with the dated dialogue and the overly adult-pleasing Henry.

9.   Campbell, Barbara. *A Girl Called Bob and a Horse Called Yoki*. New York: Dial Press, 1982. 167 pages.***

A Girl Called Bob and a Horse Called Yoki, reissued in 1986 as *Taking Care of Yoki*, is a heartwarming story that takes its readers back to the era of World War II. During a winter in St. Louis, Missouri, eight-year-old Barbara Ann Weathers, popularly known as Bob, and her friend, ten-year-old Chuckie Williams, steal a horse to save him from the slaughterhouse. Parallel to this plot runs another plot: Bob's indecision over whether she should be baptized. She's not sure she's ready: "It's a lot of responsibility being baptized. You got to try to watch what you do and what you say, trying to be a good person. It may be too much for me." The other plot that runs through the whole book is Bob missing and writing to her father, who has been away in the war for over a year.

Bob, her mother, and grandmother live in two rooms of a modest boarding house run by crazy Mrs. Beene, with her horde of cats. Bob's mother, Saree, works at a defense plant making army supplies. Her grandmother, Sweetmama, came up from the rural South to care for Bob while Saree's at work. The family isn't poor but it is frugal. Saree is saving for a house in California, which the family hopes to buy when the war is over.

The story is full of intimate conversations among family and friends, richly detailed descriptions of daily life in another time and place—from hitching up the horse to the milk wagon, to making ice cream out of snow, to preparing for Easter Sunday. Bob's black-positive classroom and the passionate black church community are conveyed through occasional sketches of classroom lessons and church services.

Bob is mischievous and prone to impulsive actions and clumsiness. She tries to do right, but usually it comes out wrong. With help from fellow animal-lover Mrs. Beene, she and Chuckie steal Yoki, a mangy, decrepit horse, and take him to safety at Mrs. Beene's son's country farm. Meanwhile, the horse owner's nephew, Roger, who wanted to sell Yoki to the glue factory, vows to prosecute the thieves when he finds them.

Ultimately, Bob cannot live with herself for violating her principles, especially as she prepares to be baptized. Sweetmama, in helping Bob decide whether to be baptized, tells a personal story of her own childhood struggles, which brings the two of them closer together and gives Bob a satisfying philosophy with which she can live: "You going to do the best you can in life. You know right from wrong, and you going to try to do right. You just do your best. . . . I know I wouldn't be perfect, but who is?" Bob decides to tell Roger that she stole Yoki, even though he may prosecute her. Then she tells her mother. When she tells the truth, regardless of the consequences, she feels ready to be baptized. In the end, there are several happy endings: Bob gets baptized, and Roger's uncle thanks Bob for rescuing Yoki from Roger.

While never didactic, *A Girl Called Bob and a Horse Called Yoki* teaches several important lessons in addition to the aforementioned lessons of doing your best and of being honest despite the risks. Other lessons include: sometimes you have to do something bad in order to accomplish something good; sometimes you need to do for others to get a better perspective on your own problems; even if it accomplishes something good, you still have to pay a price for breaking the rules; your family can love you but still be angry with you; and giving and doing for others, making sacrifices, both hurts and feels good. All of the moral points that Barbara Campbell makes are illustrated largely though Bob's actions and their consequences, rather than spoken in a summation by an adult "moral exemplar."

This book has the best ingredients of historical fiction, nature-adventure, and coming-of-age genres. Although the chief protagonist of the story is a young girl and the dominant mood is sentimental and warm, elementary and middle-school girls alike will identify with Bob's moral dilemmas and enjoy her boldness. The nature theme is a big draw for boys. Bob is a complex character. She's a mature young person. So many facets of her life are so simple, and yet even the simplest situation can present an ethical dilemma. This book moves fairly quickly, but it's a full reading experience for elementary and middle-school students. The vitality of its characters and the predicaments and messages it presents make *A Girl Called Bob and a Horse Called Yoki* a worthwhile book.

10. Carter, Mary Kennedy. *On to Freedom*. New York: Hill and Wang, 1970. 55 pages. **

In the middle of the Civil War, thirteen-year-old slave Gabe Adams wants to escape his slave masters in Charleston, South Carolina. One day in town he meets Uncle Lee, a notorious free black man who helps slaves escape north to freedom. Gabe begs Uncle Lee to help him escape, but the older man insists that Gabe talk to his parents first, to try to convince them to go with him. Although they have been timidly saving toward legally buying their freedom for many, many years, Gabe's parents finally realize that escape is their only real hope. Gabe's father works on the ship *Planter*; together with Uncle Lee, they hatch a daring escape plan to steal the *Planter* with its entire black slave crew and sail to freedom right past southern naval checkpoints. Gabe becomes almost sick with anticipation as the day for escape approaches, but in the end he acts like a real man in helping his family and many others escape to freedom.

Based on a true historical event, *On to Freedom* gives the reader a small glimpse into the minds and conditions of slaves during the Civil War. Unfortunately, none of the characters ever becomes real. They remain in two dimensions, somewhat woodenly resenting slavery and planning their escape. And despite the boldness of the actual historical event, *On to Freedom* fails to communicate the sense of excitement and immediacy necessary for a good adventure story. Most of the action focuses on Gabe's feelings, detracting from the plot. Yet even so, Gabe does not come alive enough for the reader to care deeply what happens to him. At the same time, the story clings stubbornly to a historically revisionist sexism—although female slaves actually faced as many dangers and worked just as hard as male slaves, *On to Freedom* portrays the women as followers, sleeping peacefully while the men, including young Gabe, lead and protect them.

Because of its brevity and large print, *On to Freedom* is not truly a YA book, being more appropriate for fourth to sixth graders. Because of the passivity of its few female characters, it will hold limited interest for female readers. Although readers can learn about an amazing incident in black history through this story, it never takes off as an adventure tale and thus fails to fire the imagination.

11. Childress, Alice. *A Hero Ain't Nothin' but a Sandwich.* New York: Avon Books, 1973. 127 pages. *****

American Library Association Notable Books for Children and Young Adults, 1973; Coretta Scott King Honor Book, 1974; Jane Addams Honor Book, 1974; Lewis Carroll Shelf Award, 1975; School Library Journal Best Books for Children and Young Adults, 1973

In trying to negotiate the passage from childhood to adulthood, Benjie Johnson, a thirteen-year-old African American boy from Harlem, gets hooked on heroin. *A Hero Ain't Nothin' but a Sandwich* is about how and why that happens and how everyone around him—family, friends, teachers, and Benjie himself—reacts to it.

The book's excellence lies in its format and depth. Each chapter, written in the voice of a different character, adds a new layer to the puzzle of Benjie's life. Not only does the reader get a beautifully clear picture of the people who surround Benjie but also of the complexity of personal and societal problems which intersect in this one young boy's life. Childress' characters offer varied and often conflicting views on the issues which touch Benjie: drugs, poverty, racism, abandonment by his father, schooling which deadens his sense of self, an inadequate social service system, black activism, and family members doing the very best they can in bewildering circumstances. Childress offers no easy answers, yet the story is, in the end, hopeful. She draws each of the characters with exquisite complexity and compassion and provides strong black role models in the characters of Benjie's stepfather and mother.

A Hero Ain't Nothin' but a Sandwich is a brilliant book, readily appealing to students from grades seven through twelve. Although written in the vernacular of 1970s Harlem, the issues raised are still entirely relevant today, and Childress' treatment of them (in 127 pages, no less!) is more thoughtful and multilayered than anything I've read in years. Her skillful manipulation of characters provides powerful commentary on the issues without ever editorializing. This is an interactive book—although the characters speak bluntly, each in the first-person voice, the reader must actively sift through the sometimes contradictory information to make her/his own deductions. With its unusual format, this novel also offers an excellent opportunity to teach perspective and character development.

The Black English may make some chapters difficult for younger readers, but the short chapters, gripping plot, real life issues and narrative voices which seem to speak directly to the reader all make this compelling book accessible for younger readers. But don't let the novel's size or young protagonist fool you—*A Hero Ain't Nothin' but a Sandwich* is for adults, too, and readers of any age will be moved by its insight and honesty.

12. Childress, Alice. *Rainbow Jordan*. New York: Avon Books, 1981. 127 pages. ***

American Library Association Notable Books for Children and Young Adults, 1981; Coretta Scott King Honor Book, 1982; School Library Journal Best Books for Children and Young Adults, 1981

Rainbow Jordan is a fourteen-year-old African American girl living in New York City either with her mother Kathie or her temporary foster mother Josephine. Rainbow's life is a juggling act—trying to take care of her irresponsible mother, trying to hold onto her boyfriend Eljay without giving in to his demands for sex, and trying to pretend to the world that she leads a normal family life. Rainbow's father lives in Detroit. Her mother, AFDC check in hand, leaves Rainbow for weeks at a time to travel around with a new boyfriend or to take temporary go-go dancing gigs out of town. Whenever Rainbow's social worker realizes she's been left again, Rainbow is sent to live with Josephine, a single black woman aspiring to middle-class refinement. The novel explores Rainbow's maturing relationship with Josephine and her coming to terms with Kathie's lack of commitment to motherhood.

Rainbow Jordan is not nearly as moving or poignant a novel as Childress' *A Hero Ain't Nothin' but a Sandwich*. In *A Hero Ain't Nothin' but a Sandwich*, the reader could identify with nearly every character in spite of her/his faults; in *Rainbow Jordan*, no character is sympathetic enough to identify with. Their faults are somewhat caricatured, and Childress does not give enough insight into how each woman became the person she did. Although *Rainbow Jordan* follows the first novel's format of each chapter in a different major character's

voice, the narrative lacks the gripping immediacy of *A Hero
Ain't Nothin' but a Sandwich,* and the issues are explored in
much less depth. Only in the last chapter does Childress
reveal her genius in portraying the tender-tough,
heartbreaking emotional jumble of adolescence in a
dysfunctional family.

13. Chocolate, Debbi. *NEATE to the Rescue!* Orange, NJ: Just Us
Books, Inc., 1992. 90 pages. ***

As a member of the city council, Naimah Gordon's mom
has worked to improve the city for everyone, but now David
Russell, a white racist challenger for her city council seat, is
spreading lies about African Americans trying to take over the
city. He has sponsored a bill to get the voting districts redrawn
so an influx of suburban whites into Naimah's mother's district
will threaten her chances for re-election. Thirteen-year-old
Naimah, determined to help her mother, gets together her
group of five friends to strategize about campaigning for Ms.
Gordon. The first thing they do is go door to door with
campaign flyers. But along the way, they encounter a rally for
David Russell and start shouting slogans in favor of Naimah's
mother, touching off a mini riot, with eggs being thrown and
people getting trampled underfoot. All five friends are
arrested, and their parents are not happy about having to come
down to jail to bail them out! Naimah's mother grounds her and
forbids her to work on the campaign.

Meanwhile, Naimah herself is running for a student
council president position in her junior high school,
campaigning on much the same platform as her mother's. Both
promise to work to improve conditions for people of all colors.
With an inspiring, unifying speech, Naimah sweeps to victory.

But her mother has a harder time. When the
redistricting plan wins, Ms. Gordon finds herself trailing David
Russell by eight points in the polls. Naimah is determined to

help her mother retain her city council seat in spite of her mother's ban. So with the help of her friends, she organizes a rally for all the junior high schools and high schools in the city, gathering the students together to remind them, "We're too young to vote, but we're not too young to urge our parents to vote." She reminds them that bad people can get into office when good people don't care enough to get out and vote. The television news picks up the story of the rally, focusing on the ethnic diversity, positive energy, and serious political focus of the students. With the help of the rally and the positive news coverage, Naimah's mother is re-elected.

NEATE to the Rescue! is a cute book with good intentions, but it is overly simplistic. The protagonist, Naimah, offers a great role model of somebody who sees something wrong and tries to fix it, building alliances with friends and strangers to make positive change. This is a wonderful message for young people to hear, particularly since this activist is a thirteen-year-old African American girl. However, she solves all of her problems too easily. Even though the kids get arrested briefly following their first organizing attempts, they bounce back too quickly, with no further problems. In particular, their ability to throw together a city-wide political rally, pulling together students from every school and every racial community in the city in just two days, is totally unrealistic. If part of the goal of this book is to encourage young people to become involved, offering such a facile view of political change sets readers up for failure if they try to apply it in their own lives. Debbi Chocolate would have done readers a greater service by looking seriously at some of the obstacles and discouragements that young activists face, while exploring ways they persevere to overcome those problems.

On the other hand, it's wonderful to see a young adult book featuring very proactive African American females, including both Naimah and her mother. In addition, there are a number of families in the book, including Naimah's family and her friend Tayesha's interracial family, that are intact and functional, providing support and guidance for their young people.

NEATE to the Rescue! is a relatively short book, with simple chapters and vocabulary. The reading level will work for students in fifth through seventh grade. Despite a female protagonist, there are plenty of boys and girls in the story, and because Naimah is such an active and non-stereotypical character, readers of both sexes will enjoy the book. *NEATE to the Rescue!* is the first in a proposed series featuring the same characters. If this book is any indication, we can look forward to strong characters, very positive messages, and engaging plots. I hope that the future books will go more in depth into some of the problems and solutions involved in trying to create social change.

14. Cornwell, Anita. *The Girls of Summer.* Berkeley, CA: New Seed Press, 1989. 96 pages. *

Thirteen-year-old Aurelia Riverton was the first black student to integrate Carleton City Junior High School, located in an unnamed state in 1973. Her best friend there, Eunice Hightower, is a poor white girl with troubles of her own. Aurelia's father was killed years ago in the riots following Dr. Martin Luther King, Jr.'s death, while Eunice's father lives in a shack on the edge of town, drinking himself to death. But the girls' immediate concern is how to join the boys' Small Fry baseball league to give themselves something fun to do over the summer. Aurelia secretly hopes that playing Small Fry baseball will help her get onto the high school team, which, in turn, could help her win an athletic scholarship to college. She wants to become a scientist.

Aurelia and Eunice elicit the support of Aurelia's grandmother, who marches down to baseball practice with them and confronts the current coach, who has a 0-10 losing record from previous seasons. The old coach conveniently has a heart attack on the spot just thinking about letting girls play, and Granny takes over as coach. Fortunately, she knows how to coach from her days of traveling with her husband, a pitcher in the old Negro baseball league. She immediately puts girls in all the key positions, and with some strenuous practices, the team begins to win. Few townspeople oppose the changes, except Aurelia's mother, who doesn't think baseball is ladylike.

One day in the middle of the season, Eunice has to go ask her father for rent money for her sick mother. Aurelia accompanies her. Not only is Eunice's father drunk, but he is furious to see his daughter in the company of a black friend, and he comes after them with a meat cleaver. The girls run away but Eunice trips. Her father is about to split her skull when Aurelia throws a fast ball at his head and almost kills him. Her grandmother takes Aurelia to an African American woman psychiatrist to get over her trauma and has a friendly female judge visit her to assure her that she will not be charged with a crime. So Aurelia's next greatest problem is getting to the final game of the season when her mother insists she must go to a picnic instead. Aurelia jumps from the train taking them to the picnic and hitchhikes to the game, which she wins with a special pitch her grandmother has taught her.

The Girls of Summer is every bit as foolish and unrealistic as it sounds. To begin with, the characters are unreal, particularly Aurelia who speaks like a college graduate, pitches better than anyone else in town, and single-handedly integrates the junior high school. Eunice's character is never fleshed out, serving instead as a foil to Aurelia. Granny paints her own house, coaches like a pro, raises her granddaughters alone, and intimately knows the only female judge in the county. Carleton County is backward enough to have seen the killing of civil rights workers a few years back but just happens to have an African American woman doctor practicing at the local hospital and a female judge. Furthermore, the girls' campaign to play baseball is won far too easily, with almost no resistance. As nice a dream as it is, it's a little hard to swallow.

Anita Cornwell tries to provide strong female role models for her readers, but in the process, she fails to make them human. The plot also fails, swinging between Eunice's wildly unbelievable escape from her father's meat cleaver to the mundane details of baseball games which will interest only the most avid fans.

It's too bad *The Girls of Summer* falls so flat, because we certainly can use more YA books featuring strong girls and women actively trying to improve their lives, even through sports. While many YA books focus on sports as African American boys' ticket to college and prosperity, this is the first I've seen which suggests the same avenue for girls. This, too, is part of the book's idealism—relatively few girls of any race manage to attend college on athletic scholarships, especially in the early 1970s, and baseball is simply not a female collegiate event. Perhaps more importantly, *The Girls of Summer* is unlikely to convince its readers that reading is an enjoyable or worthwhile pursuit either.

This novel's reading level is fifth to eighth grade. With a virtually all-female cast, it will not appeal to boys, but girls will also have a hard time becoming absorbed by the lackluster plot.

15. Davis, Ossie. *Just Like Martin*. New York: Simon and Schuster, 1992. 215 pages. ***

In Alabama 1963, change is sweeping across the land. Fourteen-year-old Isaac Stone has met Dr. Martin Luther King, Jr., and vows to be like him, to embrace nonviolence and to protest injustice wherever he finds it. As the Junior Assistant Pastor of Holy Oak Baptist Church and the president of the Young People's Bible Class, Stone works side by side with Reverend Cable, a personal friend of Dr. King's. Stone tries to set a good example for his peers, despite having his leadership constantly challenged by jealous Hookie Fenster. When *Just*

Like Martin opens, the Holy Oak Baptist Church, in fact all the blacks in Stone's town, are preparing to go to the March on Washington. Only Stone can't go, forbidden to participate by his Korean War veteran father who believes that nonviolence is cowardice and marching will not change anything. Stone tries to respect his father, Ike, although he's a difficult and morose man. Before Stone's mother died, she explained to him that his father changed after the war, that something terrible happened to him in Korea, from which he never recovered. So Stone struggles to understand his father and to take care of him as best he can.

When the church members return exuberant from the March on Washington, Reverend Cable approaches them with the idea of training the children to take the lead in the next marches. In a stormy meeting, the church fathers refuse, insisting that letting children lead marches is unsafe and cowardly. An elderly lawyer finally convinces them at least to offer children's workshops in nonviolence, because the children want to fight for their own future. Then a bomb explodes in the junior Bible class, killing two girls and severely injuring one boy. The congregation is devastated, but Stone takes the lead to organize a city-wide children's march against racist violence.

Realizing that he cannot keep Stone from the march, Ike decides to go along to protect him. But Stone is more concerned about his father bringing his gun along and sparking violence, so he hides his gun. Meanwhile, he practices Dr. King's "I Have a Dream" speech, to give at the rally following the march. But he never gets the chance. Despite a large but peaceful turnout and a valid march permit, the sheriff orders everyone to disperse or risk arrest. When the children refuse to leave, the police begin arresting people. Stone's father fights back and is beaten badly and arrested. Afterward, Ike refuses to talk to Stone, insisting that he would never have been so humiliated if Stone hadn't hidden his gun. Although Stone knows that Ike would probably have been killed if he had pulled out a gun, nevertheless his father blames him for what happened, snarling: "The worst thing that ever happened to me in my whole life was having you for a son!"

Ike decides they are moving to California, away from the site of his humiliation. Sadly, Stone says good-bye to all his friends, to his church, and to the only home he has ever known. Just before they move, though, President Kennedy is shot, and Ike spends a night by the grave of Lucy, his wife, trying to understand all the violence. There, he has a change of heart and returns in the morning to tell Stone his terrible secret about Korea. While over there, Ike accidentally shot a mother and baby and has never forgiven himself. Realizing that they cannot outrun their fears, Ike decides to stay in Alabama, to rejoin the community, and to try to open himself up to Stone.

Just Like Martin follows two important revolutions, the Civil Rights Movement and the opening of a father's heart. Violence, justice, and responsibility weave the two themes together, with the son teaching the father. Ike's metamorphosis is moving and realistic, showing the ways that world events can impact a despairing man's psyche. His treatment of Stone, his reaction to nonviolence and to the humiliation of a beating and jail all ring heartbreakingly true. Stone, on the other hand, provides a perfect role model. Perhaps too perfect. Although author Ossie Davis tries to show Stone struggling to stay nonviolent, he is still too good to be entirely believable. Here is a fourteen-year-old who constantly forgives his father's verbal abuse, leads his peers, excels in school, nurtures kids' strengths when others have given up on them, catches the personal attention of Dr. Martin Luther King, Jr., successfully organizes a city-wide demonstration, memorizes the speeches of black leaders, and has a principal grooming him for a scholarship to Morehouse College while he's still in junior high school. Without more exploration of Stone's internal life and conflicts, he's a little too good to identify with.

Despite this weakness, *Just Like Martin* offers a powerful look at the events of the early 1960s and how they affected blacks in one ordinary Alabama town. By making the events personal, Ossie Davis encourages young readers to picture themselves there and to envision that they, too, can make social change. At the same time, he exposes one complicated father-son relationship, exploring the way societal oppression can contaminate personal relationships and destroy lives. Ultimately, *Just Like Martin*'s message is hopeful, pointing to personal responsibility and just action as the path for both personal and societal change.

One serious weakness of the book is its exclusively male focus. While novels about coming of age *as a man* may legitimately have a strictly male focus, *Just Like Martin* is a more universal story and has no excuse for excluding females to the extent it does. All but one of Stone's friends are male, none of the three main characters has a mother, all the church's civil rights organizing is done solely by men and boys, and every leader is male. Even the church meeting about nonviolence training for the children features only men. Judging by *Just Like Martin*, one would think that women and girls never participated in the Civil Rights Movement at all, which is a misleading and damaging impression to give both female and male readers. For obvious reasons, then, *Just Like Martin* will appeal to boys more than girls. It has a seventh to tenth grade reading level.

16. DeVeaux, Alexis. *Spirits in the Street*. Garden City, New York: Anchor Press, 1973. 192 pages. **

Alexis DeVeaux considers *Spirits in the Street* a novel. This novel contains six chapters of prose poetry, news clippings, drawings, diary entries, poetry, and dialogue written in drama format. The book begins with a poem: "Do Not/pass/thru the pages/of this/book/and hear/nothin/on the way"; and a prose poem: "I write this book in recognition of the collective spirit of 3 people on 114 street. And their battle for survival. Forced to exist daily only painfully." The three people are Michelle, Charles, and Lynda, who live in Harlem. The mediator for their life stories, the narrator Alexis, writes the story at twenty-two, after she drops out of Cornell University and returns to Harlem.

Although Alexis lovingly refers to the characters and their lives as "poetry," everything about these people's lives is awful. She wants to rescue them—"Away from the block to a different space. The one every body says is peace. Cause the real fantasy of living here is surely absurd." Prison is the operative metaphor for this story, and the characters' only crime is that they are black in a racist society: "We live in a special prison. You can't see the bars and the guards. A force shield keeps us inside and locked out. Inmates. Mates in a . . . box . . . of buildings and streets. A physical obstacle. Money. Information. We don't have either squeezed in here, black. Gates . . . to discourage us . . . to beat us. They say NIGGER GIVE UP. Captured. Yields the desired effects: claustrophobia depression and exile from life. And all those other things that cause inmates to go stir crazy."

The narrator emphasizes the unsavory details of mundane existence, dwelling on inhuman living conditions and institutions, on absent families and cheap but impossible dreams. Woven among the details of daily living are indictments of bureaucracies, particularly the criminal justice system, welfare, and the job market, and reflections on political activism as a constructive outlet for anger.

Family and school receive most of the narrative's attention. Charles never learned to read in school. When Michelle hits her third-grade teacher in retaliation for the teacher's ridicule and slaps, the school blames Michelle and forces her to spend the mornings baby-sitting other "troubled" children outside the guidance counselor's office and the afternoons in class with her head on her desk as punishment. In eighth grade, Lynda challenges her teacher because she's bored. She hangs out in the bathroom with other bored students. When a teacher barges into the bathroom and grabs only Lynda and one other girl to punish them for all of the girls' loitering and smoking, Lynda, in trying to extricate herself from the teacher's grasp, slaps the teacher to the ground. She gets suspended and sent to a girls' home.

Nevertheless, the young women continue to attend school, in spite of the racist white teachers.

Alexis' father spends more time in prison than at home. When Alexis, sixteen, runs away from home because it's too crowded, the court requires her to submit to counseling at a center for emotionally disturbed children. Michelle's mother struggles alone to support six children. Her favorite brother, Melvin, is in jail. Lynda, now seventeen, essentially abandoned by her family, is the mistress of a drug dealer named Sammy. Charles, with a mother in a state hospital and a father disappeared, was shuttled along the eastern seaboard to live with assorted relatives. Charles began his criminal career when he was fourteen, spending time in "training schools." Now eighteen, Charles is a junky who spends all of his time in the street, sorting through garbage and stealing whatever he can to hawk to buy drugs.

Given the depressing material and tone of the narrative, it's easy to miss the almost upbeat ending. Alexis concludes her story with a scene from a play she finished, in which the mother and daughter characters love each other and are getting strong from their struggles.

In its intense and unrelenting analysis of racism and black youths' angry reaction to it, *Spirits in the Street* is unparalleled in black young adult literature. Despite its unusual narrative techniques, the novel is accessible to high-school readers. Its poetry is irresistibly sumptuous and compelling. But I cannot recommend *Spirits in the Street* unqualifiedly to all high-school readers. Some readers will not appreciate Alexis DeVeaux's representing Harlem as hell on earth; others will challenge the author's assertion that all white people are the enemy. However, some readers will appreciate the narrator's bluntness and "no need to explain" approach to her characters. She takes the reader into an abyss which is in itself sufficient explanation and justification for her characters' unattractive anger, violence, apathy, and substance abuse. Love is understood as the basis for telling these characters' stories, but love is missing from their stories. To some readers, *Spirits in the Street* will seem realistic and righteous, to others extreme and depressing.

Alexis DeVeaux's indictment of racist schools and teachers, and of racist bureaucracies, is poignant and absolutely on target. Unfortunately, because the author shifts abruptly from idea to incident as if each were a poem—often using poetic forms—the book seems too short, ending like a cliffhanger, after it has stirred up the reader's despair and anger. Not that the reader should expect linear plot and resolution of conflict typical of traditional narrative, since *Spirits in the Street* announces its radical, experimental departure on page one. I suspect that most readers would want to read more of Alexis DeVeaux's penetrating analyses.

The profanity, given the characters' anger, is remarkably tame. The hostility toward family needs no explanation in light of the characters' experiences. However, the author's wholesale rendering of all families as dysfunctional and dangerous, attributable solely to the racist conditions of their lives, seems simplistic and irresponsible. It contradicts the reality of the majority of black parents in Harlem who protect and nurture their children precisely because of and in spite of the hostile, racist society.

Although the narrator and two of the three central figures in the novel are female, male and female readers will feel equally involved in the story, primarily because its focus is on anger, despair, and action. Because a disproportionate number of black youth, especially young men, are inappropriately labeled disturbed and unfairly incarcerated, *Spirits in the Street* is, sadly, perhaps more relevant today than when it was published twenty years ago.

17. DeVeaux, Alexis. *Don't Explain: A Song of Billie Holiday.* New York: Harper and Row, Publishers, 1980. 151 pages. *****

Coretta Scott King Honor Book, 1981

The title of Alexis DeVeaux's biography refers to her theme and style as well as to one of Holiday's standards about love, loss, and betrayal. DeVeaux has written a prose poem, broken into four chapters or movements—"Swing, Billie," "So Much Jazz," "Blues," and "The Last Song," that reads like fiction, punctuated by occasional drama-format splices. She blends third-person narration with first-person internal monologue by Holiday about the insecurity and drug addiction that gnawed at her. The book traces the jazz legend's life in a linear fashion, from her birth in 1915 in Baltimore as Eleanora Fagan to her death in 1959 in New York as Lady Day. That is where the book's obedience to the conventions of traditional biography ends.

The elements of the legend's life on which the author concentrates make *Don't Explain: A Song of Billie Holiday* particularly compelling reading for young adults. DeVeaux dwells on Holiday's formative, fragmented family experience: her mother, Sadie, a domestic and later restaurant owner, left Billie to follow work; her father, Clarence, a jazz guitarist and trumpeter, left his wife and daughter to follow his dream of becoming a professional musician. Ten years old and in the fifth grade, mistaken for a "grown" woman, Billie drops out of school to scrub stoops to support herself and deflects unwanted male attention. After a neighbor rapes her, she is sent for two years to a Catholic institution as punishment.

Ultimately, mother and daughter, for whom family is all important, are reunited in vibrant and relatively free Harlem. DeVeaux stresses the double thrill for Billie of having a literal and figurative home, with her mother and in Harlem. Unfortunately, economics again determine the family's life, for the Great Depression and Sadie's illness strike, forcing Billie to hit the streets in search of work at the tender age of fifteen. Exhibiting the uncompromising pride which characterized her professional career, Billie refuses to slave as a domestic and, by default and a miracle, lands a job singing in a club in Harlem, Pod's and Jerry's.

Initially, she fights managers' and audiences' desire to treat her like a stripper instead of a singer. On demand, she performs popular mainstream tunes she dislikes, tunes with lyrics that "offended challenged/or blamed no one for war/or world tension," but through her handling of the tunes, she turns their meaningless words around. Not allowed the comforts of a star, she enters clubs through the back door and waits by the toilets, away from the white patrons in the clubs, until she performs. Treated as a money maker willing to sacrifice her soul and artistic vision for fame and fortune, Holiday often sacrifices her livelihood rather than cater to whites' minstrel show expectations. Disrespected by managers and audiences, and derided by fellow artists who did not understand her genius or who envied her explosive success, Holiday faces betrayal and malicious misrepresentation in recording studios, in clubs, on the road, and in films.

From her debut at the innocent age of fifteen, through her long-suffering exploitation and lack of recognition, to her two prison terms, subsequent comebacks, and finally her sudden death, DeVeaux accentuates Holiday's indomitable and defiant struggles over her triumphs and losses. The poetry takes the reader on an emotional roller coaster ride through Holiday's turbulent life and career.

The author mentions that Holiday had numerous affairs but never fleshes out these lovers. Instead of detailing Holiday's two failed marriages—to womanizer and drug addict Jimmy Monroe and to Louis McKay who could not handle his wife's powerful demons of insecurity and drug abuse, the author baldly attacks the sexism which impinged on Holiday's self-esteem. Holiday sought a man "to come sweep away her pain and self-doubt"; she internalized society's message that a man could make her a complete person. The reader feels the agony of Holiday's loneliness and generosity, which everyone else in her life abused.

Don't Explain: A Song of Billie Holiday is a thoroughly original, powerfully emotive book that young adult readers will find hard to put down—because its poetry flows uninterruptedly and because its story compels and engages. Although it is a biography, it presents feelings primarily, facts minimally. Pains and pressures, interrupted by spasms of beauty and joy, emanate from the lines. By its tragic ending, the book makes it clear how Holiday was "broke"—in the broadest sense—on her deathbed.

With her brilliantly selected and executed episodes, Alexis DeVeaux, like Billie Holiday, "transform[s] a minor singing part/into an event./With a sense of rhythm about words she knew/which ones to put/together./When to pause for emphasis./Which phrases were most powerful or scorching. She wanted her listeners to see and feel/beauty in the painful/story she was singing." The author turns the commonly understood approach to the jazz legend's life on its head: the tragedy of Billie Holiday's life was not Billie Holiday's life but the racism and sexism which brutalized her, and the economic inequality which hurt her family and her artistry. Because she was black and female, Billie Holiday was essentially a slave struggling for her freedom from agents, managers, audiences, record companies, film makers, and predatory "friends."

Don't Explain: A Song of Billie Holiday is a praise poem. The poetry describing Holiday's music is music itself. The author manages to convey the legend's personality— insecure, moody, sensitive, and proud—and style—"sassy and cool," dramatic, "mesmerizing and witchful." DeVeaux and Holiday favor(ed) serious songs. *Don't Explain: A Song of Billie Holiday* unfolds the development of the legend's signature songs, such as "God Bless the Child" and "Strange Fruit." *Don't Explain: A Song of Billie Holiday* is magnificent as a work of art and as a truly inspired biography, highly recommended for middle-school and high-school readers who are not intimidated by poetry.

18.　Dodson, Owen. *Boy at the Window*. New York: Farrar, Straus and Giroux, 1970. 212 pages.**

Coin, the protagonist of *Boy at the Window*, is nine years old, the ninth child of Oscar and Naomi Foreman. The time is 1926, the place, Berriman Street, in the Brownsville section of Brooklyn. Coin's neighborhood is home to a big cast of eccentric black, Italian, and Jewish characters who form a tight-knit community—all except for the racist and anti-Semitic Mrs. Carth, whom the neighbors pity for her self-imposed isolation in the midst of their vibrant community. The plot of *Boy at the Window* is fairly simple: when Coin's mother dies, he goes to Washington, D.C., to live with her brother, his Uncle Troy. The move involves Coin's losing his childhood innocence and growing into an adult understanding of life and death.

In the first half of the novel, Coin's mother is weak and walks with a limp. Her condition started the day Coin came into the world; she suffered a stroke during his birth. Coin feels guilty about his mother's disability and assumes responsibility for her recovery. When Mrs. Quick, the nurse, says that the Lord, through the Reverend S. Robert Blanton, heals the sick and raises the dead on Thursday evenings at the Miracle Baptist Church, Coin begs his mother to attend services. Convinced that he can cure his mother if he can get in touch with God and help his mother to do the same, Coin becomes born again during regular Sunday services at his family's church. However, Coin's mother suffers a second stroke, which kills her.

The second half of *Boy at the Window* is devoted to the death and funeral of Naomi Foreman and to how each member of the family copes with this loss. The novel ends with Coin settling into his new home with his Uncle Troy. There Coin is pounded with a rude awakening: he "accidentally" witnesses a striptease, gets drunk with his uncle's friends, and then catches his uncle in bed with a feisty lover. Yet the novel has a happy ending. Coin experiences a sort of epiphany, where he "sees" God and feels a calmness and confidence about his life and life in general.

Boy at the Window takes place in 1926, and Owen Dodson takes care to include historical details that lend the story a sense of authenticity and accuracy. Furthermore, the essential story being told here is timeless: a boy's initiation into adolescence, his painful reluctance to let go of his simple, childlike notions about sex and procreation, about life, death and the afterlife, and finally his easing into adult knowledge of sex and death. The sting of racial slurs, which the novel explores, is also, unfortunately, timeless. One minor but disconcerting aspect of the book is that Owen Dodson uses a few clichés of Indians as wild and savage to characterize some of the children's games in the street.

Boy at the Window is definitely not a book for preteens, even though its protagonist is one. The narrative is at its best when the author attempts to convey his young protagonist's childish attitudes and misunderstandings, with Coin's mind making strange leaps and easily losing his concentration. Also realistic is Coin's obsessing about adults and older siblings whom he dislikes for petty reasons that, from his perspective, are all-important. Young readers will relate to the narrative's perspective, but they will be bored and slowed down by the book. The plot is tied to inner action, to Coin's maturing sense of religious belief. Coin first sees God as a little man made out of sunshine, standing behind his mother. Later, he sees and feels God in the everyday miracle of the rising sun. There is a nice message. And this kind of action, suggested primarily through metaphors, is more accessible to high-school readers. However, high-school readers may have trouble relating to a nine-year-old protagonist. This is not a novel that will appeal more to boys than to girls, but its highly allegorical spiritual mode makes it an engaging book only for very sophisticated fifth through seventh graders, or for unusually sympathetic tenth through twelfth graders.

19. Dodson, Owen. *Come Home Early, Child.* New York: Popular Library, 1977. 221 pages.*

Ten-year-old Coin Foreman of *Boy at the Window* sneaks away from the pitiful guardians in Washington, D.C., that his father farmed him out to after his mother's death: his blind, drunk, number-playing Uncle Troy and Troy's kinky girlfriend, Mrs. Walker. He returns to his family's multiethnic, shabby Brooklyn neighborhood, to a world of dysfunction and destruction. The day he returns, his church burns down. When he is twelve, his stubborn father dies, forcing the children to relocate. When Coin is sixteen, his sister, angelic Agnes, who sacrificed her romantic longings to play surrogate mother, dies.

Coin feels guilty and perplexed. His mother suffered a stroke giving birth to him and eventually died from another stroke. He became a Christian to pray for his mother's recovery, but because she died, he stole from the collection plate to spite God. His father suffered a stroke struggling to rebuild his burnt-out family and burned-down church. His sister suffered a stroke while breaking her back to create a decent home for him, which he never appreciated. One brother, Oscar, is incarcerated; the other, Woody, a mischievous street rat, is on his way.

After Agnes dies, what's left of the family—Coin and his desperately lonely and horny sister, Bernice— disintegrates. Coin takes a room in the house of the holier-than-thou drunken Mrs. Quick, but when the house turns out to be the preferred destination for neighbors' assignations, he leaves. Homeless, he enlists in the Navy. His tour of duty as the only black yeoman on the *U.S.S. Commodore* takes him to Italy and reunites him with his childhood black friend, Ferris, the ship's cook. Along the way, he befriends the white Lieutenant Commander, Mark, with whom he reads and discusses poetry. On shore, Coin sightsees and swims or relaxes with Ferris, even though he won't accept Ferris' debauched drinking and whoring. Coin taints his one happy experience in Italy with sin: the family of his girlfriend, Fortunata, welcomes him, and for once in his life, he feels at home. However, he departs, fearing he betrayed their love and trust by possibly impregnating their innocent daughter.

Coin returns to Brooklyn at nineteen, to death. He sees: Mrs. Quick, the lone survivor of his former decrepit neighbors, in a drunken stupor; Bernice, abandoned by her lover and denied custody of her baby, living in an unseemly house to which she refuses to invite him; and his enemy and former guardian-by-default, Lucy Horwitz, laid out in a vulgar coffin with second-hand flowers. Coin stands, drunk, content, embracing death as a fact of life, and realizes that he is now a "man."

Come Home Early, Child contrasts the hellish prison of Brooklyn's slums with the heavenly freedom of the Navy and the coexistent purity and lust of Italy, as the parameters for Coin's journey from childhood to manhood. It is not necessary to read this novel's forerunner, *Boy at the Window*, in order to appreciate the characters and plot, for Owen Dodson provides key information from the first book when appropriate. Readers of *Boy at the Window* who want to follow Coin Foreman's story will not be heartened by the way his life turns out. Although ribaldry and sick humor abound, this novel is essentially tragic, overflowing with evil people and death. The title, which comes from a song Bernice sings, is telling, for even its message of arrival and comfort at home are mockingly undercut by Coin's isolation and homelessness.

Owen Dodson introduces homosexuality into the story offensively. Two of the most unsavory characters in the novel are Lucy and Franz. Lucy helps Agnes buy a house and raise Coin and Bernice, motivated by her "perverted but unconsummated affection" for Agnes. Franz, a European in Italy, objectifies Coin the black native as a rare commodity and comes on to him, which temporarily traumatizes Coin. Although the homosexual aspect of these characters is not extensively developed, it nonetheless sends the consistently negative message that homosexuals are lonely, predatory freaks.

Because this novel veils much of its meaning in dense metaphor, it shortchanges exposition of basic facts and explanations, particularly regarding Lucy and Mark. Although her name sounds Jewish, the narrative informs the reader only that Lucy Horwitz is black; in fact, she makes derogatory remarks about Jews. Then again, she could be a self-hating Jew, for she also makes derogatory comments about black features and disparages black group loyalty. If Owen Dodson intended her to be Jewish, then he viciously stereotyped her as money-grubbing, bloodsucking, and powerful. Her cynical mocking of the Foremans' religion would then take on another more distasteful meaning, too.

As for Mark, the only explanation implied for why he— a white officer of an essentially segregated ship where all of the blacks except Coin are in the galley slaving as cooks and cleaners—begins inviting Coin into his quarters for intimate conversations framed by literary talk, is the photograph of two black children tucked in with his personal effects. Implying what? Does Mark have black children? The narrative never settles this question.

Its content and style recommend *Come Home Early, Child* to a select few eleventh and twelfth grade readers who can appreciate its heavy literariness—it frequently refers to classic American and European poetry—and its numerous Christian metaphors, particularly the Crucifixion, apropos of the preponderance of suffering and death in this story. Its mysterious and figurative narrative style will baffle readers of average ability.

20. Glass, Frankcina. *Marvin and Tige.* New York: St. Martin's Press, 1977. 232 pages. *****

American Library Association Notable Books for Children and Young Adults, 1978; Coretta Scott King Honor Book, 1978

Eleven-year-old Tige Jackson lives with his mother in extreme poverty in a half-furnished Atlanta apartment. Tige's mother, a laid-off factory worker who is often sick and in pain, earns a meager living as a reluctant prostitute. Tige helps by soliciting men for his mother and by stealing food. Tige never has three meals a day, but he has his mother's love and his freedom. Then his mother dies.

To avoid the confinement of an orphanage or foster care, Tige runs away to face the street alone. There he is befriended by Marvin Stewart, a middle-aged white man who has dropped out of his white-collar job to scrape by doing odd jobs and roaming the streets. Marvin and Tige do not particularly like each other at first, but they need each other. Gradually, that need turns to love, and Marvin wants to adopt Tige. However, Tige becomes deathly ill, forcing Marvin to track down the boy's biological father, who abandoned him as a baby. Marvin asks Tige's father, Richard, for money for a doctor for Tige, but instead Richard decides to bring his son to live with him and his new family. Marvin realizes that the most loving thing he can do for Tige is to let him go, but he finds his life empty without him. Tige, too, misses Marvin, until they decide that there is room in his life for both a father and a friend.

Marvin and Tige is a uniquely moving depiction of two survivors slowly growing toward each other, overcoming their stereotypes and self-protective armor to teach each other how to love again. Their struggles in the process are warm and funny—there are no altruistic heroes here, only prickly, stubborn characters hiding tender hearts. Frankcina Glass does an astounding job of showing the slow changes in each character and the powerful bond they forge.

The importance of a father figure to a young boy is an implicit central theme of the story. Yet Glass manages to emphasize male characters without denigrating women or mothers. This makes *Marvin and Tige* appealing to girls as well as boys. Likewise, Glass deals with the theme of interracial friendship thoughtfully, describing it as one of many issues Tige and Marvin must work out. Her judicious ending, with Tige embraced by his black, biological family while he continues to treasure Marvin's love, affirms African American families without denigrating sincere interracial bonds.

Marvin and Tige is a heartbreaking but ultimately optimistic book. The vocabulary is accessible for seventh graders and up, although some younger readers may initially be slowed down by Tige's Black English. The book is long but broken up into manageable chapters for younger readers. Older readers, ninth through twelfth graders and adults, will find that the novel speaks to them also, with layers of meaning and depth reminiscent of Mildred Taylor's classic young adult novels. Marvin and Tige is an outstanding piece of work, most highly recommended.

21. Graham, Lorenz. *South Town*. Chicago: Follett Publishing Company, 1958. 189 pages. **

Although it appeared in 1958, *South Town* is included in this bibliography because two of its sequels came out after 1968. *South Town* introduces sixteen-year-old David Williams, who lives in an archetypal rural, segregated southern community. In the spring and summer of 1955, the Supreme Court decision for integration is news. David and his seven-year-old sister labor on their family's subsistence-level farm on weekdays before and after walking miles to the modest, recently desegregated Pocahontas County Training School. David dreams of becoming a doctor and returning to care for the people of South Town, although the story never explains what triggered this dream. He seems to be the only serious student in a school where classmates frequently stay home to help their families farm.

South Town is poor. Many families moved North for better opportunities, while the remaining men moved to the cities for better work. David's father, Ed, worked in a city shipyard during the Korean War and parlayed that job into postwar work in a factory. On the occasional weekend when Ed can come home to see his family, he feeds them fantastic stories of the outside world, where people are different, and there's modern plumbing and bathrooms, and better schools provide black students with adequate preparation for college. But David's father has no desire to move his family with him, for he knows that in the city they would live in a crowded apartment in a segregated slum, whereas in South Town they have a house and four acres of their own land where they're relatively isolated from whites.

Previously Ed worked as a mechanic at Mr. Boyd's dealership but left because Boyd paid the black mechanics significantly less than the white mechanics. Boyd is the Williamses' nemesis, the richest man in the county, who owns most of the property on which local black families live and farm. Boyd desperately needs David's father for his garage, but instead of making friendly overtures, he warns Ed that work in the city will run out and then he won't be able to find a job in South Town.

Boyd's son Harold is David's archenemy. David's other white classmates are relatively poor, but under Harold Boyd's leadership, they assume an air of superiority. Harold's arrogance almost causes the death of his cousin, Little Red. Harold, refusing to swim near the black boys, leads his white friends to swim in the dangerous current near the dam, despite the other boys' warnings. David risks his own life to save Little Red's life, an act of courage which transforms Harold's opinion of him. As a token of appreciation, Mr. Boyd offers David a summer job in the garage but warns him to respect the workplace's hierarchy and segregation. When David gives notice so he can return to school in the fall, Mr. Boyd attacks his ambition and then fires him.

The ultimate crisis occurs when Ed loses his job in the city due to cutbacks. Forced to seek employment in South Town, Ed agrees to work again for Boyd, but only for a salary equal to that of the white mechanics. Predictably, Boyd not only refuses him but insures that none of the other dealerships will hire Ed either. When Ed returns to persuade Boyd, the encounter escalates into an argument, and Boyd has Ed arrested for disturbing the peace. The Williamses worry about Ed's fate in jail while trying to protect themselves from reprisals by the police and the Klan. When the white man guarding their front door is killed by racists, the sheriff illogically blames the people inside the house and arrests them. Thirty-two people, including David, his sister, and his mother, go to jail. "Foreign" black lawyers from the NAACP win the case and get Ed released as well. But Ed arrives home beaten, bloody, and scarred. The final scene of *South Town* shows the Williamses fleeing to Detroit, where their many relatives sing praises of the North. Their departure, instead of signaling the promise of a new beginning, is described as if it were a funeral.

Aside from the Williams family, most of the black characters are gradualists, espousing compliance with the white power structure. Reverend Arrington prays for love and understanding. Brother Dan Jenkins, the government farm agent, advises angry friends to placate the white folks' egos at the expense of black victims' pride. Mechanic Joe Broadnax tries to persuade Ed to swallow his pride and work for Boyd, regardless of the conditions. The one exception is Israel Crawford, who argues that the educated men of the community who can speak powerfully should use their gifts to "wake the folks up." Crawford envisions an organized community working together, but the purity of his position is compromised by his bitterness and despair over losing his son in the Korean war and losing his farm in a depression.

The logical sentiment with which David greets every disaster is, "I hate white people." However, *South Town* includes a range of white characters designed to force David to question his prejudice. Dr. Anderson cares for the Williamses in the fullest sense, mentoring David's career ambitions as well as providing health care. Judge Armstead believes in applying the law equally to whites and blacks. Travis Solomon, a veteran who's committed to challenging segregation, explains to David that in Korea, black and white soldiers fought side by side, and a black medic saved his life. Another white veteran, mechanic Sam McGavock, teaches David auto mechanics. Both McGavock and Solomon join the vigil outside David's house to prevent racist whites from trying to burn the house down; they prove to the mistrustful Williamses that not all white people hate blacks.

South Town does a good job of showing individual and institutional racism at work through the details of daily life. In extensive analyses of the institutions that shape people's lives and dreams, Lorenz Graham reveals how African

Americans internalize racism and the impact it has on their self-esteem and health. In a flowing, fast-paced narrative, he offers a panoramic view of a typical southern town and its people on the edge of the Civil Rights Movement. As historical fiction, *South Town* works well, acquainting the reader with the diversity of experiences and attitudes of southern African Americans during the pre-Civil Rights period. As a meditation on racism and social change, it falters when it uses interior reflective monologues and obvious, didactic dialogue rather than action. And the uncritical reader comes away from this book with the inaccurate idea that most African Americans were complacent and passive even under the harshest of conditions.

South Town is a pacifist's delight. When David discusses the possibility of registering for the army to get training for a trade, his mother dissuades him. But the nonviolent element in the story operates on a deeper, more disturbing level, too. The black adults in David's life are tender and resilient but strive to indoctrinate him to be passive, to conciliate wounded white egos for survival. They believe that the burgeoning Civil Rights Movement may be too radical. Yet David sees nothing radical in a movement that simply insists on black people's right to live and work like anybody else. He wishes that the black adults around him would speak from their hearts and speak their minds, instead of mediating everything to make it palatable for threatened white listeners. The black citizens of South Town are disarmed psychically as well as physically although they live in a perpetual police state. This point is driven home powerfully in descriptions of the random police raid of the Williamses' household and Ed's arrest. Ironically, the war overseas proves to be a boon for the blossoming activism of South Town. The black and white veterans who return are the most militant, in a productive way. They don't advocate violence, but they are willing to fight violence with violence, in self-defense.

Sympathetic white characters show how racism hurts whites. However, *South Town* embraces some of the paternalistic tone of its white characters. For example, Dr.

Anderson explains to the Williamses why South Town whites mistreat blacks—as if any black southerner needs a white interpreter to understand racism! Whereas Dr. Anderson, as a healer, is the Williamses' literal savior, Solomon and McGavock—the most militant agitators for dismantling the racist system—are the Williamses' spiritual saviors. These white veterans get the best lines in the book, providing the most compelling analysis. Thus David reaches the patronizing conclusion that the best educated make the best leaders, denying the power and potential of grass roots activists who, though they may lack formal education, possess a wealth of understanding and resourcefulness. David feels that he must help black people overcome their "poverty and ignorance."

On the other hand, *South Town* offers an outstanding black-affirmative message. David doesn't desire to be with whites, for he cherishes the black community. He doesn't want to be white, for he is proud of his family, his community, and his heritage. What he wants are the opportunities that whites have.

Lorenz Graham has created a sensitive and strong young man whose experiences will interest readers of both sexes. David's mother is quiet but steady; she responds, while David's father is proactive. David's sister, Betty Jane, plays a minimal role, most likely because she's so young, but she does go to jail for protesting. *South Town* is an easy but rich book that is accessible to middle- and high-school readers. However, high-school readers will best be able to digest the abstractions and analyses woven into the action.

22. Graham, Lorenz. *North Town*. New York: Thomas Y. Crowell Company, 1965. 220 pages. **

North Town picks up where *South Town* left off. The Williams family never made it to Detroit. En route, they visited old friends, the Crutchfields, in North Town, and Mr.

Crutchfield got Ed Williams a job in the Foundation Iron and Machine Works there. In North Town they live in a slum, in a dingy, cramped apartment—but one with modern plumbing and a bathroom. Sixteen-year-old David Williams feels alone. Although he would have been a senior at his South Town school, the counselor here places him in tenth grade at the integrated North Town Central High School and in the vocational track rather than the college preparatory track. The story focuses on how David gingerly maneuvers his way through the unspoken etiquette of his new environment.

Through their trials in North Town, the Williamses lament the absence of family and neighbors. Lorenz Graham demonstrates how northern and urban migration weakened one of southern blacks' greatest assets, the physical and psychological closeness of kin and the sense of community. When Ed Williams resolves to move the family to a middle class neighborhood, the author uses the house hunting experience to show how segregation was enforced through exorbitant prices for houses in poor repair and through white-flight from neighborhoods once a black family moved in. Once the Williamses move to a "better" neighborhood, they fall into the credit trap while trying to furnish their new home. This debt becomes catastrophic when Ed collapses and is hospitalized—for head injuries sustained in South Town. Mr. Crutchfield gets David work at the factory to support the family while Mr. Williams is incapacitated. Again, a benevolent white doctor, Dr. Meyer, saves the day, helping Williams heal.

Lorenz Graham argues that blacks need to help whites, too, by positively depicting David's efforts to secure a job in the factory for Mike, a white friend, in spite of Mr. Crutchfield's opposition: "A white boy? How come you got to look out for a white boy? Ain't you got troubles enough of your own? What he trying to do, get your job?" Mr. Crutchfield also berates David for postponing real work in the factory in favor of the white world's seductive "tease" of school and the dream of becoming a doctor.

The test of the opportunity for true equality and friendship between the races is symbolized by Mike's teaching David football; he teaches him so well that David becomes a star player on the high school team. The crux of the book's happy ending is David's growth as an athlete and the sense of confidence and belonging he gains from it. The football fans, whose various colors David can't distinguish, become a symbol of what he is learning up North and what he values: America as a melting pot, where people are just people.

Mike, poor and white, symbolizes the optimistic success of integration. Mike is presented as an Irish Catholic stereotype, but he bonds with David around their shared poverty and interest in football. His foils are Jimmy and Alonzo, poor and black, who symbolize the pessimistic view of integration. They choose to remain separate from their white peers, warning David, "they're treacherous—smile in your face and laugh at you behind your back." David plays the devil's advocate with them, scrutinizing their opinions in light of how decently the white principal, football coach, and football captain treat him. His white classmates' distance outside of class deeply disturbs him, though.

Buck Taylor is the most complicated black character in *North Town*. His father worked his way through trade school, supported himself as a carpenter, and moved his family North, where he started a real estate business and became a lawyer. Buck espouses a similar self-made attitude, but unlike his father, Buck looks up to whites while considering himself superior to other blacks. The author counters Buck's derogatory judgments of poor black families with incisive analyses from David, other black students, and Buck's own father. Buck's selfishness is contrasted with the other black characters who care about all people and never forget where they come from.

Other black characters advance Lorenz Graham's message as well. David's father continues to play a dominant role in his moral development, instructing him that hard work will lead to success. Jeanette Lenoir, a classmate, always asks for both sides of a story and analyzes situations with such objectivity that she's almost too perfect. With her dark skin,

Jeanette also dramatizes the internalized color consciousness of black students in North Town. The minister, Reverend Hayes, is overtly political in his sermons, condemning the "slavery of poverty and unemployment . . . and the slavery of ignorance."

Lorenz Graham goes out of his way to show that the North was more hospitable to blacks than the South. He doesn't completely idealize the North, for David encounters myriad subtle manifestations of racism daily, and sometimes explosive, overt oppression. Still, whites deliver in the crucial moments of the Williamses' life. *North Town* contains the same paternalism of *South Town*, with generally positive white characters who win blacks' trust and offer needed help. There is a greater range of personalities and values with the black characters, although the majority of them are compromised in some way. David also witnesses the divisiveness of class within the black community.

David sympathizes with but distances himself from strongly black-identified characters in the story. He never questions why Jimmy and Alonzo have low expectations for themselves or why they willfully unlearn in school. Other black characters, Hap and Head, give David a ride in their stolen car, then try to convince him to jeopardize his freedom in the name of black unity and in defiance of white law. Unbelievably, the justice system proves fair, the white judge "kind," and the black rebels delinquent and mistaken. David never looks beneath the surface at their anger and despair or at their self-destructive tendencies.

There is one unusual component in *North Town* worth mentioning: the connections between blacks and Jews, which are suggested in two minor passages. Mr. Taylor uses Jews as an example when he urges Buck not to forget his roots; he warns of isolation, just as Jews look down on successful Jews who try to forget Jewish ghettos. In the second incident, Dr. Meyer is clearly a Holocaust survivor. He explains to Mrs. Williams that Mr. Williams must provide one of the essential factors in his own recovery: hopefulness. Meyer uses his survival in the concentration camps as an analogy for Mr. Williams' potential to survive.

Lorenz Graham exposes historical ways of thinking that will shock today's reader who doesn't know the context which gave rise to them. A sophisticated reader will find much to reflect on here, but a naive reader will be easily misled. *North Town* again focuses primarily on male characters, with the exception of the admirable Jeanette who, although David has a crush on her, is not objectified. Ed Williams is again the center of the Williams family's world. But he is a wonderful character: devoted and sensitive, never domineering or arbitrary. Football is one of the subplots, but otherwise this book does not alienate female readers. Middle and high-school readers will be able to appreciate the author's graceful prose and superb character and plot development. Older readers, however, are more equipped to untangle the sophisticated political issues raised.

23. Graham, Lorenz. *Whose Town?* New York: Thomas Y. Crowell Co., 1969. 246 pages. **

David Williams, the hero of *South Town* and *North Town*, is eighteen, expecting to graduate from Central High School and attend State College on scholarship. News of the black riots in most major American cities has everyone in North Town wondering if the same will happen there.

One evening, David and his friends, Jimmy and Lonnie, are insulted and assaulted by a white patron at the Plantation Drive-In. They defend themselves and the incident escalates into a brawl. The white patron who attacked David charges David with assault. The police arrest David and his friends. While they are in custody, Jimmy's car, left in a gas station, is destroyed. They return to the station to question the attendant, in hopes of finding out who destroyed the car, but the white attendant shoots and kills Lonnie, claiming self-defense, which compounds David's criminal charges—his supposedly committing a felony by threatening and attempting to rob the attendant. Buck Taylor's father defends David in court: Lonnie's death is ruled a justifiable homicide, but David's assault charges are dismissed. These incidents cause David to question whose town North Town is—the white man's town or everyone's town? He questions the analogy of America as a football team, which came to him in *North Town*, wondering which "team" to join, the team of all people for "right," or the team of all black people bound by racism.

David's girlfriend, Jeanette Lenoir, now a first year student at State College, maintains her faith in David and in the opportunity for him in "everyone's town." Even after she witnesses the drowning of a black child at the Stanton Park pool, which another friend insists was a deliberate racial attack, Jeanette blames herself for not rescuing the drowning child. Furthermore, when the police arrest her father for assaulting white men who threatened and insulted her, Jeanette has no comment.

Meanwhile, Mr. Williams gets laid off from his job at the Foundation Iron and Machine Works. As his unemployment drags on, he vacillates between despair and sullenness, hanging around town all night, drinking and smoking. Mrs. Williams picks up work as a domestic in Stanton Park, which exacerbates Mr. Williams' frustration and sense of emasculation. But then she challenges her white employer's condemnation of black activism and is fired. Ever self-conscious about not being stereotypable, Mr. Williams disdains unemployment, considering it the same as "relief," for lazy people.

Whose Town?, like its predecessors, espouses a "people are people" philosophy. However, *Whose Town?* has a preachier tone, frequently reiterating assimilationist views on race and racism, which will annoy some readers. Lorenz Graham indulges his ideological agenda in the powerful but excessive "sermons" of black North Town's religious leaders. David flirts briefly with Black Muslim and Black Power sentiments but ultimately he concludes that education, "hard work and right living" will gradually bring about widespread social change. David's experiences will not allow him to generalize about and vilify all white people: in spite of the exploitation and violence he suffers at white hands, he remembers the decent white people who befriended and supported him. Later, Reverend Hayes' urging rioters to disperse by pointing out that they are only hurting themselves—destroying businesses and homes in their own community and putting themselves at risk of police brutality—and his sermon in the aftermath of the damage about all people working together to oppose a racism really speak to David. David's idol, though, is still his father, who, despite his victimization by racists, is not angry with or hostile toward white America.

The adult family members of the young protagonists in *Whose Town?* don't understand their children's militant challenges to racism. The exceptions are Jeanette's parents, who examine the young people's passion for democracy and freedom within the context of the poor conditions that the majority of black people endure in North Town and everywhere in America; even the Lenoirs, however, suggest the youths' culpability in the racial incidents, saying that they started the "cycle" of confrontation by going to formerly all-white facilities.

The powerful white characters, in the guise of acting objectively and fairly, in fact perpetuate David's oppression. Principal Hart, who presumes David's guilt before and after the trial, threatens first to expel David, then to prevent him from graduating. Coach Henderson agrees with David that the majority of black Americans have much to despair about but rebuffs David for talking about "fighting back." Teacher Madigan patronizingly differentiates between the "bad" black people living in poverty and rioting nationwide and the "good" black people in North Town who work hard and don't complain.

A minor but excellent tangent in the novel is its juxtaposition of the headlines about racial incidents from the white and black newspapers. Whereas the "mainstream" white newspaper presents slanderous, sensationalist reports in an attempt to bias its readers' consciences and discourage public debate, the black newspaper boldly publishes the truth to incite action.

Again, Jews figure slightly but significantly in the saga of David Williams' life : his father-figure employer, Sam Silverman, who responds to the destruction of his business during the riot with, "That's all right"; his savior-lawyer, Jack Perlman, without whose help David might have been convicted; his idealized white classmate, Becky Goldberg, who campaigns for "student rights, labor rights, and civil rights, all of which she spoke of as human rights," and who knows the Negro National Anthem better than David does.

As do its predecessors, *Whose Town?* has white characters delivering the novel's major messages. Sam Silverman has the last word, and his advice to David encapsulates the essence of David's psychology throughout this series of novels: "Everything looks bad just now . . . but don't let it get you down. Sometimes just living through your trouble is success, just not giving up, just not quitting." The clemency and passivity of this finale is representative of the perspective underlying the entire novel. And this perspective, while thoughtfully laid out and dissected in the story, will not and should not appeal to the high-school readers who comprise the ideal audience for this book. *Whose Town?* is more male-centered than its predecessors, yet it will engage high-school readers of both sexes.

24. Graham, Lorenz. *Return to South Town*. New York: Thomas Y. Crowell Co., 1976. 245 pages. ***

Fifteen years earlier, David Williams' family left South Town, somewhere in the South, for North Town, somewhere in Michigan, to escape racial prejudice and violence and to seek better jobs and schools. Having completed medical school and his residency, David returns to South Town to complete his boyhood dream of becoming a doctor and serving its people. Four years ago, his beloved father finally worked himself to death. His sister teaches. His mother plans to accompany him to South Town.

David doubts the outward indications that South Town has changed. A modern skyline, mall strips, expressways, modern amenities in the newly-sprawling apartment complexes and housing tracts, a community college, and, most of all, the outlawing of Jim Crow and the relative prosperity of old friends—although the majority left. When he travels the backroads through the bottoms, he sees the appalling poverty of sharecroppers, living with a slavery mind-set, passed over by progress.

Quickly, events erode his confidence that he can practice, let alone succeed, as a doctor in South Town. Doctor Anderson, David's idol, retired, and South Town's black residents, though they cannot fathom why David would prefer to work in their backward and impoverished town instead of the progressive and prosperous North, desperately need David's services, for South Town has four white doctors, all of whom serve white people first and black people last. Black and white residents mistake David for a menial laborer or visitor and struggle to disguise their shock when they learn that he is a doctor. Unfortunately, David's boyhood enemy, Harold Boyd, also a doctor, controls the county's only hospital, built by his father. If he is to get his license from the state Board of Medical Examiners, David needs Boyd's agreement that the hospital will admit David's emergency patients and allow him to follow their care in the hospital. Immediately, David and Boyd clash about de facto segregation in the hospital, with Boyd defending it as a reasonable accommodation to white doctors' and patients' privacy and comfort. Boyd blocks David's licensing.

Catastrophes thrust David into practice—license or not—and gain him respect and rapport within the community. David mobilizes his family and friends to respond to a car accident and a plane crash. When David, the devoted doctor, follows the victims into the hospital, Dr. Von Schilling defers to David—in spite of David's not having a license and Boyd's not wanting a black doctor working in his hospital and caring for white patients! Boyd bursts into the surgery room, fires Von Schilling for insubordination and arrests David for practicing without a license. Fortunately, white Dr. Tennant of the neighboring county's Methodist Hospital secures David's license in time for David to avert court and open his practice.

What's not to like about David Williams the humanist who never objectifies or discriminates against people? He treats all people with respect: in his dealings with "rebbish" whites, he admires their "hard work and steady application" and plays down their race and class privileges that account for who they are and what they have; in his practice, he relates to patients as family rather than clients, "being with the people" instead of "doing things for them." The strong sense of community facilitates this bonding, for, as Lorenz Graham demonstrates, David is embraced as family from the moment he returns. He thinks only of others: repeatedly he dismisses others' expectations that he, as a doctor, should go where the money is; and he risks jail and his career to save the victims of a car accident and a plane crash. All high-school students, particularly aspiring doctors—there are long passages about the travails of medical school, interning, and residency—will admire and empathize with David.

Return to South Town exhibits the series' hallmark gentle but proud protagonist, extended interior monologues punctuated by thought-provoking questions, and animated dialogues. As in the three other novels, Lorenz Graham unobtrusively fills in the essential facts of David's past so that *Return to South Town* can stand on its own. As is typical of Lorenz Graham's other books, black and white people support David. Black lawyer and business professor Dr. Hart helps David settle business and legal transactions; otherwise, David has no use for Hart's "Black identity thing," whereby Hart scares assimilationist blacks and liberal whites with his tirades on black rage and the existential contest between black and white. David's hosts, the Crawfords, work hard and complain but never confront. Nasty whites with their modern plantations whose behavior receives analysis that borders on

pseudo-justification are counterbalanced by "good whites"—
Doctors Tennant and Von Schilling, principal John and teacher
Peggy Smith, and Little Red.

Again, Lorenz Graham explores male-female
relationships as a subplot—how the mass migration north and
to cities of African Americans impacts male and female
identity, relationships, and, consequently, families. However,
the characterization of nurses as "older women, cold, mother
types. And hard." is offensive, even though balanced by
David's remark that nurses typically are the most competent
caregivers and best teachers, providing care without
discriminating. Yet worldly David encourages girls who
express an interest in becoming nurses to become doctors, for the
idea of women being nurses and men being doctors is a "mistaken
idea." Meanwhile, the key women in the story, Velvet
Crawford and David's mother, passively accept their fate as
God's plan.

Fortunately, the heterosexual-marriage imperative is
foisted on a man, not a woman, in *Return to South Town*. Yet it is
women who view David's not being married as a problem. In
connection with this problem, then, the novel introduces a
"solution" in the character of Joyce Palmer, a transplanted
northern black sociology professor who is brilliant, competent,
and attractive—and, as she labels herself, "thoroughly
liberated." Through conversations between David and Joyce,
who is studying the effects of civil rights legislation,
integration, and the changing attitudes of black and white
southerners, Lorenz Graham inserts musings on the connections
and differences between race and class privilege, between
northern and southern whites, between urban and rural
communities, plus the differences between white people who
admit their prejudice versus white people who claim to be
without prejudice. These conversations are meaty, albeit too
brief.

25.   Greenfield, Eloise, *Sister*. New York: Harper Collins Publishers, 1974. 82 pages. ***

   Sister is a very short novel in twelve chapters which are capable of standing on their own as separate short stories. It opens with Doretha Freeman of Washington, D.C., going to a concert which gives her a magical feeling she struggles to hold on to as she returns to her troubled home. Her mother, Thelma, comes home so exhausted from toiling in a laundry that thirteen-year-old Doretha runs the house. Thelma is devastated from the loss of two loves and the seemingly inevitable loss of her older daughter, sixteen-year-old Alberta, who has dropped out of school and disappears for days at a time with her delinquent friends. After the concert, Doretha flips through her journal while she waits for Alberta to come home. When she finishes, her waiting and hoping haven't effected Alberta's return, but Doretha resolves to remember the hard times conjured up by her journal because woven around and through them are good times, too.
   The opening and closing chapters sandwich ten episodes told in flashbacks from Doretha's first journal entry at age nine through her latest entry at thirteen. In one story, the reader learns how she acquires her journal to entertain herself while recovering from a broken ankle. Three of the stories explain how her father's sudden death from a heart attack during his birthday party traumatizes Alberta, then thirteen. Alberta becomes numb and distances herself from her mother and sister. One of the best stories describes Doretha learning about her family's personal experience of the abuses and losses endured under slavery and their legacy of resistance to it embodied in her spirited great-grandfather, Jack. Doretha survives losses in two other stories: her teacher is replaced by a nasty, long-term substitute, and her neighbor gives her his flute in preparation for his death. Another excellent story relates how Thelma, her spirit renewed because she's fallen in love again, is heartbroken when she learns that her boyfriend is married. There are stories of a surrogate mother, Aunt Mae, who helps Doretha learn to deal with the streets, and a surrogate sister,

Sister Shani, who directs the Afrocentric after-school program that helps Doretha boost her academic skills and her black pride.

The short chapters and illustrations in every chapter make this book most appropriate for elementary-school readers, though middle-school students will find the plot engaging. *Sister* will resonate strongly for girls in fourth through seventh grades, the slice of Doretha's life described in the book. The book is distinguished by its sensitive and rich exploration of female relationships. Although her father's death catalyzes profound changes in Doretha's life, the book doesn't dwell on the death itself. The title refers to the characters' calling each other "Sister," an endearing expression signifying the strength and beauty of their relationships, and their respect for each other.

Sister takes the reader on a roller coaster ride of events through which its protagonist remains remarkably stable. Fortunately, Doretha inhabits a world of generally caring adults, strong, supportive families and kinship networks, and loyal friends. But none of these characters or relationships is idealized. *Sister*'s realistic ending is neither happy nor sad. On the one hand, Alberta doesn't revert back to her old self and return home. On the other hand, Doretha copes healthily with the hardship that has taken its toll on her mother and sister.

Although some of their behavior hurts Doretha, Thelma and Alberta are sympathetically portrayed. Thelma is a positive mother, though a sad woman. For instance, while Thelma is composing a sad song as part of her grieving process for her deceased husband, Doretha intrudes, demanding Thelma's undivided attention and pity. Thelma explains to her, "Right now, I need this song. I can't be Mama for a little while. I got to be just me, just Thelma. Just for a little while. And after that, I'll be stronger and I can help you." Doretha thus learns to care for as well as to be cared for, an important ingredient in her growing up. Likewise, Thelma helps Doretha understand Alberta's behavior in a way that empowers Doretha to recover and mature.

The story contains many Afrocentric elements. In addition to the story about the proud legacy of survival and resistance to slavery, there are frequent references to Afros and dashikis, which transport the reader back two decades without detracting from the story's immediacy. The description of the Afrocentric program that Doretha joins, with its celebration of black history and culture, is certainly far from being a relic of the past.

26. Greenfield, Eloise. *Koya DeLaney and the Good Girl Blues.* New York: Scholastic, Inc., 1992. 124 pages. **

Eleven-year-old Koya DeLaney is known and loved by everyone at Barnett School for her brilliant sense of humor and irrepressible laughing fits. During the month of April of her sixth grade year, two significant events take place. Koya's cousin, Del, an emerging music star, visits her town to perform a benefit concert for a homeless shelter. Koya basks in the popularity she enjoys temporarily as Del's cousin. Meanwhile, her best friend, Dawn, distances herself from Koya because she envies the attention her classmates are lavishing on Koya. Dawn, who co-captains the school's Double Dutch team with Koya's sister, Loritha, hurts Loritha by excluding her from a new event in the Double Dutch competition. What hurts Loritha more than Dawn's action is Koya's refusal to take Loritha's side; when Koya insists on excusing Dawn's behavior, Loritha labels her "Miss Good Girl" and decides to shun Koya until Koya takes a stand against Dawn. Koya refuses to get angry and she fears other people's anger, so she makes jokes, and if joking doesn't diffuse the tension, she makes excuses for people's hurtful behavior. However, she hates being taunted with Loritha's variations on "Miss Good Girl," which gives her the blues of the book's title.

At Del's concert, however, Koya loses self-control and throws an angry fit when applauding fans drown out Del's singing of her favorite song. Losing it is a breakthrough for Koya, for it feels good and is over soon. She constructively confronts Dawn and Dawn apologizes to Loritha.

Koya Delaney and the Good Girl Blues is a pleasant story, loaded with details of Koya's everyday school and home life, of Loritha's Double Dutch practices and contests, of Koya's Drama Club practices and Variety Show performance, and of Del's visit to their school and his concert. However, fourth through sixth graders will not find the details tedious or dense. Given that the central characters are Koya and Loritha and the central concern is their sisterly relationship and Koya's friendship with Dawn, girls will find it easier to enter into the novel. With feisty Koya and Loritha, their hard-working and motherly mom, good-natured dad, and tender Del, the reader gets healthy antidotes to sex-role stereotypes. An additional unusual but unobtrusive feminist touch is Eloise Greenfield's referring to every woman in the novel as Ms., even Koya's mother.

Koya's parents are great role models, working hard and saving for their dream of opening their own drug store, where Koya's father will be the pharmacist and her mother the accountant. They are also great parents, consistently warm and concerned, always there for their children. The family joyously spends quality time together every day. Del, portrayed as a person first and a celebrity second, is a sweetheart, warm-spirited and grounded. The teachers at Koya's school are superb and respectful educators who are firm but friendly.

Lest everything seem too perfect, the DeLaneys are not superhuman or heroic. For example, Koya has an unrequited crush on her classmate Winston; Loritha wins second place in the Double Dutch contest; and their parents live comfortably but frugally. Realistically, the parents struggle with how to resolve the conflict between the daughters and, when they reach an impasse, retire to the privacy of the kitchen to argue in whispers. Mr. DeLaney believes that Koya should not be pressured into action, particularly against her friend, while Ms. DeLaney wants Koya to become more assertive and expressive, and "to take a stand for what's right." The novel's focus on anger is unique and useful. In presenting their divergent views on whether Koya's fear of confrontation and anger is healthy, the author presents a balanced discussion and includes Koya's candid rationale for her behavior—although, in such an ideal family and school, the reader may wonder how anything, including anger, could disturb Koya, given the constant affirmation and support she receives.

27. Griffin, Judith Berry. *Phoebe and the General.* New York: Coward, McCann and Geoghegan, Inc. 1977. 47 pages.*

The protagonist in *Phoebe and the General* is thirteen-year-old Phoebe Fraunces, the general is George Washington. Phoebe's father, Sam Fraunces, owns the Queen's Head Tavern in New York City, a popular dining and meeting place. Because Fraunces is patriotic, he knows and serves famous colonist patrons who plan there, in privacy and safety, their treason against the King. On the eve of independence, in 1776, Sam overhears a British loyalist plot to assassinate Washington, a skilled general and an invaluable rallier of the colonial masses, while he lodges at nearby Mortier House. Sam sends Phoebe to work at Mortier House during Washington's visit and to spy, to try to figure out who plans to kill Washington and how he plans to do it and then to warn Washington in time. Suspense mounts slightly as time almost runs out before Phoebe uncovers the assassin. The mystery element, cute but simple, brings the reader alongside Phoebe as she collects fragments of information and races to put them together just in time—she warns Washington as he's about to put peas, poisoned by bodyguard Thomas Hickey, into his mouth.

Phoebe and the General introduces readers to an exciting situation and time. The narrative tells the reader more than it makes the reader feel the distrust and tension in the air, as people try to guess their fellow citizens' political sympathies without giving away their own and as some people's loyalties are easily bought with bribes and rewards for information. Although Sam warns Phoebe that they would be killed if the "enemy" discovered their spying, the story itself doesn't have a sense of danger. Handled well but too quickly is the political situation from the black angle. The Fraunces family, unlike the majority of African Americans in New York City during this era, were free blacks, and Sam articulates his confusion and frustration with his patriotic mission: he respects Washington, but Washington owns slaves; he supports the colonists' freedom but knows the new government will not immediately free enslaved blacks. There is also the suggestion that Phoebe could "slip" among the guests at Mortier House because the white patrons would not notice her, i.e., she was invisible as a black and a servant.

The story itself renders Phoebe invisible, too. The ideas and dialogue mainly come from Sam. The happy ending of the story pertains to Sam, who, the reader learns, becomes Washington's steward after American independence. For a book whose title and hero is Phoebe, it's annoying that it ends with, "No one knows what happened to Phoebe after that."

Although its basic plot will interest readers of all ages, the illustrations and read-aloud simplistic narrative style of *Phoebe and the General* make it suitable for elementary-school students, not for young adults. *Phoebe and the General* was also published as *Phoebe the Spy* in 1977.

28. Grimes, Nikki. *Growin'*. New York: The Dial Press, 1977. 107 pages. ****

When Yolanda Jackson's father dies in an automobile accident, Yolanda struggles to adjust to her father's absence, a new neighborhood, and a new school in an unspecified city. Yolanda prefers to be called Pump, short for Pumpkin, her father's nickname for her. Because her mother, Renee, is strict and discourages her from writing poetry, Pump feels that her mother hates her. After her father's death, Renee tries to get closer to Pump, with no success, for Pump is "mad at Daddy for leaving me, and mad at Mama for still being alive when she knew I loved Daddy best, and mad at God because it was His doing."

Pump gradually replaces her father with a new friend, classmate Jim Jim. Jim Jim is a lovable contradiction: in school, he bullies his classmates, but at home he is a teddy bearish "man of the house," caring for his five siblings while his mother works. What makes Pump and Jim Jim uncannily compatible, however, is that Pump dreams of being a poet and Jim Jim of being an illustrator, and they take each other seriously. Together, they critique Pump's poems and Jim Jim's drawings, and even create joint story books.

The turning point in Pump and Renee's relationship occurs by accident. Pump, in perusing her mother's high school yearbook, finds poetry written by her mother. Renee justifies her jaded attitude with: "When I was your age, I used to write poems and short stories. Everybody said I was gonna be a great and famous writer someday. . . . Then, when I got older, I sent my poems out to magazines and publishing houses. But nothin' ever happened. Came time to make it on my own, all I knew how to do was write and type. Never wanted to know anything else. So today, I work for an insurance company, typing." Pump comes to understand that her mother discourages her to protect her from suffering the same rejection and frustration. Renee comes to understand that her daughter deserves the chance to try to make it as a writer, despite the risk of failure. They grow closer as they share memories of their deceased husband/father and their passion for writing. As Pump realizes how she is very much her mother's daughter, she grows to feel deeply that her mother loves her.

Growin' is an outstanding novel. One of its greatest assets is its holistic approach to its characters and their relationships. None of *Growin'*s characters are one-dimensional foils or types; none of their sentiments are simplified or sugar-coated.

Although he isn't in the story for long, Pump's father is a wonderful husband and father figure. He nurtures Pump through intimate conversations, friendly handball games, and encouragement for her poetry writing. Particularly impressive is his ability to support both his wife and his daughter, who want him to take sides. He doesn't get sucked into Pump's tirade against her mother. When Pump criticizes her mother and says that her mother hates her, he insists that her mother loves Pump and that she's different from them, which is neither good nor bad: "[Y]our mother worries about money. She thinks that goin' to school and gettin' a job is the most important thing. You have to make a livin' no matter what. Your mother loves you. Just as much as I do. Maybe more."

Nikki Grimes devotes her storytelling to developing the evolving relationships between Pump and Renee and between Pump and Jim Jim. Mother and daughter grow closer as they struggle to communicate honestly and to respect each other's reality. The significant stages in the youths' friendship revolve around the unstated but understood "tests" that they subject each other to, especially their unexpected and embarrassing moments of vulnerability. The shifts in these relationships are portrayed through short but effective episodes.

Nikki Grimes shows how society's male conditioning and violence require Jim Jim to adopt a tough stance in order to survive; he sacrifices his potential to be close to other people, hides his sensitivity, and guards his emotions. Relatedly, the characters in *Growin'* defy sex role stereotypes. Pump fights. Jim Jim caretakes. Pump plays marbles. Jim Jim plays hopscotch.

There is a minor cast of eccentric characters in the neighborhood. Pump and Jim Jim, unlike the adults, accept and respect these outcasts. Each character, despite her or his unique history of powerlessness and heartbreak, treats all people kindly, especially the children. The author suggests that ordinary people with a lot of love and constancy are essential and can serve as role models; they need not be successful professionally.

The author criticizes traditional schooling as she contrasts the routine and conformity of school with the youths' creativity and individuality. For example, their teacher Miss Morris punishes Pump for writing poetry and Jim Jim for drawing during an English lesson of rote memorization and recitation and then orders them to write on the board after school, "I will pay attention in class," one hundred times. The youth skip school sometimes because they want to develop their talents, and because, when Miss Morris catches them writing or drawing in class, she denigrates their work and calls them stupid. They know better than to share their extracurricular story books with her.

Because the author fleshes out the characters of both sexes equally, even though her central character is a girl, *Growin'* will appeal especially to readers of both sexes who share a passion for the arts. *Growin'* includes two poems and a short story by Pump and a poem by Renee—all excellent. Pump's age is never indicated, but she's at least in sixth grade. Upper elementary-school readers and middle-school readers who are not put off by the six short chapters and seven handsome illustrations are, therefore, the appropriate readership for this novel.

29. Guy, Rosa. *The Friends*. New York: Bantam Books, 1973. 185 pages. *****

American Library Association Notable Books for Children and Young Adults, 1973; School Library Journal Best Books for Children and Young Adults, 1973

The Friends is a coming-of-age story about Phyllisia Cathy, a fifteen-year-old girl transplanted with her family from the Caribbean to Harlem. The opening scene chronicles her fights with U.S.-born classmates, who hate Phyllisia for her intelligence, pride, and foreignness. But one student befriends

Phyllisia—Edith Jackson, an impoverished, motherless ragamuffin whom Phyllisia is not sure she wants as a friend. Phyllisia's pride and snobbery, inherited from her father, battle against Edith's warmth and caring until Phyllisia is forced to decide what kind of person she wants to be.

Together with her seventeen-year-old sister Ruby, Phyllisia also has to cope with the illness and death of their mother and their father's increasing rage and iron-fist control. In the end, only Phyllisia's newfound commitment to Edith enables her to stand up to her father to break through to his humanity and preserve them all as a family.

This beautifully crafted story is told in Phyllisia's voice, making the overwhelming passion of adolescence and the confusion of displacement into a new culture immediately accessible to the reader. *The Friends* offers a vivid examination of the differences between Afro-Caribbean and African American cultures and the struggles of immigrants to adjust to their new lives. At the same time, it examines the disturbing near-collapse of Phyllisia's family from the tensions of her mother's death, her father's pride and domination, the family's constant economic struggle, and the girls' rebellion against the old ways.

The novel's plot is tight and compelling, the characters well developed, and the fast-paced style perfect for adolescent readers. For all these reasons, I highly recommend *The Friends* for readers ages thirteen to adult. Although the story is told in an adolescent voice, its tone and issues are never condescending. Phyllisia's father's character is somewhat caricatured as the domineering West Indian patriarch, but careful readers will recognize clues that Phyllisia's perception of him, and of herself, are biased by her own personality and adolescence. Although *The Friends* focuses on girls, readers of both sexes will be drawn in by the masterly storytelling. This is a book that's impossible to keep on the library shelves and has students fighting each other for a chance to read it next. And anyone who hates to leave the characters at the end of this novel can read the sequels *Ruby*, which picks up the tale from

Phyllisia's older sister's perspective, and *Edith Jackson*, which details her friend's trials.

30. Guy, Rosa. *Ruby*. New York: Viking Press, 1976. 217 pages.****

American Library Association Notable Books for Children and Young Adults, 1976

   Ruby is the second novel in *The Friends* trilogy, following Ruby Cathy, Phyllisia's older sister, through her junior year of high school in Harlem. The Cathys are a transplanted West Indian family whose mother died several years ago and whose tyrannical father dominates his daughters' lives with his rules and suspicions. Ruby is a warm and lonely girl in desperate need of affection—from her family, her teachers, anybody. When the cool, intelligent, and arrogant Daphne Duprey deigns to notice Ruby in class, Ruby falls hopelessly in love with her. The two girls begin a passionate affair which fills Ruby's need for love for perhaps the first time in her life. Under Daphne's tutelage, Ruby begins to think for herself and to separate somewhat from her father. But when Daphne leaves Ruby in disgust over Ruby's neediness and out of her own desire to leave the city for college and upward mobility, Ruby has nothing to live for and attempts suicide. Her father saves her and, in one moment of tearful closeness, affirms his love for her.
   Another strong book from Rosa Guy, *Ruby* gets inside the characters' heads and exposes all the pain and confusion of growing up. Like the other novels in the trilogy, Ruby is written in the first-person narrative voice, this time from Ruby's perspective. The author's genius is obvious in the different tone, language and reality she creates in each novel, simply by telling the story through a different character's persona. When Daphne attacks Ruby's neediness at the end, the reader

suddenly sees events in a different light, having previously identified totally with Ruby's perspective.

Because of the immediacy of the narrator's perspective, the plot is compelling and the events believable. Mr. Cathy's character is a little overblown, a little too evil, but again, this is his daughter's perspective, not an objective truth. My only criticism is that Miss Gottlieb is an identifiably Jewish teacher who despises the students and whose emotional twistedness is symbolized by a crippled body. A writer with Guy's talent does not need to stoop to oppressive stereotypes, either of Jews or of disabled people, to get her point across. In contrast, the book's lesbian relationship is handled gracefully and realistically, without either romanticization or vilification. Without minimizing the social pressures against them, the novel focuses on Ruby's and Daphne's relationship, its ups and downs and disillusionments, rather than on the fact that they are two girls. This is an excellent way to demystify lesbian love and makes the story accessible to heterosexual readers also. Ninth through twelfth graders will greatly enjoy *Ruby*, though it may appeal more to girls than boys since all of the major characters are girls and it is essentially a love story.

31. Guy, Rosa. *Edith Jackson*. New York: Viking Press, 1978. 187 pages. *****

American Library Association Notable Books for Children and Young Adults, 1978

The third of *The Friends* trilogy, *Edith Jackson* tells seventeen-year-old Edith's story in her own words. Orphaned at fifteen, Edith keeps her family together in a run-down Harlem apartment by hiring herself out for daywork. But when her older brother is shot and killed by police and her baby sister dies of malnutrition, the Department of Social Services steps in to ship the four remaining sisters to an orphanage and then to foster homes. Vowing to find a job on her eighteenth birthday and create a real home for her younger sisters, Edith waits out her time with the girls' third foster family. Meanwhile, she falls in love with a neighbor's nephew, James, and is confused by his aunt's lectures about finishing school and becoming someone who "counts."

When Edith's thirteen-year-old sister Bessie runs off with their foster mother's boyfriend, the other sisters are returned to the orphanage. Eleven-year-old Minnie escapes via her street smarts, charming a white family into adopting her, and twelve-year-old Suzy is shipped off to another foster family in Brooklyn. Edith works in the orphanage's nursery, nurturing babies who, like her, have no one to love them. Then Bessie turns up dead, and Edith runs off in search of James. She hopes he will marry her when he learns she is pregnant. When he refuses, Edith, who longs for a baby and a home, chooses instead to have an abortion and to work for her own future.

At last, an honest and contemporary look at some of the problems facing African American *girls*! Granted, Edith's troubles are magnified by being an orphan and trying to hold her family together, but on a smaller scale she faces the same problems as many poor and working-class African American girls: sexual harassment, having to take care of younger siblings at the expense of her own childhood and possibly her future, looking for love to save her, unplanned pregnancy, and fighting a social service system that would turn her into another statistic. She looks at upwardly mobile blacks and wonders what they have in common with her. Adults have all the power in her life, yet their help always has a price—such as splitting up her family. She looks at the choices in her life: welfare, struggling to finish school for uncertain rewards, working for her siblings and putting her own needs permanently on hold or being selfish and abandoning her sisters. Edith struggles mightily with these difficult, no-win choices throughout the book. However, this is a sad but not hopeless story, for Edith's caring and her will to survive help her to reach a more mature understanding of her life and to make necessary choices without losing her humanity.

Edith Jackson is just as well written as Rosa Guy's earlier novels, with strong characters, narrative voice, plot, and themes. If possible, I would recommend it even more highly than the other two in the trilogy, because Edith grows throughout the story and her narration is so finely drawn. Never does the author suggest right and wrong answers for the difficult questions she raises; rather, she affirms African American youth for their simple survival against all odds. *Edith Jackson* is especially sensitive to girls' struggles but should appeal to all young adult readers from ages thirteen and up.

32. Guy, Rosa. *The Disappearance*. New York: Delacorte Press, 1979. 246 pages.***

American Library Association Notable Books for Children and Young Adults, 1979

The Disappearance introduces Imamu Jones, a sixteen-year-old African American sleuth. Imamu has just been released from jail after standing trial for a crime committed by his friends. Emotionally abandoned by his alcoholic mother, Imamu is drawn to the Aimsleys, a middle-class black family living in Brooklyn. When Mrs. Aimsley invites him to come live with them, he reluctantly accepts but continues to feel responsible for taking care of his mother. In Brooklyn, Imamu finds himself in another world—locking horns with Mr. Aimsley, worshipping Mrs. Aimsley, and falling for Dora Belle, the Aimsley girls' godmother. But when eight-year-old Perk Aimsley disappears, Mrs. Aimsley turns Imamu over to the police, who arrest and beat him. Seventeen-year-old Gail Aimsley believes in his innocence, though, and together they solve the mystery of Perk's disappearance.

As a mystery, *The Disappearance* works well, weaving suspense and tension into a surprising conclusion. As a commentary on social issues—police violence, class differences, alcoholism, and male-female relationships—the novel's tone is more superficial. For instance, the Aimsleys recover far too quickly from Perk's disappearance and death. Similarly, Imamu's feelings about the events in his life are on the surface; somehow Rosa Guy seems not to integrate them into his character.

The Disappearance lacks the immediacy and narrative brilliance of Guy's *The Friends* trilogy, and might have done better to stay purely as a mystery instead of attempting simultaneously to address social issues. Though not great literature, *The Disappearance* is a good mystery. Male and female readers in grades eight through eleven will enjoy it.

33. Guy, Rosa. *New Guys Around the Block*. New York: Dell Publishing Co., 1983. 199 pages.***

Parents' Choice Award, 1983

The setting is a contemporary, bombed-out block in Harlem. Imamu Jones, an African American boy in his late teens, shares the neighborhood with hustlers, junkies, and winos. His goals for the summer are to find a job, stay out of jail, and repaint the apartment he shares with his mother before she returns from the alcoholism rehabilitation hospital. Along the way, he meets Olivette and Pierre Larouche, eighteen- and fourteen-year-old brothers. Olivette is like no one Imamu has ever met, part philosopher, part saint, and he opens Imamu's eyes to new ways of understanding Harlem's destitution. At the same time, Imamu tries to stay clear of an old friend, Iggy, just released from jail after serving time for murdering a storekeeper. Imamu also gets drawn into trying to solve a series of burglaries and searching for Gladys, an eighteen-year-old neighbor who disappears shortly after a fight with Iggy. Underlying the plot are Imamu's tension about whether his mother can ever truly recover from her alcoholism and his moral dilemma over whether to turn his criminal friends in to the police.

This book is about despair and the waste of human potential in Harlem. Opening with a dream sequence about rats charging to their deaths, Rosa Guy drives home the point that some segments of the black community are inexorably trapped by the circumstances of their lives—arbitrary arrest and police brutality, extreme poverty, drug addiction, and crumbling neighborhoods. One would prefer a more powerful protagonist engaging more actively with his life, but Imamu is probably a more realistic character. Guy does an excellent job of describing the devastation of inner city life, which makes this a depressing book. The most hopeful character turns out to be the biggest hustler of all, but somehow Imamu finishes the summer with renewed hope.

New Guys Around the Block is appropriate for older high-school readers, grades ten through twelve, both because of its disturbing descriptions and its sophisticated moral dilemmas. Teens who are not familiar with urban life may find the plot and setting implausible, but inner city teens may welcome the book's reflection of the reality of their lives and limited choices. All the major characters are male, so male readers are likely to find more to identify with. Unlike *The Disappearance*, this novel presents an involving moral dilemma in the midst of a good mystery.

34. Guy, Rosa. *Paris, Pee Wee, and Big Dog*. New York: Dell Publishing Co., 1984. 116 pages. **

Paris, who is almost twelve, lives with his mother in Harlem. His real name is Charles Junior, but he changed it to Paris to protest his father's leaving the family the year before and to symbolize his hope that his father will return to fulfill his fantastic promise to bring them to France one day. One spring Saturday, when Paris' mother leaves him home to clean the house while she goes to work, all hell breaks loose. Paris' best friend Pee Wee, thirteen, persuades Paris to go roller skating; Pee Wee promises that, after roller skating, he will help Paris clean up. Pee Wee is a manipulative troublemaker. Another friend, Big Dog, follows them; Big Dog, an over-confident, precocious nine-year-old, is the pesky "little brother" Paris loves and loves to hate. The older boys run away from Big Dog all day, but Paris always returns to take care of him.

This is the story of roller skating gone wrong. First, by roller skating through an intersection, the boys cause a car crash. Then they find a bike that has been stolen and abandoned in some bushes, and get accused of stealing it. Later, while fishing for eels in the Hudson River, Big Dog falls in and almost drowns. After they order hot dogs, they realize they don't have enough money to pay for them. At sunset, they play in an abandoned tenement and avert a near-fatal accident.

Punctuating each turn in the action are five recurring themes. Joanne, a girl on whom Paris has a crush, appears in the beginning and end of the story. Marvin, a fourteen-year-old bully, surfaces from behind every building and tree to terrorize the boys and take their skates. In the end, though, he apologizes and returns the skates after Paris saves his life. Paris worrying about his mother's anger and punishment is another theme. After every event, Paris feebly attempts to return home, but Pee Wee lures him in the opposite direction. Ironically, by the time he walks in the door, with his bloody face and ripped jeans, crying uncontrollably from the aftershock of the day's events and in anticipation of his mother's anger, she greets him with affection and concern, asking, "What happened . . . to my baby?" Another recurring theme is the father-son relationship. Paris misses his father, while Pee Wee longs for the father he never knew. And Big Dog's bragging about all the special times he shares with his father drives the older boys crazy with jealousy. The older boys believe that fathers always break their promises; yet they also believe that fathers are essential and irreplaceable. The final theme, of caretaking and gender, ties in with this. When Pee Wee hurts himself and goes to the hospital, Paris wants to hold his hand to comfort him but reflects that boys don't hold hands. Paris also notes that, even though Pee Wee is in pain, he's tough and won't cry because boys don't cry.

Rosa Guy provides a fast-paced story, with an easy-to-follow, tangible plot that's not heavy with philosophical digressions yet works in a few things to think about. *Paris, Pee Wee, and Big Dog* is a book for boys. Male bonding and adventure are the crux of the story. Because the average age of the three characters is eleven, readers from third through sixth grade will relate most easily to this story. Some middle-school readers will enjoy the action, but the illustrations will put off older readers.

The author develops her three characters through their actions, without detail or reflection. These are wholly believable, enjoyable characters. Rosa Guy tangentially explores two particularly noteworthy facets of Paris' emotional development. While he defers to rigid sex role stereotypes, he questions them and, occasionally, challenges them: he holds Pee Wee's hand briefly in the hospital; he acts tough with Pee Wee but tender with Big Dog; and he cries with his mother. Unfortunately, Guy doesn't satisfactorily develop the theme of the father-son relationship. Paris reflects often that fathers always break their promises, but the narrative never offers explanations of why some fathers abandon their sons and why those sons continue to desperately want their fathers. Young readers would probably benefit from a better development of this theme.

35. Guy, Rosa. *And I Heard a Bird Sing.* New York: Dell Publishing Co., 1987. 232 pages.***

And I Heard a Bird Sing continues the Imamu Jones' mystery series. Imamu is an eighteen-year-old African

American trying to find his place in the world and solving mysteries along the way. In this novel, he has created a home in Brooklyn for himself and his mother, a recovering alcoholic whom Imamu supports, worries about, loves, and resents. Through his job as a delivery boy, Imamu becomes caught up in a murder at the Maldoon mansion and tries to discover who killed Margaret Maldoon. With the help of his girlfriend Gail, Imamu solves the mystery, and, with the help of his foster family, he makes some important decisions about his own future.

This novel is entertaining, with a quick-moving plot and an intriguing mystery which helps propel the action. Author Rosa Guy integrates important issues into the plot, such as how Imamu sees himself and how others see him as a young black man, whether people are born into immutable fates, and the complex nature of guilt and responsibility within families. Imamu's character is developed to moderate depth, more so than the novel's other characters. Overall, this story is fun, with fewer of the sophisticated moral dilemmas and despair that characterized the second Imamu Jones mystery, *New Guys Around the Block*. This book is light reading appropriate for eighth through eleventh graders, boys and girls.

However, the Imamu Jones mysteries just do not display the talent that Rosa Guy showed in *The Friends* trilogy. The brilliance and simplicity of those novels are not apparent here, perhaps because the earlier novels integrate more of Guy's own life experience or perhaps because the mystery format got in the way of carefully-developed characters and narrative voice. Guy's attempts to address significant social issues through the mysteries fall somewhat flat, especially in comparison to her outstanding earlier books. Nevertheless, the Imamu Jones mysteries are enjoyable reading.

36. Guy, Rosa. *The Ups and Downs of Carl Davis III*. New York: Dell Publishing Co., 1989. 113 pages.**

When Carl Davis III's parents send him from Harlem to live with his grandmother in South Carolina without any warning, he is devastated. He cannot understand why his parents don't want him around. He always tries to be considerate when his mother, a nurse, is studying for her Ph.D., and when his father, a physician, is trying to rest. An overly intellectual and overweight twelve-year-old, Carl Davis has trouble making friends in South Carolina. Not only does he think he's smarter and better than everyone he meets there, but he also insists on giving black history lessons to both the teacher and the other students in his history class. This does not go over well with his stuffy, white social studies teacher, and even his black classmates are angry at him. They have just recently been allowed admittance to the public school for gifted students, and they are afraid that Carl Davis' calling attention to himself will get them all thrown out.

Underlying all his misery is Carl's confusion over why his parents sent him away in the first place. The story is written as a series of letters from Carl to his parents and to his two closest friends in New York City. He can't understand why his closest friend, Russell, doesn't write back to him, until one day he learns that Russ has died of a drug overdose. Feeling guilty, Carl thinks back to the time when he saw Russ start to use marijuana. Although he suspected Russ was also using harder drugs, Carl didn't tell anybody because he was afraid that if his mother found out, she would forbid him to hang out with older friends like Russ. Carl didn't have a lot of friends in New York, either, and he was unwilling to risk his friendship with Russell.

Russ' death finally moves Carl's mother to explain to Carl that they have sent him to South Carolina to protect him from the drug influences of New York. Carl is outraged that they would think he is so weak, until he finds out that his own father was addicted to heroin as a teenager and only barely managed to turn his life around with the love and support of his family.

At the same time he starts to understand why his parents sent him away, Carl also starts to adjust to life with his grandmother. He starts to appreciate the nature that surrounds him there, and he finally makes a friend, even if it is just an old dog. At school, though, he still has major problems. When his history teacher assigns them a report on a hero of their own choosing, Carl picks Malcolm X. His teacher is so outraged that he has chosen a drug addict and revolutionary as his hero that she berates Carl in front of the whole class. Unable to stand her tormenting anymore, Carl walks out of school and refuses to return.

When his grandmother finds out a week later that Carl has not been attending classes, she marches down to school with him to straighten things out. There, in front of his class, the teacher and the principal, she talks from the heart about the importance of black history to all Americans, not only the history of slavery but the history of the civil rights struggles of the 1960s and 1970s which changed her life and the lives of her family and neighbors. She tells the story of having to go North with her son just so he could get a decent education. Everyone is clearly moved by Carl's grandmother, including him, and he starts to think that maybe she's a little more intelligent than he gave her credit for. He confides to her his trouble making friends. She suggests that instead of trying to impress everyone all the time, he speak from the heart more often. Carl tries this, and finds, to his surprise, that it actually works. By the time Carl's parents' call him home, reassured of his intention to stay off drugs, Carl is not sure he wants to leave South Carolina.

The Ups and Downs of Carl Davis III is a silly book. At times it is hilarious, making fun of Carl's over-intellectualization, but this theme grows tiresome fast. Rosa Guy manages to insert some very interesting history into the story, including a history of Columbus from the Native Americans' perspective and a quick history of Malcolm X's life and beliefs. Unfortunately, neither these enlightening history lessons nor the absurdity of Carl's personality is enough to keep the book interesting. The plot moves along, but Carl Davis just never seems real enough for the reader to care what happens to him. This novel lacks the immediacy and impact of many of Guy's other books; one feels like a disinterested observer throughout the novel.

Guy starts to address Carl's disillusionment with his father when he learns of his troubled past. However, she skims over the topic, suggesting that Carl's intellect alone is sufficient to help him overcome such an adolescent disillusionment. We get a glimpse of his grandmother as a wise and determined woman, but since everything is distilled through Carl's foolish first-person viewpoint, we never get to know her well. Due to the epistolic format, no other character except Carl's is developed in any depth. One strength of the novel is that Guy presents both good and bad, clear-sighted and foolish people among blacks and whites; her world isn't divided neatly by color.

The Ups and Downs of Carl Davis III is a short book with a very easy reading level, appropriate for fourth through seventh grade readers. It is completely focused on a boy so male readers may enjoy it more, but Carl's personality is so pompous that I think most readers will have trouble identifying with him. By the end of the story he is becoming more human, but Guy will have lost most adolescent readers by then. They may enjoy the laughs that *The Ups and Downs of Carl Davis III* offers, but their experience of this book is unlikely to go deeper than that.

37. Guy, Rosa. *The Music of Summer*. New York: Delacorte Press, 1992. 180 pages.**

American Library Association Notable Books for Children and Young Adults, 1993

Seventeen-year-old Sarah Richardson is a dutiful daughter, studying hard and practicing piano constantly, as her strict mother demands. Her single mother, Lottie, sees Sarah's musical talent as her ticket to a successful future, free of the incessant worry over poverty that Lottie and her relatives have known. Sarah and Lottie live in a Manhattan apartment which they moved into only after suing to gain admittance. Clarise Johnson, Lottie's closest friend, helped them win that battle, but lately Lottie and Clarise have had a falling out. Sarah's closest friend since childhood is Cathy Johnson, Clarise's daughter, but lately Cathy has snubbed her, forming a clique instead with other light-skinned blacks from her private school.

When Mrs. Johnson invites Sarah to spend the summer on Cape Cod with them, Sarah leaps at the chance to take a rest from her serious piano study and to try to patch things up with Cathy. The house is lovely and Cathy's grandmother Mama Dear is a warm, insightful hostess, but Sarah soon learns that Cathy has invited her clique of friends up to the house and plans to spend the summer belittling and snubbing Sarah. Only the arrival of Mama Dear's friends from Martinique assuages Sarah's misery. She quickly grows close to twenty-nine-year-old Jean Pierre, a handsome, idealistic activist with plans to dedicate his life to Africa.

To Sarah's surprise and confusion, Jean Pierre asks Sarah to marry him and join his work in Africa. At this point, Cathy's jealousy turns deadly as she attempts to drown Sarah. Sarah survives, only to face the most difficult decision of her life—to follow Jean Pierre to the life of adventure, joy, and dedication he offers or to return to her family and take up her duty and musical talent.

The plot of *The Music of Summer* is outlandish and implausible. Teenage girls form cliques, jealousies and rivalries, but rarely do they attempt to murder one another. Teenage girls dream of romance with handsome, older men, but rarely do these older, exotic strangers actually swoop down to rescue them. Taken at face value, the fantastic romance of *The Music of Summer* may turn off some teens. However, I strongly suspect that author Rosa Guy intends the story to be read as a parable, with the different characters representing different paths open to African Americans: the path of indiscriminate assimilation played by Cathy and her upper-class, light-skinned friends; the path of rejecting the West to return wholly to African roots played by Jean Pierre; and Sarah as the struggle to create a meaningful synthesis of past and present, of African and American.

Guy's greatest strength, as always, is her characters. Each is a multi-layered composite of dreams and fears, insecurities and longing. Race is an ever-present issue in the book, but *The Music of Summer* goes well beyond simple categories of black and white to explore the nuances of class, color, assimilation, and personal jealousies which threaten blacks as a community. Yet the novel's ultimate message is one of forgiveness, responsibility, and growth. The book details the difficult choices facing African American youth, particularly the perils of financially successful blacks assimilating right into a hateful disdain of other blacks.

Guy is an excellent writer whose thoughtful young adult novels assume that teenagers can handle thematic subtleties and complexities of character. *The Music of Summer* offers many layers for the careful reader. Its reading level is appropriate for eighth through twelfth graders. Girls will probably enjoy it much more than boys, because the protagonist's perspective and concerns are completely female, and the few male characters are all portrayed solely through female eyes.

38. Hamilton, Virginia. *The House of Dies Drear*. New York: Collier Books, 1968. 279 pages. *

E.A. Poe Award, 1968; New York Times Best Books for Children and Young Adults, 1968

The House of Dies Drear is a contemporary mystery featuring Thomas Small, an African American boy transplanted from North Carolina to Ohio when his family moves into the old house of Dies Drear, a murdered abolitionist. The house, a former stop on the Underground Railroad, is reputed to be haunted by the ghost of Drear and two slaves who were killed with him. A somewhat surrealist blending of reality with Thomas' overactive imagination provides most of the "mystery," and the story is not a mystery in the traditional sense—the question of ghosts, underground passageways and hidden treasure is solved mid-story, leaving only the task of scaring away would-be looters for the second half of the novel.

This book received several awards, but I'm not sure why. As a mystery, it falls flat, with mild suspense being created by intimation, dream, and atmosphere rather than by actual events. Its attempt to integrate the history of the house and the Underground Railroad into the plot is the most interesting aspect of the book but is not pursued very far. The character development is lazy, with such inconsistencies in Thomas' character that it is hard to know if he is a mature ten-year-old or an immature fifteen-year-old. As a protagonist ridden with immature fears and insecurities, he is too young to appeal to high-school students, yet the novel's style and length are too much for younger readers.

In addition, the sole adult female, Thomas' mother, is an entirely passive character who needs Thomas' and her husband's protection just because she is a woman. The family is middle class, but this issue is never addressed as one possible cause of Thomas' isolation from other kids, and their African American identity is an aside which explains their interest in black history and the black church but which otherwise does not affect their lives at all.

Although this is not a terrible book, neither is it especially interesting, either as a mystery or as a novel of adolescence.

39. Hamilton, Virginia. *The Planet of Junior Brown*. New York: Collier Books, 1971. 217 pages. **

John Newbery Honor Book, 1972; Lewis Carroll Shelf Award, 1972; School Library Journal Best Books for Children and Young Adults, 1971

    The Planet of Junior Brown focuses on the friendship between Junior Brown, a two-hundred and sixty-two-pound, eighth-grade piano prodigy, and Buddy Clark, a tender and loving classmate who lives in bombed-out Harlem tenements (called planets) and works nights at a newsstand to earn food money for himself and the horde of younger homeless kids he takes care of. Surrounded by fat, Junior is simultaneously the object of ridiculing attention and entirely invisible and unheard—his piano teacher will not permit him to use her grand piano but instead makes him tap out pieces on her coffee table. His piano at home is lined with felt so that no sound disturbs his resting, sick mother, Junella, and his father, Walter, never makes it home from work in New Jersey to visit on the weekends. The only music Junior hears is in his head. He also hears voices.
    Junior and Buddy grow close as they skip two straight months of school, spending their days in the school basement with Mr. Pool, a disillusioned teacher-turned-janitor. Mr. Pool and Buddy build a mechanized, moving model of the solar system and add an extra planet—the planet of Junior Brown. When the boys are caught skipping classes, the solar system is dismantled, and Junior decides to run away from his suffocating and depressing home before his mother finds out what's happening. Over the course of the novel, Junior is becoming more divorced from reality, imagining a decaying relative in his piano teacher's apartment, painting grotesque figures on a canvas, and hearing voices more frequently, but Mr. Pool and Buddy vow to look after him. They find an abandoned tenement for him to rebuild the solar system in, reestablishing the planet of Junior Brown.

This is another slow-paced novel from Virginia Hamilton, with little action, unrealistic characters, and a boring abundance of detail about the solar system, piano lessons, the public transit system, and painting. The boys are supposed to be eighth graders, but their size and experiences are more realistic for eleventh or twelfth graders. Buddy's character is resourceful and appealing, but Junior's character is very difficult to access, especially as Hamilton switches from third- to first-person voices without warning and expresses Junior's internal monologue without quotation marks. And overall, the novel is simply confusing: Hamilton provides no explanation of why the boys are cutting school in the first place, and Junior's deterioration into psychosis is depressing and demoralizing. Also, the boys' parents are clichés—the usual absent father (both boys), one abandoning mother (Buddy's), and one neurotic, controlling, dependent mother with a life-threatening illness and middle-class aspirations (Junior's).

The theme of this novel is nice: "We are together because we have to learn to live for each other." But its development is too confusing. Only advanced readers, eleventh through twelfth graders and up, will be able to fully appreciate *The Planet of Junior Brown*, but there may be too little action to hold their interest.

40. Hamilton, Virginia. *M.C. Higgins, the Great*. New York: Collier Books, 1974. 278 pages. ****

American Library Association Notable Books for Children and Young Adults, 1974; Boston Globe-Horn Book Magazine Award, 1974; John Newbery Medal Award, 1975; Lewis Carroll Shelf Award, 1975; National Book Award, 1975; New York Times Best Books for Children and Young Adults, 1974

M.C. Higgins is a thirteen-year-old African American boy who lives on Sarah's Mountain, North Carolina, surrounded by his family and the ghosts of his ancestors. His days are spent swimming, hunting rabbits, watching his younger siblings, and playing games with his friend Ben. But M.C. is also scheming about how to get his family off the mountain before they are buried by the mound of strip mining waste which inches closer with every rainfall. He hopes that James Lewis, the stranger who has come to record mountain people's songs, will be so taken by his mother's voice that he will offer her a recording contract and relocate the entire family to Chicago. M.C. hates the thought of leaving the mountain, despite the continuing destruction of strip mining. Through all this, he experiences his first attraction to girls and his relationship with his father changes as he stands up for himself and finds a way to protect his family without leaving the graves of their ancestors.

This is a very fascinating, mystical book with enough of a plot to keep it interesting. M.C. is a believable character, and the folks who people his life are intriguing, if odd. The mountain itself is an important character in the story, and Hamilton's descriptions of its ever-changing moods and nuances are a great strength of the book. The theme of M.C.'s maturation is nicely understated, implied in actions and changing relationships. *M.C. Higgins, the Great* is appropriate for tenth through twelfth graders, but I wonder if urban high schoolers might have trouble relating to the mountain locale which is so central to the story. The book has accessible language and a straightforward plot but can also be read on an entirely allegorical level—the shortsighted foolishness of miners who, in trying to own a living thing (the mountain) can only destroy it; the ever-threatening mound of waste; and the younger generation's task of honoring the past without sacrificing the future to it.

41.   Hamilton, Virginia. *Arilla Sun Down*. New York: Greenwillow Books, 1976. 248 pages. **

American Library Association Notable Books for Children and Young Adults, 1976; School Library Journal Best Books for Children and Young Adults, 1976

Told in the first person, shifting between partially-remembered dreamlike flashbacks and the present, *Arilla Sun Down* features Arilla Adams, a twelve-year-old girl who lives in Cliffville, Ohio. During the course of the novel, Arilla tries to work out two interrelated matters. The first is her identity. Arilla's mother is black and "settled" into the community in which she grew up, while her father is black and Cherokee, recognizes only his Native American background, and disappears on periodic escapes from the "white man's world" to his hometown. To her family and friends, Arilla looks black, but in her brother's and her own mind she is Native American. Her second concern is her sixteen-year-old brother, Jack Sun Run, her competitor for her parents' and friends' attention. Everybody worships Jack the scene-stealer and "radical Indian" who flaunts the community's image of a traditional Indian. Arilla regards Jack with a chaotic mixture of love, fear, and jealousy.

Whereas her brother has a Native American middle name, which expresses his personality, Arilla has no middle name at all. But after she saves her brother's life (he is thrown from his horse during a hail storm) and retrieves her father from one of his escapes to bring him home permanently, she claims a Native American middle name, Arilla Sun Down, which resolves her identity crisis and draws her closer to her father and brother.

The themes of *Arilla Sun Down*, interracial identity and sibling rivalry, are important and interesting, but the book's development and its experimental narrative technique are flawed. Hamilton introduces a topic in need of much exploration in young adult literature—interracial identity, especially as it applies to African Americans and Native

Americans—but she does not do justice to it. Part of the confusion about Arilla's identity stems from her mother's ambivalence about embracing a Native American identity for the whole family and part from her father's separation from the family home. Hamilton confines the issue to the interpersonal dynamics of the family, and, with the exception of one minor comment, neglects to introduce the sociopolitical context which makes interracial identity a conflict. Furthermore, the stream-of-consciousness and fusion of dreams and reality drag on the story rather than enriching it. And unfortunately, some of the action and dialogue in the "Indian dream scenes" sounds clichéd.

42. Hamilton, Virginia. *Justice and Her Brothers*. San Diego: Harcourt Brace Jovanovich, 1978. 282 pages. **

Coretta Scott King Honor Book, 1979

The first book in a science-fiction trilogy, *Justice and Her Brothers* follows eleven-year-old Justice Douglass as she tries to negotiate changing relationships with her family and discovers her own extrasensory powers along the way. For one long, hot summer, Justice's mother returns to college, leaving Justice at home alone all day with her twin thirteen-year-old brothers. Justice misses her mother's constant presence and feels spooked by the empty house. Worse yet, her brother Thomas torments her constantly and ensures that she remains an outsider among the neighborhood gang. Justice is convinced that winning the Great Snake Race, decreed by Thomas, and impressing the boys with a fantastic bicycle stunt she has taught herself will win her acceptance among the gang. Instead, the Great Snake Race ends with her humiliation and she is almost hit by a car while showing off her bicycle stunt.

Finally, Justice's summer begins to change when Mrs. Jefferson, her neighbor, introduces her to her extrasensory abilities. Gradually, Justice learns of her own power to mind read and even to transport herself to the future. But her most important power may help to save her brother Levi's life. For Justice learns that Thomas also has extrasensory power and has been using it for years to torture Levi. Levi is the sensitive twin, the brother who is kind to Justice and tries to protect her from Thomas. Now Justice must battle Thomas for Levi's sake, as the gentle twin weakens under Thomas' torment and predicts he will not live long. In doing so, Justice claims her own power and emerges a stronger person.

Virginia Hamilton has a fine imagination, and this book becomes interesting once she starts to use it. Unfortunately, the first 100 pages or so, until Justice's extrasensory powers appear, are tedious and should have ended in the editor's trash. The next 180 pages, while interesting, are actually the elaborate lead-in to *Dustland*, the second book in the series. The final pages of *Justice and Her Brothers* contain a discordant plot shift which is a transparent attempt to hook the reader into reading the sequel. In addition to these problems with plot, certain characters are two dimensional. For instance, Hamilton never bothers to provide any explanation for Thomas' evilness; neither basic sibling rivalry nor overcompensation for a stutter adequately explains the primal evil of this young character, and this is a major fault with the novel.

However, if you can get past these considerable weaknesses, *Justice And Her Brothers* is entertaining reading. As one of very few young adult science fiction novels with African American characters, it offers black science fiction fans a chance to see themselves reflected in the protagonists. It offers a feisty female protagonist and two entirely different models of African American teenage boys (neither of whom is entirely admirable). At the same time, this story brings a new, extrasensory slant to sibling rivalry which will leave the reader chilled but hooked. The model of a caring, two-parent black family is also remarkable, with both parents trying to balance their own needs with their kids' needs.

Like many of Hamilton's books, it's hard to know for whom to recommend *Justice and Her Brothers*. The book's length, vocabulary, and long chapters demand an older audience (of tenth graders and up), but the youth of the protagonists could turn off older readers. However, the book should appeal to girls and boys. Readers should skip the first four chapters of the book so that they don't give up in boredom before the plot turns interesting.

43. Hamilton, Virginia. *Dustland*. San Diego: Harcourt Brace Jovanovich, 1980. 214 pages. ***

Dustland, book two in the "Justice Trilogy," continues the adventures of Justice Douglass and her twin brothers. In this story, the three siblings team up with Dorian, a neighbor boy, to form a unit that can time travel. Together they transport themselves to Dustland, a barren, hostile world which may be Earth in the distant future. While adapting to the harsh conditions of Dustland, they meet Miacis, a cross between a dog and a lion, and the Slaker colonies, which are almost human except for their wings and three legs. The Slakers want nothing more than to escape Dustland, and Justice, communicating with them through telepathy, pledges to assist them. First, however, she must find her brother Thomas, who has run away in rebellion against her leadership. Without Thomas, the unit is broken and cannot return home. Meanwhile, Thomas' twin Levi is weakening fast, and Justice fears for his life if they do not return soon.

Dustland is a far more interesting story than *Justice and Her Brothers*, the first book in the series. Because the characters here spend most of their time in Dustland, author Virginia Hamilton gives free rein to her imagination, painting vivid pictures of a totally alien world. The story line holds the reader's attention, swinging between the children discovering new creatures, warding off the dangers of Dustland, and fighting among themselves for dominance in the unit. Thomas' character is slightly more complex in this novel than the completely villainous role he played in the first book. And the development of each character's extrasensory powers is creative and fun to read. The major weakness of *Dustland* is its self-conscious position as the second book in a trilogy. Instead of resolving the plot, Hamilton offers a temporary climax which leads into book three. This leaves an unsatisfying ending and the sense that Hamilton could have accomplished much more in this novel if she hadn't been stretching it into a series. Still, for the science fiction fan, *Dustland* offers young African American protagonists exploring a startlingly original planet. Justice's role as the unit's leader offers female readers a strong female role model who is neither afraid of her power nor of her own growth. The male characters run the gamut, from jealous, powerful Thomas, to Dorian, the healer, to Levi, who suffers for them all. The adults' minuscule role in this story is limited to the Douglass parents' struggles to accept how different their children are from normal kids.

The length and vocabulary of *Dustland* make it appropriate for ninth- to twelfth-grade readers, and they will be able to identify with the characters; although the protagonists are just eleven and thirteen, they are not stuck in petty sibling rivalries as they were in *Justice and Her Brothers* but instead struggle with survival and adventure in a new land—conflicts which older readers can easily appreciate. All in all, *Dustland* is a treat for science-fiction fans.

44.   Hamilton, Virginia. *The Gathering*. San Diego: Harcourt Brace Jovanovich, 1981. 179 pages. **

American Library Association Notable Books for Children and Young Adults, 1981

Book three in the "Justice Trilogy," *The Gathering* chronicles the Douglass children's final return to Dustland. The Douglasses—eleven-year-old Justice, thirteen-year-old twins Levi and Thomas—and their neighbor, Dorian, join their extrasensory powers to travel into the future of the planet Earth, which has become Dustland. On this trip, they must meet gangs of identical children who run together for survival and communicate through musical tones. Justice, her brothers, and Dorian help the children evade Mal, the evil force which imprisons them in Dustland, to escape to the protected dome where they were born. Once there, the Douglass children meet Colussus, half machine and half god, and discover their true purpose in traveling to Dustland.

The Gathering is a story which never gels. Events float past, but the theme is too vaguely defined to be coherent. Dustland is bad and then it's good. It demands a constant struggle for survival and wearies the spirit of those who live there, but they are free to be individuals—free within the physical imprisonment of Mal, that is. The dome, on the other hand, is good but then it's bad. Governed by the all-loving godlike Colussus, it offers the hope of new life for the planet. Yet it creates creatures which are exact duplicates of each other, with each reduced to playing its role as a small cog in the overall machinery of the society. There is a hint that Justice's power will complete Colussus', expanding its wisdom to create a more varied society. But this is only a veiled hint and perhaps not what Hamilton means at all. It's hard to know. So this story ends up being frustrating and confusing.

Hamilton is as creative as ever, but it's much harder to visualize *The Gathering*'s ethereal descriptions than the more immediate descriptions in *Dustland*. *Dustland* is science fiction adventure. *The Gathering* sacrifices action and adventure to an unfocused spiritual message which never does become particularly clear. Early chapters describing life among the children of Dustland are interesting and promising. Unfortunately, Hamilton soon sacrifices characters and plot to her theme. The characters become shadow plays—flat images going through the motions of predestined action and dialogue to make a point. But it's hard to figure out what that point is.

45.   Hamilton, Virginia. *Sweet Whispers, Brother Rush*. New York: Avon Books, 1982. 215 pages. ****

American Library Association Notable Books for Children and Young Adults, 1982; Boston Globe-Horn Book Magazine Award, 1982; Coretta Scott King Award, 1983; International Board on Books for Young People Honor List, 1983; John Newbery Honor Book, 1983; New York Times Best Books for Children and Young Adults, 1982; School Library Journal Best Books for Children and Young Adults, 1982

Fourteen-year-old Teresa "Tree" Pratt lives in Wilberforce, Ohio, with her retarded older brother, Dab, and her mother, M'Vy, a homecare attendant who's hardly ever home. Isolated, with only Dab for company, Tree starts seeing the ghost of Brother Rush, her uncle who committed suicide years before. Brother Rush takes Tree on journeys through her family's history, where she becomes her mother, seeing events through her mother's eyes that happened before her birth and during her infancy, and where she becomes herself as an infant, where she sees events she vaguely remembers. Through the dream journeys, Tree unravels the secrets her mother has kept from her: that her father abandoned them, that her mother abused Dab as a child, and that all of the men in her family have porphyria, a rare debilitating disease. Porphyria, brought to Africa by Dutch colonizers and carried to the U.S. on slave ships, fills the men's lives with pain, makes them unable to go out into the light lest their skin burn and scar, and in combination with alcohol and/or drugs, kills them.

Ironically, Tree passes into the dream journeys—the power to do this is a "mystery" inherited from her African ancestors—by walking into the light, and Brother Rush then offers her the secrets and the memories she needs to know in order to understand her life. When Dab dies from porphyria and barbiturates, Tree must confront her mother with her new understanding and then learn to forgive her. At the same time, M'Vy's boyfriend Silversmith and his son Don enter the picture, providing the love and attention Tree needs. With the addition of the homeless Miss Pricherd, whom M'Vy hires to move in and help take care of Tree, Tree finds herself surrounded by an emerging supportive family for the first time in memory.

Sweet Whispers, Brother Rush is one of Virginia Hamilton's best books. The journey sequences are suspenseful and interesting, slowly unfolding layers of the mystery which is not completely solved until the end. The metaphor of porphyria may be difficult for young readers to understand but is nevertheless powerful. And this novel offers a bridge to complicated, supernatural "adult" African American fiction, such as the works of Toni Morrison and Gloria Naylor— Hamilton's narrative is experimental and yet still accessible to high-school students reading independently.

In addition, the characters are beautifully drawn. Tree is realistic as a lonely fourteen-year-old with her fantasies about Brother Rush, her anger and confusion about her parents, and her love and resentment toward Dab. Dab's level of retardation is inconsistently rendered (it's hard to believe that someone who bathes fully dressed and forgets to eat dinner would nonetheless manage to seduce and pleasure as many different girlfriends as he brings home!), but it's refreshing to see a retarded black character, particularly one who is described as beautiful. M'Vy's character is believable though disturbing, and Silversmith and Don are very sweet, mature black men, showing only respect and caring toward M'Vy and Tree.

The reading level of *Sweet Whispers, Brother Rush* is appropriate for eleventh through twelfth graders. Readers need a good attention span to remember all of the journey sequence details which are necessary to understand the novel's mystery and metaphors, so the book might lose younger readers. This book offers unique and engaging reading.

46.   Hamilton, Virginia. *The Magical Adventures of Pretty Pearl*. New York: Harper and Row, Publishers, 1983. 309 pages.
* * *

American Library Association Notable Books for Children and Young Adults, 1983; Coretta Scott King Honor Book, 1984; New York Times Best Books for Children and Young Adults, 1983; Parents' Choice Award, 1983

Pretty Pearl, a god child, lives on Great Mount Kenya with her brother John de Conquer, the best god, and other god children. Lying around one day with nothing to do, she pushes her sight down to the human level, and sees Africans being enslaved and boarded onto ships. Pearl's heart cries out for the slaves, and she convinces John de Conquer to come down off Mount Kenya with her and follow the slave ships across the ocean. Pearl begs him to intervene to end slavery, but John de Conquer, in his greater wisdom, tells her that humans have to correct their own problems. Unwillingly, she waits with him for two or three god days, two or three centuries of human time, watching slavery, the Civil War and Reconstruction come and go. Then he agrees to let Pearl slip into human form to help a small African American community hiding in the Georgia hills from bandits, Ku Klux Klanners, and white bosses who would enslave them again through trickery and tenant farming. To help protect Pearl, John sends three mischievous spirits with her, as well as Mother Pearl, Pretty Pearl's own self grown up into a woman god. He also gives her John de Conquer root to wear around her neck, to contain her power.

Pretty Pearl quickly becomes part of the human world, forgetting at times that she is a god child. The hidden community of Promise embraces her, Mother Pearl and the spirit Dwahro, believing that they are endangered free blacks like themselves. Her new friend Josiah teaches Pretty Pearl the secrets of Promise—how they stay hidden, their work digging ginseng, and the help they receive from the Real People, Cherokees also in hiding from whites. But Promise is no longer safe. As the new railroad comes closer and closer, through forests and mountains, the people of Promise are bound to be discovered. So Old Canoe, the leader of the Real People, and Black Salt, their own leader, secretly move the people to Ohio, where they can farm together openly. They are helped in their journey by John Henry Roustabout, the black giant of railway legend, who is actually Pretty Pearl's oldest god brother, self-exiled from Mount Kenya in his jealousy over their other brother, John de Conquer.

As Pearl spends more time with humans, she becomes more human herself. One day, in a fit of pique and jealousy, she lets one of her spirits out of her John de Conquer root to scare the other children. But this is breaking one of John de Conquer's cardinal rules, and Pearl is punished by becoming truly human. Before she leaves Pearl to return to Mount Kenya, Mother Pearl tenderly makes the child forget her former god status, leaving her in the good care of Black Salt's family. Pretty Pearl's only memory from god days are the legends she shares around the fire of John de Conquer god and his love for his African people in exile.

A mythical and lyrical tale, *The Magical Adventures of Pretty Pearl* offers a unique perspective on African American history. Weaving legend, fantasy, and history, Virginia Hamilton focuses on an era in black history rarely addressed by young adult books: the period immediately following Reconstruction, when freed blacks were enslaved by poverty and white trickery. Although her subject matter is serious, her approach is playful, giving more attention to the daily travails of the god child Pretty Pearl than to historical facts. Hamilton obviously delights in playing with language, in spinning sounds and puns and chants to create a unique story with a memorable cast of characters. The rhythm of the story beautifully reflects the rhythm of oral storytelling, and *Pretty Pearl* might best be read aloud.

The main weakness of the book is its slow plot development. The many middle chapters describing daily life in Promise drag on, interrupting the plot's momentum. As much as I wanted to like the novel for its whimsical storytelling and fresh approach to black history, I was bored. In addition, Pearl's banishment from Mount Kenya and god life simply for making the relatively small mistake of jealousy seems an excessive sentence. It is understandable as a plot device to bring the god legends to human ears, but for those young readers identifying with Pearl, it may be too strong a punishment, reinforcing the common childhood fear that abandonment is the price for not pleasing adults.

The Magical Adventures of Pretty Pearl is accessible to female and male readers. Although the protagonist is female, male characters play major roles. In fact, it is annoying that the all-good, all-knowing, and paternalistic best god is male, as are the leaders of both Promise and the Real People. Mother Pearl slightly balances this out with her female wisdom and soft-spoken guidance, but she expresses this in a very traditionally female way by becoming the surrogate mother for the whole community. Readers of fantasy aged twelve to fifteen are most likely to enjoy this novel, if they can stay with the sometimes slow plot. I would recommend it only for high-level readers because of its elaborate word play. Although it is beautifully written, *The Magical Adventures of Pretty Pearl* lacks the immediacy to pull in many teenage readers.

47. Hamilton, Virginia. *Willie Bea and the Time the Martians Landed*. New York: Greenwillow Books, 1983. 208 pages. *

American Library Association Notable Books for Children and Young Adults, 1983; New York Times Best Books for Children and Young Adults, 1983

Twelve-year-old Willie Beatrime Mills lives on her family's farm homestead in Xenia, Ohio, eighteen miles outside Dayton. The action of *Willie Bea and the Time the Martians Landed* spans Halloween and the day after, in October 1938. The first half of the story describes the children's pranks around the farm, the extended family's preparations for Sunday dinner, and the children's preparations for trick-or-treating. Amidst tough times, Willie Bea's family of sophisticated and prosperous farmers with their hundred-year-old homesteads ride out the Depression in style. They find strength in the extended family. Willie Bea's father, Jason Mills, is tender but firm; the "worst farmer in the family," he excels as a gourmet baker and earns respect for his college education. Her mother, Marva, is a spitfire, "strong and country-smart." Aunt Leah, whom Willie Bea adores, is a feisty yet flaky single woman who tells fortunes and reads numbers.

Everyone is on edge, however, because sirens blast frequently to warn of fires and tornadoes, and radios broadcast sudden warnings about the war in Europe and Asia. Everyone is unusually vulnerable, fearing a Nazi invasion. On Halloween, they hear a radio announcement that Martians invaded New Jersey and New York. Not until the next morning, after widespread chaos and panic, is it revealed that the "news" was actually Orson Welles' radio production of H.G. Wells' *War of the Worlds*. Of course, the supernatural-oriented Aunt Leah runs to the Mills' household with the "news." The family gathers at their grandparents' homestead and waits for impending doom. Hearing that the Martians reached Kelly's farm on the north side of town, Willie Bea and her cousins sneak out to spy. Willie Bea believes she sees the Martians, but they are actually Kelly's combines, one of which hits her and gives her bruises and a concussion. Embarrassed and disappointed by reality, Willie Bea, shored up by Aunt Leah, nevertheless holds on to the possibility that someday aliens from outer space will visit Earth.

Willie Bea and the Time the Martians Landed is plodding reading. Its plot receives only the last third of the book. The author tells the reader about the panic of the 1938 Halloween radio broadcast but never makes the reader feel that panic or suspense. More than half the novel consists primarily of descriptions of and dialogues between the relatives, whose characters are generously drawn. Virginia Hamilton reinforces a sense of a strong, highly-educated, successful black family impervious to racism. Nicely, the country dialect and young characters' mispronunciations are rendered clearly in the dialogue.

There is an interesting and successful reversal of sex role stereotypes in the characters of Jason and Marva Mills and of Willie Bea's cousins, Big and Little Wing. Little Wing is a scrappy, mischievous girl who manipulates her brother, Big Wing, into foolish and dangerous actions. The characterization of Big leaves much to be desired, however. Is he retarded, of poor judgment, undisciplined, shy, or uncoordinated?

Willie Bea and the Time the Martians Landed contains the ingredients of potentially good historical fiction but they are used clumsily. Hamilton provides ample detail to recreate the sense of this different place and time. Yet, as Willie Bea's world is circumscribed by how far she can walk, this focus is microscopic. Willie Bea quotes extensively from the shows and commercials on the radio, but the quotes are excessive and distracting rather than informative. Willie Bea does reflect on the reports of Hitler's persecution of Jews, and how, if Hitler invaded America he would certainly persecute African Americans; unfortunately, this reflection is brief and undeveloped.

Using Orson Welles' radio broadcast as the catalyst for the novel's action is different but not particularly engaging. Readers familiar with the historical incident may appreciate this novel somewhat. The story is too slow for elementary-school readers but too simple and superficial for middle-school readers. Readers interested in a slice of old-fashioned farm life and family dynamics will not be disappointed. Readers interested in suspense and science fiction will be very disappointed.

48. Hamilton, Virginia. *A Little Love*. New York: Berkley Books, 1984. 207 pages. *

Boston Globe-Horn Book Magazine Honor List, 1984; Coretta Scott King Honor Book, 1985

Sheema, seventeen, overweight, a slow learner studying cooking in a vocational school, hooks up with Forrest, eighteen, skinny, a faster slow learner at her school training to become a chef. Forrest is Sheema's lover but he is also a surrogate for the father she longs to know and possess. Sheema lives with her grandparents in Harrison, Ohio, because her mother died in childbirth and her father, devastated by the loss and blaming his daughter for it, abandoned her. Her father, Terhan "Cruzey" Hadley, a professional sign painter, sends child-support money to his wife's parents to care for his daughter, but he never sends a letter or provides a return address. Yearning for the parents she never had—"a little love" (and security)—Sheema sleeps around until she meets Forrest, and then she sneaks out nightly to make love with him in his car. She also eats like crazy.

Frantic about a possible end of the world (she lives near a military base) and about her grandparents' imminent death (they're both becoming senile), Sheema decides to track down her father during the summer. Forrest drives her down to find Cruzey in Georgia. The meeting, uncomfortable and unproductive—Cruzey and Sheema discuss why he left her and what they do, or don't, mean to each other—forces Sheema to realize that she's been in love with the idea of a father but not with her real father. She realizes she must redefine and recreate her own family. At the end of the book, Sheema and Forrest plan to marry and hope to have a child.

A Little Love's strong characterization and intense emotionality compensate for its awkward stream-of-consciousness narrative that skips from internal monologues and musings to actual conversations which are not set off in quotes. The themes of family secrets and finding/knowing one's biological parents are drawn out thoughtfully here, although it's not clear enough why Sheema never thought about her father before or why she fixes so suddenly on finding him. The worst aspect of the book is that Hamilton infantilizes Sheema: Forrest calls her and treats her like a baby, basically spoon feeding and chaperoning her through every minute of her life, and she desperately needs him to do it. How realistic is it that a teenage boy would be concerned about and care for his girlfriend the way Forrest does?

Sheema's overeating and sexual issues need to be developed much more. High-school readers might not understand that she overeats and sleeps around to fill her emptiness, her hunger for "a little love." Hamilton never makes a judgment about whether Sheema's coping mechanisms are healthy, but, rather, takes them for granted and passes on to how her father's passed her off to her grandparents who'll pass her off to her boyfriend to be taken care of for life. Especially terrible as a model for young women is Hamilton's enthrallment in describing how passive Sheema is in her sexual relationship with Forrest. *A Little Love* may be Hamilton's idea of a happy ending, but it leaves a lot to be desired.

49. Hamilton, Virginia. *Junius Over Far.* New York: Harper and Row, 1985. 274 pages. *

Coretta Scott King Honor Book, 1986

Fourteen-year-old Junius Rawlings lives in an unspecified northern city. He actually lives in his own world, though, ever since his Grandfather Jackabo returned home to Snake Island in the Caribbean. When Grandfather Jackabo lived with him, Junius rushed home from Bethune High School to him, forgoing peer friendships in favor of intimate talks with his grandfather. Now that Jackabo is gone, and Junius' parents are always at work, Junius drifts on the periphery of his peer group, hanging out at Mary and Slim's luncheonette and drooling over a classmate, Sarietta Dobbs. When Sarietta asks Junius to tutor her in geometry, he uses the one-on-one tutoring situation to gradually transform the friendship into a romance. In Jackabo's absence, Junius also pursues a closer relationship with his father, Damius, whom he doesn't understand. Damius is aloof and disdainful of the island and its dialect, even though Snake Island is his homeland.

The third person narrative alternates between Junius' story and Jackabo's. Jackabo returns to Snake Island to rightfully claim and share his family's deteriorating plantation with a nasty white cousin, Burtie Rawlings. Burtie grudgingly acknowledges their kinship but preys on the seventy-six-year-old Jackabo's ailing health in hopes of driving him out of the house. Burtie also connives to extort Jackabo's savings. Next door to the estate is a new neighbor, Gerard Kostera, engaged in undercover activity. In his letter to Junius' family, Jackabo sounds disoriented and ill, so Damius and Junius fly to Snake Island during Christmas break to investigate.

Then the police arrest Burtie for stealing Jackabo's money, and Kostera for smuggling arms and munitions. Burtie's going to jail leaves the estate to Jackabo. Jackabo agrees to return to the States with Damius and Junius for his health's sake and for Junius' sake. But Damius reconnects with his homeland during the visit and resolves to bring the family back every summer.

Ironically, girls will probably enjoy this book more than boys, even though the protagonist is a boy and his relationship with his father and grandfather are central to the plot—because of Junius' strong, open affection for his father and grandfather and his corny infatuation with Sarietta. Sarietta is a realistic and affirmative character. She asserts herself when Junius starts pawing her and demands that he respect her strict mother's etiquette for behavior between the sexes. Although Junius is almost fifteen, he feels and acts younger than his peers. His immaturity makes this book more appropriate to younger readers, probably sixth to eighth graders.

Junius seems unrealistically impervious to peer pressure. His classmates' teasing about his grandfather and his girlfriend doesn't bother him. He's amazingly un-self-conscious. Also, how does he have $900 to pay for his own airline ticket to Snake Island? His parents are comfortable professionals, but the book never mentions Junius working. Another curious aspect of his personality is his obsession with Jimi Hendrix. Weaving Hendrix's verse into the story, Virginia Hamilton offers a novel interpretation of some of the lyrics. However, given Junius' obsession with the Islands, it seems strange that he listens to calypso or reggae only once. "Junie-mahn"'s most annoying character trait is his dialect. He speaks like an "island man" to bond with his grandfather, but since he grew up in the States and his parents don't speak in dialect, his voice seems affected and excessive.

It's unclear why Hamilton introduced the character of Gerard Kostera. If she was trying to make *Junius Over Far* into a mystery, it's disappointing that Junius' family then played no part in solving the mystery.

Junius' developing relationship with his father and his growing insight into his father's demeanor during their trip to Snake Island are described with an economy of dialogue and reflection and satisfactorily resolved. The formality of their interactions dissolves. Junius learns how living in the self-contained and suffocating colonized society of the island limited his father's ability to realize his potential. Damius sternly counters Junius' romantic observations about "simple" ways of life and the street vendors with realistic analyses of how poverty and racism are at work in all he sees. Through the character of Burtie, Hamilton demonstrates the racist legacy of colonization; through the character of Chief Downing, she explores the mixed blessing of tourism and the illusion of the island as paradise for the people who inhabit it.

50. Hamilton, Virginia. *The People Could Fly: American Black Folktales*. New York: Alfred A. Knopf, 1985. 178 pages. ***

American Library Association Notable Books for Children and Young Adults, 1985; Boston Globe-Horn Book Magazine Honor List, 1985; Coretta Scott King Award, 1986; International Board on Books for Young People Honor List, 1986; New York Times Best Books for Children and Young Adults, 1985; School Library Journal Best Books for Children and Young Adults, 1985

In *The People Could Fly: American Black Folktales*, Virginia Hamilton retells, as faithfully to the original source as possible, twenty-four classic black folktales of African and African American origin. The first section, "The Lion, Bruh Bear, and Bruh Rabbit . . . and Other Animal Tales," presents in seven stories the paradigms for those black folktales which use animal protagonists and illustrate allegorically how the underdog slave, through resourcefulness and spiritedness, outsmarted the powerful master.

In the six stories grouped in the next section, "The Beautiful Girl of the Moon Tower . . . and Other Tales of the Real, Extravagant, and Fanciful," the little animal or person with smarts, lies and riddles, hard work, and allies, beats a seemingly omnipotent opponent. These stories include mythical monster-creatures versus people or animals playing the part of tricksters.

The final section, "Carrying the Running-Aways . . . and Other Slave Tales of Freedom," contains six stories based on true events. All of these stories show the range of imagination that slaves employed to keep the dream of freedom alive in their hearts and minds. The author focuses on the slaves instead of the masters, which makes this an upbeat section. The book's title comes from the final story of the same name, about slaves who, in Africa, could fly, but who couldn't take their wings with them on the slave ships. Hamilton notes that the slaves who couldn't "fly" kept the story alive of the people who could fly to set them free through their imaginations.

Despite its large-book format and illustrations, *The People Could Fly: American Black Folktales* is not just for young readers. Though high-school readers will get the most out of Hamilton's introduction and notes, readers of all ages will enjoy its variety of stories rendered in a smooth style. A useful introduction provides a cultural-literary history of black folktales, situating the tales within the history of Africans and African Americans, noting the folktales' oral and written genesis, providing an overview and analysis of key themes and a discussion of the dialects used by the tales' creators and by Hamilton in recreating the tales. When she uses dialect, she provides a glossary of difficult vocabulary. For the younger reader or reader of any age who has little experience reading dialect, it may be difficult to focus on the action because of the challenging language.

The comments at the end of each story are also outstanding. Hamilton situates each story within the larger tradition of black folktales and of world folktales. In addition to presenting fascinating comparative folklore, she notes historical and psychological approaches to the texts and raises questions that gently guide the reader into multilayered interpretations of each story. The author tries to help the reader appreciate the creative impulse and genius behind each tale. Even the mediocre stories seem better after reading the notes.

There is an inverse correlation between length and quality of stories: the shorter the story, the better. Some of the stories fall flat, failing to build intrigue or suspense; they ramble on for pages and end up delivering no more information or action than stories half their length.

This would be a better book if it included more female protagonists. Nineteen stories contain only males. Hamilton isn't doing women any favors when she does include them in five of the stories: in each, the female characters are secondary to the male hero and are portrayed as passive girls, lovers, or mothers, either being pursued by a man or a wolf, or helping the hero of the story escape danger.

Despite these flaws, this book is a gold mine of information on the parallels and variations of themes, motifs, and genres of folktales from Africa and the African disapora as well as from around the world. One other noteworthy feature of the book is that it includes a substantial amount of information about and material from Cape Verde.

51. Hamilton, Virginia. *The Mystery of Drear House.* New York: Collier Books, 1987. 217 pages. **

The Mystery of Drear House is not actually a mystery and is stronger for that reason. The protagonist, Thomas Small, an African American boy of indeterminate age, has moved to Ohio with his family to live in the Dies Drear house. Drear was a an ardent abolitionist and his house, which served as a stop on the Underground Railroad, has a series of secret tunnels and passageways within it. In this sequel to *The House of Dies Drear*, Thomas learns more about the house's history as he tries to protect the treasure hidden in the tunnels below from the marauding Darrow family. When his great-grandmother arrives from North Carolina to offer a reconciliatory solution for protecting the treasure, Thomas becomes friends with some of the Darrow family. He also becomes closer to Pluto, the old black man who lives in a cave near the Drear treasure.

This book is better than *The House of Dies Drear*—more interesting, shorter, with fewer clumsy attempts to create mystery out of what is essentially a mild adventure story. Thomas' character is more believable here, too, with none of the too old-too young inconsistencies of the first novel. However, none of the characters are particularly well developed, nor is the plot strong enough to compensate for the lack of character development. The women remain feeble, even to the point of needing to have house paint mixed for them— presumably they are either too dumb to decide what shade they want or too weak to stir it up.

The book's style and vocabulary make it appropriate for high-school students, but I doubt that students above ninth grade would find the plot or protagonist interesting. It's not a bad book but not memorable either. And students brought up on Stephen King mysteries and ten-murders-a-minute adventure films will probably be bored by it.

52.   Hamilton, Virginia. *A White Romance*. San Diego: Harcourt Brace Jovanovich, 1987. 233 pages. **

Talley Barbour's high school becomes a desegregated magnet school, and suddenly the halls are filled with rich white kids. The black and white students keep a cautious distance for awhile, but gradually Talley grows close to Didi, a beautiful, blonde runner who turns out to be as poor as Talley. Among other things, Talley, a slightly prudish virgin, is fascinated by Didi's sexual relationship with drug-addicted Roady. So when white, handsome David Emory sweeps her off her feet, Talley quickly becomes intimate with him. Talley is unable to resist her passion for him, even after she realizes that he mistreats her and deals drugs. By turns tender and controlling, David finally leaves Talley heartbroken.

A White Romance is dense and distractingly surreal. The novel loses credibility immediately with a stream-of-consciousness, pseudo-Black English that is overdone, fake, and tedious. Then, inordinate time is spent detailing Talley's running (and thinking about running), her first sexual experience, and a Judas Priest concert. Only the sex will hold young adult readers' attention for the amount of time Hamilton devotes to it. In contrast, she glosses over more important topics, such as Talley's coming to terms with her own repressed sexuality, her realization that David deals drugs, and the problems caused by differences in their racial and class backgrounds.

On the positive side, Hamilton explores well the interplay of race and class issues at Talley's school and in her friendship with Didi. Hamilton's continued focus on the girls' friendship, even after Talley falls for David, legitimizes the importance of female friendship. Complex but sympathetic characters are another strength of *A White Romance* as is Talley's changing relationship with her father. Finally, the story's ending is positive, with Talley finding support from white friends and potential love with a classmate who is more suitable not simply because he's black but also because he's clean and cares deeply about her. Unfortunately, these strengths do not overcome the plodding plot and unrealistic narrative voice.

A White Romance's reading level is tenth to twelfth grade, with strong male and female characters. However, most readers will not have the patience to get through the first nine chapters.

53. Hamilton, Virginia. *Anthony Burns: The Defeat and Triumph of a Fugitive Slave*. New York: Alfred A. Knopf, 1988. 193 pages. ***

American Library Association Notable Books for Children and Young Adults, 1988; Boston Globe-Horn Book Magazine Honor List, 1988; Coretta Scott King Honor Book, 1989; Jane Addams Book Award, 1989; New York Times Best Books for Children and Young Adults, 1988; School Library Journal Best Books for Children and Young Adults, 1988

Anthony Burns escapes his Virginia slave master in March of 1854 by stowing away on a ship with the help of a black sailor. In May of the same year, he is arrested in Boston by bounty hunters taking advantage of the Fugitive Slave Act to capture him in the free North to return him to southern slavery. Despite a legal defense by sympathetic northern lawyers and vigorous opposition to his deportation by thousands of abolitionists, Anthony loses his case and is returned to slavery. Federal troops must be called in to quell the Boston riots in Anthony's support, and never again is a fugitive slave deported from Boston.

While awaiting trial in the Boston jail, Anthony flashes back over his life as a slave and his escape to freedom. His return to slavery threatens to break his spirit, particularly when his slave master makes an example of him to other potential runaways, starving him, chaining him, and abusing him in a Virginia jail. Less than a year later, though, northern supporters find him again and buy his freedom. Anthony returns North as a hero and becomes a minister to free black Canadians. However, his health ruined by his mistreatment as a slave, he dies of consumption at the age of twenty-eight.

Anthony Burns: The Defeat and Triumph of a Fugitive Slave is historical fiction, based on the documented case which Virginia Hamilton imaginatively embellishes. The case itself is important and interesting but would make a stronger story with more imagined detail, particularly of the characters. The novel is strongest during Anthony's flashbacks, which are not based on historical record, presumably freeing Hamilton to invent likely events. Where the novel stays closest to the historical record, during the trial and protests, it reads woodenly, without adequate character or plot detail to make it come alive. This is a real loss, as the story has great potential for teaching history and evoking empathy for a slave's internal experience of slavery as Toni Morrison does in *Beloved*. Despite these flaws, *Anthony Burns: The Defeat and Triumph of a Fugitive Slave* is still worth reading.

The book's reading level is accessible to eighth through twelfth graders and contains no horrifyingly explicit violence inappropriate for younger readers. All of the substantive characters are male, including the slaves, slave masters, and abolitionists, which distorts historical reality and blocks female readers from fully identifying with the events. On the other hand, the novel shows both black and white characters struggling against slavery, acknowledging the important role of each group. Similarly, the honest portrayal of southern slave masters running the continuum from very cruel to relatively kind emphasizes the book's theme that slavery is unconscionable under any conditions.

54. Hamilton, Virginia. *The Bells of Christmas*. San Diego: Harcourt Brace Jovanovich, 1989. 59 pages. ***

American Library Association Notable Books for Children and Young Adults, 1989; Coretta Scott King Honor Book, 1990

The Bells of Christmas is a long short story, told by twelve-year-old Jason Bell. Jason describes two days in 1890—Christmas Eve Day and Christmas Day—in rural Springfield, Ohio. Life is good for the Bells, a family proud of their one hundred years of history in Ohio. Jason plays with his seven-year-old sister Melissy, and his thirteen-year-old friend, Matthew, with whom he shares a crush on Cousin Tisha. Papa Bell, his three oldest sons, and Uncle Levi have a virtual monopoly on construction, carpentry, and woodworking in the area. Mama Bell has her own seamstress business at home. Jason has much to anticipate: a snowstorm, surprises from Santa Claus, a feast with extended family, a church celebration, exchanging gifts with relatives, and a visit from Uncle Levi and Cousin Tisha. Jason longs for snow, for then sleighs with bells instead of wagons will come down the National Road.

Virginia Hamilton provides just enough detail to lend authenticity to the story's setting. These details not only paint a picture but also educate readers about a way of life in a particular time and place. The clever ending of the story effectively serves this purpose when Jason, riding the sleigh home from church, imagines the future of the National Road and of transportation, pondering the concept of horseless carriages and flying sleighs. The author handles her heavy dose of history and tradition masterfully.

Although the protagonist is twelve years old, readers of this age may not appreciate the innocence and interests of this character. Jason lived in a time when only childhood and adulthood existed. Today, with the interim stage of adolescence, twelve-year-olds are unlikely to identify with Jason's childlike sentiments, although they may relate to his surprise and joy in family and gifts, his crush on his cousin, and his sense of waiting an eternity for Christmas to arrive. Jason's voice is not consistent, sometimes sounding childlike, at other times waxing poetic, but mostly just sounding old-fashioned. *The Bells of Christmas* is best suited for nine- to ten-year-old readers, male or female, though some of the vocabulary and figurative language may be challenging for these elementary-level readers.

This story provides a rare representation of a physically challenged character in young adult literature. Papa Bell lost one of his legs in a wagon accident, but the loss does not disable him. In everyone's eyes, Papa's disability is simply a physical difference. Papa Bell is the epitome of the Bell family's pride, self-sufficiency, and success. *The Bells of Christmas* portrays a strong, loving black family who are physically and psychically unafflicted by the racist society around them.

55. Hamilton, Virginia. *Cousins*. New York: Philomel Books, 1990. 125 pages. ***

American Library Association Notable Books for Children and Young Adults, 1991; Boston Globe-Horn Book Magazine Honor List, 1991; New York Times Best Books for Children and Young Adults, 1990

In August, eleven-year-old Camilla attends day camp while her mother, Maylene, goes to work. She sneaks into the nursing home to visit her ninety-four-year-old grandmother, Gram Tut, and rides around her small, unnamed Ohio town with her sixteen-year-old brother, Andrew, in his pickup truck when he's not working at the service station. Gram Tut, though she weaves in and out of consciousness and time, is vital enough that Cammy can continue to deny her grandmother's impending death.

Intertwined with Cammy's family is the family of Maylene's sister, Cammy's Aunt Effie Lee. Effie Lee, a homemaker whose husband owns a prosperous car dealership, is overly proud of her perfect house and perfect, overprotected children. Cammy envies and hates Effie Lee and her daughter, cousin Patty Ann, and regards them as enemies for their ostentation and conceit. Effie Lee and Patty Ann put down Cammy and her family for their ordinariness and working-class standard of living and for the freedom Maylene allows her children. Effie Lee's perfect family has problems, though, of which she seems ignorant: Patty Ann is bulimic and son Richie is an alcoholic who cannot hold a job for more than a month. Patty Ann brags and berates others to make herself feel better; Richie tells lies to overcompensate for his insecurities.

Cammy, Patty Ann, and their third cousin, Elouise, attend a day camp sponsored by the Christian Shelter, where Elouise lives while her mother is away working as a migrant farmer. Elouise is starving for inclusion and attention from anyone. Cammy only associates with Elouise out of pity or when Patty Ann pays attention to Elouise. In the climax of the story, Elouise falls into the Little River and almost drowns. Patty Ann jumps in to rescue her; Elouise gets out, but Patty Ann goes down, and Cammy, from the riverside, watches her cousin drown.

In September, Cammy cannot successfully return to school. Feeling guilty for having hated and not tried to rescue Patty Ann, Cammy suffers weeks of nausea and nightmares. Effie Lee encourages the students to dwell on Patty Ann's death. She starts a rumor that Elouise is possessed by Patty Ann. Elouise, ostracized by the townspeople who hold her responsible for Patty Ann's death, drops out of school and joins her mother as a migrant worker. She tries to convince Cammy that Patty Ann will possess her, too.

A series of events helps Cammy recover. Cammy's father returns to take care of her while Maylene is at work. Elouise reassures her that no one was to blame for Patty Ann's accidental death. And Gram Tut visits and helps Cammy to feel more comfortable discussing Patty Ann's death and death in general. In the end, Cammy gains understanding and a real relationship with her father.

Cousins is well paced, with a balance of action and reflection. It addresses the serious issue of death with depth. However, readers have to wait until the final fifth of the book to get to the heart of the story, Cammy's coping with Patty Ann's death. Stylistically, *Cousins* is Virginia Hamilton in top form. Regrettably, the novel is marred by two weaknesses: prejudices expressed by the characters are never critiqued, and there are several unresolved minor plot threads.

Cammy's competitiveness and envy—and its consequent disdain—are realistic. Upper elementary- and middle-school girls, the ideal readership for this book, will find her character believable, if immature in some respects. Yet Virginia Hamilton leaves some inappropriate sentiments unchallenged. Cammy values her mother primarily because her mother is beautiful. She ridicules Patty Ann's bulimia as pathetic. Maylene chastises Cammy's visits to Gram Tut as unhealthy. By contrast, Cammy at least confesses that she's ashamed of herself for feeling ashamed of impoverished, near-homeless, and desperate-for-attention Elouise.

Virginia Hamilton represents a range of familial relationships, some positive, some negative. The animosity between the two families illustrates the truism that people can choose their friends but not their families. Money and appearances are divisive. Sadly, relatives who are in a position to help each other—especially Elouise's desperately poor family—distance themselves from each other. Maylene's is a close-knit family except for her ex-husband, who lives in another town. When he returns to help Cammy recover, remarkably, the family resumes business as usual, except that Cammy now has a father. Why Effie Lee doesn't know or care about her children's problems is never revealed. Why Effie Lee sends Patty Ann to a day camp for children whose parents work all day or who don't have parents, is also never explained. What's even more troubling than these inconsistencies is that Effie Lee is blamed for all her children's problems. In the end, Hamilton renders even Effie Lee's grief over Patty Ann's death as dysfunctional and she remains an unsympathetic character.

56.   Hamilton, Virginia. *Many Thousand Gone: African Americans from Slavery to Freedom*. New York: Alfred A. Knopf, 1993. 151 pages. ****

American Library Association Notable Books for Children and Young Adults, 1993; Coretta Scott King Award, 1993; School Library Journal Best Books for Children and Young Adults, 1993

Many Thousand Gone: African Americans from Slavery to Freedom reads like historical fiction. Virginia Hamilton manages to provide readers with a many-faceted understanding of the institution of slavery and the range of African Americans' conditions and responses under it. In the first story, Hamilton starts in 1619, when the first slaves were brought to America, to what was then the colony of Jamestown in Virginia. In the last story, it is 1863, when the Emancipation Proclamation was announced and slaves were theoretically free.

The stories in this book are not arranged chronologically, but thematically. Hamilton divides her book into three sections and establishes the cultural, political, and social background behind the events. Hamilton's introductions to the three sections are superb: they are succinct, yet manage to do justice to the complex and numerous factors that influenced the course of events described. Because the introductions are more sophisticated than the stories themselves, a high-school reader will get the most out of them.

Part One, entitled "Slavery in America," contains six stories about people born in Africa and America. The difference of homeland allows Hamilton to explore several important topics: the role of Europeans and Africans in the slave trade in Africa, the Middle Passage, the Triangle Trade, "seasoning" in the West Indies, the auction block, and the transmission of culture and the heritage of resistance carried from Africa and the West Indies to America. The majority of the stories take place in Massachusetts, which is an effective surprise, since the average reader will probably come to this book with the expectation that the setting for most of the stories will be the South.

Part Two, called "Running-Aways," the longest section of the book, includes fifteen stories which present a range of situations. Most of the stories are about the Underground Railroad and uprisings, but Hamilton also weaves in accounts of slaves using the courts to fight for their rights and against slave codes and fugitive slave laws. In some of the stories, the characters are successful, while in others, they are caught and returned to their owners, resold, or killed. As in the first section, there are stories that acknowledge some European Americans who possessed the moral integrity and courage to work to end slavery and help African Americans escape to freedom. Maryland and Virginia are the most common settings for these stories, but some take place in Massachusetts and Canada. Some of the characters will be familiar to the reader, while some will be new.

Titled "Exodus to Freedom," the final section of the book has thirteen stories about famous and unknown figures. Thematically, this section differs little from the previous one. There is a wider range of settings, though, with Ohio figuring prominently because of its strategic significance on the Underground Railroad en route to Canada. The last seven chapters are about the Civil War and the Emancipation Proclamation, with the last story bearing the book's title, in which African American soldiers in the Union Army sing a song about the auction block whose last line is "Many thousand gone." It's a poignant moment in history and a fitting finale to the book, incorporating a tribute to the millions of Africans who suffered slavery and a turning point in African Americans' struggle for freedom.

The stories in *Many Thousand Gone: African Americans from Slavery to Freedom* are from two to seven pages long, a perfect length for the reader who likes to pick up a book for occasional reading or for the restless or short attention-span reader. For the most part, the stories are suspenseful and fast-paced. They don't simplify or sanitize the horrors of slavery, but they focus more on their characters' spirit, strength, and resourcefulness to cope with and triumph over near-impossible situations. The content is appropriate for upper elementary through high-school readers. The illustrations and the fact that it reads like a storybook instead of a history book don't detract from its appeal to older readers. It is engaging and thoroughly accessible for readers of all ages.

What makes this book different from a traditional study of slavery is Hamilton's storytelling technique. She is at her best when she builds in an element of surprise, which hits the reader in one of two ways. One way is when Hamilton doesn't reveal the character's name until a pivotal moment in the action, letting the reader realize all of a sudden that s/he has been reading about someone about whom s/he already knows. This late-breaking revelation forces the reader to see the famous figure in a new light. The second way that Hamilton works her storytelling magic is even more fun, particularly for the older, more meticulous reader: Hamilton includes minor details, some bizarre, some private, that seldom appear in standard profiles, but which are just the kinds of things that young people love to learn about famous people in order to think of them as real people.

Only about a third of the stories are about women. However, this book does not strike the reader as male centered, for some of the best stories are about female characters.

It's ironic that Hamilton concludes a book that shows how African Americans fought for their freedom with stories that portray them as more passive characters, the grateful beneficiaries of European Americans like President Lincoln "giving" them their freedom. In the afterword, Hamilton mentions the problems and promise in the aftermath of the Civil War and the Emancipation Proclamation. She concludes with, "For 125 years [African Americans] have continued to struggle and to survive." However, Hamilton downplays the fact that despite the Emancipation Proclamation, millions of slaves were not free, and that, even after 1865, even today, millions of African Americans rightfully argue that they are still not free. This contradictory image and conclusion are the only weaknesses of the book.

57. Hamilton, Virginia. *Plain City*. New York: Blue Sky Press, 1993. 194 pages.***

American Library Association Notable Books for Children and Young Adults, 1993

Winter weather brings dramatic changes into twelve-year-old Buhlaire-Marie Sims' life, as she begins to learn why everyone in Plain City, Ohio, antagonizes or ostracizes her. Their mistreatment stems more from their response to her icy reserve than, as she had previously assumed, her unique appearance, odd-acting family, and the unusual way they live. Seventh-grade classmate Grady Terrell, who, like his peers, taunts Buhlaire in school but follows her admiringly outside of school, unwittingly helps her see herself in a new way and, in the process, becomes her friend.

Buhlaire lives with her father's family in the Water Houses, rough-hewn tree houses suspended on stilts above the river on the edge of Plain City. They keep a sparsely furnished household, with no documents or photographs, and all personal possessions locked away. Buhlaire's aloof, egotistical, and exhausted mother, Bluezy, is a songstress and exotic dancer whose work takes her away from home too much; her absence makes Buhlaire feel discarded and worthless. Communing with nature and witnessing her relatives' special relationship with the river, Buhlaire realizes that they live in the Water Houses, not, as others incorrectly assume, because they are too poor to afford a traditional house in the center of Plain City but because they choose to live harmoniously alongside the river.

To protect her from the truth, Buhlaire's mother and her father's family tell her that her father, Junior Sims, died in Vietnam. But Junior is very much alive and in Plain City: mentally unstable and homeless, he lives on the outskirts of the city in a freeway underpass. He adores his daughter but cannot take care of her. Still, he does what he can, shadowing her protectively during her isolated walks. When Buhlaire loses her way in a blinding blizzard, he rescues her and introduces himself. Buhlaire learns that Junior is the biracial son of an outcast white stepmother ultimately rejected by his black father and half-siblings—which explains why Buhlaire stands out physically, for she, like Junior, with gray eyes, blond hair, and orange skin, appears neither white nor black.

Buhlaire then rescues Junior in turn by getting him the "stash" he needs to "get going," her life savings of three hundred dollars. Rather than test her father's promise to take her with him, she returns home to greater intimacy with her mother and other relatives, forgiving them for misrepresenting Junior's status and realizing that they care about her even though she has never recognized it before.

When her relatives bring her to one of her mother's shows at Delmore's Club, Buhlaire gains a first-hand appreciation for Bluezy's talent and magnetism. She bonds with her mother when Bluezy invites Buhlaire onto the stage so that they can sing together. She learns why Bluezy and Sam have no investment in her father's return, that they have been clandestinely and guiltily involved romantically for years.

When her father hands her an envelope stuffed with memorabilia and photographs, Buhlaire suddenly realizes that her relatives' place was barren of such objects not because they wanted to deny her existence but because her father routinely broke in and snatched them. By reappearing in Buhlaire's life and returning to her the envelope of personal effects, Buhlaire's father gives her life in the broadest sense: she gets what she calls her "back time."

Still disappointed with her home life, Buhlaire frequents the homeless shelter, A Shelter From *Any* Storm. In her mind, the welcoming and caring shelter exhibits more ingredients of a real home than the Water Houses, which are cold and lonely. The shelter cares for people, instead of "killing them off," as her family attempted to do with her father.

Plain City unfolds like a mystery, which it is for Buhlaire, but some aspects of her story remain unclarified and confusing. For example, two of the novel's purportedly central themes, biracial identity and finding an unknown or lost parent, receive short shrift. Biracial readers will not feel affirmed or enlightened by this novel. The reader knows how Buhlaire sees herself, but what does it all mean? Why does everyone treat Buhlaire as if she is different yet avoid stating the obvious? How does Junior's biracial identity affect him? Did the war break him or was he always fragile and angry?

Told in a third-person voice that rarely establishes objectivity or offers facts—except to elaborately describe the emotional and physical landscape—the narrative is further muddled with italicized and unquoted first person stream-of-consciousness thoughts from Buhlaire. These italicized passages convey Buhlaire's confusion, stubbornness, and anger; unfortunately, the device seems contrived and will confuse some young readers. These boringly repetitive passages seem at times like a rambling self-indulgence of angst and aggression. The broad outline of the novel's plot indicates major events, yet the narrative provides so little concrete information that it seems as if little happens. Ironically, Virginia Hamilton tries to do too much and ends up doing too little. However, she deserves praise simply for tackling two difficult and seldom addressed topics, biracial identity and homelessness.

Readers looking for real action will be thrown by the book's interior, reflective focus, its impenetrable literary veneer, and amorphous plot. Furthermore, the use of some colloquial expressions—like "snap" and "bwoy"—will quickly date the story, if they do not already. Although the novel's protagonist is twelve, its style suits a high-school readership. Some of Buhlaire's figurative expressions seem extraordinarily literary and sophisticated for a twelve-year-old, even if she is in the Talented and Gifted Program for her writing skills! Granted, the metaphors of the blinding snowstorm and the flood-causing thaw work well: she meets her father and sees herself and her family more clearly after the snowstorm; and the thaw serves as an appropriate metaphor for her rite of passage, for her world which breaks apart and flows together as she forces a new openness with her family.

Virginia Hamilton does do justice to the other challenging issue she writes about in *Plain City*, homelessness—even if she strains credulity with the coincidence that the two key figures in Buhlaire's new life— her father and friend Grady—have a history of homelessness. Although the author concentrates primarily on detailing the operations of the shelter and only develops two characters to concretize that experience—the successful Mr. Terrell and the unsuccessful Mr. Sims—she dramatizes their proud struggle, their hard road to making a home for themselves, defined differently for each of them. In her descriptions of the shelter, the author demonstrates the magnitude of the problem of homelessness, as well as the power and potential in the camaraderie and positive spirit of some individuals and agencies.

In her descriptions of Junior, the author accurately portrays a mentally ill and homeless man, unkempt and smelly, prone to abrupt mood swings, his thoughts spinning off, helpless and yet remarkably resourceful at the same time. Junior is all too human, and so is his daughter. Realistically, the narrative captures Buhlaire's ambivalence, her love and fear of her father, her wanting to both help him and get away from him.

Fortunately, there are not the typical Hamilton simple dichotomies between male and female characters, with the former being good and the latter bad, though there are more positive male characters. Because of its excessive focus on Buhlaire's appearance and her distinctly female dynamics with teachers and classmates, *Plain City* will not appeal to male readers, but those elements will not necessarily make it appealing to female readers, either. Overall, its treatment of homelessness recommends it for all readers.

58. Hansen, Joyce. *The Gift-Giver.* New York: Clarion Books, 1980. 118 pages. ****

Fifth-grader Doris hangs out on her block on 163rd Street in New York City with her friends, Sherman, Yellow Bird, Big Russell, twins Mickey and Dotty, and the new kid, Amir. Together they have fifth-grade worries and adventures— beating the sixth graders at basketball, getting yelled at in school, competing for the Social Studies award, becoming friends with tough girls from the next block through a jump-rope competition. But occasionally, more serious worries intrude: a boy is randomly shot to death on their playground; Doris' father gets laid off, and she pitches in to watch her baby brother while her mother looks for work; Sherman runs away when the state scatters him and his siblings to different foster families.

Through all of the changes, Doris struggles to fit in. More than anything else, she wants to be part of her crowd. However, Amir is different. In his quiet, watchful way, he simply is who he is. He likes to draw, he never joins in the good-natured insults the other kids pass around, and, instead of playing basketball, he acts as the informal coach. Yet as different as he is, Doris' friends like and respect Amir. Slowly, Doris learns from Amir that it's okay just to be herself.

The Gift-Giver is a wonderful slice-of-life novel that incorporates serious themes into the everyday adventures of middle-school age kids. The kids' characters are warm, funny, and outrageous, each one unique. The plot is lively and entertaining, with realistic dialogue. And the underlying message—that young people do not have to sacrifice their authentic selves to be accepted and liked—is vitally important.

The Gift-Giver is highly recommended. Hansen tells a good story, and makes the reader care about her characters so that small adventures become engrossing and the plot flows nicely. The characters' ages and the relatively non-threatening issues addressed by *The Gift-Giver* make it appropriate for fifth- to eighth-grade readers. Its reading level is also accessible for this age group. Hansen avoids sex role stereotyping, and the healthy mix of female and male characters will attract readers of both sexes. Adult characters play a reassuring but peripheral role in the story; the main focus is the peer group and the strength and wisdom that African American kids can draw from each other. Best of all, readers who grow to love Doris, Amir, and the other kids can look for them again in *Yellow Bird and Me*, the sequel.

59. Hansen, Joyce. *Home Boy*. New York: Clarion Books, 1982. 181 pages. ****

Sixteen-year-old Marcus' parents rudely transplant him from St. Cruz to the Bronx in search of a better life. Trying to escape the cycle of poverty and to give their children access to education, Marcus' parents work two jobs each in New York to save money to bring his five younger siblings over. Marcus, however, experiences much difficulty trying to adjust to his new home, where poverty means violence and burned-out buildings so different from the turquoise sea and communal poverty of St. Cruz. The new kid at school, Marcus must fight his way to acceptance. His teachers place him in a special education math class and an English as a Second Language class, although English is his native language. Frustrated with school, Marcus starts cutting classes and eventually begins selling drugs to earn quick money for himself and his mother. The stress of New York life becomes too much for his parents, and Marcus' father, with whom he has always had a stormy relationship, leaves the family. Marcus finds solace only through his growing friendship with Cassandra, a serious girl with family problems of her own.

When Marcus' drug supplier is murdered in front of him, he and his friend Ron vow to turn over a new leaf. But on the very first day of the new school year, Marcus' old adversary Eddie pushes him too hard, and Marcus stabs Eddie. Frantic, Marcus spends the day riding the subway, thinking back, in a series of flashbacks, about his life in St. Cruz and in New York. Remembering his beloved grandmother's faith in him, Marcus turns to his father, and together they go to face the police.

Home Boy is a beautiful book about one island boy's coming of age on the mean streets of New York. Marcus' seemingly thoughtless descent into crime and truancy, while remaining a deeply confused, caring young man underneath, rings true. So does his parents' strict West Indian discipline unraveling into exhaustion and frustration as they learn that New York streets are not paved with gold after all. Marcus' father Rudy is an especially heartbreaking and true-to-life character. An uneducated orphan, Rudy shows his children love in the only way he knows how, by working hard for them and uprooting them all to try to break the cycle of poverty. But Rudy cannot talk to his children, and Marcus, the eldest, desperately needs his father's love and guidance. Only at the end, when Marcus nearly kills a boy, does Rudy break through his own isolation to support his son.

Home Boy alternates by chapter between Marcus' fleeing the knife fight and his flashbacks to St. Cruz and early days in New York. Although somewhat discordant and distracting, this literary device highlights the contrast between life in St. Cruz and New York. The sense of Marcus' running through the whole book builds suspense, and the plot is always interesting.

The novel offers strong male and female characters, both adults and children: Marcus' grandmother and Cassandra, two wise female voices pushing Marcus to live up to his potential; and his parents, struggling to do their best, and sometimes failing, under very difficult circumstances. The mix of characters should appeal to male and female readers, and the reading level is appropriate for eighth- through eleventh-grade readers.

Anybody who has faced the trauma of adjusting to a new, hostile culture will identify with *Home Boy*. Anybody who feels misunderstood by her/his parents, dreams of dropping out of school to strike out on her/his own, or feels drawn by the enticements of the street, will understand Marcus' world. And anybody who simply enjoys a good story has a treat in store with *Home Boy*.

60. Hansen, Joyce. *Which Way Freedom?* New York: Walker and Co., 1986. 120 pages. **

American Library Association Notable Books for Children and Young Adults, 1986; Coretta Scott King Honor Book, 1987

Obi is nineteen or twenty, a slave on a small farm in South Carolina. Sold away from his mother at six or seven, Obi has a burning desire to return to her Sea Islands off the South Carolina coast to find her. In the meantime, he works the fields with thirteen-year-old Easter and eight-year-old Jason, and together they form a new family. As word of the Civil War filters down to the slaves, Obi decides that the war's chaos will provide an excellent cover for running away. Together with Easter and Buka, an ancient African who guides them, Obi runs away. They make it as far as the South Carolina coast before being caught and re-enslaved in the service of Confederate soldiers. Buka dies shortly after they arrive, but Obi and Easter watch carefully for another chance to escape— Obi to the Sea Islands, Easter to find Jason and bring him back with her. When the Confederate soldiers are attacked by sea, Obi escapes to the island in a boat he made of reeds. His mother is gone, sold from the island long ago, and the island is now controlled by Union troops. After a while, Obi joins the

Union Army and is nearly killed in battle. He survives, however, determined to leave the past behind and to claim a new, free identity for himself.

Which Way Freedom? is a disappointing book about a fascinating topic. The history of slaves escaping and fighting in the Civil War deserves more compelling treatment than this novel offers. There is little character development, which makes the plot and dialogue somewhat wooden and makes it hard to care very much about the characters. In addition, the story ends without any plot resolution, which is singularly unsatisfying. We don't learn whether Easter ever escapes or reunites with Jason or Obi. We know that Obi survives one battle, but we leave him in the middle of a war. All we learn is that he claims a new name for himself and gives up on the search for his mother. Although the symbolism of abandoning the past to embrace the future is legitimate, in this case there are too many threads left hanging.

Which Way Freedom?'s writing style is simple and straightforward, appropriate for sixth- through eighth-grade readers. The lack of substantial female characters—Easter is a mere shadow—will annoy female readers. This might be less of a problem if Obi's character were more real, but even boys may have trouble identifying with the flat portrayal of him. *Which Way Freedom?* is a promising skeleton of a story which is never fleshed out. Each chapter opens with intriguing historical quotations from ex-slaves, soldiers, and President Lincoln. Unfortunately, the fiction that follows does not live up to the animation of the quotations. Hansen's writing style is more suited to elementary-school readers and I suspect that these young readers would enjoy *Which Way Freedom?* if it were shorter.

61. Hansen, Joyce. *Yellow Bird and Me.* New York: Clarion Books, 1986. 155 pages. *****

Parents' Choice Award, 1986

Bronx sixth grader Doris Williams is mourning the loss of her best friend, Amir, who moved to a foster home in Syracuse. Since he left, nothing is the same. Her old friends seem foolish, and she has nobody with whom to share her thoughts or poems. Determined to earn enough money to go visit Amir, Doris starts working at Miss Bee's Beauty Hive, answering the phone and running errands for tips. Doris continues to sneak to her job every Saturday even after her overprotective parents forbid her to work.

Then Doris decides to help Yellow Bird with his schoolwork, thinking it might make her feel closer to Amir. Before Amir left, he and Doris helped Yellow Bird together. Although Yellow Bird is always playing the fool and getting into trouble, Doris tries to see inside him, behind the facade, as Amir always urged her to do. As she grows closer to Yellow Bird, Doris realizes that he cannot read and that his cutting up in class is an attempt to hide his academic problems. Although he improves a little with Doris' help, he is put into a special education class for remedial work. Ashamed, Yellow Bird tries to duck his old friends, but Doris stands up for him and wins them over.

When a new drama teacher comes to school, Yellow Bird excitedly auditions for the play. With Doris' coaching, he learns his lines and brings down the house on opening night. Doris confides in the drama teacher that Yellow Bird is smart but just reverses letters and numbers so that he can't read or do math well. This sympathetic teacher helps to diagnose Yellow Bird's dyslexia and gets him returned to the regular classroom with a special reading tutor. Yellow Bird's success on the stage teaches all the kids that everybody has their own strengths. Meanwhile Doris matures through the process of helping Yellow Bird, and she finds that with his friendship, she does not miss Amir as acutely. Having integrated some of Amir's kindness and insight into her own actions, she feels close to him even when they are apart.

Yellow Bird and Me is an excellent example of a high-quality book for young teens. Never didactic or condescending, it addresses young teens' concerns about friendship, peer approval, and discovering one's own talents. Although the plot centers around the same daily preoccupations as other many other middle-school-level books, this novel is set apart by its strong characters and themes of acceptance and compassion. The plot moves at a good pace, holding reader interest. More significantly, the characters are so likable that the reader is pulled in to their lives, wanting to know what happens next to them. The growing friendship between Doris and Yellow Bird is particularly moving as is Doris' own internal maturation process. At the same time, the characters never come off as goody-two-shoes, realistically testing limits with both their teachers and their parents.

The adult characters in *Yellow Bird and Me* are similarly well drawn. Doris' parents are by turns caring and unreasonable, at least from her perspective. The sixth-grade teacher who torments Yellow Bird so mercilessly in the beginning becomes much more understanding once she recognizes his learning disability. Perhaps the most moving aspect of each character's development is that it is described through Doris' eyes, a product of her own deepening insight into human nature. Doris' narrative voice is perfect, at once believable, age appropriate, and insightful.

With young characters and a moderately easy reading level, *Yellow Bird and Me* is an excellent choice for sixth- to eighth-grade readers. Both girls and boys will find characters to identify with, and the school setting is general enough to appeal to readers from urban or rural backgrounds. *Yellow Bird and Me* can be enjoyed alone, but reading it after *The Gift-Giver* allows one to spend more time with Doris and her friends. In either case, this moving story should not be missed.

62. Hansen, Joyce. *Out from This Place*. New York: Walker and Company, 1988. 135 pages. **

American Library Association Notable Books for Children and Young Adults, 1988

Out from This Place continues the story of the final days of the Civil War, which Hansen began in *Which Way Freedom?* Slaves Obi and Easter have run away to the South Carolina Sea Islands, controlled by the Union Army; there they are paid wages for working abandoned plantations. *Out from This Place* takes up fourteen-year-old Easter's story after Obi leaves her to join the Union army. It is a time of confusion and danger, with soon-to-be-freed slaves running away from plantations in large numbers, marauding bands of Confederate soldiers, and deserters raiding plantations. Despite the risk, Easter is determined to find and rescue Jason, her adopted "little brother" whom she and Obi left behind when they ran away from their slave masters. Traveling alone, Easter is reunited with Jason, and together they return to the safety of the Sea Islands, along with an entire band of runaway slaves from their plantation.

On the Sea Islands, the Union army offers all former slaves a deal: work the former island plantations in return for a small wage and ultimate ownership of the acres they cultivate. Although Easter hates fieldwork, she joins the small community of former slaves, providing childcare in exchange for a small portion of their wages. The community grows and organizes itself, creates a church, an informal local government, and a school. When Easter learns to read, the northern missionary teacher offers her a scholarship to a teacher-training school in Philadelphia. However, Easter has her mind set on leaving the island to search for Obi.

Meanwhile, the federal government changes its policy and demands that former slaves return the land they have been cultivating to its white former plantation owners. The people of Easter's community rebel, vowing to fight for their land, despite government threats to send in the army. When Rayford, one of the community leaders, is shot dead in the ensuing conflict, Easter joins with the others to negotiate a settlement to buy some of the land and to avoid further bloodshed.

Joyce Hansen demonstrated her storytelling and character-creating talent in *The Gift-Giver*, but somehow these skills evade her when she attempts an historical novel. *Out from This Place* focuses on a fascinating period of black history rarely addressed in young adult books. But this novel has many of the same faults of *Which Way Freedom?* Although it describes epic events, the plot is not particularly gripping. The flat characters never come alive enough for the reader to care much about them. Actually, the novel reads more like a history book, with the characters added as an afterthought to try to personalize the history a little. This is really too bad, since the history of Reconstruction is powerful and exciting, providing rich material for adventure-filled, educational novels.

Another disappointment of *Out from This Place* is its random jumble of major events and minor personal worries. For instance, Easter's indecision about whether she should attend teacher-training school or search for Obi constantly detracts from the historical events she's living through. Although the plot should climax with Easter's role in resolving the land battle and helping the freed slaves own land for the first time, Hansen creates an anticlimax by having Easter decide to attend the training school shortly afterward. Although interweaving personal dilemmas and major historical events can make history come alive, in this novel it simply doesn't work.

One strength of the book is its portrayal of a whole range of personalities and opinions among African Americans responding to Reconstruction. The novel acknowledges that individual freed blacks had many different priorities following freedom from slavery, including land ownership, education, keeping the family together, maintaining friendly relations with whites, safety, and economic survival.

Out from This Place has a sixth- to eighth-grade reading level. Although its main protagonist is female, male characters play an integral part in the story as soldiers and community leaders, so both male and female readers will find characters of interest.

63. Harrison, Deloris. *Journey All Alone.* New York: The Dial Press, 1971. 120 pages. **

Thirteen-year-old Mildred Jewell is a self-conscious adolescent who daily feels inferior because she's poor, dark-skinned, physically underdeveloped, and shabbily dressed. The world of Harlem and her school in midtown Manhattan confirm her negative self-perception. Nobody, not even Mildred herself, regards her strengths—her intelligence and her competence at managing domestic responsibilities—as assets. The other black freshmen at her high school tolerate her as a hanger-on but seldom include her in their intimacies. While her stylish, wealthier "friends" flirt with boys at parties and around town, Mildred harnesses herself obediently to the household tasks of cooking, cleaning, laundering, and parenting her nine-year-old brother, Michael, while her mother works from sunrise to sunset at menial jobs to support the family. Mildred herself also shoulders worries about the family being thrown out on the street.

Not only is Mildred alienated from her peers, but she feels acutely alone within her own family. Her father Nat wants her mother Izola to support him while he quits his factory job to try to realize his talent as a jazz pianist. When Izola refuses to support what she considers his latest selfish scheme, Nat moves out. Izola grows overworked and overwhelmed by anger, fear, and sadness about Nat's abandonment, while Michael withdraws into the streets. For Mildred, a Daddy's girl, Nat's fantastic stories and schemes provided the only distraction she had from her ugly world. So she transfers her daydreams to Angel Rivera, a handsome Puerto Rican tennis instructor in the neighborhood park whom she has seen but never met. But Mildred's dreams are totally shattered. Angel turns out to be a sleazy pothead. When her father returns to the family half a year later, it's only to try to get money from Izola for an expensive musician's union card. Izola refuses, and fists fly, accompanied by unforgivable insults. Mildred figuratively and literally loses her father forever: not only does he leave for good, but his emotional and physical abuse of Izola is too obvious even for Mildred to ignore. As if Mildred's emotional innocence has not been violated enough, three boys try to rape her in the park.

Then Mildred develops a breakthrough friendship with Gene, despite her initial reflex to reject him because he's short, fat, dark, and poor. But he's also winningly genuine, thoughtful, funny, and a nonconformist. In learning to respect Gene, Mildred reassesses her own self-perception, and starts to value herself as a person of substance.

Journey All Alone is a depressing if realistic account of a black girl's coming of age in an alienating, impoverished world. Race, color, and class divide people and damage the few relationships that manage to cross such boundaries. The narrative divides everyone into dark or light and, by taking this color prejudice for granted, reinforces it. No character or event in the novel repudiates or contradicts effectively this bias. Similarly, the narrative offers, without comment, Mildred's and Izola's prejudices about Puerto Ricans. And Angel and Chico, the only Puerto Rican characters developed in the story, fulfill negative stereotypes as greasy, drug-abusing, sexual predators in provocative clothing.

Most depressing is that acceptance, affection, praise, and attention is almost nonexistent for all of the young people in the story. Mildred's character is overly selfless and obedient, never challenging her mother. On the other hand, readers who are oldest children in difficult families will easily identify with Mildred: she is the ultimate parentified oldest child, caught in the crossfire between embattled parents. Deloris Harrison does a fine job of inviting the reader into the workings of Mildred's head and heart.

Harrison's clear prose renders the novel accessible to junior and senior high-school readers, but its plot recommends it most for young adolescent girls. Particularly because the novel will appeal most to young women, it's disconcerting that the author doesn't delve into how sexism impacts Mildred and her mother. In fact, the novel's only examination of sexism contradicts itself. As Aunt Vi cleans the blood off Izola's face, she asks Izola how she provoked Nat's beating and warns her to stand behind her man, since black men's lives are so difficult. Izola comes back with, "What about us? What about black women?" But the discussion is promptly dropped.

The final message of *Journey All Alone* strangely glorifies Mildred's rite of passage into adulthood as into "alonehood." Her family has been trying to teach her "to stop looking to others to make [her] life better and stand on [her] own two feet and make [her] way in life the best way [she] knows how"; she strives to follow a lesson from a spiritual, for which the novel is named—"Without a father, without a mother, you gotta make this journey all alone." Self-sufficiency is a positive attribute, but is not being able or willing to count on any other person—especially a parent or friend—an ideal condition for which young people should strive? *Journey All Alone* provides no pat resolution of the challenges and conflicts it sets in motion; rather, it ends with Mildred's life's work just beginning.

64. Haynes, Henry Louis. *Squarehead and Me*. Philadelphia: Westminster Press, 1980. 143 pages. *

Twelve-year-old David Stevenson will only treat his neighbor and fellow sixth grade classmate Bobby Palmer semi-respectfully when they are alone. All of the kids in their Washington, D.C., neighborhood ignore or taunt Bobby, whom they call Squarehead, because he seems stupid and immature. When in the presence of other kids, David also mistreats Bobby. No one, including Bobby's mother, understands him; in fact, Mrs. Palmer is determined that summer school will transform her son into a student, despite Bobby's protests that summer school has failed him every year.

One day, close to the start of summer school, when David breaks his promise to play with Squarehead by walking off to flirt with Denise Inchfield, Bobby runs away. David tracks him down and follows him to a farm in Prince George's

County, Maryland. One of their classmates, Sharon Van Pelt, vacations there with family friends, the Olsons, and had invited Bobby to visit anytime. During their weekend stay, David sees Bobby in a new light: Bobby knows how to swim, has been on an airplane, and gets along well with the Olsons and Van Pelts. Also, Sharon confides to David that she invited Bobby out to the farm so that her mother, who runs a special education program, could informally assess Bobby's "problem"; Sharon explains that Bobby probably has a language disability, like Jimmy and Tommy Olson.

Because the story is told in the voice of eleven-year-old David, it spends too much time on the details of games and gossip and too little time on the serious issues which the plot introduces. Readers are likely to find Mrs. Palmer's flowery speeches about aging women confusing and irrelevant and Mr. Olson's rambling Viking sagas weird and long-winded.

Squarehead and Me is intended for readers without disabilities, even with the somewhat enlightened perspective that Sharon provides. Readers with disabilities are likely to be hurt by David's insensitive comments about Bobby. The novel captures David's offensive attitudes, but fails to portray his changing understanding of Bobby. David learns so little about Bobby's disability that he, along with the reader, is left shocked and puzzled at the end of the story when he learns that Bobby has a higher IQ—125—than he does. And the reader never learns what's going on inside Bobby's head. The ending, where Bobby asks David to call him Squarehead, after he's been rightfully rejecting that pejorative nickname for years, comes out of nowhere and never gets explained. For most of the story, guilt and pity chiefly motivate David to deal with Bobby. At the end of the story, David won't have to juggle his changed relationship with Bobby with his peers' teasing, since Bobby will be attending another school with a special program. Tommy Olson serves as a "success story" that reinforces the desirability of a norm—he attended an alternative educational environment, where he learned to harness his intellectual skills and to manage his disability, and now does satisfactorily in a mainstream school.

Why did Henry Louis Haynes have white folks without disabilities be the saviors here? Sharon identifies with Bobby because as one of a few white students bussed in, she, too, is an outcast at their school. As an outcast with the intellectual and communication skills to articulate what Bobby must feel, she chastises David for always taking "the easy sure road," for bowing to peer pressure and for not speaking up when one of his peers is hurting someone else. And Mr. Olson, by sharing his personal struggle with his learning-disabled sons, is the first and only person to successfully challenge Mrs. Palmer's perception of her son and to let him be assessed. It took a twelve-year-old white girl to identify Bobby's special need? What was wrong with Bobby's mother and teachers over the years? While *Squarehead and Me* attempts to demystify learning disabilities, it implicitly infantilizes and objectifies people with disabilities by giving voice to only able people's perceptions and ideals.

65. Higginsen, Vy, with Tonya Bolden. *Mama, I Want to Sing.* New York: Scholastic Inc., 1992. 183 pages. **

When *Mama, I Want to Sing* begins in 1946, Doris Winter is twelve, the apple of her parents' eye. Daughter of a minister, her life centers around Mt. Calvary Church in Harlem. During her twelfth year, though, two events occur that change her life. First, the brilliant music minister recognizes Doris' talent and invites her to join the adult choir. Second, her father dies of a heart attack, sending Doris into a year and a half of grief. Only gospel music and time finally heal her, allowing her to go on with her life.

As she becomes a teenager, Doris' musical interests turn to blues and soul. She dreams of a singing career but must sneak around behind her mother's back just to hear records of the popular, secular black singers of the day. Her mother, convinced that show business is the devil's work, refuses to let

Doris stray from church music. Doris rebels and, at seventeen, forms a singing group with three friends to appear at amateur night at the Apollo. When the group not only wins but is offered a contract by a famous manager, Doris begs her godmother, Sister Carrie, to intercede for her with her mother. Sister Carrie had a singing career in her younger days but left it behind when she realized it held no joy for her. Sister Carrie warns Doris about the temptations of the road, about holding on to her calling and her values in the midst of everything. Then she helps to convince Geraldine Winter to let go of her daughter. Doris sets off on a singing career that eventually brings her fame, wealth, and happiness but that never manages to separate her from her roots or the people she loves.

Though loosely based on the real-life experiences of the author's sister, *Mama, I Want to Sing* is a fairy tale. The characters are all a little flat, moving through their experiences without divulging any real depth of character. The adoration that the Winter parents shower on Doris is a bit much, although Mrs. Winter finally becomes more real in her frustrated reactions to Doris' teenage rebellion. Doris' simple path to stardom is hard to believe as is her completely unsullied response to fame.

On the other hand, the plot moves nicely, providing easy and interesting reading. The values that the characters espouse offer a refreshing look at entertainment, one traditional African American path to success. Between Mrs. Winter's reactionary view and Doris' naive one, Sister Carrie espouses the centrist opinion that the content of one's career path matters less than her motivation for choosing it. She stresses to Doris that no one is successful without meaning and joy in their lives. For herself, helping to build the church with her beautiful singing brought Carrie real success. She urges Doris to follow her dreams but to hold on to her values at the same time. One hopes that young readers will understand that this, more than Doris' worldly success, is the true message of the book.

Occasionally the authors' turn of phrase is truly inspired, giving words a life of their own. Unfortunately, they also give considerable space to insipid entries from Doris' diary, which do little to advance the plot. Although Doris is growing up during the novel, her dated sensibility and the moderate reading level make this novel appropriate for younger young adult readers, grades six through nine. Despite a primarily female cast of characters, Doris' sense of self and expression of struggle are not strongly female, so the book should appeal equally to boys and girls. I would rate *Mama, I Want to Sing* as an even balance of strengths and weaknesses. While not an especially memorable book, it offers an entertaining and worthwhile message.

66. Hunter, Kristin. *The Soul Brothers and Sister Lou.* New York: Avon Books, 1968. 192 pages. *****

Lewis Carroll Shelf Award, 1971

Louretta Hawkins lives on Southside, the poor black section of an unnamed northern city, where teenagers hang out on the street corners because there's nowhere else to go, and cops beat up black boys because there's no one to stop them. Fourteen-year-old Louretta lives crammed into a three-bedroom apartment with her mother, seven brothers and sisters, and a niece. Since her father left them in despair, her older brother William supports the family with a post office job. But William dreams of opening his own printing shop, and at Louretta's urging, he rents a storefront to house his press. Louretta then convinces him to let her convert some of the rooms into a clubhouse for the neighborhood kids. She hopes that if she invites them in, the neighborhood boys will let her join their street corner singing group, which has always excluded girls.

As the neighborhood teenagers move in, events spiral beyond Louretta's control. Fess, a young enraged revolutionary, wants to print a weekly newspaper, a call to action. He also tries to sway the kids toward violence, although he's confused about whether the target should be a rival black gang, suspected informers within their own ranks, local businesses, or the police. Meanwhile, the music-making takes off, with the coaching of Blind Eddie Bell, an old blues singer reduced now to begging. When some of the boys decide to raise money for instruments by robbing a store, Louretta suggests a fundraising dance instead. But the dance ends in disaster, with cops storming the room, humiliating the black dancers, closing down William's print shop, and "accidentally" shooting Jethro, one of the boys.

When Jethro dies, the kids, led by Fess, plan their revenge. In despair, Lou vows to quit school and tries to deaden her dreams for a better life. She convinces herself that nothing matters and nobody cares, even after supportive teachers, black and white, get William's print shop reopened. But with the help of friends, Louretta finally finds healing in music, composing a song about Jethro. The kids come together to put out a newspaper decrying police violence. In the end, their action succeeds, although they cannot bring Jethro back. The newspaper mobilizes the community to press for the suspension and transfer of the worst cops. William's printing business grows. And an agent for Jewel Records hears Louretta and her friends sing at Jethro's funeral and signs them to a record contract. Louretta's song, "Lament for Jethro," becomes a hit single, earning The Soul Brothers and Sister Lou more money than they've ever dreamed of.

The Soul Brothers and Sister Lou is hard to put down. With sympathetic, believable characters and a fast-moving plot, it brings the reader right into Louretta's life in the city. With Lou, we watch each character react differently to the poverty and injustice of ghetto life—with unceasing hard work or hopelessness, with revolutionary fervor, indiscriminate rage, or faith in the hereafter, with self-centered egoism, high-reaching dreams, or no dreams at all. Kristin Hunter makes every response understandable as she vividly describes African American life on the poor side of the city.

Every character in *The Soul Brothers and Sister Lou* is believable. The sibling rivalry in Lou's family, the guilty favoritism her mother shows her oldest sister, and Lou's resentment at having to care for her younger siblings all ring true. Hunter fulfills the first requirement of an excellent novel—spinning an absorbing story—while packing it with powerful, heartrending lessons. Despite the overly optimistic and somewhat rushed ending, many African American readers from the inner city will find their world reflected in the experiences of Lou and her friends. Meanwhile, readers with more privileged lives will be rewarded with a glimmer of insight into Lou's world. Unfortunately, the story is as timely today as it was twenty-five years ago when Hunter wrote it.

One relatively minor weakness of the book is its portrayal of all black revolutionaries as dictatorial and violent. The fact that Fess converts to a fanatical belief in capitalism with his first taste of money also denigrates the many committed black revolutionaries of the 1960s and 1970s. I wish Hunter had included at least one admirable revolutionary to counterbalance the overwhelmingly negative portrait of Fess and his "comrades." In addition, the book's ending is unbelievable, with Lou and the boys' overnight success. However, this is remedied by the sequel, *Lou in the Limelight*, where Hunter shows the harsh realities of becoming successful entertainers.

The Soul Brothers and Sister Lou is an excellent book for urban teenagers who can read well but are disaffected with literature that does not speak to realities of their lives. Its reading level and subject matter are appropriate for grades eight through twelve. With a majority of male characters but a female protagonist, it will appeal to female and male readers. And it shows a nice array of both adult and teenage strengths and foibles—the adults' best efforts may not be quite enough, but neither are the kids forced to solve all their problems alone. *The Soul Brothers and Sister Lou* was a best seller, and it's easy to see why.

67. Hunter, Kristin. *Guests in the Promised Land*. New York: Charles Scribner's Sons, 1973. 133 pages. *****

Christopher Award, 1974; Coretta Scott King Honor Book, 1974

 Guests in the Promised Land offers seven luscious short stories, each featuring a young African American narrator or protagonist. The best stories in the collection include "Hero's Return," in which a nineteen-year-old man, just paroled, teaches his adoring younger brother what prison is really like. In "Two's Enough of a Crowd," a black teenage boy who can't dance and can't curse finds affirmation and the courage to be himself in the arms of a crippled, self-assured black girl who also doesn't fit in. "The Scribe" describes a young boy who sets up shop, offering free letter reading and writing for illiterate older folks right in front of an exploitative check-cashing shop that charges people for the same services. Lastly, the title story chronicles the resentment of a group of black city boys invited to spend one summer day at an expensive, exclusive white country club.
 Guests in the Promised Land is a prize find. Each elegantly crafted story focuses on a different aspect of African American life: fitting in, class aspirations, gang violence, Movement rhetoric, hypocrisy, demeaning social services, a dog's funeral, and authentic self-expression. Although societal racism and black-white relations set the context for many of the stories, as a whole, *Guests in the Promised Land* is a very Afrocentric collection, focusing its critique on African American culture with all its strengths and failings. Kristin Hunter takes a hard look at African American teen culture in particular, raising important questions about the sense of cultural and/or racial identity dislocation that black teens may feel if they don't share popular peer values.
 While addressing important issues, Hunter never sacrifices character or plot to make a didactic point. However, many of the negative characters are caricatured, serving simply as foils for the protagonists, with no examination of their complexities or of the events that brought them to

negative positions. Partly this may be due to the short length of each story. There is also a subtle sexism running through the collection; for instance, many of the stronger negative characters are female, and stories with female protagonists tend to center around clothes, dancing, and social acceptability. While the male-centered stories address peer acceptance, they also cover a whole range of other issues as well. Remember, though, that these stories were originally published in 1968, so a certain amount of sexism can be expected.

Despite these faults, *Guests in the Promised Land* is a collection of gems. This book will be enjoyed by seventh-through twelfth-grade readers, male and female. The stories also each stand on their own and may be read individually. Start with "Hero's Return" and try to stop your favorite reader (or yourself) from reading straight through to the last story's damning conclusion: "[I]t ain't no Promised Land at all if some people are always guests and others are always members."

68. Hunter, Kristin. *The Survivors*. New York: Charles Scribner's Sons, 1975. 308 pages. ***

American Library Association Notable Books for Children and Young Adults, 1975

Lena Ricks, a middle-aged African American seamstress, values her hard-won independence. After leaving her childless marriage to a grandiose and increasingly violent alcoholic, she supported herself with her small dressmaking shop, living in the store's basement for four years. Now a modestly successful businesswoman, she enjoys her solitude and self-reliance. Then one morning she meets BJ, a physically disabled thirteen-year-old who lives by his charm and his wits. Slowly, against Lena's better judgment, BJ works his way into her heart, making her realize how lonely she has been. Just as she begins to care about him, Lena's worst fears about BJ are proven true; after secretly living in her basement, he helps friends rob her shop. Disillusioned and angry, Lena throws BJ back out onto the street.

Lena continues to worry about BJ, though, sending her blood pressure to dangerously high levels. She goes to visit him in the unheated, dark squatters' apartment that he shares with his father. Although BJ is very sick with a high fever and a bad cough, Lena flees. But worry causes her to have a stroke shortly thereafter, and she refuses to be taken to the hospital unless the ambulance also goes after BJ. At the hospital, Lena signs his bills as his "mother."

After their release from the hospital, Lena finds BJ's help indispensable at her shop, as the stroke has permanently impaired her memory. Although BJ tries to conform more to her straight-laced sense of morality, his father's associates demand that he "earn his keep" by helping them rob a market. He is arrested at the scene and faces many years in juvenile detention unless a parent claims responsibility for him. So Lena must decide once and for all if she loves him—or anyone—enough to accept the messiness that comes with human relationships.

The Survivors is another beautifully written, vivid account of inner-city African American life by Kristin Hunter. Her characters are poignant, struggling against great odds and finding imperfect solutions. In particular, she does a wonderful job exploring the clash of values between black middle-class morality and the demands of the street. She adds to this Lena's need for independence, heightened by her disillusionment with relationships, and BJ's naked need for acceptance, accentuated by his lack of a stable family and by the physical disabilities which set him apart from other boys. Although the plot is interesting, the novel's real strength is its characters. This is a very human story about survival, caring, and compromise. It explores racism indirectly in the hollow remains of BJ's drunken father, BJ's own poverty, and the limited choices available to everyone on the black side of the city.

Treatment of BJ's disability is generally excellent—frankly acknowledging its effects without defining the boy by the disability. Although some characters inadvertently demean BJ by making him their pet and calling him elf-like (because of his shortened, twisted legs and hips), the same characters have foolish or misguided opinions about other topics as well. BJ responds believably to these characters, taking advantage of their misconceptions, like any street-smart kid struggling to survive.

The story line, themes and reading level of *The Survivors* are appropriate for those ninth- to twelfth-grade readers who read well enough to handle its 308-page length. Although BJ plays a central role, Lena's older perspective dominates the book, so some young adult readers may not be as hooked by this story as by Hunter's others. However, like all her novels, *The Survivors* is unflinching but ultimately hopeful.

69. Hunter, Kristin. *Lou in the Limelight.* New York: Charles Scribner's Sons, 1981. 296 pages. ****

Coretta Scott King Honor Book, 1982

The sequel to *The Soul Brothers and Sister Lou, Lou in the Limelight* follows sixteen-year-old Lou's singing career as it takes her to New York and Las Vegas. Lou's mother virtually banishes her as soon as she starts performing "that Devil's music," and their manager Marty is no better, ready to auction the group off to the highest bidder. Show business offers Lou, Frank, David, and Ulysses many traps: drugs, prostitution, selling-out artistically to make their music whiter, and dropping out of high school to perform full time are all peddled as the paths to success. Thoroughly confused, Lou turns to Frank for support and they become lovers. But Frank's head is turned by the many pretty girls on the road and by Las Vegas' big stakes gambling. He and David quickly run up a $27,000 casino debt, enslaving the group to continue performing at the casino indefinitely. Only the help of a United States Attorney frees Lou and the boys, in return for their testimony against the casino owners.

Freed from their nightmare in Las Vegas but blocked from advancing any further in show business, Lou and the brothers tour the South, playing churches, college halls, and local stages. Lou is initially frightened of southern racism but experiences a strange sense of homecoming in Georgia. There she lands in the hospital from exhaustion and pill-popping, only to discover an entire extended family which her mother kept secret. Slowly coming to the realization that show business is unhealthy for her, Lou decides instead to move in with an eccentric, cultured Georgia cousin who promises to send Lou to college. With her self-possessed cousin, Lou feels she will be able to develop into her own person.

Lou in the Limelight is a fast-paced, entertaining novel which tackles important issues of integrity and success. The characters' responses to these conflicts is entirely believable—few teenagers can resist the pull of easy sex, drugs, and big money. But the ultimate triumph of their characters, fueled largely by fear but partly by inner strength, offers a more worthy definition of success. It's refreshing that Lou, the only girl, leads the way, and that the young characters turn to trustworthy adults in their life when events become too overpowering for them to handle alone. The boys' characters are also well defined, avoiding gender stereotypes: steady Ulysses, motivated by the desire to earn money for his family; flirty Frank, who cares for Lou but is seduced by the fast life; and young David, who follows the crowd. Lou's struggles with her mother are equally insightful, especially once she uncovers her mother's hidden past. The adult women characters are wonderful and varied: earthy Jerutha Jackson, who rescues the children in Las Vegas; the hooker Tina, who befriends them; and cousin Julia, who shows Lou (and the reader) a strong, independent model of female self-expression.

Because of its length, *Lou in the Limelight* is most appropriate for tenth to twelfth graders. Despite a female protagonist, the boys' concerns are given almost equal time, so male and female readers can see themselves in the plot. And the novel's message is important for all readers—that integrity and self-definition are ultimately greater indicators of success than fame or fortune.

70. Jackson, Jesse. *Tessie*. New York: Harper and Row Publishers, 1968. 243 pages. **

Tessie is the story of a fourteen-year-old girl who wins a scholarship to attend the exclusive Hobbe (rhymes with snob) School, a private day school in Manhattan. Tessie's mother prophesies disaster, and her forecast proves, for the most part, to be accurate. The reader is immediately thrust into the dislocation and frustration Tessie experiences as the first black at Hobbe who then comes home to Harlem. Tessie's neighborhood friends keep her at a distance as they assume she will drop them when she starts at Hobbe. Her best friend, Floe, plans to drop out of school to help her mother make ends meet. And her classmates at Hobbe are generally hostile, treating her like a mascot at best and a mistake at worst, a token who could never be their equal intellectually or socially. Tessie vacillates between feeling ashamed of herself and being angry at her classmates and teachers at Hobbe for their racist and classist attitudes.

In the midst of all this pain, Tessie makes some important and unexpected discoveries about her world which empower her to view the people and situations in her life with greater understanding. However, she has to go through everything alone, being reluctant to open up even to those Hobbe classmates who make sincere overtures of friendship toward her. Happily, at the end of the story Tessie and Floe renew the primacy and intensity of their friendship. Tessie confides in Floe all the self-doubt, anguish, and abuse she's experienced at Hobbe, and Floe decides to go back to school. Tessie figures out how to balance her need just to be herself with the responsibility thrust upon her to represent and achieve for other black students. She realizes that, unlike the more privileged Hobbe students, her achievements are truly her own, attained with hard work and pure grit. And as Tessie feels more sure of herself and her right to be at Hobbe, she reclaims home, as well.

Author Jesse Jackson manages to make the reader worry about his protagonist's worries and feel his protagonist's feelings, quite an accomplishment. Tessie is a realistic and fully realized, vulnerable teenager. Her struggle to reconcile two worlds as she also confronts the routine developmental challenges facing every teen—bodies, boyfriends, parents, siblings, etc.—is compelling and accurate. The third person narrative provides ample pauses in the action for the author to go inside Tessie's head to reveal her ongoing questioning and answering.

In order to dramatize the intense and all-consuming nature of her worries, he focuses obsessively on a handful of the rites of passage that Tessie faces her first semester at Hobbe. It's puzzling that Tessie unquestioningly embraces all of these rites. She is so ungrounded that she doesn't see how embarrassingly stupid some of the rituals are, and then she can't understand why her Harlem friends are uninterested in them. Jackson dramatizes how the experience of attending school involves much more than the mere attending of classes. The episodes in classmates' homes and at the local soda fountain provide sketchy but provocative explorations into the extracurricular life that is integral to any school experience yet almost impenetrable for Tessie. The author also exposes how multifaceted and pervasive racism is within an institution, even when some individuals are anti-racist. For example, the only African Americans Tessie sees at Hobbe are janitors; at her classmates' homes, cooks and servants. The school play, the cornerstone of extracurricular life, contains only one black character, a maid, whose part requires her to spout colloquial expressions to humor a white audience.

In 1968, *Tessie* must have seemed a remarkable book. It is poignant that the story's essential points are still relevant today. Unfortunately, some dated expressions and dialogue, which probably added a sense of authenticity in 1968, today sound contrived and silly.

A few character descriptions in the story are troublesome. Bea Ficarra is described as being "as dark as an Arab"; Katy Brady is beautiful because she has "blue eyes and copper-colored hair"; Eve and Tessie refer to Tessie, the only black girl, as a "redskin among palefaces"; and Tessie and Floe use Columbus as an analogy for Tessie's integrating Hobbe.

On the positive side, the author does not reduce all the characters to stereotypes. Tessie has friends and enemies in Harlem and at Hobbe. The role the peer group plays in reinforcing prejudice and segregation is strongly suggested. Tessie's best friend at Hobbe, Eve Cohen, weathered her classmates' anti-Semitism. Eve lives on luxurious Long Island. However, her father, who grew up in Harlem above his father's store and who works in a Harlem hospital, doesn't distance himself from his humble roots and doesn't avoid black areas of the city as the other Hobbe families do. But, to the author's credit, Eve isn't perfect. When Tessie spends the weekend at her house, Eve makes some ignorant generalizations about Tessie's family based on her limited exposure to black people through the Cohen's servant, Sarah. Through the character of Eve, Jackson ably demonstrates how segregation and tokenism deny the truths of individuality and diversity for Tessie and her community.

The most serious problem with *Tessie* is that all of its villains are female. There are few male characters in the story, but all the male characters affect Tessie's life positively: her Pastor gets credit for summer camp; her father gets credit for permitting her to attend Hobbe; Jimmy gets credit for settling the confrontation between Tessie's Harlem and Hobbe friends at a youth center dance in Harlem; Irving Fox, a Hobbe classmate, helps Tessie rebound gracefully from a social slight off campus; and Mr. Shugg is her supportive counselor and the only politically sensitive teacher at Hobbe. Why does Tessie's mother, Ethel, have to play the part of the hardened parent? Even Tessie can't comprehend it. She assumes Ethel will support her desire to go to Hobbe, since Ethel worked as a maid to put herself through nursing school. Ethel's concern that going to Hobbe will confuse Tessie and alienate her from herself and her home is important and legitimate, yet Ethel's concerns, couched in venomous language, sound spiteful. Ethel's maternal love and racial pride produce the unexpected: instead of instilling self-esteem in her daughter, she berates her, instead of protecting her, she limits her. Ethel presents a dramatic contrast to Ed, the always-supportive, pleasant parent. The other dominant adult in Tessie's home life is Mrs. Blue, the sensible and strict librarian who challenges Tessie without cutting her down. She teaches her tough values and nourishes her staying power to help Tessie succeed at Hobbe, since that's what Tessie wants.

Tessie speaks best to girls in middle and high school. At times embarrassingly silly and dated, it nevertheless packs some important food for thought for all African American readers who are attending a predominantly white school, private or public.

71. Jackson, Jesse. *The Sickest Don't Always Die the Quickest.* New York: Doubleday and Co., Inc., 1971. 185 pages. *

In 1920, in Columbus, Ohio, twelve-year-old Stonewall Jackson delivers newspapers, picks up odd errand jobs, spews profanity, experiments with conjure recipes, dabbles in Catholicism—a slight to his Baptist and Methodist family—fights, and plots mischief with his friend, Steeplehead, both of them having been expelled from the public and private schools.

Stonewall faces pressure from his mother, Maybell, to "get saved." She reasons that, since God saved Stonewall when he almost died from a "spot on his lung," Stonewall owes God, not to mention that a sinning son tarnishes Maybell's reputation as a member of the Soul Savers at church. However, Stonewall is reluctant, doubtful of some of the religion's tenets and scared that he will drown in the river during the baptism. After he gets a "sign"—he sees his first naked woman on the delivery route—Stonewall allows himself to be tricked into the conversion. Stonewall fears that he will fail an upcoming tuberculosis test and be sent to a sanitarium, where "Blacks die like flies." That his archenemies, the Coffin brothers, sons of the undertaker, taunt him by ordering him a casket, does not alleviate his anxiety. In the end, Stonewall gets a clean bill of health.

As is customary on Sunday afternoons after church, Stonewall lunches with his Aunt Hettie Jones, another "confirmed sinner," a forty-year-old rebel, still feisty after three former "varmit" husbands have left with younger women and with her money. The title of the novel comes out of Hettie's mouth; to reassure Stonewall before his tuberculosis test, she says, in her ironic style, "The sickest don't always die the quickest." On his circuitous route home from Hettie's, Stonewall becomes ill and loses a bottle of wine that Hettie gave him to bring to his parents. Even Hettie assumes that Stonewall got drunk after his conversion and cuts him off. Fortunately, Aunt Lucy, called Aunt Lucifer by Stonewall, vindicates Stonewall by reading her Ouija board.

The bulk of *The Sickest Don't Always Die the Quickest* is devoted to detailed church services scenes in which Jesse Jackson pokes fun at the pomp and corruption of the preachers and the parishioners, their perverse hierarchizing and backstabbing, their obsession with color and class and style. For readers who relish detail, Jesse Jackson's style will delight. However, most high-school level readers, unless they can relate to the church dynamics, will lose interest in the funny but lengthy church scenes. As for Stonewall, few readers, male or female, will identify with him in his dispassionateness, nay saying, and aimlessness.

Lesser subplots revolve around the dichotomized personalities and antagonisms in Stonewall's family: Stonewall's parents, Ben and Maybell, are a study in contrasts, as are Stonewall and his brother, Moses, whom he affectionately calls Pisseyes, and Maybell and her sisters, Hettie and Lucy. Perhaps readers will enjoy Stonewall's family's problems.

There are a few expressly serious points made in the novel. The hypocrisy of men comes under the microscope: Hettie argues that women are not, as men insist, to blame for problems which inherently involve a man and woman; teenage Delilah is not the only one to blame for becoming pregnant, nor is Hettie the sole cause of her ex-husbands' philandering and pilfering.

There is also the repeated motif of the newspaper headlines about race riots and temperance crusades, introduced to establish the historical context for the story as well as to parallel the hypocritical intragroup conflicts in Stonewall's church and neighborhood: the Backsliders and the Soul Savers split the church; white leader of the city Harry Bolt flies in liquor from Canada and binges in his basement; Deacon Randolph impregnates a teenager in the church; Sweeney serves medicinal liquors in his pharmacy-bar; policeman Tyree operates a still in his backyard.

Stonewall's two religio-philosophical questions—Does his being black make him inherently sinful?, and, Does God hear the prayers of suffering people such as Hettie?—are raised without any attempt at a response.

72. Jackson, Jesse. *The Fourteenth Cadillac*. Garden City, New York: Doubleday and Co., 1972. 184 pages. **

The antihero of *The Fourteenth Cadillac*, seventeen-year-old Stonewall Jackson, is the ultimate bumbler and failure of Columbus, Ohio, in 1925. Stonewall, failing to graduate from high school, simply wants to make enough fast money so that he doesn't have to work long and hard all his life. His only ambition is to marry the pretty and proper Talitha, with whom he has a strained relationship. With his best friend, twenty-year-old Steeple, expelled from school for truancy and placed in training schools for delinquency, Stonewall engages in a series of foolish stunts.

The novel's title refers to its opening scene. When Stonewall's practical Aunt Hettie dies, her husband, Ernie, ironically, gathers fourteen Cadillacs for her funeral to create an awesome impression on the community surrounding their Seventeenth Street. Stonewall spent most of his time with Hettie, a surrogate parent who was "[n]ot like . . . his parents or other adults, always laying down the law to him about what he should do and preaching and going on like he didn't know up from down." When discussing scripture, Hettie would jokingly reply to the heavy questions, Where is wisdom? Understanding?, with, "Search me."

However, at Hettie's funeral, when Reverend Hitchcock dials God on his hotline to heaven, he gets no dial tone, i.e., no verification that Hettie's reached heaven. The community pressures Stonewall to save himself and join the church to expedite Hettie's ascendancy to heaven. At the next Sunday's service, when the congregation expects him to declare himself to the church, Stonewall backs down sheepishly.

Stonewall's parents, Maybell and Ben, arrange an intolerable apprenticeship for him with the greedy undertaker, Ed Coffin. To escape the "vengeful tribunal" that he calls his family, Stonewall joins Steeple to work as an exerciser of horses, traveling the country on the horse show circuit. With enjoyable work that pays well, Stonewall believes he is on the way to finding freedom and himself. Connected to this first step on his journey toward self-knowledge is the remembrance that working with horses is in his blood: when he was four years old, he visited his mother's family in Kentucky, learned to ride from his grandfather, and watched other black horse owners and riders competing in competitions.

Jesse Jackson presents an extremely animated cast of eccentric characters in *The Fourteenth Cadillac*, the majority of whom the reader will not be able to identify with, for they verge on parody. Stonewall himself is rather nondescript. However, readers may identify with Stonewall's confusion about his future and his contempt for work. Neither male nor female readers will identify strongly with him otherwise.

While *The Fourteenth Cadillac* is not difficult to read, it may strike middle-school readers as slow. Jesse Jackson's work will be appreciated most by high-school readers with an eye for details and asides. The reader doesn't need to catch the author's myriad allusions to historical figures and literary works in order to appreciate the story. However, s/he will then miss the metaphors and punchlines woven into the fabric of the narrative. Some of the allusions enhance the development of the story's characters and its setting: for example, references to diametrically opposed figures such as Booker T. Washington and W.E.B. DuBois add another dimension to the author's efforts to relate his characters and their foils' outlook on the gamut of issues. For example, an understanding of the nature of Ohio, particularly of its uniquely not-North/not-South identity and of its evolving urban steel-industry which factored in the Great Migration of southern blacks, adds significance to the story's setting. Some readers, not knowing the historical references, may lose interest in whole paragraphs or pages in which the author indulges his broad knowledge base.

Jesse Jackson builds an almost encyclopedic volume of information and explicit commentary about black religious and fraternal/sororal institutions into the novel. Readers who agree with the author's and the protagonist's cynical view of organized religion, especially with its emphasis on performance and profit, will enjoy the ironic treatment of Aunt Hettie's funeral, Reverend Hitchcock's sermons, the entire community's obsession with Stonewall's being born again by joining the church, and the hypocrisy of some of its preachiest members.

The characterization of Stonewall's parents through infrequent descriptions and dialogue is problematic. Stonewall has a good parent, his father, and a bad parent, his mother. Ben, an impressive foreman at the steel plant, pushed around by no one, always forgives Stonewall's foolishness. Stonewall wants to be like his father but feels inadequate. Maybell, a pitiful cook and petty laundress, bosses everyone around and constantly chastises Stonewall. When Stonewall decides to strike out on his own as a horse exerciser, Ben overrules Maybell's objections and encourages Stonewall to do it. Whereas Maybell evaluates Stonewall's behavior in terms of how it makes her look in other people's eyes, Ben thinks purely of how Stonewall sees and thinks about himself.

Through several vignettes, Jesse Jackson demonstrates the pervasiveness of racism: Uncle Ernie's feeling self-important because his white employer pays respects at the funeral for his wife; Harry Bolt's firing Uncle Ernie because Ernie follows Marcus Garvey; the churchwomen's animosity toward the minister's wife because she can pass for white but graduates as the first black from Oberlin College; the white workers at the steel plant refusing to work for or with Ben; Stonewall's struggle to even get a job interview with white bosses; Stonewall's wondering about the supposed brotherhood and unity of religion within segregated churches of the same denomination; and the contrast at the horse shows between the white horse owners and riders and the black grooms. These sketches successfully present historical and psychological realities without depressing the reader or seeming superficial or sensational.

73. Johnson, Angela. *Toning the Sweep*. New York: Orchard Books, 1993. 103 pages. ****

American Library Association Notable Books for Children and Young Adults, 1993; Coretta Scott King Honor Book, 1993; School Library Journal Best Books for Children and Young Adults, 1993

It is the summer of 1992 and Emily and her mother are spending several weeks in Little Rock, California, helping Grandmama Ola pack and say good-bye to her home in the

desert. Ola must move into their apartment in Cleveland until
she dies from cancer. In between packing, Emily and her
mother, Diane, take a final look at Ola with her eccentricities
and the desert with its strange beauty. Having visited Ola
every summer of her fourteen years, Emily reflects on her
relationship with Ola, the desert, and Ola's neighbor, sixteen-
year-old David Two Star. Emily uses a video camcorder to
record interviews and toasts, to capture images of the house,
the desert, and the community, for Ola to bring with her to
Cleveland. In the process of videotaping, Emily gains new
insight into her Grandmama and her mother, who grew up in
Little Rock. In packing Ola's belongings, Emily happens upon
old family photographs and letters that also fill in some of the
blanks of the years before Emily was born. The crux of the
mystery that Emily unwittingly unfolds is this: Ola and Diane
fled their home in Birmingham, Alabama, in 1964, after some
white people murdered Ola's husband/Diane's father for being
an "uppity nigger," which they spray painted on his beautiful
new Buick, for which he'd slaved and saved to grace his
family's otherwise spare existence. Ola drove that Buick
straight across the country and settled in the desert, which
evoked total escape and freedom and suited her wild
nonconforming personality. Diane resented Ola and the desert,
for she felt that Ola did not allow her time to grieve the loss of
her father, childhood innocence (she found his dead body), and
the place that she would always consider home—Alabama, not
California. Diane's spirit refused to settle in California.

The story culminates with the community throwing a
major picnic to celebrate and to usher off Ola the day before the
moving van is to arrive. The morning of the picnic, Emily and
Diane perform a private ritual, "toning the sweep": "[W]hen
somebody dies in an accident or suddenly, their souls just stay
here. It's better if someone knows you're dying; then people are
around to tone the sweep. [W]hen someone died, a relative
would get a hammer and hit a sweep, a kind of plow, to let
everybody know . . . [Y]ou had to do it right after to ring the
dead person's soul to heaven." In toning the sweep, Diane puts
her father's restless soul to rest and disperses the core anger and

sadness she's carried since her childhood. In toning the sweep, Emily and Diane announce to the desert Ola's departure—to Cleveland for now and to heaven forever, setting in motion the process of mourning they'd like to avoid but know is imminent, given that Ola's cancer is terminal.

Toning the Sweep is an unusual novel—which is meant both as a compliment and a warning. Angela Johnson has crafted a positive family story full of love and wonder. Johnson tells the story from the perspective and voice of Emily, making the narrative relatively straightforward and concise. The conversational style, colloquial language, and simple plot make this novel accessible to middle- and high-school readers. The emphasis in the story is on the subtle shifting and deepening of perceptions and relationships; there's not a lot of action. Furthermore, this is a strongly woman-centered story. These last two aspects—the interiority of the action and the intense focus on three generations of women in a house in the desert—make *Toning the Sweep* more engaging for girls, especially those who share a close relationship with their mother and their grandmother.

Emily takes after her Grandmama in eccentricity, and she's precocious when it comes to analyzing emotions and spiritual matters. The novel's meditative mood makes it most appropriate for a high-school audience. As it accentuates poetry more than plot, *Toning the Sweep* suits readers who like to sink their teeth into rich figurative language and reflection. This is a different kind of book—not a guaranteed great experience for all young adults but substantive and provocative for the sensitive reader.

74-82. Johnson, Stacie. The *18 Pine St.* series. New York: Bantam Books.

The *18 Pine St.* series, written by Stacie Johnson but "created" by Walter Dean Myers, currently contains nine novels, featuring the same basic cast of characters, with several new novels being added each year. The basic "crew" at 18 Pine St. includes five girls and two boys, all African American except one, all in the tenth and eleventh grade. Each book has a primary plot and several subplots with plenty of fast-paced, clever dialogue. An individual description with a brief critique is included with each novel's listing, but the following strengths and weaknesses are shared by all of the novels in the series.

As a whole, the *18 Pine St.* series quickly pulls readers into the action and into the characters' heads. Although some characters initially seem to be stock types, over the course of the series they emerge as sometimes surprising individuals. Author Stacie Johnson has a finely tuned ear for dialogue, and much of the action and the characters' growing self-awareness takes place through conversations. The main topics of interest are friends, school, clothes, sports, and dating—realistic topics for teenagers. Afrocentric elements are woven seamlessly throughout the novels. In addition, many of the novels provide excellent social analysis and political commentary that offer insight without being heavy handed or didactic. The books tackle themes that are central to African American teenagers, including sexism, social responsibility, the role of sports versus academics in future success, interracial dating, and adolescent rebellion.

On the down side, the plots are sometimes weak—predictable or too focused on the minutiae of teenagers' days. However, teens who like fiction and identify with these characters are unlikely to be bothered by the plot weaknesses. There is also a heavy, unexamined emphasis on physical appearance as a determinant of overall attractiveness and popularity. Every member of the crew is very attractive and has the means to buy fashionable clothes. The novels feature much unquestioned materialism. Although the crew lives in a multiethnic, economically diverse community, they themselves are all financially comfortable and "in the mainstream" of their community and school's happenings.

These faults, however, never overshadow the series' strengths: likable characters, readable plots, authentic Afrocentrism, realistic dialogue, and relevant themes. The series offers active, intelligent, and strong female characters, so rare in young adult books. At the same time, it offers teenage characters, female and male, who are actively involved in their lives, making choices and reaching for goals. The stories will appeal most to seventh- to tenth-grade girls, as they focus primarily on female interests, often from Sarah's perspective. However, boys who want an inside glimpse of female life and older girls who like light fiction will also enjoy *18 Pine St.* While not "great literature," these high quality novels tackle difficult issues thoughtfully and speak directly to the concerns of African American teenagers.

74. Johnson, Stacie. *18 Pine St. #1: Sort of Sisters*. New York: Bantam Books, 1992. 149 pages. ***

Sort of Sisters introduces Sarah Gordon, who will be a central character in all of the *18 Pine St.* novels, and her cousin, Tasha, both sixteen years old and in the eleventh grade. Tasha has recently come to live with Sarah's family in Madison, New Jersey, after her own parents died in a car crash. Although the girls like and respect each other, they also have typical sibling rivalries. Sarah likes to meddle in everybody's business, to take care of people and solve everyone's problems. Tasha is fiercely independent and extraordinarily multitalented—garnering the whole school's attention as a scholar, athlete, and musician, and beauty—attracting much male attention as the new girl in town.

Sort of Sisters' primary plot involves the crew's fundraising efforts for Hamilton High School, the alternative high school for dropouts and learning disabled kids, where Sarah's father is the principal. Although the crew all attend Murphy High School, the college-prep school, they recognize that Hamilton kids get short changed on resources like video equipment and decide to organize a service auction to raise money. During the course of organizing, Sarah and Tasha have conflicts over personality differences and boys. At the same time, Sarah's snobbery and her negative assumptions about kids with learning difficulties are challenged as she becomes friends with kids from Hamilton and meets adult graduates who are successes in the community despite never attending college.

A subplot describes Sarah's growing romantic interest in Dave Hunter, the boy next door. When Tasha attracts Dave's attention instead, Sarah begins dating another boy, Roy, to explore her feelings and, on some level, to make Dave jealous and to show Tasha that she can do it. But Roy is too fast for Sarah, and she pulls back—only to find that Dave wants to date her after all. Always respectful and gentle, Dave's expression of masculinity contrasts dramatically with that of the other men Sarah and her friends date throughout the *18 Pine St.* series. Sarah calls the shots in their relationship, asking him out on their first date and telling him that she wants to be just friends indefinitely while she sorts out her intense feelings.

Sort of Sisters shares most of the strengths and weaknesses of the entire *18 Pine St.* series. The plot drags at times with Sarah's realistic but annoying obsessing about boys and relationships and grooming. However, author Stacie Johnson handles the subplots skillfully, exploring issues such as inequalities in education, young people's empowerment, and non-college routes to success. Johnson lets pass unexamined the characters' opinions of Tasha as stunning, with her lighter skin and long, curly hair, while Sarah, with darker skin and more traditionally African features, is considered merely attractive. On the other hand, Sarah has a fine, supportive, black-identified family who are almost unbelievably good—a lawyer mother who warmly welcomes Tasha into the family, a reform-minded principal father whose discussions help Sarah shed old stereotypes, and a pesky, adoring eleven-year-old

The Future
and Other Stories

Ralph Cheo Thurmon
with an introduction by
Margaret Walker Alexander

Cover from *The Future and Other Stories* by Ralph Cheo Thurmon (Chicago: Third World Press, 1991). Cover illustration by Dennis Price. Cover design by Gina Minor Allen. Courtesy of Third World Press.

Cover of *Let the Circle Be Unbroken* by Mildred D. Taylor (New York: Bantam Books, 1981). Cover art by Wendell Minor. Courtesy of Bantam Books.

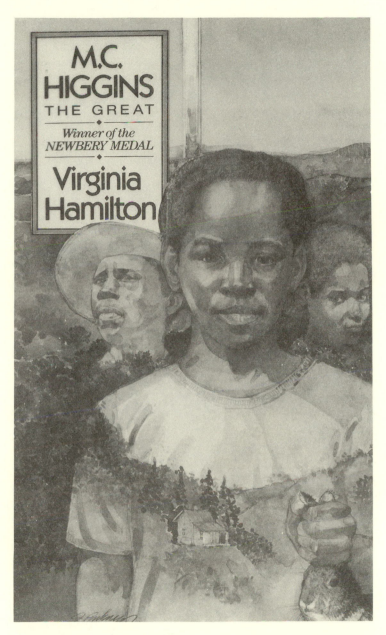

Cover from M.C. *Higgins the Great* by Virginia Hamilton (New York: Collier Books, 1974). Courtesy of Jerry Pinkney.

LIFE IS TOUGH.
LIFE IS REAL.
FRIENDSHIP
IS BEAUTIFUL.

THE AWARD-WINNING NOVEL THE
NEW YORK TIMES CALLS "A HEART-SLAMMER"

THE FRIENDS

BY ROSA GUY
AUTHOR OF RUBY AND EDITH JACKSON

Cover of *The Friends* by Rosa Guy (New York: Bantam Books, 1983).
Cover art by Max Ginsburg. Courtesy of Bantam Books.

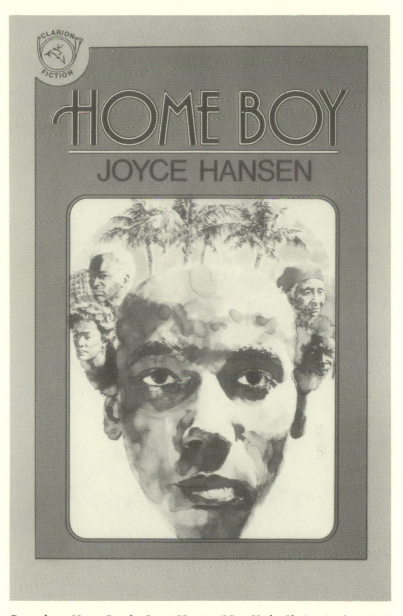

Cover from *Home Boy* by Joyce Hansen (New York: Clarion Books, 1982). Jacket illustration by Ted Lewin. Courtesy of Clarion Books.

Cover from *The Gift-Giver* by Joyce Hansen (New York: Clarion Books, 1980).
Cover illustration by Martha Perske. Courtesy of Clarion Books.

Cover from *Fallen Angels* by Walter Dean Myers (New York: Scholastic Inc., 1988). Courtesy of Scholastic Inc.

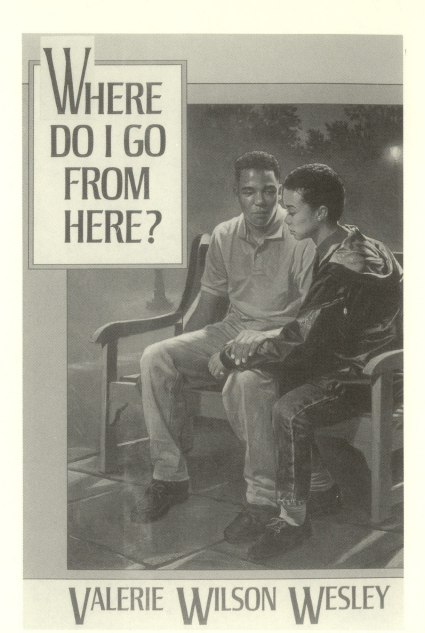

WHERE DO I GO FROM HERE?

VALERIE WILSON WESLEY

Cover from *Where Do I Go from Here?* by Valerie Wilson Wesley (New York: Scholastic Inc., 1993). Jacket painting by Derek James. Courtesy of Scholastic Inc.

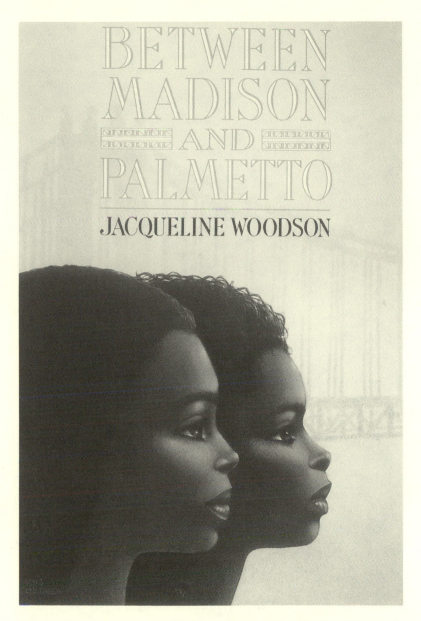

Cover of *Between Madison and Palmetto* by Jacqueline Woodson (New York: Delacorte Press, 1993). Jacket illustration by Leo and Diane Dillon. Courtesy of Delacorte Press.

sister, Allison, with whom younger readers will identify immediately.

75. Johnson, Stacie. *18 Pine St. #2: The Party*. New York: Bantam Books, 1992. 150 pages. ***

Jennifer Wilson is a sixteen-year-old "poor little rich girl" whose divorced parents try to buy her love instead of spending time with her. Her parents are distracted by their professional careers, and her father, by his new twenty-five-year-old wife, whom Jennifer disdains. Feeling all alone and trying to grow up fast to outgrow her needs and feelings, Jennifer decides to throw a party for the entire junior class of Murphy High School one weekend while her mother will be away. Although her friend Sarah tries to dissuade her, Jennifer is determined to have the party.

Much of the plot revolves around plans for the party, arguments with Sarah, and discussions about the merits of rap music, since Jennifer invites a wild rap group to perform as a drawing card. A subplot follows Sarah and Dave Hunter's on-again, off-again romance. At one point, Sarah tries dating a smooth talker and athlete, Billy, but breaks up with him after his ex-girlfriend describes how he dropped her when he started to move up in the world.

As expected, the party is a disaster. The rap group hired, Def Cru 4, sleazy drinkers and druggies, appears with an entourage of "babes." Ego contests between the rappers and some of the party-goers result in valuable furniture and the deck being destroyed; the police break up the party after neighbors' complaints. Although she warned her friend against the party, Sarah organizes the crew in cleaning up afterwards and in finding odd jobs to make money to help pay for repairs.

Despite an overly predictable plot, *The Party* examines some important themes. It looks at the experience of "latchkey" kids and at a daughter's stress over a parent's remarriage. In the course of the novel, Jennifer begins to understand that clothes and popularity are so important to her because she's feeling neglected by her parents. Sarah struggles with her own maturing moral development, starting to shift from living by the rules to defining for herself what she thinks is right and wrong. And Linda, Billy's ex-girlfriend, articulates the difference between loving somebody for who they are versus loving somebody for their education or possessions.

The rap group's sleaziness is too stereotypical, and the party's ruin too pat. In contrast, Sarah and Dave's relationship is developed nicely, exploring issues of both emotional and physical intimacy without sexual intercourse. Meanwhile, Jennifer's superficial, image-oriented femininity is quickly revealed as her attempt to fill the lonely void within her.

76. Johnson, Stacie. *18 Pine St. #3: The Prince.* New York: Bantam Books, 1992. 151 pages. ***

In *The Prince*, Cindy Phillips, Sarah Gordon's best friend, falls in love with a new student, Ibrahim Yusef Zayad, who claims to be a prince from the west African nation of Guinea Bissau. Under his influence, Cindy starts studying African history, politics, and cultures and tries to refashion herself as the authentic African woman he wants. Ibrahim insists that women in his culture—*real* black women—are supportive and respectful of men, standing behind them in every way. Cindy's friends Sarah and Tasha take issue with this sexist ideal, pointing to their own strong, independent mothers as fully realized black women. In addition, Cindy's friends take issue with Ibrahim himself, who likes to spend all his time alone with Cindy. Sarah, in particular, feels jealous that her best female friend no longer has time for her once a boyfriend is in her life. For her part, Cindy feels guilty about deserting Sarah and about sneaking around behind the backs of her strict West Indian parents in order to spend time with

Ibrahim. At the same time, Ibrahim makes Cindy feel excited and vital.

Because Ibrahim never wants to spend time with Cindy's friends, they become suspicious of him. When Kwame researches facts about Guinea Bissau which contradict Ibrahim's descriptions of his homeland, the crew decides to follow Ibrahim home one day. They follow him right to his home in Willowdale, a somewhat dangerous, rundown section of the city, where he has friends who call him Russell! When they bring Cindy to show her Ibrahim's deception, she confronts him. He apologizes, explaining that, ashamed of his background and poverty and feeling that he had no future, he transferred to a new school and created a new identity in hopes of attaining respect and pride.

The Prince's subplot centers on more personality conflicts between Sarah and Tasha Gordon and their fight over whether the big event of the year, the Junior Jump, should be pure entertainment or activism. Sarah wants a play, Tasha wants a food drive. Since most of the students agree with Sarah, they undertake an updated and hilarious version of *Romeo and Juliet*. In the end, however, they compromise by taking the production on the road to raise money for a food pantry.

The Prince explores some interesting and important themes. Sarah and Tasha's disagreement leads to discussion about the need for social activism as well as the risk of becoming overwhelmed with guilt and the demand of too many social needs. Cindy's experiences permit an excellent discussion of sexism and whether women can judge other cultures by American standards of sexual equality. Furthermore, Cindy wrestles with issues of "going back" to Africa—not just learning about her roots but trying to become what she thinks is more authentically African.

Other strengths of this novel include the mystery of Ibrahim's true identity, which adds momentum and interest to the plot. Also, it takes a realistic look at some girls' tendency to abandon female friends in favor of a boyfriend and at the hurt feelings that engenders. Similarly, the novel does an excellent job of exploring Cindy's ambivalent feelings about her relationship with Ibrahim—her excitement, guilt, willingness to be molded by his expectations, and ultimately, her re-evaluation of her self-identity. Despite Ibrahim's deception, he is drawn as a sympathetic, if ultimately sad, character.

No male characters are trashed in this novel, and male readers may enjoy the subplot about the Junior Jump play and the mystery of Ibrahim's identity. Female readers will definitely connect with the story, as female characters play lead roles and the romance is viewed from a female perspective.

77. Johnson, Stacie. *18 Pine St. #4: The Test.* New York: Bantam Books, 1992. 150 pages. ****

Despite strong opposition from her high school math teacher, Tasha Gordon competes in a countywide math contest for college scholarship money and prestige. Not only did her teacher, Mr. Cala, only tell male students about the contest, he aggressively tried to dissuade Tasha from competing, using timeworn sexist arguments about girls' inability to do math and lack of competitive drive. Tasha, the daughter of a late professional football player, knows she has plenty of drive and proves it by coming in third in the math competition. Unable to believe a girl could do so well, Mr. Cala accuses Tasha of cheating and apologizes only when Tasha's aunt and uncle threaten to sue him for slander.

At the same time, Tasha tries out for the basketball team and sprains her wrist going up against Anna, an overly aggressive white girl trying to prove her merit on a black-dominated team. However, the girls become friends, and Anna supports Tasha through her conflict over the math competition. On the boyfriend scene, Tasha dates Billy (dropped by Sarah previously) but stops when things become too passionate. Billy volunteers at a community center with troubled kids, and, through him, other members of the crew get involved there.

Finally, as the fourth anniversary of Tasha's parents' death approaches, her aunt and uncle want her to participate in a church memorial service for them. In the struggle over whether she will attend or not, her uncle's ambivalent feelings about Tasha's father emerge—although he loved his younger brother, he was also jealous of his success as a professional football player. With the support of her aunt and uncle, Tasha starts to understand that adults, too, have mixed-up feelings, and she allows herself to start experiencing emotions that she couldn't face alone after her parents' death.

The Test is the strongest book so far of the *18 Pine St.* series, largely because of Tasha's dynamic character. The story demonstrates clearly how much power teachers have to affect students' self-image and how negatively that power can be used by a sexist, racist, or simply uncaring teacher. Characters are well balanced, with both African American and white teachers portrayed positively and negatively; some hard-working, caring teachers are African American and some are white. Mr. Cala, the worst offender, is African American but so are Tasha's aunt and uncle, whose activist stance counteracts his negative influence. Anna, Tasha's other strongest supporter, is white. At the same time, the novel explores how girls come to believe they can't do math, while challenging that assumption via Tasha's success and the example of Mrs. Feder, the math department chair who ultimately forces Mr. Cala to apologize to Tasha.

Like the other books in the series, *The Test* has only a few faults. Mr. Cala's character is overblown, almost a caricature; it's hard to believe he expects to get away with such blatant sexism in this day and age. Similarly, the troubled kids at the community center are too stereotypical and change too quickly as a result of their brief relationships with the crew. Finally, the memorial scene at the church is rather corny.

On the other hand, we get to know Billy better, learning that he has depths beyond the smooth-talking surface we met in *The Party*. Tasha herself has been fleshed out into a likable, ambitious, strong, and competent young woman of whom we hope to see much more in future books.

78. Johnson, Stacie. *18 Pine St. #5: Sky Man*. New York: Bantam Books, 1993. 149 pages. ***

When Bill Hodges, nicknamed Sky Man, transfers to Murphy High School, he puts Murphy's basketball team in the spotlight. A national prospect as a basketball player, Sky Man knows he can get a full scholarship to any colleges he chooses, then go on to the NBA despite his academic weakness. At first the other students at Murphy are thrilled to have him and the attention he brings them, but gradually resentments build. Other members of the basketball team feel overshadowed; they know that hard work and teamwork win games, but everyone gives all the credit to Sky Man. Kwame, a serious student, feels offended that the community rallies around Murphy's basketball team instead of its excellent academic programs. Other members of the crew are angry that Sky Man can write his own ticket to college, while they have to struggle hard academically to make it. When they realize Sky Man can hardly read and offer to tutor him, he confidently rejects their offer. At each high school he attends teachers and principals overlook his academic failings until the basketball season ends, and then he transfers to avoid flunking out. Basketball builds his ego, assures his short-term success, and makes him popular with the girls but it also robs him of a quality education.

In a subplot, Jose Melendez's infatuation with Sarah makes her question whether she wants to date boys of other races. In talking with the women in her family, she decides it's all right, since dating is not a lifelong commitment. Jose is very romantic and passionate, but Sarah feels confused about her feelings for him and uncomfortable with his family. Following her date, Sarah's mother helps her sort out her prejudices about

Puerto Ricans from her discomfort at the unfamiliar food, language, and family dynamics that she experiences at his house.

Sky Man tackles another vitally important issue for African American youth, the role of athletics versus academics as a path for success. Accurately describing the adoration and financial rewards that accompany top athletic prowess, *Sky Man* also portrays the costs. While it is clear that Sky Man will attain one kind of success, it is equally clear that, when his basketball career ends, he will still not be able to read. In an equally sensitive manner, the novel addresses interracial dating and the interactions between different peoples of color. Without coming down strongly for or against interracial dating, *Sky Man* details the confusions and conflicts that it can raise within people and the prejudices that some African Americans hold against other people of color. The book counteracts certain stereotypes of African American culture: *African American* youth protest the adoration of athletes above more serious achievers, and Sarah's mother challenges her daughter's reactions against Jose's family life. As usual for the *18 Pine Street* series, author Stacie Johnson develops her themes through action and dialogue, never preaching.

A few minor weaknesses mar *Sky Man*. Jose's character is somewhat stereotypical as the passionate and flamboyant Latin, although this is balanced by the very positive portrayal of his sweetness toward Sarah. The novel never deals with how Jose feels about Sarah's decision, in the end, not to date him anymore. Similarly, it never explores Dave's feelings when Sarah dates other boys without telling him, although he ultimately finds out. While this may be because *Sky Man*, like the other novels, is written strongly from Sarah's perspective (though not in her voice), it sometimes makes it seem that the boys don't have feelings.

Because of the issues it addresses, *Sky Man* will be more relevant to male readers than some of the previous books in the series, though female readers will enjoy it as much. This is another fine novel from Stacie Johnson.

79. Johnson, Stacie. *18 Pine St. #6: Fashion by Tasha.* New York: Bantam Books, 1993. 150 pages. ***

Tasha Gordon hopes to become a professional fashion designer, so she's thrilled when her aunt asks her to design clothes for a fundraising fashion show for Mother Belva's Home for Young Women, a home for teen mothers. Impressed with her talent, a visiting Dutch businessman who sees the show invites Tasha to submit designs to his international clothing company. He promises her $1,500 for each design accepted and asks her to submit a dozen designs in three weeks. With visions of instant fame and riches, Tasha throws herself into the designs but the pressure drives her crazy. She neglects her schoolwork, is irritable with her family, and lets her basketball team down by taking a leave of absence just when they face some of their toughest competitors. Along the way, her family and teachers try to convince her that she needs to finish high school and go to college to achieve long term success, not be seduced by this "big break." Tasha finally sees their point when only one of her designs is accepted. In counterpoint, Dave Hunter receives a full athletic scholarship from Polytechnic University, dependent only on his continuing his hard work to complete his studies.

A subplot involves Orchid Smith, a beautiful, fashionable, and sexy teenager who comes to live with Dave's family for a short time. All the boys fall for her, including Tasha and Sarah's boyfriends Billy and Dave. Orchid, a confused young woman, uses boys for their attention. She taunts Sarah, suggesting that she and Dave are romantically involved, although Dave denies it. Sarah and Tasha are angry and appalled that even the best boys they know will fall for a pretty body.

A second subplot follows April Winter, the crew's only white member, as she runs away from home several times. Her father and stepmother are fighting all the time as they expect their first baby. April is worried that her irresponsible father, who divorced her mother shortly after April was born, will divorce his new wife after the new baby comes. She's equally worried that the new baby will supplant her. The crew supports her and reassures her that when parents fight, it's not the kids' fault and it doesn't always lead to divorce. Finally, she has a long and reassuring talk with her father and starts to build a closer relationship with her stepmother.

Fashion by Tasha's plot stresses the value of education for its own sake, as well as for long-term professional/financial success, and cautions against seeking short cuts. Although this is an important message for African American teens to hear, this novel's tone is elitist at points, making the assumption that everyone should go to college and that college is the only legitimate path to success. Similarly, in disparaging the GED, the high school equivalency exam, *Fashion by Tasha* potentially alienates a particular audience who might otherwise find that the story speaks to them. The Dutch businessman's offer to Tasha is unrealistic, though it's very realistic that what promises to be a fantastic opportunity, a short cut to success, does not pan out. Tasha's character, as usual, is dynamic and attractive. The adults around her offer concerned advice, while her friends try to support her and build her confidence. In return, despite her disappointment, she spends some of the money she earns on thanking them, donates a large portion of it to Mother Belva's Home, and saves the rest for college.

The subplot about April's family sensitively explores the problems of divorce and changing families but would have been stronger if the author recreated the discussions between April and her parents instead of just having her report on them to the crew.

Female readers who have ever been passed over in favor of sexier girls will relish the book's totally female perspective on boys as dogs who will chase after any pretty body. The story offers a discouragingly realistic look at the difference between what most boys and most girls are looking for in a relationship, although Dave ultimately redeems himself. On the other hand, it slips into dichotomizing girls between the pretty, smart, good girls and the stupid, sexy, bad girls. Nevertheless, the male-female interactions in *Fashion by Tasha* will reflect the experiences of many female readers and will appeal much more to them than to male readers.

80. Johnson, Stacie. *18 Pine St. #7: Intensive Care.* New York: Bantam Books, 1993. 151 pages. ****

Jennifer Wilson gets her learner's permit the same day her mother unexpectedly leaves on a business trip, giving up the little time they have together. Against her own better judgment, Jennifer borrows her mother's new Saab to go to the mall with Sarah Gordon. But along the way, freezing rain begins, and a truck smashes into the Saab, forcing it off the road. While Jennifer wakes up with just a whiplash, scrapes, and bruises, Sarah slips into a coma. Because there's no evidence of another vehicle at the scene, the police, the insurance company, and most of the crew don't believe Jennifer's story about the truck and think instead that she simply drove off the road in bad weather. Wracked with guilt, having nightmares about Sarah lying in her hospital bed looking dead, and fearful of the crew's rejection, Jennifer turns to her mother. Mrs. Wilson comes through for her daughter, punishing her for taking the car but helping her through the crisis.

Each member of the crew reacts differently. Tasha, who lost her own parents in a car crash several years ago, is furious, blaming Jennifer for the tragedy. Sarah's boyfriend Dave feels guilty that he cannot face visiting Sarah in the hospital, although finally he sneaks in one night to whisper loving messages in her ear (which her roommate reports to Sarah after she wakes up!). Kwame, the first crew member to believe Jennifer's story, helps her track down the dented truck and then convinces the police of her innocence. *Intensive Care* ends with Sarah waking up at the last possible moment. In the meantime, Jennifer and her mother grow close, and Jennifer starts to accept her mother's new boyfriend without worrying that he will supplant her.

In the subplot, April and transfer student Steve have broken up for unknown reasons. Misunderstanding something April says, Cindy concludes that Steve tried to date rape her and tells her friends. Soon the rumor is all over school and Steve starts receiving hate mail. Only it turns out that they broke up because *April* was too aggressively, publicly romantic with Steve.

Intensive Care is one of the best books of the *18 Pine St.* series, accomplishing an enormous amount in very little space. Because annoying Sarah is in a coma for most of the book, we finally get to see events from other characters' perspectives. It becomes clear that Jennifer acts more grown up than she is in order to avoid emotional dependence on her parents, whom she feels are not there for her; the depth of her pain over their divorce becomes more apparent. On the other hand, *Intensive Care* offers the first view of Jennifer's mother as a fully realized character, self-respecting and caring within the constraints of trying to support herself and her daughter alone.

Although the plot's happy ending is predictable, author Stacie Johnson does make readers wait until the very last moment before delivering Sarah's recovery. The description of Jennifer waking up after the accident, her terror in wondering if Sarah died, is so vivid that it pulls the reader right in. Furthermore, the experience of teenage car accidents is all too realistic, including the emotional scars that everybody involved bears afterward. The other characters' reactions to the accident are equally believable and moving.

Because it focuses less on relationship drama than previous books in the series and because Jennifer's experience with the accident could apply equally to girls and boys, male readers may like *Intensive Care* as much as female readers. With quirky, likable characters and a fast moving plot, *Intensive Care* is a very strong book, highly recommended.

81. Johnson, Stacie. *18 Pine St. #8: Dangerous Games*. New York: Bantam Books, 1993. 146 pages. ***

When the boys at Murphy High School decide to play KAOS—Killing as Organized Sport, an assassination game with water guns—real chaos breaks out. Fights start at school, and the boys neglect their girlfriends. The girls in the crew are appalled by the simulated violence; as Tasha argues, the last thing they need is black men killing each other, in sport or reality. The girls decide to boycott the boys until they end their game. Then, spurred on by Debby Barnes, a snotty, trouble making cheerleader, the girls initiate a game of their own, Kissing KAOS, where each girl is assigned other girls' boyfriends to kiss. A host of misunderstandings and jealousies ensue, particularly since the boys are unaware that the girls are playing a game. Finally, the boys are put on probation, ending their game, while Sarah and Tasha end the girls' game by humiliating Debby in front of the entire school.

In a subplot, Kwame wants to apply to Yale University's summer internship in African American history. His African American guidance counselor, Mrs. Brewer, tries to convince him to apply instead for the math or science internships, arguing that Yale uses the African American Studies program to ghettoize and use African American students instead of integrating all their programs. When Kwame protests that he loves African American history, she challenges him to explore programs at historically black colleges instead. Finally, he does apply to Yale's internship program and is wait-listed. Then Mrs. Brewer tells him to do something extra to show Yale who he is and how much the program means to him. He follows her advice and is admitted when another student drops out.

Dangerous Games is a novel of trashy intrigue, which nevertheless addresses several important themes. It offers excellent insight into the pervasiveness of violence in our culture, embedded as it is in our language, games, and other forms of entertainment. The story also thoroughly explores the issue of colleges ghettoizing African American students and students' options in responding to this reality. The guidance counselor presents a sophisticated argument for her point of view but ultimately helps Kwame achieve his own goals. Despite Kwame's academic strengths, reaching his goals is realistically presented as a struggle without a fairy-tale ending. Finally, the importance of academics is stressed through Kwame's personality, a healthy teenage boy with a passion for learning about his people's history.

Male readers may connect with Kwame's character and with the boys' game of KAOS, but *Dangerous Games* remains a primarily female book. Like the other novels of the *18 Pine St.* series, it is written from a female perspective and offers girls' insights into adolescent dilemmas.

82. Johnson, Stacie. *18 Pine St. #9: Cindy's Baby*. New York: Bantam Books, 1993. 151 pages. ****

Cindy Phillips' parents are leaving her home alone for the first time in her life, as they return to Jamaica to visit a sick grandfather. Before Cindy can plan her "vacation," though, an old classmate of hers calls, begging her to baby-sit for her son Andy for one night. Sixteen-year-old Vietnamese-American Karin Tran dropped out of Murphy High School to have a baby last year. Now she lives in a dangerous and dilapidated apartment, trying to raise her baby all alone. Her parents, angry over her pregnancy and over the fact that the baby is half-white, offer no support. Karin won't tell anyone who the baby's father is. Isolated as she is, Karin finds it very hard to be a good mother, and she describes to Cindy how having a baby has completely changed her life, making her despair that her future will ever hold any promise. Feeling sorry for her, Cindy agrees to baby-sit.

However, Karin does not return for her baby! She calls to say that she is overwhelmed and needs more time away and makes Cindy promise to take care of Andy. When the crew arrives to help Cindy baby-sit, at first they are charmed by

Andy but soon become frustrated by his constant demands. The boys try to entertain him with "boy" games, while the girls expect him to watch television patiently—neither group being at all realistic about a baby's needs. Then the girls experience racist reactions when they take baby Andy out in public, with a teacher accusing them of becoming teenage mothers to sponge off of welfare.

The crew decides to unravel the mystery of who the baby's father is, to force him to take the baby. They learn that he's a white football player, Frank Boccio, who brags about being a stud but publicly denies fathering Andy. The boys and girls of the crew have an excellent discussion about a father's role in raising a child, about who is responsible for birth control in a relationship, and who is responsible if the girl decides to bear a child instead of getting an abortion. The boys sympathize with Frank, arguing that he should not have to give up his college scholarship to help raise Andy. The girls question why Karin should be the only one to give up her future. In the end, though, they learn that Frank works full time after school to help support the baby financially and that Karin took responsibility for her own decision to bear the child because she wanted someone of her own to love.

After more than twenty-four hours of caring for Andy with the crew, Sarah Gordon confides to her father that Karin has left. He, in turn, alerts Social Services, who take the baby into protective custody. But not before Cindy's parents return home unexpectedly to find the house a disaster and Cindy skipping school to care for Andy. They are furious at her, as is Karin, when she returns a few days later. Cindy feels guilty but also relieved not to have responsibility for the baby anymore. Ultimately Karin's life improves as well when Social Services forces her parents to care for her until she turns eighteen; Karin moves back in with them and they slowly grow to love Andy.

A small subplot involves Jennifer tossing over one boy for a more desirable date to the school dance, even after she gave her word. At the same time Cindy and a boy she never noticed before start to look past appearances to see the person underneath. Meanwhile, some African American members of the crew briefly become angry at all whites after seeing a movie about slavery.

Cindy's Baby takes an eye-opening look at the difficulties of being a teen mother. It offers a realistic and sympathetic portrait of how frayed Karin is, how she's a child struggling alone to support and raise her child. The story's elaborate detail about the minute-by-minute demands of a baby leave the reader feeling as tired and depressed as Cindy feels every time Andy cries. The story shows how easy it is for a parent to lose patience when Cindy starts to shake Andy in frustration after less than a day of caring for him.

Cindy's Baby manages to explore teen motherhood without making any of the crew bear a child, which would be less realistic, given their middle-class milieu. (Pregnancy may be equally prevalent, but abortion is a more likely choice as women move up the socioeconomic scale.) In introducing another character to bear a child, however, why did author Stacie Johnson choose an Asian American when the series has no other major Asian characters? Certainly it would have been valid to introduce another African American character, given that the prevalence of teenage pregnancy is much higher among African American girls than among Asian American girls. Still, the novel subtly raises issues of race and gender as they affect teen parents. It honestly explores the no-win choices available to both mothers and fathers, without caricaturing either Karin or Frank.

Cindy's Baby is an excellent novel, full of surprises, which packs a lot into its 150-odd pages. With its sympathetic portrayals of male and female characters, it will appeal to readers of both sexes and should especially be read by any teenager who thinks it might be fun to have a baby in the near future.

83. Jordan, June. *His Own Where*. New York: Thomas Y. Crowell Company, 1971. 90 pages. **

School Library Journal Best Books for Children and Young Adults, 1971

His Own Where tells the story of Buddy Rivers, a sixteen-year-old Brooklyn boy, totally alone—until he falls in love with fourteen-year-old Angela Figueroa. Buddy grows to know Angela during his daily visits to the hospital to watch over his dying father (his mother abandoned the family years before); Angela's mother is the attending nurse for the patient who shares Mr. Rivers' room, and Angela visits her mother every day after school. Buddy becomes protective of Angela as he witnesses her distressing family situation: her parents imagine her sleazing around on the street, despite the fact that they require her to perform all of the domestic chores and care for her four younger siblings every day, and they insult and beat her occasionally. When Mr. Figueroa beats Angela so badly that she must go to the hospital, Buddy pledges to help and love her. The Court sends Angela to a Catholic shelter, and Buddy breaks her out of it and takes her to "his own where," a retreat from the harsh world where they can be together and make love constantly—ironically, in a cemetery. The book ends with Angela and Buddy hoping for a baby and imagining a better life for themselves together.

This novel is essentially poetry in fragmented verse form, a narrative technique which makes for different but at times difficult reading. Only sophisticated readers will appreciate its nuances. And younger readers will be frustrated with the dreaminess and incompleteness of the plot—*His Own Where* focuses on feelings much more than on action. The feelings it emanates are love and fear—from struggling against hatred and injustice in the family and in society. Angela's and Buddy's relationship is very sweet and the lovemaking scenes are juicy without being graphic. This novel touches on many important issues: child abuse; sex education; classism and racism; and religious hypocrisy. Unfortunately, Jordan doesn't develop her points adequately. For example, she doesn't provide enough insight into the Figueroas to explain the hatred and violence they direct toward their children. Also, the couple's excitement about Angela's possibly being pregnant seems unrealistic (escapist) and scary, given that they haven't resolved any of their familial problems, they have no source of income, and they're supposed to finish high school. Any high-school student could read this book, but few would "get into" it or "get it."

84. Kai, Nubia. *The Sweetest Berry on the Bush*. Chicago: Third World Press, 1993. 121 pages.*****

The Sweetest Berry on the Bush contains nineteen stories set in Africa, the Caribbean, and the United States, and suffused with the basic tenets of Islam.

Ten-year-old Regina Williams of "Harlem Stone" grudgingly leaves her Harlem neighborhood for a private, predominantly white, parochial school on the Lower East Side because her parents consider her Harlem school "too rundown and rowdy." When she complains to her parents about the white nuns and students treating her meanly and hatefully, her parents tell her to persevere and prove her worth through academic achievement. One day, Regina finds a black stone on her steps, a "Harlem Stone." When Regina looks at herself in the stone in Harlem, her features are "full of joy and life," but when she looks in the stone at school, it "would not shine or mirror her face." Her neighbor Mrs. Alderberry explains that the stone comes from Africa and "is a mirror to [her] true beauty," shining when she's among her people at home in Harlem, connected to their roots, seeing her for who she is and loving her as they love themselves.

Teenager Bucky of "Cop the Robber," who lives in an unspecified American city, refuses to help his friends rob an elderly lame man at a liquor store, and warns them that "the old man keeps a gun under his coat." He watches the man gun down his friends when they try to rob him.

"A Lie That Cost Five Lives" is another story about senseless violence. Sixteen-year-old Damon kills five friends of a boy named Craig after Craig comes out of a Coney Island diner and jokes that the five boys were laughing at him and planning to beat him up.

Identical twins Michelle and Rochelle, of "Misery Loves Company," receive identical, precious necklaces from Egypt from their Aunt Ilene. Vain Rochelle disobeys her mother's rule about wearing the necklace to school and, predictably, loses it. Rochelle then jealously flushes Michelle's necklace down the toilet. Guilt and regret cause her to gain weight inexplicably, and "[t]he sassy, confident young girl they had known before was now self-conscious, insecure and withdrawn." When a classmate finds Rochelle's necklace, Rochelle says her neck is too fat and asks Michelle to take the necklace, while confessing that she was responsible for the disappearance of Michelle's necklace. Michelle accepts the necklace and forgives Rochelle. Unburdened and forgiven, Rochelle miraculously sheds her excess weight and returns to "normal."

In "The Misfit Who Became a Hero," ten-year-old, special education student Eric Waters learns in spite of the dumbing-down schooling his teachers try to impose on him. He becomes a hero when he evacuates the school moments before it is destroyed by a gas leak explosion, which he detects during his punishment time in the hall. The media, clergy, and educational and medical experts then offer a host of explanations to account for the discrepancy between his previous misfit status and his new hero status, while his classmates honor him.

There are animal tales. "The Snake and the Bull," featuring "Bruhs" Bull and Snake in the vicinity of the Garden of Eden, teaches: "[B]e glad of what yah is and don't try and be what yah ain't." "Why the Spider Brings Money," set in Ethiopia, explains how the superstition of not killing spiders originated. The moral of "Beware of Dog" is that cats and dogs, i.e., women and those men who are "dogs," shouldn't mate because they're natural enemies; it's a dog's nature "to use a cat's body, then cast her off or kill her." "Tale of the Curious Crows," set on a farm somewhere in America, holds individuals and American society responsible for drug abuse. In "CARICOM Meets Anansi," Anansi the spider trickster comes to a conference in Cuba to advise the CARICOM collective on how to truly liberate the Caribbean nations from racial and economic oppression, and challenges them to unite, be willing to sacrifice and take risks—perhaps to die—for their liberation. Fish in the Detroit River swim to the Gulf of Mexico to escape pollution in the unusual environmentalist and Muslim-inspired dietary code promotional "You Are What You Eat." They learn survival strategy from an imprisoned fish named Joe, who advises the fish to keep a strict organic, vegetarian diet of food untouched by pollution; the fish survive, and the humans kill themselves with their own pollution. Brer Rabbit comes back from the grave to Chicago in "Brer Rabbit Comes to Town" and finds out that he's not clever enough to contend with today's hustlers; hard experiences convince him to apply his cleverness to solving the interconnected problems of economic oppression and black-on-black violence.

There are mythic tales. The lesson of the bitterly ironic "The Story of Jabbar," which centers around adolescent Jabbar and his mother Sala in Guyana, is: "[Y]ou should never, ever, steal." In "Let There Be Peace on Earth," the sons of King Sefuwa in Chad dramatize the power of forgiveness, generosity, and peace in a political leader. Eleven-year-old Kima Canek of Mexico makes the most of her hard life of abuse and suffering in "The Fantasy Bird," and never loses her compassion for all humanity and her commitment to her principles.

Tales of young adults in Africa and the Caribbean round out this collection. Sixteen-year-old Jamaican Dalton Andrews of "Dem Dread in de Head or Dem Dead" misuses the Rastafarian lifestyle to seduce girls and to condescendingly preach to his non-Rastafarian peers; he learns to take the religion to heart after he loses his superficial observance of it, his popular dreadlocks. "Adimissa Will Live" affirms its Ghanaian adolescent protagonist's freedom and "right to marry who and when she chooses." In a similar feminist bent, "Seek Knowledge From the Cradle to the Grave" relates, in fairy tale style, the true story of how Sia Kalabi of Mali defies her father's authority. Following the higher authority of Allah's teaching that men and women "should pursue knowledge," a sheik pays for Sia Kalabi to be the first woman from Mali to come to America to earn a Ph.D. in engineering. The final story, "Longo," developed around the KiKongo marriage ritual, praises "the basic African philosophy governing marriage and family ties," wherein the union of man and woman is imperative and essential for life, and marriage unites families and creates an indestructible community through kinship.

Nubia Kai is a master storyteller and every piece in her collection is rich and wonderful reading for young adults and adults. The lessons and sociopolitical analyses of the stories will be apparent to readers of all ages, and sophisticated readers will find, upon each rereading, new layers of meaning and nuances of narration. The stories in *The Sweetest Berry on the Bush* will engage the most reluctant reader and will spark lively discussion.

"The Harlem Stone" examines incisively the myths of meritocracy and education as the great leveler. The Harlem Stone's magic functions as a metaphor for Regina's being grounded, literally and figuratively, in her community and their heritage.

"A Lie That Cost Five Lives," like "Cop the Robber," keeps action at a premium and message at a minimum. But its ending with the shocking murder of Craig's five friends can distract the reader from the story's message about the vanity of pride and the violence of insults and threats.

"Misery Loves Company" celebrates true sisterhood and attacks sibling rivalry as self-destructive. This story dramatizes the impact of materialism and the desperate want and competition that it fosters. Its one problem is that, instead of indicting Rochelle strictly for her behavior, the author implicitly condemns her also for being overweight. Society, with its obsession with appearance and tyranny of slenderness, needs to be chastised, not an overweight girl.

"The Misfit Who Became a Hero" adroitly critiques traditional educators' esteem for homogeneity and control in general and the notion and practice of special education in particular: "They said he was a misfit. [I]n the dictionary it meant 'something that does not fit.' He didn't see himself as something that didn't fit. Didn't fit what? He fit himself fine. What else was he supposed to fit?" To his peers, accustomed to the arbitrariness of teachers' assessments and open to the possibility of change and growth, Eric's heroism is no mystery, "'cause the dumbest kid often turned out to be the smartest. And the child that was cursed yesterday is honored today. Life is funny like that."

The following stories deserve special mention. "Tale of the Curious Crows" is an astute and searing analysis of the individual and societal dimensions to drug abuse, its causes and effects, and its consequences for the black community. "CARICOM Meets Anansi" is a funny yet penetrating psychological examination of the role that Africans in the diaspora play in perpetuating their oppression and of the importance of self-help and unity for liberation. Anansi, in her expertly-rendered patois, tells a story within the story to illustrate the interrelated, deep-rooted effects of racism, nationalism, and colonialism. "Brer Rabbit Comes to Town" manages to entertain and eye-open with speed and style. Brer Rabbit learns firsthand that times have changed and people have lost perspective and, with it, purpose. "Never before had rabbits stole from one another or cheated and tricked each other. [T]hey wasn't trickin master no more . . . onliest each other. They wasn't trickin to find a way to freedom; they was trickin for the crumbs from master's table." Nubia Kai takes the animal tale to another level with Brer Rabbit's reflecting on himself as a literary-historical figure with a powerful political message about black liberation then and now.

Easy to overlook, given the fairy tale context of most of the stories, is the conventional focus on the female characters' appearance. It is noteworthy that the author rarely mentions the physical traits of her male protagonists, while she always includes the physical aspects of her female protagonists and, in several significant instances, builds a key element of the plot and point around their physicality. Additionally, while the author develops strong and independent female characters, she includes in the majority of the stories only one model for adult women in the personal realm, that marriage is a given and ultimate good.

But every story in this collection is strong. Nubia Kai's writing talent, her Afrocentrism, and the tasty variety of themes, genres, narrative structures and techniques, languages, and settings make this an outstanding book.

85. Lester, Julius. *To Be a Slave.* New York: Scholastic, Inc., 1968. 160 pages. ****

John Newbery Honor Book, 1969; New York Times Best Books for Children and Young Adults, 1968; School Library Journal Best Books for Children and Young Adults, 1968

Although *To Be a Slave* is nonfiction, short stories are at the heart of the book; these "stories" are oral histories from interviews with former slaves and narratives in which Lester recreates settings, moods, and situations. This book is an outstanding complement to Lester's fiction, *This Strange New Feeling* and *Long Journey Home*.

Using abolitionists' arguments against slavery, recordings of narratives and memoirs by slaves who escaped to the North before and during the Civil War, and Depression era interviews with ex-slaves, *To Be a Slave* is a powerful book. It mixes primary sources and Lester's analysis of the meanings embedded in those sources, and fuses history, politics, psychology, and sociology into a seamless whole. *To Be a Slave* teaches how history is recorded at the same time that it makes the reader understand what slavery was and what it did to European Americans as well as African Americans.

Lester begins with the Portuguese slave traders in Africa in the sixteenth century and ends with the Ku Klux Klan in the southern United States at the turn of the twentieth century. Between the prologue and epilogue he arranges the material thematically into seven chapters: "To Be a Slave," "The Auction Block," "The Plantation," "Resistance to Slavery I and II," "Emancipation," and "After Emancipation." Besides telling "the story," he stresses how enslaved African Americans retained and transformed their cultures in the diaspora despite their oppressors' efforts at assimilation and annihilation. And he examines the inter-workings of economic, racial, and sexual exploitation and of nationalism and colonization.

Its descriptions uncensored and graphic, its language straightforward and poetically full, its selection of primary sources strategically arranged, *To Be a Slave* is a book that can make slavery brutally present for its readers. It is concise and complex, making it accessible to high-school age readers while giving them a depth of analytical as well as emotional understanding that thick, scholarly tomes seldom manage to do. Lester has a gift for presenting sophisticated and sometimes contradictory ideas in a clear way.

86. Lester, Julius. *Black Folktales*. New York: Grove Press, Inc., 1970. 159 pages. ***

Julius Lester provides an excellent introduction to his collection of stories: "The stories in this book are told in the cities and villages of Africa and on the street corners, stoops, porches and wherever else in America black people gather. The stories in this book come from the black people of Africa and Afro-America. Most of them have been written down before, in different words and for different times." The earlier versions for the African American stories come from Arna Bontemps,

Langston Hughes, and Zora Neale Hurston; some were "told in the South for so long that nobody knows where they came from."

The stories in the "Origins" section are about exactly what their titles indicate: "How God Made the Butterflies," "Why Apes Look Like People," "Why Men Have to Work," and "How the Snake Got His Rattles." They also illustrate the greed, waste, and selfishness of humankind, particularly of colonizing whites. In the "Love" section, "The Girl with the Large Eyes" explains how water lilies were created, while "The Son of Kim-ana-u-eze and the Daughter of the Sun and Moon" demonstrates how resourcefulness, rather than brute strength, proves necessary for a mortal to beat the gods and get his girl. Continuing the theme of the underdog triumphing, "Jack and the Devil's Daughter" relates how Jack outsmarts the Devil, who is "simply looking for an excuse to kill" him.

"High John the Conqueror" and "Stagolee" comprise the "Heroes" section. Set in Mississippi, the first story describes how High John out-tricks his master, by appealing to his greed and smug sense of superiority, into killing his mule and killing himself. "Stagolee," set in Georgia, describes how Stack brazenly kills the first white sheriff who hates his "walking around like he was free" and how he defies the second white sheriff who, with the Ku Klux Klan Alumni Association, attempts to hang him. Stack, with his fearless resistance and guns, proves a match for Death, but God finally sends a thunderbolt when Stack's time runs out. With pleasure, Stack rules hell (thinking the predominantly white heaven the true hell).

The final section is entitled "People." After his wife dies, the old man of "The Old Man Who Wouldn't Take Advice," set in Louisiana, marries a young woman who welcomes his money but refuses to tolerate his impotence on their wedding night. He acquires a concoction from a root doctor but neglects to follow her directions and becomes blind. A hawk offers to restore his "powers" if he surrenders the pigeon it's been chasing, and the pigeon offers to restore his sight if he protects it from the hawk. He ignores the advice of his best friend and his wife, tricks both creatures, and regains his "powers" and his sight. The lesson: make up your own mind.

"The People Who Could Fly," set in South Carolina, describes how slaves risked everything—including their lives—to escape slavery; on a particular plantation, a witch doctor helps all of the slaves to fly back to Africa when their mistreatment becomes unbearable. What was the word that the witch doctor uttered that enabled the slaves to escape their past and present misery? What word can an African American utter to heal the pain of her or his history in racist America?

In the final story, "Keep on Stepping," Tennessee house slave Dave saves his master's children and produces a year's extraordinary harvest on the promise of freedom. When he frees Dave, the master lets Dave's body go free, but keeps yelling, "Remember, you still a nigger," while Dave walks on to Canada. The lesson: "You ain't free long as you let somebody else tell you who you are. We got black people today walking around in slavery 'cause they let white folks tell 'em who they are. . . . Just keep on stepping when you know you're right. Don't matter what they yell after you. Just keep on stepping."

In *Black Folktales*, Julius Lester explicitly states his political viewpoints, but there is a literary quality to the statements that makes the reader delight in their expression as much as in the artfully rendered metaphors and dialogue. These stories are meditations on power—its uses and abuses, the struggle for it and sharing of it, the triumph of the underdog—and the nature of evil. Ultimately, the collection affirms the necessity for self-definition and self-determination.

Except for the three stories in the "Love" section, all of the stories contain numerous indictments of racism. The "Heroes" and "People" sections offer a sustained exploration of racism in America. "High John the Conqueror," set in slavery, and "Stagolee," set immediately after slavery, penetrate the warped psychology of the slave master and the slave's strategies of resistance that capitalize on the slave master's assumptions of superiority and control.

Some of the allusions to the history of the 1960s may be lost on young adult readers. For example, the panther in "Why

Apes Look Like People" uses the jargon of the Black Panthers. "How the Snake Got His Rattles," an exploration of the semantic and philosophical differences between self-defense and terrorism, is also a barely veiled discussion on the Black Panthers. In "High John the Conqueror," the narrator's comments about house slaves and field slaves, and about black intragroup dissent, betrayal, and violence, come straight out of Malcolm X's mouth. Stack of "Stagolee" is the archetypal black fantasy and white fear of an armed Black Power militant advocate; also within the story are jibes against the president and Vietnam.

As Julius Lester states in his introduction, the point of these stories should be pretty obvious: "These stories are told here not as they were told a hundred years ago, but as I tell them now only because they have meaning now." Lester's narrative technique, with its contemporary elements, colloquial dialogues, and political insertions, is as important as the plot. God is a cigar-smoking, coffee-guzzling, grouchy, and indignant old man who rocks on his porch. The anthropomorphized animals nearly burn out in their attempt at consensus decision-making in their organizational meetings. God, the animals, and the human characters in these stories are explicitly black; if the reader missed the many cues, the illustrations accompanying the stories complements them. The assumed audience is also black, and this sense of insiderness will be a powerful draw for young adult readers.

The glaring weakness to this collection is its depiction of women. All of the significant characters, whether God or Devil, human or animal, are male. The secondary female characters, like Mrs. God and Mrs. Snake, are homemakers who henpeck their husbands or, like Lady Moon and the Devil's daughter, are adoring helpmates. The only story featuring a female protagonist, "The Girl with the Large Eyes," defines female characters through marriage, the other typical depiction of women in this collection. White women, predictably, fare even worse: helpless and whining, deserving of violence.

Julius Lester is a brilliant storyteller. He spins magical stories that seamlessly inject relevant and provocative political statements into pure entertainment. Middle-school and high-school readers will laugh at and mull over the mixture of comedy and tragedy. *Black Folktales* lends itself to multiple interpretations, which makes it accessible to a wide readership.

87. Lester, Julius. *Long Journey Home*. New York: Scholastic, Inc., 1972. 147 pages. ***

Lewis Carroll Shelf Award, 1972; School Library Journal Best Books for Children and Young Adults, 1972

Long Journey Home contains six stories about slavery and emancipation, all based on historical fact. "Satan on My Track" follows Rambler, a blues guitarist who travels from plantation to plantation playing for black sharecroppers. Although slavery is officially over, whites still control blacks through permanent debt peonage, and Rambler vows never to stay in one place long enough to come under whites' power. "Louis" is the story of a Virginia slave who runs away to Ohio to avoid being sold. However, after living safely in Ohio for a time, Louis is captured and tried under the Fugitive Slave Law, which would return him to slavery. In the midst of sentencing, Louis daringly escapes again and continues north to Canada. "Ben" is written in the first-person narrative voice of a white northern man who is slowly seduced by the genteel South and slavery. The story chronicles his ideas about Ben, a Kentucky slave who has no voice until he escapes to freedom; then he responds to the narrator with a rhetorical question that packs a fierce punch. "The Man Who Was a Horse" introduces Bob Lemmons, a black Texas cowboy and ex-slave who is exquisitely attuned to the mustangs he tracks and captures. "When Freedom Came" is the tragic tale of Jake, who, freed from slavery, goes in search of his wife and children only to find that his wife has remarried since she was sold away from him. Finally, in "Long Journey Home," the narrator tells her/his family's stories of slave days, touching on capture and the Middle Passage, prayer and resistance, and an incident where fifty Ibo slaves walked into the sea to head back to Africa.

Long Journey Home is not quite as strong as *This Strange New Feeling*, Lester's other young adult book of African American stories based on historical fact. "Ben" and "When Freedom Came" are superior stories, with a strong narrative voice and piercing insights into slavery. The other stories in this collection have potential but are simply not developed far enough. However, all of the stories demonstrate Lester's poetic vision and his luscious way with words.

Five of the six stories focus on men, and in the sixth story, "Long Journey Home," the narrator's sex is not disclosed. The title story does feature two feisty women characters, but overall this is a very male-focused collection. The writing is accessible for ninth through twelfth graders. In spite of *Long Journey Home*'s faults, it must be recommended for its fine writing and a couple of very special stories.

88. Lester, Julius. *Two Love Stories*. New York: The Dial Press, 1972. 180 pages. **

Only the first of *Two Love Stories* features African American characters. "Basketball Game" features fourteen-year-old Allen Anderson, whose family moves from Kansas City to Nashville one summer. Nashville takes some getting used to, with its segregated lunch counters and the multitude of "for sale" signs that go up in front of houses all up and down the street when the Andersons move into a formerly all-white neighborhood. Allen feels lonely until Rebecca, the white girl next door, befriends him. Then he feels nervous. First, his father berates him: "A rattlesnake be a better friend to you than a white girl." Then white townspeople, including Rebecca's father, get up in arms at seeing a black boy with a white girl. In addition, Allen's relationship with Rebecca is strained by her naiveté and his need to be extremely careful around her. Although they finally become friends, Rebecca ultimately proves Mr. Anderson's warning true by snubbing Allen the first time she runs into him while in the company of her white friends.

Despite the book's title, "Basketball Game" is not a love story, but the story of two lonely teenagers negotiating a complicated friendship. Julius Lester does a good job of describing Allen's internal landscape but limits Rebecca to being a foil to Allen's character. We never come to know her as a real person. Perhaps this is intentional—Lester's comment on the impossibility of blacks and whites becoming truly intimate within racism's confines. On the other hand, perhaps it simply reflects Lester's exclusively male focus, which plays out also in his drawing of Allen's parents. Allen's father is a complex, at times contradictory, character, a proud and stern black preacher who believes in African Americans keeping to their own yet marries a woman who looks white, and then moves his family into an all-white neighborhood. He teaches Allen to show just enough "respect" to whites to stay alive. Of Allen's mother, we learn only that, "It was good she didn't talk much, because when she did, it was never anything good." This insultingly harsh depiction of Allen's mother adds nothing to the story. Similarly, we never get any sense of the girls' characters in the description of Allen's romantic relationships with black peers Gloria and Eloise. Again, this may be intentional, a reflection of teenage boys' self-absorption, but it seems that the females' characters simply don't matter, and this weakens the story.

Another weakness is Allen's unbelievable ignorance about sex: at fourteen, he supposedly does not know the difference between girls' and boys' anatomy. This will make him look silly to teenage readers.

Despite these weaknesses, "Basketball Game" explores an important topic—racism as it affects a southern teenage boy's relationship to his family, his neighbor, and himself—with sensitivity. Allen defies stereotypes. He is an artist, a basketball player, and a rebellious son. As his father taught him, he stands up for his beliefs, integrating the white public library and continuing to see Rebecca even after he has been warned not to. In these ways, he is an admirable role model for teen readers.

"Basketball Game" is suited to seventh- to tenth-grade readers, and will likely appeal more to boys than to girls.

89. Lester, Julius. *This Strange New Feeling*. New York: Scholastic, Inc., 1981. 164 pages. ****

Coretta Scott King Honor Book, 1982; Parents' Choice Award, 1981

This Strange New Feeling contains three stories about slavery and freedom, each written from a slave's perspective and each based on a true story. The title story is about Ras, a young man who, with the help of his uncle and a southern white farmer, escapes to freedom in Maine. Betrayed by another white man, he is captured and returned to his plantation, where he helps other slaves escape. In "Where the Sun Lives," Maria's mistress dies and Forrest Yates, a free black man whom Maria loves, buys her to be his wife. Maria begs him to free her, but since Georgia law prohibits this and they would have to move up North, Forrest refuses. Instead he promises to free her in his will. But when he dies in a horseshoeing accident, Maria is sold to pay his debts. The third story, "A Christmas Love Story," describes the experiences of Ellen and William Craft, slaves who posed as a master and slave to flee up North. They became outspoken abolitionists and escaped slave hunters who pursued them to Boston.

The topic of slavery is approached honestly, yet the stories are empowering rather than depressing. Slaves are presented as courageous actors in their own lives, not merely victims. Lester has successfully made slave stories come alive, combining historical fact with creative imagination to make characters whose humanity is undeniable and whose lives are both brave and tragic. With beautiful language, *This Strange New Feeling* forces the reader to imagine what being a slave must have felt like. However, Lester tends to marginalize and make passive the women characters, especially Ellen Craft, and tends to portray the men as teaching the women how to be free. (Contrast Lester's story with Dorothy Sterling's account in *Black Foremothers* of the Crafts' escape, which credits Ellen with a powerful role and never relegates her to the role of an invalid.) Aside from this one serious weakness, though, *This Strange New Feeling* is an outstanding book, appropriate for ninth- to twelfth-grade readers.

90. Mathis, Sharon Bell. *Brooklyn Story*. New York: Hill and Wang, 1970. 56 pages. ***

Vi and Eddie haven't seen their mother Della for five years. They've lived in Brooklyn with their grandmother since their father died in the Korean War when they were little. When Della finally comes to visit, fifteen-year-old Vi falls all over herself trying to get close to her. But older brother Eddie is angry, first staying out all night, then coming home to taunt Della about not being a real mother.

During Della's visit, Dr. Martin Luther King, Jr., is killed. Eddie, out in the streets watching the rioting, is shot in the chest. At first the crisis threatens to tear the family apart as Della tries to flee and Vi accuses her of abandoning them because she never loved them. Then Vi's grandmother explains that Della left them before because she had a nervous breakdown after their father's death and entered a hospital for many years. With this new knowledge, Vi forgives her mother and helps Eddie to forgive as Della stays on to help him recover from his bullet wound.

Brooklyn Story moved me to tears. The multifaceted, honest characters pull the reader in immediately with their heartbreaking struggle to come to terms with difficult family relationships. Each character is unique but real—Vi's eagerness to please, Eddie's sarcastic rage, their grandmother's rough, scolding tenderness, and Della's painful longing to reestablish a bond with her kids. The dialogue, though somewhat dated, rings true and provides most of the plot momentum. The one weakness of the story is Eddie's shooting—an unnecessarily sensational plot device to resolve the conflicts which would have been better accomplished by having the characters slowly evolve in their understanding and tolerance.

Because of its short length and quick pace, *Brooklyn Story* is accessible to fifth- and sixth-grade readers, but will also be appreciated by readers of all ages. Male and female characters are drawn with equal insight. Despite the artificial plot resolution, the strength of voice and character makes this a very special story.

91.   Mathis, Sharon Bell. *Teacup Full of Roses*. New York: Puffin Books, 1972. 125 pages. *****

Teacup Full of Roses is a story of African American men told with a loving eye and poetic language. Joe Brooks, an African American seventeen-year-old living in Washington, D.C., is about to graduate from night school. His younger brother Davey is a basketball player and a brain—the Brooks brother most likely to succeed. Older brother Paul is an artist and a heroin addict; just one day out of a rehab program, he already has his family revolving around him and his drug habit. The more strung out Paul becomes, the less attention his mother Mattie has for anyone but him. Meanwhile, Isaac Brooks, the father, is too sick to work, so he sits at home reading the newspaper and watches television to block out his wife's nagging. Aunt Lou rounds out the family with her visions of death and her lapses into crazy talk.

This is a story about people, about Joe's love for his brothers, his girlfriend Ellie, and his parents. A middle child and a storyteller, Joe tries to save everyone in his family but learns that he can save only himself. He loses Paul to drugs, his mother to Paul, and Davey to street violence. His final story, told over Davey's dead body, sends his brother off to a place where "All the mothers love you . . . And all the fathers are strong. The sisters are pretty. And the brothers help each other. It's a love place. A real Black love place."

Teacup Full of Roses is an incredibly moving, heartbreaking novel. In a gentle and loving tone, it focuses on the disintegration of a family and the hopeless efforts of one son to hold his world together. The characters are wonderfully drawn and the focus on human response rather than on drugs or street violence itself sets this story apart from other black-families-dealing-with-drugs stories. The description of a family system skewed by one son's addiction is realistically portrayed, although far too much blame is placed on the mother. My one criticism is that Mattie Brooks comes off as the villain, while all the men are portrayed sympathetically as victims or strugglers.

Still, I highly recommend *Teacup Full of Roses* for ninth to twelfth graders. Although the publishers consider it appropriate for ages ten to fourteen, only high-school age readers can fully appreciate the beauty of Mathis' language and the complexity of her characters' feelings for each other. This book is fine literature made accessible to young adult readers.

92. Mathis, Sharon Bell. *Listen for the Fig Tree*. New York: Puffin Books, 1974. 175 pages. **

American Library Association Notable Books for Children and Young Adults, 1974

Marvina is a sixteen-year-old African American girl who lives with her mother in New York City. Although blind, Marvina takes care of herself and tries to take care of her mother, too, as Leola sinks into an alcoholic depression following the murder of Marvina's father. Marvina's main supports are her quiet boyfriend, Ernie, a Black Muslim, and Mr. Dale, the loving man upstairs who has taught Marvina to sew and is always there for her. As the first anniversary of her father's death approaches, Marvina becomes overwhelmed by her mother's increasing emotional deterioration. She focuses on sewing the perfect dress for herself, fantasizing that if she can just hold on until the upcoming Kwanza celebration, everything will be all right. But when Marvina is attacked by a would-be rapist the night before Kwanza, the holiday takes on deeper meaning for her as it reaffirms her sense of community and helps to heal her.

Listen for the Fig Tree is a nicely written book with well-developed characters and dialogue. The theme is community and people's responsibility to each other. It's refreshing to read a book where a character's blindness is not the story's focus but simply an incidental attribute.

However, I take issue with several components of the book. First, Marvina is a teenager trying to cope all alone with an alcoholic mother. Yet when she becomes overwhelmed and does self-protective things, such as dream about Kwanza or leave her mother's vomit on the floor to clean up later, Ernie berates her and the reader is supposed to agree with him. Co-dependency was not a well-known concept in 1974 when Mathis wrote this book, and the story certainly urges co-dependent behavior. Second, Mathis' theme of community never addresses the issue of why Marvina is left alone to deal with her mother; Mathis implies no criticism of the adults (all men) in

Marvina's life who support her but never intervene with her mother. Third, when Marvina is almost raped, Mr. Dale—the voice of wisdom in the novel—explains the attack with, "You know why this happens to Black women? . . . All of you—each one, nobody left out—are so incredibly beautiful, profoundly beautiful . . . And, see—people like to touch that." An affirmation of African American women's beauty is great, but as an excuse for rape? Spare me.

The novel is very black affirming, particularly its powerful ending, which includes a beautiful, if somewhat didactic, description of a Kwanza celebration. In spite of this, I would not recommend *Listen for the Fig Tree* because it inappropriately holds Marvina responsible for more than a teenager can control, a damaging message for teens.

93. Mathis, Sharon Bell. *Cartwheels*. New York: Scholastic, Inc., 1977. 96 pages. **

The ten chapters and forty-five photographs which comprise *Cartwheels* are devoted primarily to three weeks of twelve-year-old Zettie Page's practicing for and winning a summertime gymnastics contest at her neighborhood recreation center in Brooklyn. First prize is fifty dollars. Zettie wants the prize money so that she can buy herself a bus ticket to go back to her aunt's in South Carolina, where she lived until a year ago and which she greatly prefers to New York. Her basement apartment, which she shares with her mother (her father is dead), is dark and cramped. The neighborhood girls, Thomasina, Connie, and Bernice, insult her and throw bricks and trash against her door.

To make matters worse, her mother invites a near-homeless and destitute former coworker, Sylvia Deering, and her deceased sister's fourteen-year-old daughter, Fawn, to stay with them indefinitely. Bossy Fawn "takes over everything," including Zettie's dreams: if Zettie wins the prize money, Fawn expects Zettie to take the two of them away from their problems and to South Carolina. Fawn also befriends Thomasina, Connie, and Bernice, and, gradually, they include Zettie in their circle. Thomasina, who plans to compete in the contest, begs Zettie to let her win so that she can buy her baby brother Billy a winter coat from Goodwill, as her mother has trouble providing for Thomasina's ten siblings. Zettie wrestles with her pride and pain; she's the best gymnast, and proving it by winning the contest will raise her status in her peers' eyes. And all year, she's suffered loneliness and harassment on account of Thomasina. Zettie tries, unsuccessfully, to teach Thomasina some fancy moves.

Fawn, an aspiring writer, tries unsuccessfully to enter the play competition, and so she runs away, only two hours before the contest; Zettie almost misses the contest. Zettie helps Fawn by letting her write poetry to accompany the music and choreography for Zettie's performance.

However, Sharon Bell Mathis introduces one more obstacle to Zettie's victory: an unknown contestant, Daisy. Of course, Zettie wins and she helps Fawn and Thomasina. After she splits her winnings three ways, Zettie doesn't have enough money to go to South Carolina, so she gets paint to put a mural of a tree, the sun, and a bird on the walls of her room.

Cartwheels is a simple, sweet story about a young girl who takes after her mother by having a big heart. Zettie is also resilient and spirited. However, all the characters in *Cartwheels*—and all of the characters are girls—seem younger than their twelve to fourteen years, and the photographs reinforce this impression. For this reason, the book seems most appropriate for upper elementary-level girls. Simple sentences, rapid-fire dialogue, and linear plot development with no subplots or tangents make the book easy to read. While the story isn't boring, it also isn't suspenseful.

The one surprise in *Cartwheels* is when Thomasina shifts responsibility for her mistreatment of Zettie onto Zettie. For the first half of the book, Sharon Bell Mathis presents only Zettie's perspective on Thomasina, Connie, and Bernice, who appear hostile for no apparent reason. When Thomasina explains to Zettie why she wants to win the gymnastic contest, Zettie wonders why she should forgive and help Thomasina, given how badly Thomasina has treated her so far. But Thomasina offers a radically different perspective on the situation: Zettie complained so much about Brooklyn and kept distant from the neighborhood kids initially, acting superior about her former home and her athletic ability, that Thomasina felt Zettie didn't want to be around them, let alone friends with them. This revelation—that the animosity worked both ways—shocks Zettie, but also enables her to start over in building a friendship with Thomasina. The author puts a nice spin on the story by shifting perspective, alerting the reader to the narrator's bias, as well as the adage that there are two sides to every story. Furthermore, given Thomasina, Connie, and Bernice's nastiness in the beginning of the story, it's useful to gain insight into their personalities and the motivation for their behavior.

94. McCannon, Dindga. *Peaches.* New York: Lothrop, Lee and Shepard Co., 1974. 126 pages. *

In the first chapter of *Peaches*, Millicent Johnson is being welcomed into the world by her grandmother. The grandmother nicknames Millicent Peaches, because peach trees remind her of youthful, happier days in her native Georgia, and she "figured that when [she] started to get up in age and closer to God, [she]'d need a pretty memory." In the last chapter, Peaches is mourning her grandmother's death. Peaches lives with her grandmother, Elizabeth, whom she refers to as Ma, in Harlem. Across the street live her mother, whom she calls Hally, short for Hallelujah, and her stepfather, Benton. When her grandmother goes into the hospital, Peaches moves in with her mother and stepfather, but the mood is tense. Peaches takes after her grandmother, too, in her artistic talents and in her gifts for picking the numbers, and she's strong willed. Despite warnings from teachers and family members that a person, especially a black woman, cannot make a living as an artist, Peaches is determined, from the third grade, to become a professional artist.

Peaches is feisty and mischievous. Most of the episodes revolve around her stealing, cursing, cheating, and drawing when and where she's not supposed to, from the age of six to fourteen. Peaches is also bright, and so she gets promoted into an accelerated junior high school program that will allow her to skip from seventh to ninth grade. She possesses a vivid imagination into which she retreats when she's not creating enough excitement in the "real" world.

Although Hally slaves as a domestic worker for Mrs. Markowitz, her relatives seldom work, and the entire extended family relies primarily on hitting the numbers for an income. The young people in the family are generally happy, the adults cranky. When Elizabeth becomes ill, Peaches lives with Hally, who makes Peaches miserable with her dictatorial and always-critical style. Thus, when Elizabeth dies, Peaches not only mourns the loss of her grandmother but dreads the future with her mother.

Peaches has potential. It leaps from anecdote to anecdote, some of which are humorous, some inspiring, some mildly titillating. Although Dindga McCannon develops her protagonist's character, she rarely develops her episodes, and she never explores deeply or resolves satisfactorily the problems that she introduces. It seems as if, as soon as the reader realizes what's happening in the story, the story's jumped to another time and place. Why does Peaches live with her grandmother, when her mother lives nearby? Why does Peaches' mother treat her with contempt and pessimism? The author feels no compulsion to provide insight into this dysfunctional family.

Describing the omnipresence of humongous rats, exploitative grocers, mean-spirited teachers, and messed-up relatives and neighbors in a matter of fact manner is okay. However, Dindga McCannon throws in some disturbing sexual scenarios and treats them just as off-handedly, which is unhealthy and potentially disturbing for young readers. For example, for some unknown reason, Peaches' friend Gloria jumps her and kisses her until Peaches breaks away. There is no explanation of where the behavior came from, no commentary on this as a sexual assault instead of an odd and random experience. When Jeannie's brothers, Ernie and Billy, try to rape Peaches, she worries about her mother, her friend, and the boys' reputations, instead of herself. Out of nowhere, the attempted rape begins, and then, when Peaches manages to talk them out of it and runs out of their house, it's completely over—no processing, no aftershock, nothing.

From fifth grade on, Peaches occasionally drinks wine with family and friends. With friends, she drinks to get a buzz. Is this okay with the author? What's the author's point in including this troubling behavior? The reader has no way of knowing.

Although Peaches is obsessed with the opposite sex, she adheres to a strict code of sexual standards: she kisses and feels but doesn't undress or have intercourse. Granted, she sneaks around a lot, which is suggestive. Yet the adults around her assume the worst. Her boyfriend Mickey's boss asks her, "Did he make your pants wet yet?" People stare at her as if she's a prostitute when they see Leroy repaying her the money he borrowed. Jeannie wonders if Peaches, instead of going to camp, went somewhere to have a baby. She knows there's no point in her reporting that Ernie and Billy attempted to rape her because no one would believe her. Dindga McCannon doesn't explore the contradictions in Peaches' behavior and in her milieu's mixed messages about being sexually active.

Basically, *Peaches* presents such a variety of themes and events that its variety sabotages the overall impact of the story. *Peaches* needs less variety and more depth. As some of the material seems inappropriate for middle-school readers, the ideal reader would have to be a girl of Peaches' age, fourteen, but rare will be the reader who identifies with her.

95. McCannon, Dindga. *Wilhelmina Jones, Future Star*. New York: Delacorte Press, 1980. 202 pages. **

Wilhelmina Jones, a.k.a. Willi, lives in Harlem, where she has few friends and is generally misunderstood and unappreciated. Her mother Orphelia, often drunk, keeps Willi at a distance, works her as if she were a servant, and talks to her only to curse, dictate to her, or berate her. Willi dreams of being a professional artist, but Orphelia forces her to attend Commerce High School to learn secretarial skills so she won't repeat her mother's mistake of working in a low paying factory job. Orphelia further deters Willi from developing her art by throwing out her art supplies and intruding on her creative time. In contrast, Willi's secret boyfriend Skeeter affirms her unique style and sends her money to buy more art supplies. Drafted in the Vietnam War and sent to the front lines as a cook, Skeeter writes often. His letters are full of informative and ironic reflections about black soldiers being drafted to fight a war abroad when all black people are essentially at war in America, about the groundbreaking radical activities of the black liberation struggle in America, and about the horrors of the military and war.

Willi gets involved with a local chapter of the multiracial Congress of Racial Equality. In CORE, she meets Joe, a foil to Skeeter, who just wants the opportunity to amass capital and move as far away from Harlem as he can. He projects his values and dreams onto Willi, criticizing her in the name of "improving" her. But he does tell her about a black artists' cooperative, and coins her artistic pseudonym, Tamu, which means beautiful in Swahili. Joe, too, is sent to Vietnam, where he is killed.

Through the artists' cooperative, Willi learns about a wide range of styles, sells some paintings, wins an award at the Harlem Outdoor Art Exhibition, and finagles her first exhibition. When Skeeter returns from Vietnam and Willi reaches her eighteenth birthday, they marry, move into their own apartment, and work hard. However, the ending to *Wilhelmina Jones, Future Star* is succinct and semisweet:

"Skeeter and I stayed married for seven years, had one child, and then divorced. . . and I went on to make myself a 'famous' artist. Years later, I was finally able to squeeze out a living from the works I created with my hands."

Expression is the dominant theme in *Wilhelmina Jones.* Willi wants the freedom to find herself without others' preconceived expectations. The novel laboriously depicts Willi's hard work of pursuing her dream to become an artist. Its message, that her success depends ultimately on her, will challenge and inspire young artists. The book offers excellent analysis of the challenges facing African American artists: is Willi an artist who happens to be black or a black artist? Will the white patronage and appreciation on which her professional success depends force her to compromise her subject matter and style? Will those blacks who can afford to do so support black artists?

In the sexual realm, Willi is presumed promiscuous by everyone around her except Skeeter. Her behavior contradicts this offensive and unfair assumption, but she never wonders where it comes from or explicitly condemns it. Men are depicted as amusingly predatory, with many badgering her to date them, but women are always blamed, including by other women characters, for any real or imagined sexual activity. When an uncle tries to molest her, Willi never considers seeking protection from her family, for they "would probably accuse me of starting it." Skeeter and Willi make love only after he pressures her, the night before he is shipped to Vietnam, to make their last night together memorable. Skeeter lays on the lines thick, arguing that a man "needs it." Although this scenario is realistic, with Willi consenting because she loves Skeeter, it is disappointing that, as the self-assured rebel, she does not do something dramatically different, such as countering his lines with her own clever, barbed replies and seeking intimacy through everything but intercourse. On the positive side, the portrayals of young love take it seriously without idealizing away its vicissitudes and obstacles. The novel stresses the importance of Willi and Skeeter finding themselves and learning about each other before they marry.

The explicitly Afrocentric elements in the novel add a philosophical dimension to it. For example, there are recurring discussions of black political movements and figures, cultural icons of the era such as Miriam Makeba and Nina Simone, and analysis of semantics around the use of "black" versus "Negro" and "nigger." Willi is the quintessential black activist and artist, politically committed and culturally rooted. But there is also a lot of drinking and toking.

The author subtly suggests that the unsympathetic character, Orphelia, is held hostage by the combined oppressions of race, class, and gender. Feeling trapped by her circumstances, she unwittingly perpetrates the cycle of oppression on her daughter. Young readers who feel similarly tortured by a domineering parent or a volatile parent-child relationship will identify with Willi's struggles with Orphelia. The flaw in Dindga McCannon's characterization of this relationship is Willi's remarkable courteousness toward her mother. Willi possesses superhuman compassion and self-control; she repeatedly expresses gratitude to Orphelia for providing a home and values, while she simultaneously asserts her need to grow up and become independent of her. The novel provides a modicum of hope to young readers with the epilogue's discussion of the gradual reconciliation between Willi and Orphelia, in spite of Orphelia's vow never to speak to Willi again after she moves out.

Aspiring artists, teens with troubled parental relationships and frustrated love affairs—these are the ideal readers for *Wilhelmina Jones, Future Star*. Despite the male-centered perspective of some of the female characters, this is a strongly female story. The age of the protagonist and the subject matter of the novel recommend it for high-school readers.

96. McDaniels, William. *Abdul and the Designer Tennis Shoes*. Chicago: African American Images, 1990. 79 pages. ***

Sixteen-year-old, eleventh grader Abdul Johnson is on the Thurgood Marshall High School basketball team because he is almost seven feet tall, not because he possesses natural ability. Distracted by the basketball season and tired of senior Slim Perkins, the handsome, sportscar-driving star of the team, humiliating him in practices, Abdul neglects his studies; yet, without at least average grades in his classes, he cannot play on the team. He enlists the help of his neighbor and longtime friend, classmate Tina Brown. Tina is good enough for Abdul to flirt with in the privacy of his home but not "his type" when it comes to publicly acknowledging her as his girlfriend. Instead, he takes Slim's cousin, sophisticated and gorgeous Diane, to the big dance. He nearly loses Tina as a friend, and does lose Diane after smoking her reefer and drinking scotch to impress her, only to end up too wasted even to dance.

In the aftermath of his humiliation, Abdul is visited by a promotions man from a shoe manufacturing company who asks him to test a unique pair of tennis shoes that will supposedly improve his basketball game; the catch is, if the labels come off of the sneakers, the sneakers will lose their "powers." From that moment, Abdul's life changes as he becomes touted as the best high school basketball player not only locally, but nationally. Meanwhile, Tina undergoes a transformation: her braces and bifocals come off, and she dons a gown that accentuates her previously camouflaged shapely figure to win the title of Homecoming Queen.

Before the state championship basketball game, the labels on Abdul's sneakers disappear, and his confidence goes along with them. He plays so miserably in the first half of the game that Coach Phillips puts him on the bench. At half-time, Tina pries the secret out of him and preaches: "Abdul, it's not in the label. It is all in your mind. If you put as much confidence in yourself and in your God-given abilities, you can succeed!" Abdul internalizes her message in time to recover and win the game.

William McDaniels explores the role that peer pressure plays in shaping young people's values and the importance of separating the shadow from the substance. Thurgood Marshall High School is a multiracial institution where students cross differences of neighborhoods and economic brackets to form genuine friendships; however, having fancy clothes, driving a sportscar, and dating the most beautiful student celebrities cause envy and admiration. When Abdul witnesses the prestige that possessions bestow on Slim, he rapidly succumbs to showmanship, striving to best Slim in every respect by buying more and better of everything and by hustling several beautiful girls at the same time. And none of the adults and friends who previously espoused basic values in other facets of his life—for example, believing in oneself, valuing education, not drinking or using drugs, respecting women, etc.—seem bothered by Abdul's unreal existence; in fact, everyone around Abdul is swept up in his exhilarating experience, living it vicariously through this "winner." This is realistic: America is a country of idol-worshippers and labelers, and young people are victimized most by this. In such a climate, basic values become relative or irrelevant. In the end, Abdul loses some of his magical aura without losing the real ability and hard work that boost his self-esteem. He understands that he "can succeed without the labels," and he slightly revises his yardstick to measure success.

The "experienced," substance-abusing Diane, who passionately explains how gangs murdered her best friends, is a just a stereotype that proves a point to Abdul. On the other hand, if one character has to carry the burden of being an emotionally detached party animal, it's refreshing to have it be a girl instead of a boy.

William McDaniels repetitively represents some young men's annoying objectification of women. A woman's appearance determines everyone's estimation of her; attractive girlfriends are commodities; and being a man means having emotional and sexual access to as many desirable women as possible. Abdul even objectifies Miss Thompson, his gym teacher, whom he purposely seeks out and respects for her advice. The only instance where the author counters the male protagonists' sexism is ineffective because it is somewhat contradictory: Tina makes statements about not caring what other people think of her and believing in herself, yet nevertheless seeks traditional validation of her beauty through the Homecoming Queen contest. She wins for her beauty as much as for her dancing and public speaking. And Abdul finds Tina attractive not because of her inner beauty alone, but because of her legitimated outer beauty, too.

When William McDaniels blows Abdul's meteoric rise to stardom beyond local celebrity, he appeals to some young people's fantasies. Abdul, recruited by colleges, is wined and dined across the country, introduced on national television to NBA stars like Magic Johnson and Michael Jordan, featured in *Sports Illustrated*, and paid enough for promoting products to buy a Corvette, stylish clothes, gold jewelry, new furniture and appliances for his family's home. While the fairy-tale element of the magic sneakers easily stretches the reader's imagination, the hyperbolic rise to celebrity may break the reader's suspended disbelief. Then again, including actual famous basketball stars in the novel provides the author with an opportunity to implicitly critique the appropriateness of professional athletes as role models for today's African American young men. After Tina "converts" Abdul, he teaches others to believe in themselves, in their natural, God-given talent and beauty within, and becomes an inspiration to young people nationwide; clearly, Abdul represents the ideal role model. But need a role model be a celebrity? Abdul, despite his newfound down-to-earthness, is still a star, not an ordinary person.

While the author relies on telling more than showing as his key narrative technique, and he states his points rather obviously, he manages to engage the reader with his straightforward style. One particularly noteworthy stylistic element is his unobtrusive insertion throughout the novel of an assortment of Afrocentric elements, ranging from history lessons on significant figures of African descent to details about clothing, dance, hairstyles, and music which incorporate an African cultural frame of reference.

97. McKissack, Patricia C. *The Dark Thirty: Southern Tales of the Supernatural.* New York: Alfred A. Knopf, 1992. 122 pages.
* * * * *

American Library Association Notable Books for Children and Young Adults, 1992; Coretta Scott King Award, 1993; School Library Journal Best Books for Children and Young Adults, 1992

Inspired by the ghost stories based on real people and circumstances that her Grandmama told her when she was a child growing up in the South, Patricia McKissack created ten original ghost stories "rooted in African American history and the oral storytelling tradition." The "dark thirty" refers to "the half hour just before nightfall. We had exactly half an hour to get home before the monsters came out," as well as the time when her Grandmama told her ghost stories.

"The Legend of Pin Oak" tells how the slave master of Pin Oak plantation in Tennessee, Harper McAvoy, jealously attempts to sell his half-brother, a slave named Henri DuPriest. But Henri is free and cannot be sold, so Harper decides to sell Henri's wife, Charlemae. Henri, Charlemae, and their son run away but slave dealers ambush them at Topps River, by a waterfall. Instead of returning to slavery, the runaways dive into the waterfall. Three birds arise from the mist, circle the slave dealers, then fly north. Transfixed, Harper steps onto the ledge by the waterfall, yelling at the birds, and falls into the water. The authorities label Harper's death an accident. Henri, Charlemae, and their son either commit suicide or escape into a cave behind the waterfalls and then on to freedom on the underground railway.

"We Organized" is a story poem based on an actual interview with a former slave. Ajax, the slave narrator, relates how the slaves on his plantation "organized" and used hoodoo or mojo to punish their master for his abuse and lying. On his deathbed, desperate to get rid of his spiritual assassins, the master frees the slaves and orders them to hurry away.

When white Riley Holt is killed in Tyre, Mississippi, in "Justice," Ku Klux Klansman Hoop Granger falsifies evidence to pin the murder on black Alvin Tinsley. The uneducated and poor Granger hates Tinsley, a graduate of Tuskegee Institute and a successful veterinarian. When Chief Burton Baker believes Tinsley's story, Granger organizes his friends to hang Tinsley themselves. He mocks Tinsley's warning that he will come back from the grave to prove his innocence. Within two weeks of Tinsley's murder, Granger begins having nightmares, seeing images of how he killed Miz Jasper's cat and framed Tinsley for it twenty years earlier and of how he murdered Holt and Tinsley. Begging Chief Baker to stop Tinsley from terrorizing him, Granger confesses to Holt's and Tinsley's murder. As he confesses, his gas station explodes.

The title of "The 11:59" refers to the Pullman Porters' figurative term for death: the 11:59 is the phantom Death Train. When retired Pullman porter Lester Simmons, of St. Louis, feels a pain in his chest, he tries to postpone the inevitable. As Simmons experiences a heart attack, he sees his deceased friend, Tip Sampson, conducting the 11:59, crashing into his apartment to pick him up. Two days later, Simmons' friends find his body and notice that his watch stopped at 11:59.

In "The Sight," Amanda Mayes encourages her son, Esau, to keep his psychic powers a secret so that no one in St. Charles, Missouri, will manipulate him to use those powers "for the wrong reasons." But Esau's neglectful father, Tall, kidnaps and forces Esau to help him win at gambling. While helping his father to pick the winning horses and numbers, Esau loses his vision; his father nearly beats him to death and returns him to his mother. Esau's sight returns when he begins having nightmares that his wife and sons will be killed by a fire. He tries to protect them from the imminent danger, and succeeds in the final moment by sending them a telepathic message to get out of the house just before it explodes in flames.

The Montgomery Bus Boycott inspires "The Woman in the Snow." White bus driver Grady Bishop treats the riders on his route contemptuously. During a severe snowstorm, he almost hits a scantily clad woman clutching her baby. The woman begs Bishop to take her to the hospital and to let her ride for free, because her baby is sick and she has no money. Even though she offers Bishop her wedding ring and promises to bring him the fare in the morning, he shoves her off the bus. The next year, during another snowstorm, Bishop sees the same woman, hits the brakes, skids and crashes, and dies. Twenty-five years later, the first black bus driver in this unspecified southern city awaits his run-in with the ghost of Eula Mae Daniels and her baby. During a bad snowstorm, he picks up Eula Mae for free and drives her to the hospital. When he drops her off, he adds, "About the bus fare. No need for you to make a special trip back. Consider it a gift." Eula Mae smiles and vanishes forever.

When Josie Hudson of "The Conjure Brother" wants a brother, she seeks the help of a conjure woman, Madam Zinnia. Josie botches Madam Zinnia's directions, however, and gets an older brother who gets on her nerves. When she complains about her brother, Adam, to Madam Zinnia, she gets a baby brother. Then Madam Zinnia and Adam disappear, leaving Josie to wonder if they ever really existed at all.

Nonviolent activist Leddy Morrison, the protagonist of "Boo Mama," takes her two-year-old son, Nealy, to live "away from the world" on a farm in Orchard City, Tennessee, after her husband is killed in Vietnam and Martin Luther King, Jr., and Robert Kennedy are assassinated. Nealy falls off a ledge and disappears for over a year. When he returns, he is in remarkable health, despite the trauma he experienced from the fall, but he exhibits animal-like features and tendencies. She learns that a tribe of Big Foot or Sasquatch healed and raised him. Nealy's Sasquatch mother, Nos, temporarily returns him to Leddy because she cannot ignore Leddy's constant vigil and crying. When Nos reappears to claim Nealy, she invites Leddy to join her people, who "had conquered disease, overcome hatred and greed, and harnessed resources within the earth to prolong life." Leddy, the die-hard idealist, accepts, leaving the townspeople eternally wondering about Leddy and Nealy's mysterious disappearance.

Laura, in "The Gingi," buys an ebony figurine of a woman in the Mother Africa Shop, despite shopkeeper Mrs. Aswadi's warning that the figurine is a Dabobo spirit that will invite disaster into Laura's house. Mrs. Aswadi insists that Laura also take a straw and cloth monkey doll called a gingi, a protective doll. Although a series of gruesome near-disasters strikes Laura and her family, she refuses to acknowledge the power of the dabobo or the gingi, but she burns the two dolls on the barbecue. Nevertheless, the dolls' spirits remain until the family abandons their home forever.

In "The Chicken-Coop Monster," a semi-autobiographical story, protagonist Melissa Russell stays in rural Tennessee with her grandparents while her parents rearrange their lives after their divorce. Melissa, a member of the St. Louis chapter of the Monster Watchers of America club, is convinced that a monster inhabits the chicken coop. Her grandfather, James, advises her to face the monster. Armed with support from James and the advice that "[t]here is no fear in love," Melissa approaches the chicken coop. She never sees the monster and believes that it couldn't come out of the coop because "I was getting stronger and it was getting weaker."

Even the weakest story in this book is wonderful; indeed, there are no weak stories in the entire collection. Patricia McKissack has assembled an eclectic and intriguing collection. Her injection of people, events, and beliefs from African American experience into the stories adds an unusual dimension to the genre of ghost stories in general and provides another layer of meaning to each story's cultural, historical, political, and spiritual message. Her focus is on fun as much as edification, and a reader can devour these stories for sheer entertainment. At the same time, the reader cannot help but learn interesting tidbits about conjuring, midwifery, Pullman porters and the Underground Railroad.

The author employs a range of storytelling styles, all successful. Humor, history, traditional wisdom, and, of course, unpredictable horror, suffuse the collection. Although an illustration accompanies each story, thereby suggesting a young audience, *The Dark-Thirty: Southern Tales of the Supernatural* is particularly juicy for high-school readers: its complex character and plot development, rich figurative language, elaborate symbolism, and vivid imagery invite the sophisticated reader. Middle-school and high-school readers who appreciate good stories in general and ghost stories in particular will greatly enjoy the suspense and mystery of this collection. Six of the ten stories feature young people as significant characters, which will further engage young adult readers.

The Dark-Thirty: Southern Tales of the Supernatural is a groundbreaking and outstanding book, a prime selection for any reader, regardless of reading skill.

98. Meriwether, Louise. *Daddy Was a Number Runner*. New York: The Feminist Press at the City University of New York, 1986. 208 pages. ****

School Library Journal Best Books for Children and Young Adults, 1970

Twelve-year-old Francie Coffin is growing up black and poor in Harlem during the Depression, surrounded by the love and familiarity of her community. Mother works hard and worries about money; Daddy lights up the house with his smile, plays blues piano, and runs numbers; brother Junior is arrested with his gang for killing a white man; brother Sterling, the "smart one" who was supposed to get an education, left school to become an undertaker's assistant; and best friend Sukie is angry at her life, at her drunk father and prostitute sister, and therefore beats up Francie regularly. Francie's world is also peopled by the boys goofing on the corner; the white men who try to feel her up in the movies, at the bakery, and at the butcher's; the suspicious, skinflint social worker who can grant or deny the Coffin's welfare; and all the blacks in Harlem who alternately take care of each other, riot, preach about returning to Africa, and dream about winning the numbers.

Daddy Was a Number Runner offers a lush description from an adolescent girl's perspective of Harlem in the 1930s. Yet the story is not dated and could easily have been written this year. Francie's perspective is the insider's view, the shot from the midst of the whirlwind, offered up by somebody who is just coming into her own. Meriwether's rich detail and understated perceptiveness are a joy and the plot's kaleidoscope of events and images moves along quickly and compellingly. The novel's language is accessible to younger high-school readers, but Meriwether's insight and the beauty of her writing will also appeal to adult readers.

Daddy Was a Number Runner is honest yet compassionate, showing the mix of love and trouble that sustains life in a black neighborhood. The characters are fully human, and their lives both touching and tragic. For its superb quality of writing and vision, I highly recommend it, especially for tenth through twelfth graders.

99. Moore, Emily. *Something to Count On*. New York: Puffin Books, 1980. 103 pages. ***

Ten-year-old Lorraine Maybe lives in a bombed-out, mugger- and rat-infested, African American and Puerto Rican community in the Bronx. When their father moves out to a nicer but distant Queens neighborhood, he rarely sees Lorraine and her baby brother, Jason. When he does take the children for the weekend, he inevitably loses his patience. As her father shatters her idealized image of a father, Lorraine begins to admit to herself that, even when he lived at home, he "was always too busy, too tired, or didn't feel like being bothered." Ultimately she comes to accept that her father loves her, but for him, being a father means providing food and clothing for his children, and being a mother means providing "the rest."

Initially, Lorraine worries that she drove her father away with her brattiness at home and her failing grades and fights in school. However, her fifth grade teacher, Mr. Hamilton, never lectures or reprimands Lorraine, just questions and spurs her to reflect deeper on her family problems and to communicate better with her parents. He also encourages Lorraine to develop her artistic talent, which nurtures her self-esteem while channeling her energy into a constructive outlet.

Lorraine's mother frequently becomes angry and impatient with Lorraine. Ma is stressed by juggling full time work and fashion design school by day, raising two hellish children by night, and trying to buffer the children's volatile feelings about their father. After an especially painful conversation with her father, Lorraine has a breakthrough conversation with her mother wherein she stops thinking about the divorce solely in terms of herself and recognizes that it drastically improved her mother's life. She finally acknowledges that the changing family dynamics provide an opportunity to redefine and strengthen relationships between herself and her parents.

Through the immediate and authentic voice of her protagonist, Emily Moore represents—with depth and sensitivity—all the players in this very real family drama. The reader understands that the divorce stems from the parents' changing needs and does not signify the father's desire to move away from his children. The parents love the children in different ways and though the father doesn't meet all of the children's needs and wants, he's not a villain. Rather, he is a product of socialization into traditional roles in the household, which are implicitly critiqued here. *Something to Count On* suggests that divorce can be a healthy solution for a troubled household.

Through the school scenes, Emily Moore indicts the traditional system of tracking and the blaming-the-victim mentality of teachers who fail to teach but hold their students solely responsible for failing to learn.

Something To Count On features young protagonists, which suggests an upper-elementary-level audience, yet it addresses with complexity and sophistication a situation relevant to the majority of today's young adults. Middle-school readers who can overlook the book's jacket illustration and some of Lorraine's infantile behavior will benefit from its exploration of divorce. Although its central concern is the daughter's search for her father—or for a father figure such as Mr. Hamilton—boys and girls will relate to the host of changes and challenges that a parent's moving out ushers in. In light of the apparent care that Emily Moore puts into developing her characters and themes, the absence of an explanation for Lorraine's nasty attitude—which preceded her parents' divorce—perplexes me. Lorraine is a feisty girl, some of whose anger is righteous, a response to disrespectful teachers and classmates, and some of whose hyperactivity is understandable if undesirable, a strategy designed to attract the attention of self-absorbed or distracted parents. Still, her propensity for emotional and physical violence deserves the narrative's attention.

100. Moore, Emily. *Whose Side Are You On?* New York: Farrar, Straus & Giroux, 1988. 134 pages. ***

Sixth-grader Barbra is failing math, while her twin brother Billy is in the special class for intellectually gifted students. At her mother's insistence, Barbra is assigned a peer tutor, T.J. Brodie, who has teased and tormented Barbra for years. Initially, Barbra feels mortified, but slowly her relationship with T.J. changes and they become friends. Then T.J. disappears, sent to a group home for boys. Angered at this injustice, Barbra demonstrates with placards and chants outside T.J. 's grandfather's apartment. The only one who will join her demonstration is Kim, a fat classmate whom Barbra and her friends enjoy teasing. Then everything changes. Barbra finds herself standing up for Kim, even at the risk of losing her own best friends. She learns the truth about T.J.'s exile to the group home and tries to convince him to come home. And she masters math.

Set in Harlem, *Whose Side Are You On?* is a wonderful book for fourth- to seventh-grade readers, particularly girls. The characters are believable and sympathetic as they struggle with issues of prime relevance to young adolescents: peer groups, changing relationships between girls and boys, and the growth of a sense of self. In addition, Moore has Barbra confront injustice on very personal fronts, offering a model of an increasingly empowered African American girl. Barbra's mother raises her twins carefully and well, setting high expectations and helping them to grow in their understanding of life. For example, when Barbra's protest turns out to be misinformed, her mother forces her to make amends to T.J. 's grandfather while at the same time applauding her spirit that demands she confront injustice. The book's male characters, T.J. and Billy, have smaller but still sympathetic roles. However, there are no adult male characters, Barbra's father having died many years earlier.

This story works so well because the situations are real and the characters react in real ways. Every young reader will be able to identify with some situation in the book, whether it's feeling like adults make all of the important decisions affecting kids' lives or feeling stupid because an academic subject is just too hard. At the same time, the reader can watch these characters grow and change, becoming more powerful actors and decision-makers in their own lives.

101. Moore, Emily. *Just My Luck*. New York: Puffin Books, 1991.
103 pages. ***

Nine-year-old Olivia feels cheated. Her best friend,
Wei Ping, moved to California, and, now alone, she faces fifth
grade with her cliquish, cruel classmates. Olivia wants a
puppy, "something to love me and stay by my side," but her
parents—her mother works grueling twelve-hour days to climb
the corporate ladder as a certified public accountant and her
father takes a risky sabbatical from his college English
teaching job to write a book—don't have the money or time to
spare on a pet. The one person who is desperately eager to
befriend her she rebuffs: her Lower East Side landlady Mrs.
Dingle's awkward nephew, Jeffrey. Jeffrey is adjusting to
isolation at home—his parents recently divorced and sent him
to live with his aunt—and at school.
     Olivia falls in love with a Beagle named Cleo at the
neighborhood pet store and connives to scrape together the two
hundred dollars to buy the puppy. Her schemes fail but,
conveniently, Mrs. Dingle's poodle, Pearl, disappears and Mrs.
Dingle offers a two hundred dollar reward. Since Jeffrey wants
Pearl, Olivia wants money, and both share a wild enthusiasm
for mysteries, they form a detective partnership to search for
Pearl. Initially, they suspect Mrs. Wise, the owner of Connie's
Bakery downstairs. Eventually, they learn that Mr. G.,
another neighbor, dognapped Pearl in order to help Olivia
raise the money to buy Cleo. Although Mr. G. is willing to face
the consequences when Mrs. Dingle learns that he stole her dog,
Olivia fears the trouble he may have to handle for her sake;
she coerces Jeffrey into pretending that Pearl simply returned
home on her own. When she sacrifices the reward to protect her
friend, Mr. G., with Jeffrey's help, she realizes that her
friendship with Jeffrey beats having a pet and finally treats
him like a best friend.
     Just My Luck will appeal to third- to sixth-grade
readers. Olivia is a very real young person whom readers will
accept, though they may not like her obsessing and sulking.
Sometimes the narrative seems annoyingly thick and slow. The

mystery, an unusual subplot within the novel, is brief but surprising.

Emily Moore portrays expertly the experiences with which young readers will be all too familiar: sibling rivalry; transparent attempts to manipulate parents; children's mortification at the outfits their parents want them to wear to school; the cliquishness and callousness of school groups; the insincerity and inequality of some children's friendships; the radically different world view of children; the prison-like atmosphere of school; and the fear of befriending the unpopular. The author works these elements into the novel but does not privilege any of them with an extensive treatment.

She does, however, accentuate another facet of Olivia's experience—the unconventional division of labor within the household. While Olivia's mother works at her high-powered job to support the family, her father cares for the children and cooks the dinners. Both of her parents are preoccupied and overwhelmed with work; neither is a hero nor a villain. Refreshingly, the father does not get extra credit for assuming domestic responsibilities and, in fact, praises his wife for working so hard to provide for the family. Jeffrey, sensitive and affectionate, is also a nicely realized contrast to male stereotypes.

Olivia's father and Mr. G. introduce important lessons for life, backing up their teachings with examples from their own youth. Olivia's father teaches her that everyone experiences failure occasionally, that sometimes one has to postpone trying to fulfill a wish, and that "sometimes you have no control over what happens, but most of the time, only you can make the all-important decisions. And they can change your entire life." The affectionate and compassionate Mr. G. helps Olivia to reevaluate her feeling of "being cheated"; he teaches her that there is a solution to every problem. In its depiction of the wonderful relationship between Olivia and Mr. G., the novel testifies to the potential and transformative power—for young and old equally—of cross-generational friendships and informal kinship networks, a unique dimension to this novel. *Just My Luck* doesn't end with Olivia's putting all of these beliefs into practice; it realistically depicts her sorting through and experimenting with them.

102. Moore, Yvette. *Freedom Songs*. New York: Puffin Books, 1991. 168 pages. ***

It's the 1960s and fourteen-year-old Sheryl leaves Brooklyn, her parents, and two brothers to visit her extended family in North Carolina. Sheryl loves North Carolina until she comes face to face with Jim Crow: whites-only water fountains; broken-down school buses, desks, and books for black students; and exclusionary voter registration practices. Then she learns that her Uncle Pete, just nineteen years old, has joined the Civil Rights Movement, working to register black voters, to desegregate lunch counters, and to establish a Freedom School in nearby Hendersonville. Awed and inspired by Pete's work, Sheryl vows to raise money to support the Civil Rights workers when she returns to Brooklyn. With the help of friends, Sheryl organizes a hugely successful Freedom Concert and raises over five thousand dollars. In the meantime, though, a bomb planted in the Freedom School kills Pete, and his mother is nearly run off the road by racist whites. Sheryl finds herself unable to cope, until she accepts the support and faith of her friends and community.

Freedom Songs' quality is mixed. Its important topic and well-drawn characters provide depth, but sometimes the plot loses momentum. The first part of the book, in particular, moves very slowly, and some of Sheryl's discoveries of Jim Crow seem clichéd. Also, the story's first-person voice, supposedly Sheryl's, rings false: no fourteen-year-old speaks in as flowery a manner or as descriptively as this book's narrator.

The second half of the book picks up, with more action and more interesting interactions between characters. Sheryl's preoccupation with girlfriends and a boyfriend provides a strong, believable subplot that will interest teenagers.

Realistic, too, and powerful is the depiction of Sheryl's emotional swings between stress over planning a major concert, grief and loss of faith over her uncle's death, and joy in her own triumphant contribution to a cause as important as the Civil Rights Movement. The story is also strengthened by the many voices of older and younger African American characters representing different perspectives on civil rights struggles.

Although the protagonist is a girl, the story is not particularly gender specific, so both sexes can identify with it. Strong male and female characters abound, from young Sheryl and Pete to their older uncles, aunts, and grandmother. Despite its faults, *Freedom Songs* is a book worth reading. The book could have been shorter and the descriptive writing a little less effusive. As it stands, the novel is appropriate for eighth through eleventh graders. *Freedom Songs* sends a powerful, historically-proven message: that even young people can make a tremendous difference when they join forces for justice.

103. Myers, Walter Dean. *Fast Sam, Cool Clyde, and Stuff.* New York: Viking Press, 1975. 190 pages. ****

American Library Association Notable Books for Children and Young Adults, 1975; Coretta Scott King Honor Book, 1976

Francis "Stuff" Williams is twelve years old when his family moves to Harlem and eighteen when this story finishes. In the intervening years, the kids on his block help each other survive Clyde's father's death in a forklift accident, Gloria's parents' separation, several unfair arrests, and Carnation Charley's drug addiction. Together they also share talks about sex, a basketball championship, Clyde and Sam entering a dance competition with Clyde in drag, and Stuff breaking his foot to impress a girl. Through their adventures, they learn the irreplaceable value of good friends who care for each other.

In *Fast Sam, Cool Clyde, and Stuff,* Walter Dean Myers achieves just the right combination of adventure, emotional depth, and humor. The story, told in Stuff's voice, catches teenage dialogue and perception beautifully, without ever taking itself too seriously. At the same time, Myers explores important everyday issues with considerable complexity; especially moving are the passages where Stuff and Sam try to comfort Clyde after his father's death, where the whole gang figures out what it means to be a friend, and where the girls set the boys straight about sex. Myers also touches on the themes of drug addiction and the threat of arrest which African American men run every time they walk down the street.

The characters are young teenagers, and all of these themes are approached at a level appropriate to their ages, twelve to fifteen. But although the discussion is simple, it is never superficial, and, in fact, these young characters show a great deal of insight. The characters' openness to new ideas, commitment to each other, and all-around good-heartedness make them endearing as they struggle to grow up. The novel's ending is weak, brushing quickly over Carnation Charley's death and the 116th Street friends going their separate ways as they grow up. But this is my only criticism of the book. On the whole, it is a pleasure to read about African American teenagers who are good, whose parents are not falling apart, and whose lives are not entirely defined by tragedy. The book's reading level is accessible to seventh to tenth graders, though older readers may also smile through *Fast Sam, Cool Clyde, and Stuff.*

104. Myers, Walter Dean. *Mojo and the Russians.* New York: Viking Press, 1977. 151 pages. *

The spring of their sixth grade year is a time that friends Dean, Kwami, Judy, Leslie, Wayne, Anthony, and Kitty will never forget. When twelve-year-old Dean accidentally crashes on his bicycle into Drusilla, the scary Mojo lady from Louisiana, he and his friends fear she will use her Mojo powers to kill Dean. The young people approach their friend, Long Willie, who happens to be Drusilla's boyfriend, to see if he will intervene on Dean's behalf before Drusilla starts her spell. Dean barely gets a chance to explain his problem to Willie before some Russians in a limousine drive up to Willie's Harlem stoop and the plot veers off in crazy directions.

The friends form "Operation Brother Bad" to spy on Willie. They hope to use proof of his working as a spy for the Russians to force him to intercede with Drusilla. The novel details the array of Operation Brother Bad's investigative schemes—some imaginative and suspenseful, some predictable and silly.

Mojo and the Russians is told primarily in the first person from Dean's perspective. Surprisingly, however, Dean is not well developed as a character. The other key players are Dean's best friend, Kwami, and the lone white member of the clique, Judy. Kwami is the self-appointed leader of Operation Brother Bad. He is naturally inclined to put people down and to see everything in a negative light. Furthermore, he distrusts all white people. In Judy, Kwami has met his match. Judy is an equally brassy character. She fights with her parents to hang out uptown. She uses her friends' colloquialisms, despite their protests, to assert her belonging. And she idealizes black culture. Whatever the issue, Kwami and Judy diametrically oppose each other. As the story unfolds, however, they reluctantly and secretly grow to like each other.

The chief adult characters are Drusilla, Willie, and the police. Occasional chapters written in the third person from Drusilla's perspective provide a comical counterpoint to the friends' fear of her—the reader learns that Drusilla indeed possesses Mojo powers, but she never seriously entertains the thought of wasting them on Dean, whose "crime" was forgettable. The police come across as generally good-natured, responsive, but simple-minded guys. They figure prominently in the end of the story, when they arrest the friends for trying to put an "Atomic Mojo" on the Russian Consulate. During the interrogation at the police station, Dean spills the story about how Willie may be spying for the Russians. Questioning reveals that Willie was negotiating with the Russians to develop a cultural exchange program whereby Harlem youth could go to college on scholarship in Russia. The Russians expected no secrets in return.

Although some of the clever or humorous elements of *Mojo and the Russians* would appeal to a middle-school reader, upper-elementary-school readers would like it best. The characters sometimes seem young for their age. Clearly, Walter Dean Myers intended *Mojo and the Russians* as light reading. Whether the reader will appreciate the author's humor is hard to predict. Most of the action is preposterous and foolish.

Dean's friend, Kwami, is not a sympathetic character—it's hard to understand how the sensitive Dean tolerates him, let alone counts him as a best friend. Kwami's most bothersome habit, for this reader, is his penchant for expressing his every thought in rhyme. The author creates a more palatable character in Judy, and her friendship with the group is believable. Portraying the police as innocuous is another signal, if the reader needs one, that *Mojo and the Russians* belongs in the genre of comedy-fantasy. Because there are as many strong female characters—in fact, the most powerful character in the book is a woman, Drusilla—as there are male characters, this book would appeal equally to readers of both sexes. This book has lost much of its potential charm with the changing times. Today's young reader has not experienced the Cold War context which made this plot remotely imaginable though silly. And the colloquial expressions which the author uses excessively in dialogue are out of date.

On the other hand, the author has created a refreshingly positive group. The members of Operation Brother Bad are an extremely happy, healthy peer group. Also, there are no sex stereotypes in this story; the girls are as brave and able as the boys. Prejudice is the one serious, albeit minor, theme explored here. Walter Dean Myers explores this theme casually and gently through the character of Judy. The friends accept her as an equal but acknowledge her difference. They are themselves around her. And they encourage her to be herself around them. Being yourself, they try to show her, is more important than being alike or fitting in. This inspirational message is somewhat buried in the overall silliness of the story.

105. Myers, Walter Dean. *It Ain't All for Nothin'*. New York: Viking Press, 1978. 217 pages. **

American Library Association Notable Books for Children and Young Adults, 1978

Twelve-year-old Tippy has lived a protected, nurtured life with his grandmother in Harlem ever since his mother died in childbirth and his father "disappeared" to jail. Grandma Carrie and Tippy struggle to pay the bills, but somehow they make it through by relying on one another. Then Grandma Carrie gets sick and ends up in a nursing home, and Tippy must go live with his father Lonnie, whom he hardly knows. Tippy's father spends his time drinking, entertaining women, and hanging out with men friends. His disgust at having to take in Tippy eases when he begins collecting welfare money for the boy, but he rebuffs Tippy's attempts to get close to him.

Then Lonnie takes Tippy with him to rob a store. Tippy, guilt-ridden, confides in a streetwise friend, Motown, and begins drinking to relieve his unhappiness. Lonnie keeps promising that each robbery will be their last, until finally his friend Bubba gets shot during a hold-up. They bring Bubba back to Lonnie's apartment, promising he'll be fine without a doctor. But Bubba gets worse, and Tippy knows he will die without help. However, the men will not permit Bubba to go to the hospital, so Tippy sneaks out and calls the police. Although he doesn't want to turn his own father in, Tippy realizes he will not be able to live with himself if he allows a man to die because he is too scared or too passive to help him.

It Ain't All for Nothin' is a mediocre book, somewhat dated by its dialogue and its concern with alcohol and marijuana as drugs of choice. Tippy's character does not quite ring true for a twelve-year-old boy in Harlem, even a protected one. For instance, his favorite response to stress is to cry, which makes him seem closer to seven or eight years old. He is not a character that most readers, male or female, will want to identify with. On the other hand, Lonnie's character is believable, particularly the glimpses of caring and optimism that show through his normally aloof facade when he finds a legitimate job. Myers does a good job of tracing Lonnie's development, showing us glimpses of his pain and sense of failure as he tries to steer his son into a better way of life even as he involves him in robberies. And we see Tippy's longing for closeness with his father fighting against his attempts to live morally.

This novel's vocabulary and writing style are appropriate for sixth to ninth graders, but its length may intimidate them. Once Grandma Carrie is out of the picture, the only female characters are just male appendages and are all nineteen or older, so young female readers may find little of interest in the book. On the other hand, male readers loathe to identify with Tippy's immaturity and his incessant ethical confusion may also have trouble being engaged by *It Ain't All for Nothin'* unless they are drawn in by the despair of Lonnie's character.

106. Myers, Walter Dean. *The Young Landlords*. New York: Avon Books, 1979. 156 pages. ***

American Library Association Notable Books for Children and Young Adults, 1979; Coretta Scott King Award, 1980

Told in the first person from the perspective of fifteen-year-old Paul Williams, *The Young Landlords* describes a summer in the life of The Action Group, a group of friends who band together to "do good" in their community—Gloria (from *Fast Sam, Cool Clyde, and Stuff*), Dean, Bubba, Omar, and Jeannie. When The Action Group complains to a slumlord about his neglecting a building in their Harlem neighborhood, the owner—for a dollar and some signatures—transfers the building over to them, challenging them to manage it better than he did. The building, the bombed-out but overoccupied Stratftord Arms, consumes much of Paul's time and much of the book's focus. Paul, the young landlord, reveals his frustration at balancing business (trying to manage and improve the property, preferably for a profit) and "doing good" (trying to support the people who live in the building and set an example for the community).

The Action Group spends most of its time negotiating relationships with the generally hostile tenants, but it also searches for evidence to exonerate friend Chris, set up by his boss for a burglary scam he didn't commit. Other subplots include Paul's struggle to transform key relationships in his life with his father and with Gloria. As he proves to his skeptical and always-lecturing father that he is thoughtful, responsible, and rightfully idealistic, the two communicate better and grow closer. Paul also confesses his crush to Gloria and stumbles backward into the relationship.

The Young Landlords focuses on a clever but unlikely plot. It is entertaining and enlightening, with a likable, rebellious narrator. It demonstrates a nice point, too, about cooperation and community, with a refreshingly positive peer group. Some of the tenants seem more like parodies or clichés than portraits. And The Action Group's gender polarizing—the boys do stupid things like making rash decisions and fighting with tenants to resolve problems, while the girls carefully weigh all factors before making decisions, use diplomacy to resolve conflict, and go on about the business of performing most of the repairs—also seems too pat. The subplots restore the reader's interest when the details of being a landlord become tedious. The best part of *The Young Landlords* is Paul's unfolding crush on Gloria. Gloria is a wonderful character—smart, strong, funny, fresh, and generous with people's feelings and finances. She is forward in tackling problems and direct in discussing her emotions.

This book is fun but nothing special. It would pose no problem for seventh through twelfth graders, but younger readers would probably identify more with Paul.

107. Myers, Walter Dean. *Hoops*. New York: Dell Publishing Co., 1981. 183 pages. ***

American Library Association Notable Books for Children and Young Adults, 1981

Seventeen-year-old Lonnie Jackson doesn't have that much going for him: he fights with his mother, has a boring job, a confusing relationship with his girlfriend, and few plans for the future. But he has basketball. Through basketball, Lonnie has a chance to attend college. And through basketball he finds Cal, a surrogate father, ex-NBA pro and a drunk, who slowly reveals more of himself to Lonnie, helping him make a commitment to his own life and to integrity. When Lonnie and Cal stand up together to the hustlers who got Cal thrown out of the NBA, Cal is killed and Lonnie must move forward alone.

This book is easy to read, interesting and fast paced, but its treatment of issues and character development are decidedly superficial. Cal is the most interesting character—a fallen hero trying, with limited success, to pull together the shreds of his life. Lonnie is likable but seems to be essentially a reactive character, tossed around by the events of his life. The relationship between Lonnie and his girlfriend Mary-Ann also lacks depth, though Lonnie's relationships with his male friends, especially with his best friend Paul, are more satisfying.

Hoops' reading level is appropriate for junior high and young high-school readers, and its focus on male characters and concerns will interest boys more than girls.

108.   Myers, Walter Dean. *The Legend of Tarik.* New York: Scholastic, Inc., 1981. 180 pages. ****

Walter Dean Myers spins a rich tale in this fantasy. From long ago and far away—vaguely central Africa and the Mediterranean basin during the Middle Ages—comes the legend of Tarik, the black knight. Although his age is never specified, it is clear that Tarik is a teenager. Tarik sees the tyrant El Muerte kill his family and fellow villagers of Oulata, but he is powerless against the conqueror. Tarik survives El Muerte's mass execution and finds refuge in the Garden of Shange, where a blind scholar named Nongo and a priest named Docao nurse him back to health and prepare him to avenge the murder of his people by killing El Muerte.

To take on El Muerte, Tarik needs to collect three accouterments, each of which is not easily had: the sword of Serq, the Crystal of the Heart's Truth, and the wild stallion Zinzinbadio. When El Muerte learns of Tarik's impending assassination plot, he captures and kills Docao and Nongo. The story ends when Tarik, with the assistance of Stria, a survivor of another of El Muerte's conquests, tracks down and kills El Muerte and then modestly returns to his homeland.

The Legend of Tarik is packed full of action and advice. It reads quickly, and readers of all ages, male and female, will enjoy it, though some may have a hard time digesting its richly detailed narrative. The centerpiece of the story is Tarik's warrior training. The core of what Docao and Nongo try to accomplish in training is, like the quest on which Tarik embarks to track down El Muerte, an obvious metaphor for the adolescent's rite of passage. Tarik is being tested emotionally, intellectually, physically, and spiritually. He is constantly forced to figure out who he was and who he will be. He develops his skills and courage. But most of all, he develops restraint: reason and mercy are preferred to rage and brute force. The tales that Nongo tells Tarik and the exercises that Nongo gives him are designed to help Tarik tame his pride, impulsivity, blinding anger, and hatred. The tales and exercises challenge Tarik to go deeper, to cut through facile assessments of problems and delusions of simple violent solutions to pursue the truth. The ultimate goal is to make Tarik powerful and to imbue him with the understanding that power is not inherently evil—it depends on how one uses power and to what end.

All of the messages that Myers has embedded in this text are made obvious without detracting from the story. The moral principles are defined more in practical than in theoretical terms, highly effective and embraceable for adolescent readers. Readers can interpret Tarik's quest as the adolescent quest for selfhood and moral development or as a fantastic tale that describes allegorically the European invasion and conquest of Africa.

It's refreshing to see the clichéd and racist symbolism of the white knight reversed. It's also nice to see a woman, Stria, second in command; it would've been even nicer if her character had been developed further. On the quest, Stria serves as a foil to Tarik, for she represents the danger of excessive emotionality, of unbridled bitterness. However, the author attributes this character flaw to El Muerte as well, thereby avoiding stereotyping the female as emotional. Stria is, stereotypically, a nurturer, despite her venom. Again, however, the author defies traditional roles by portraying Docao and Nongo as nurturers, too. But why does God have to be He? It would've also been interesting to see the author experiment more with the conventional dichotomy between day and night, light and dark, good and bad, since he made one of his heroes black and another female.

109. Myers, Walter Dean. *Won't Know till I Get There.* New York: Puffin Books, 1982. 176 pages. ***

Parents' Choice Award, 1982

This book is comprised of journal entries to TWIMSY (To Whom It May Concern) written by fourteen-year-old Stephen Perry, who lives in Harlem. Steve enjoys being an only child until his parents decide to adopt a thirteen-year-old foster child with a criminal record, Earl Goins. Ironically, Steve is the only troublemaker in the story: he spray paints a subway car to impress Earl and gets himself, Earl, and two other friends sentenced to work for the summer in an old-age home, the Micheaux House for Senior Citizens. Steve's journal entries describe his work with the House's six feisty inhabitants who force him to see older people in a new light. His other entries describe his growing appreciation of Earl and his parents— "deep conversations" with Dad and "heart-to-hearts" with Mom. At the end of the summer, Steve encourages his parents to adopt Earl and periodically visits the House's evicted residents, now scattered around the city and country. The lesson he learns from his summer, his final journal entry, is that understanding is essential for living in this world if you want to make it better, but it's impossible to understand some things until later: "I guess I won't know till I get there."

Won't Know till I Get There beautifully assaults the stereotypes and limitations pertaining to young and old folks. It also offers a subtle critique of the bureaucracy, corruption, and idiocy behind many Human Services agencies—in this case, adoption agencies and old folks' homes. Steve's journal entries explore subtly the notions of life and death, love and sex, smarts and craziness, independence and passion—in his family's and his older friends' lives. Myers never gets dogmatic. However, is it believable that a fourteen-year-old boy would be so involved in writing and reflecting in his journal as Steve is?

110. Myers, Walter Dean. *Motown and Didi*. New York: Dell Publishing Co., 1984. 174 pages. *****

Coretta Scott King Award, 1985; New York Times Best Books for Children and Young Adults, 1984

    Motown and Didi is a tender, compassionate story of two black teenagers trying to find love amidst the violence and ruin of Harlem. Motown lives alone in an abandoned building, searching daily for work and visiting the Professor, an African American bookstore owner and visionary. Didi, a high-school senior with dreams of escaping Harlem through a college scholarship, spends her days dreaming, taking care of her ill mother, and trying to get her younger brother Tony off of drugs. One day Motown saves Didi from rape at the hands of vengeful drug pushers, and the two begin a tentative relationship. Didi sees in Motown a trap, anchoring her to the ghetto, but ultimately she cannot deny her love for him. And Motown is willing to make the ultimate sacrifice for Didi—going to kill the drug dealer who gave Tony a fatal overdose. But the Professor steps in, bringing the story to a hopeful and moving ending.
    This is one of the strongest of Walter Dean Myers' novels, offering stunning depth of characters and theme. Motown is thoroughly lovable as a shy but caring African American man whose strength comes from self-reflection, love for his people, and an unwillingness to seek trouble but the courage to face it if it comes calling. Didi and Tony are also entirely believable in their different ways of escaping ghetto life. *Motown and Didi* will appeal to high-school age readers. The plot is tight, and the novel works both as a love story and an adventure story. But this novel has a deeper message than simply surviving the inner city—the Professor tries to teach Motown and Didi that, as African American youth, they are members of a body and the only way to save themselves is to work for the strength and survival of the whole body. That message alone makes the novel special. And heartwarming

characters, realistic dialogue, and believable situations make *Motown and Didi* one of my favorite books.

111. Myers, Walter Dean. *The Outside Shot*. New York: Dell Publishing, 1984. 185 pages. ***

Parents' Choice Award, 1984

The Outside Shot follows Lonnie Jackson, introduced in *Hoops*, as he wins a basketball scholarship to Montclaire State College in Indiana. When Lonnie arrives at Montclaire State, he has to learn a whole new set of rules than those that governed life in Harlem—rules about college basketball, surviving on an all-white campus, keeping up with his classes, and getting close to an African American woman with middle-class pretensions. Along the way, Lonnie forges a friendship with his roommate, Colin, a white farm boy from Illinois. And he becomes a big brother and surrogate father for a young boy, Eddie, who has withdrawn into himself. But Lonnie's biggest tests come when he faces charges of taking money to shave points off his team's score and when he faces the suicide of a would-be basketball player who reminds him of himself. In coming to terms with these events, Lonnie starts to put basketball in perspective and to build a life beyond the game.

The Outside Shot suffers from the same weaknesses as *Hoops*: superficial treatment of the themes and limited character development. Myers fails particularly in his description of female-male relationships; Lonnie's relationship with Sherry lacks depth and motivation, at least until Sherry rescues Lonnie from his despair over point-shaving charges. It's also disturbing that almost no mention is made of Mary-Ann, whom Lonnie was supposedly in love with in *Hoops*, and whom he apparently drops, with no internal conflict, for Sherry. Lonnie's relationship with Eddie is equally unrealistic; it's unlikely and too easy that a boy so withdrawn would respond so quickly to Lonnie's attention. However, the novel does a better job with Lonnie's and Colin's character development, and their relationship is more believable.

Like *Hoops, The Outside Shot* is fast-paced, enjoyable reading in spite of its faults. It is easy enough for junior-high-aged readers, but Lonnie's age (eighteen) and college experiences will interest high-school readers as well. I suspect the book will appeal more to boys than girls, not only because of the men's basketball theme but also because all of the well-developed characters are male.

112. Myers, Walter Dean. *Crystal*. New York: Laurel-Leaf Books, 1987. 198 pages. ***

Parents' Choice Award, 1987

At sixteen, Crystal Brown is a rising star, a model on her way to a movie deal. All of a sudden, people in her Brooklyn neighborhood look at her differently, and she starts to drift away from her old friends and interests. Everybody sees their own dreams in Crystal: her mother, whose dreams of becoming a professional singer ended with pregnancy; her photographer, who hopes to build his career on her success and pressures her to pose nude; the agencies, who see her as a product to be sold for their gain; and the powerful men who control the modeling business and expect sexual favors in exchange for choice assignments. Modeling demands that Crystal fit an exotic, sexy, "not too Black" image that threatens to bury her real identity. She must constantly make choices about what she will compromise and what she will not, as she balances the expectations of her parents, friends, agent, and photographers with her own need for a normal adolescence. In the end, her model friend's suicide clarifies Crystal's own values and gives her the strength to turn back to herself.

Crystal is a realistic, unflattering account of the glamour and dangers of professional modeling. As usual, Walter Dean Myers captures a teenage perspective, exploring adolescent concerns without condescension. He skillfully depicts Crystal's dilemma in making choices for herself and the pressures on her from all sides. At the same time, he draws each character with complexity, avoiding the facile good-bad categories. And like Myers' other novels, *Crystal* ultimately offers a message of hope, as a sixteen-year-old claims her own, innate power and sense of self-respect despite the confusing and demoralizing world around her.

The reading level of the book makes it fine for eighth through eleventh graders, but its focus on modeling and female characters limits its interest for boys. *Crystal* deals sensitively, without sensationalism, with the topics of sexual harassment and economic exploitation. Crystal's African American identity plays a relatively minor role in her modeling career but underscores her personal life and relationships. The novel provides adult role models in Crystal's parents, who are imperfect and struggling but ultimately supportive. Crystal herself is the strongest and wisest character and will appeal particularly to teenage girls.

113. Myers, Walter Dean. *Sweet Illusions.* New York: Teachers and Writers Collaborative, 1987. 142 pages. ****

Sweet Illusions devotes one chapter each to the feelings, reflections, and experiences of eleven teenagers who are dealing with pregnancy. The girls are sixteen to nineteen, African American, white, and Latina and have made a variety of choices about their pregnancies. Gloria gave her baby up for adoption, and now works at the Piedmont Counseling Center, which provides counseling and referral for pregnant girls. Maria, due in one month, hopes to raise her baby with her musician boyfriend Bobby since her father threw her out.

Jennifer, just four months pregnant, is confused about her pregnancy and also about why she had sex with the baby's father in the first place. Sandra, just sixteen years old, is raising her three-year-old son with her mother's help and fears she's pregnant again. And Ellen, whose affair with a married man ended abruptly when she became pregnant, decides to have an abortion. Each girl talks about discovering her pregnancy and the many issues she considered in deciding what to do. The girls also muse about why they decided to have sex and how they feel about themselves and their boyfriends now.

Alternating chapters go inside the heads of the babies' fathers. We hear from Harry, who thinks that becoming a father will give him the motivation to find a job and support his baby. Vernon thinks he's advancing the black nation by creating as many new babies as he can with different mothers, even if he doesn't help raise them. Bobby doesn't know what to think. Although he's not ready to be tied down and doesn't have much to offer, he loves Maria. His little brother Angel, born with disabling spinal curvature, can only dream of loving a woman. Kwame's mad at Gloria for giving "his" baby up for adoption, though he wasn't there for her during the pregnancy or birth. Jerry, the married man, just wants to protect his marriage. Each of the men has somebody to challenge their opinions, to make them think a little harder about what they're doing. "What does it really mean to be a man?" they're asked, "To be a father?" "How did your own father treat you? How did you feel about that?" Some of them move, little by little, toward understanding; some of them run.

Sweet Illusions is many pieces of a kaleidoscope, examining the issues of love, sex, pregnancy and parenting through the experiences of different characters. In a "Seven Years Later" chapter, we get a glimpse of how things turned out for each of them, but only a glimpse. This is somewhat frustrating, but these stories are not about a climax and a resolution, they're about the process of taking stock and making decisions for oneself. At the same time, the stories are very compelling. Each person's character unfolds not only through their thoughts but also through their actions, including flashbacks to earlier choices which brought them to their current dilemma. The characters' voices are extremely authentic, perhaps more so than in any other young adult book I've read. Teenagers *will* see themselves and their friends in this book, even if they have never been pregnant. This is a book for any teen who has had sex, who is thinking of having sex, or who is thinking of postponing sex—in other words, for every teen.

Author Walter Dean Myers' talent at drawing real teenage characters is obvious in *Sweet Illusions*, but he also does an excellent job getting inside both female and male perspectives in this most divisive issue of pregnancy. Furthermore, the book is never preachy, allowing for expression of a wide range of choices while examining the benefits and costs of each. *Sweet Illusions* doesn't preach abstinence, but it does strongly challenge teenagers to think about why they have sex, and to consider whether those reasons are self-affirming or a self-negating surrender to peer pressure. Most of all, the book constantly challenges teens to think and make active choices about their lives.

Each chapter of *Sweet Illusions* ends with a writing exercise asking readers to envision themselves in the character's place. The book introduces this unusual format in an non-threatening way, assuring readers, "You can read the story the way you read any story, or you can help create the story." These exercises are helpful, both as a way to explore the issues brought up by the story and as writing practice. However, some teens may find the exercises corny, and for them they may detract from the immediacy and impact of the story. Whatever the format, though, *Sweet Illusions* demands discussion of these all-too-relevant issues. It offers an excellent lead-in for parents and teachers to open discussion with teens of how they make important choices in their lives about sex, pregnancy, and parenting. And because the book never preaches, it won't alienate teens.

Short chapters and easy reading level make *Sweet Illusions* accessible to readers as young as eleven or twelve, which is an appropriate age to open discussion of sexual decision-making. On the other hand, teens as old as eighteen or nineteen will also find *Sweet Illusions* relevant and illuminating. Both girls and boys will be drawn in by the story. I highly recommend it for any teenager.

114. Myers, Walter Dean. *Fallen Angels*. New York: Scholastic Inc., 1988. 309 pages. ****

Boston Globe-Horn Book Magazine Honor List, 1988; Coretta Scott King Award, 1989; School Library Journal Best Books for Children and Young Adults, 1988

Richie Perry went to Vietnam right after high school, leaving his alcoholic mother and beloved brother Kenny behind in New York City. *Fallen Angels* is the story of his experiences there, as told in his own voice. Describing, alternately, his squad's military actions and the long periods of waiting between battles, Perry chronicles the developing relationships between the soldiers and the ways each of them copes with war. Perry's fear of death pervades the novel, and important questions are raised but left unanswered: Why is the United States at war? Who is the enemy? What is a good enough reason to kill another human being? Why do good people die?

This well-written, fast-paced book is hard to put down. The characters are believable and varied and the dialogue superb. The writing is simple enough for ninth graders but never condescending, and since most of the characters are between seventeen and twenty-three, older students will also identify with them.

Fallen Angels touches upon many vital issues—the futility and tragedy of war, racism within the military, homophobia, coming to terms with death, the lack of economic choices for black civilians, male bonding, and more. However, most of these issues come up in conversation, only to be passed over quickly by men trying to stay alive. While this is undoubtedly a realistic portrayal of soldiers' conversations, I believe the book would have been much stronger if it had gone into these issues in more depth. Half of the soldiers, including Richie Perry, are black; some students of color and working-class students reading this book may be considering enlisting and therefore *Fallen Angels* has a responsibility to raise the moral issues of war in a more compelling way to force students to reconsider their preconceptions about the military. However, despite this flaw, high-school students are bound to enjoy *Fallen Angels* as an adventure story, and they will benefit from its clear-sighted depiction of men under the stress of war.

115.   Myers, Walter Dean. *Me, Mop, and the Moondance Kid.* New York: Delacorte Press, 1988. 154 pages. ***

Eleven-year-old Tommy Jackson, a.k.a. T.J., and his younger brother Billy, a.k.a. Moondance, spent eight years at the Dominican Academy, a home for orphans, until six months ago, when the Williamses adopted them. T.J. tells in the first person the story of one summer spent adjusting to his new home in Lincoln Park, New Jersey, which coincides with the Little League Baseball season. T.J. and Moondance join the Elks team to help Mop, their best friend at the Dominican Academy, who will be sent to another facility with the other orphans when the Academy closes. Mop devises a plan to impress Elks coaches Jim and Marla Kennedy with her athletic abilities so that they will adopt her.

However, nothing turns out as expected. The Williamses run an organized household, with Family Discussion Day, House Day, and Church Day, but being organized doesn't help them cope with the chaos of their adopted children's feelings and thoughts. Mrs. Williams, a teacher, worries excessively. Mr. Williams, a former professional baseball player turned businessman, makes corny jokes and frequently loses his patience. Marla Kennedy becomes the Elks' primary coach and the team performs so well under her less experienced coaching that it goes from last place to first in the league. T.J., who sees himself as the star of the team and expects to impress his new dad with his athletic prowess, proves to be clumsy and scared of the ball, but he blames others or creates elaborate excuses for not catching balls and striking out. In the bleachers, Mrs. Williams takes on T.J.'s disappointment while Mr. Williams looks mortified. Moondance, who initially cared little for baseball, becomes the pitcher and demonstrates talent that impresses Mr. Williams.

Mop, mouthy, tough, manipulative and precocious, becomes so self-conscious because she's worried about impressing the Kennedys, that she is atypically quiet and cries at games. When the Kennedys adopt Mop, she lets down the defenses she'd employed for survival as an orphan and becomes a big baby.

Funny and fast-paced, *Me, Mop, and the Moondance Kid* focuses on baseball but makes serious points about life, too. With its equally strong male and female characters and its clever exploration of adoption and sportsmanship, it is quality reading for third through sixth graders of both sexes. Middle-school readers who aren't offended by the juvenile illustrations will also laugh and ponder over it. Tensions among the Elks, a generally united, multiracial team, arise because of insecurities, jealousies, and frustrations; some of the boys have difficulty accepting the three girl players. Race is never a source of conflict; in fact, the friendship among the three for whom the book is named serves as a paradigm for racial relations. The boys' sexism is dwarfed by that of their archenemy, Mr. Treaster, the coach of the leading team, the Eagles, who mocks the Elks for their female coach and players. The Elks prevail over "evil," though, by beating the Eagles in the championship.

The figure of Mr. Williams allows the author to comment on sex-role stereotyping, providing enough insight into this character so that he remains realistic and understandable.

Mr. Williams is determined to do some male seasoning—"grow up" and "don't be a sissy"—with his sons. He practices baseball roughly with them. He expects T.J. to beat up a bully who beat up Moondance. Mr. Williams becomes so focused on the Elks' winning that T.J. fears he's disappointed with them as sons. Mrs. Williams basically has to raise her husband, with his infantile tantrums and delicate ego, along with their sons.

This novel introduces adoption in an appealing format through occasional vignettes that never lapse into melodrama or heavy reflection. Since his parents died in an accident when he was too young to remember them, T.J. wonders about his "real" parents although he calls the Williamses mom and dad. Unknowing adults remark that the boys look like their adoptive parents. Related to adoption is the strong emphasis on family in the broadest sense. The nurturing and honest relationship between T.J. and Moondance portrays them as best friends as well as brothers. Their experience at the Academy instilled in them an alternative framework for family. Even though they are adopted, they consider their peers from the Academy to be "family forever." They bond with Peaches the wino, as another "homeless" person. The Elks are also like a family. Jim and Marla encourage them to play as a team, focusing more on cooperation and support and less on competition and put-downs. This model works for the Williams family as well. Everyone wins in the end. T.J. and Moondance, whose impetus for playing baseball was to help Mop, symbolize the story's message: the biggest obstacle to winning in life is not "the other team" but oneself, and one should regard another's gain as a blessing and not as one's personal loss.

Several key adult characters distinguish this book: the energetic and progressive nun, Sister Carmelita, who used to play Little League and helps coach the Elks and whose expressions of hope, humility, and patience the orphans mimic in times of crisis; and the homeless wino, Peaches, a former professional baseball player, who helps train the Elks and assists the nuns with a community outreach program. Sister Carmelita and Peaches encourage the boys to be sensitive and socially responsible.

116. Myers, Walter Dean. *Scorpions*. New York: Harper and Row, 1988. 216 pages. ****

American Library Association Notable Books for Children and Young Adults, 1988; John Newbery Honor Book, 1989; New York Times Best Books for Children and Young Adults, 1988

Jamal Hicks is a twelve-year-old who is being inducted into the Scorpions, a Harlem gang. Mack, a Scorpion, convinces Jamal that he must take his brother Randy's place as their leader; Randy is in jail for murder. Jamal's mother, whose temporary jobs force her to leave Jamal and his younger sister Sassie alone for days at a time, focuses her energy on worrying about Randy and trying to raise money for his trial. Jamal, a quiet "mama's boy" interested in art and committed to his family, is an unlikely Scorpion. But Mack forces the gang's sole gun on Jamal, pointing out that he can make enough money with a few Scorpion crack deals to pay for his brother's defense. Jamal's best friend, Tito, a gentle and caring Puerto Rican boy, tries to protect Jamal; as Jamal gets sucked into the gang anyway, he gets in trouble in school, loses his part-time job, and almost shoots someone. When Jamal finally decides to quit the Scorpions, gang members beat him severely and Tito, coming to his defense, shoots one of them in the scuffle. Tito becomes very disturbed, and his grandmother sends him back to his father in Puerto Rico, leaving Jamal to face his life without his only friend.

Scorpions is a tautly-written book which reads quickly, using simple sentences and dialogue to convey complex ideas. It has great character development, keeping its empathic focus on a few tasty characters. For instance, Sassie is an insightful, smart-mouthed third grader whose caring relationship with Jamal is well drawn out. Mama is depicted as a hard-working, exhausted single mother who nonetheless had the strength and self-respect enough to leave her abusive, alcoholic husband. And Tito's character is tender and loyal, going against the tough facade demanded by teenage boy stereotypes. It's nice to see male friends loving one another and to see a single black mother who is not dysfunctional. *Scorpions* also presents positive images of the power of religion and the strength of sibling relationships.

Other interesting issues include a school administration which pegs Jamal as trouble and chooses to sedate him with drugs rather than address his problems, and the recognition that fear rules Jamal's life—fear of violence, fear of not fitting in, fear of admitting to his anger toward and dislike for his father and brother, fear of being alone.

Jamal and Tito, at twelve, are very young for the events happening to them. Although the book is sad, it is ultimately hopeful, with Jamal showing signs of growth and working through his anger toward his father, brother, the gang, and other bullies who have beat him up. For seventh- to tenth-grade students, *Scorpions* is a good choice, although it's not so much about gangs as it is about guns, peer pressure and power.

117. Myers, Walter Dean. *The Mouse Rap*. New York: Harper Trophy, 1990. 186 pages. *

American Library Association Notable Books for Children and Young Adults, 1990; Parents' Choice Award, 1990

Fourteen-year-old Mouse has a whole summer to fill with his friends in Harlem. He devotes much time to playing basketball with his friends Styx and Omega, then gets suckered into practicing dances for a talent show with Sheri and Beverly. Beverly surprises Mouse by proclaiming them boyfriend and girlfriend, but Mouse recovers in time to enjoy making out with her. In fact, he even becomes jealous when Beverly's sights stray to Styx, and for the first time in a long friendship, Mouse and Styx find a wedge driven between them. While Mouse tries to sort out his feelings about that, his "ex-father" comes back into his life after an eight-year absence, with big ideas about winning his Mom back over and being

Mouse's father again. And finally, the whole gang is occupied with searching for treasure left behind somewhere in Harlem by gangster Tiger Moran when he disappeared.

Through a series of twists and turns, Mouse's parents get back together; Styx starts dating Sheri instead of Beverly; Mouse dumps Beverly because he's scared of her pet snake; and the friends find Tiger Moran's treasure—almost $50,000.

The Mouse Rap is a silly book which even as light summer reading will not hold a reader's interest. In fact, I had to force myself to finish it. With a short rap beginning each chapter and a desperate attempt to sound hip, Mouse's voice succeeds only in being annoying. For instance: "The Mouse does not like things that crawl on their belly and do not go woof-woof or tweet, my man, tweet. Nor could the Mouse dig himself in a lip lock with his eyes closed so he could not peep where the creep was creeping." And since Mouse's is the narrative voice, the entire book is written like that.

Although Walter Dean Myers brings up some interesting issues, such as the way male-female friendships change when one friend gets a girlfriend, ultimately, these issues are not enough to save the book. The search for Tiger Moran's treasure is an attempt to rescue the novel from "what I did over the summer vacation" monotony, but this subplot takes a wildly unrealistic turn by having Mouse actually find the $50,000. Myers can write quality books with carefully-crafted plots and complex characters. Unfortunately, *The Mouse Rap* does not display his talent.

The novel's reading level and subject matter make it appropriate for sixth to eighth graders. The primary focus on boys' concerns does not offer female readers much of interest but boys may also find the plot, characters, and dialogue foolish.

118. Myers, Walter Dean. *Mop, Moondance, and the Nagasaki Knights*. New York: Delacorte Press, 1992. 150 pages. ***

In this sequel to *Me, Mop, and the Moondance Kid*, twelve-year-old T.J. details the pre-Little League Baseball season, which revolves around a "goodwill program" to promote international understanding and cooperation. Teams from Mexico (Los Hermanos), France (Les Cavaliers), and Japan (the Nagasaki Knights) play the three best teams in Lincoln Park, New Jersey; the winning American team will travel to Japan to participate in a baseball tournament there. Again, Coach Marla Kennedy tries to teach the team that making friends is more important than winning. However, cultural misunderstandings abound and fights ensue: the French team's Stefan challenges T.J. to a duel; the Japanese team's Akiro challenges Mop to a sumo wrestling match. On the serious side, there is still the sexist and now racist Mr. Teaster who, coveting the championship for his team, the Eagles, tries to change the rules mid-tournament and oust the Japanese team.

Mop carries on her shoulders the burden of proving that girls are "better and smarter" than boys. As if she needed pressure, Jim Kennedy, the Elks' ex-coach and her new father, invests winning with great significance: if people see the champion Elks lose the tournament, then they'll think that the whole country is falling apart. Mr. Williams is still aggressive and short, and T.J. still worries that his dad doesn't like him. Yet Mr. Williams is beginning to redefine his judgment of T.J. as he notices T.J.'s sensitivity and social responsibility. Mrs. Williams is pregnant, and the boys worry about being outdone and replaced by their sibling.

Sister Carmelita and Peaches play lesser roles in this sequel. However, Walter Dean Myers introduces another key character, Gregory. Gregory is mysterious and always mad. The team struggles to deal with him because it needs him—he hits home runs when the Elks are behind in the last inning—but as a "problem" he can't be easily or satisfactorily resolved. When T.J. discovers that Gregory and his mother are homeless, he agonizes. On the theoretical level, he grapples for understanding: life is unfair. On the practical level, he wants to get involved, but he doesn't want to interfere, to "get another kid in trouble," a lesson from his orphan days. Peaches assures T.J. that it's better to do something—even though it's hard and the results may be mixed—than it is to do nothing but worry and talk. Finally, T.J. asks his father for help, risking that he'll lose control to an adult/authorities. The boys identify with and feel scared for Gregory, who is temporarily separated from his mother and placed in a children's shelter. They also dread Gregory's anger at them for trying to solve his problem.

Walter Dean Myers manages to sustain the strength of *Me, Mop, and the Moondance Kid* in every respect in this sequel. With its exciting descriptions of baseball games, its ongoing exploration of adoption, its jabs at racial, sexual, and economic injustice, *Mop, Moondance, and the Nagasaki Knights* offers thoughtful reading on an easy level. Because it contains no illustrations and its protagonist is twelve, it will appeal to middle-school students more than its predecessor. Girls will appreciate the spunky Marla and Mop. Boys will appreciate the range of strong and sensitive male characters. This book will appeal more to wanna-be athletes than to serious jocks since, for all of T.J.'s boasting, it's clear that he's more bumbler than superstar. And all readers will relish Mr. Treaster's defeat.

The author starts and finishes the story with a serious framework: when Carla explains that the Japanese team comes from a city on which the United States dropped an atomic bomb during World War II, the players struggle to understand the why and how of America's behavior. After T.J. reports Gregory's homelessness, the mayor's office and the nuns help Gregory's mother find work, but she has a hard time holding onto a job; T.J. learns about the myriad obstacles to her struggle to become stable and establish a home. For both of these subplots, the story offers no easy solutions, just the message that understanding and social action are necessary.

119.   Myers, Walter Dean. *The Righteous Revenge of Artemis Bonner*. New York: Harper Collins Publishers, 1992. 140 pages.
***

American Library Association Notable Books for Children and Young Adults, 1992

As a western, this novel is unique in the field of young adult literature. The story is recorded in the first person by fifteen-year-old Artemis Bonner of New York City. He describes his trials and tribulations of 1880-1882. His Aunt Mary offers him a two hundred dollar reward for killing her husband's murderer, Catfish Grimes, and for figuring out how to decipher a treasure map her husband left behind. Since Catfish copied the map, Artemis must race to find the treasure first. He and his partner, twelve-year-old half-Cherokee Laughing Bear, a.k.a. Frolic D. Brown, chase Catfish and his girlfriend Lucy Featherdip, to Tombstone, Arizona; Lincoln, New Mexico; Juarez City, Mexico; Sacramento, California; Seattle, Washington; Anchorage, Alaska; San Francisco, California; and back to Tombstone.

The story climaxes with a shoot-out between Artemis and Catfish. Artemis shoots before Catfish finishes counting to three and, seemingly, manages to kill Catfish. Burnt out from the road, Artemis and Frolic settle for revenge but give up the search for the treasure, and they return to New York City to work for a trading company. Just as they are reacclimating to "civilization," Artemis receives a letter from Lucy in which she explains the shoot-out was a hoax designed to shake Artemis, that Catfish is alive and enjoying the treasure, and that, much to her chagrin, he is enjoying the treasure with another woman. Lucy propositions Artemis: kill Catfish and his new girlfriend, claim the treasure, and take Lucy along. Angry, Artemis plans to kill Catfish but not to take Lucy for a girlfriend.

Walter Dean Myers goes to great lengths to detail Artemis' modes of travel and his accommodations. The travelogue affords the author an opportunity to take readers back to a different time and place, but more importantly, to emphasize the presence of African Americans in the West and explore integration and segregation in this territory. The foreground of the story is silly, but the background is interesting historical fiction.

The author debunks stereotypical notions of Indians. Every time Artemis sees and fears Indians because he's heard that they're wild and murderous, nothing happens, and the naiveté and ineptitude of Indian character Frolic disproves Artemis' assumption that Indians are "natural" fighters and trackers. Myers also pokes fun at Artemis' sexist notions. Each time Artemis catches Catfish, he fails to kill him or leave him for dead because he underestimates Catfish's partner, Lucy. Artemis considers Lucy, because she's a woman, to be innocuous and weak; however, every time she goes on the counteroffensive, she rescues Catfish and seriously wounds Artemis with her biting, spitting, clawing, kicking, and punching.

The Righteous Revenge of Artemis Bonner exhibits the stock elements of a western, with its battle between good and evil, but it's a light book. Myers introduces the comic ingredient of Artemis' antiquated voice, which lends authenticity and develops character: Artemis is a religiously strict, overprotected boy who misses his mother; he experiences a tension in values, for the code of behavior required to survive in the West contradicts his upbringing. The humor is funny but not slapstick. The plot takes several turns, keeping it varied, unpredictable, and engaging. While Artemis' circumstances and voice seem older than, but not implausible for his fifteen years, his naiveté and playfulness make him seem younger. Therefore, this novel will appeal more to readers in sixth through eighth grades. Although the protagonist is a boy, girls will also enjoy the action, particularly the heroics of Lucy Featherdip.

120. Myers, Walter Dean. *Somewhere in the Darkness*. New York: Scholastic, Inc., 1992. 168 pages. ***

American Library Association Notable Books for Children and Young Adults, 1992; Boston Globe-Horn Book Magazine Honor List, 1992; Coretta Scott King Honor Book, 1993; School Library Journal Best Books for Children and Young Adults, 1992

    Jimmy Little, nearly fifteen, is almost flunking out of tenth grade. He just can't seem to get up his interest enough to go to school after his Mama Jean leaves for work in the mornings. Mama Jean is not Jimmy's real mother, who died when he was young; he can't remember his father, who's been in prison for many years. Then one day, his father Crab shows up on Jimmy's doorstep in New York City, claiming that he's out on parole and wants to start a new life with Jimmy in Chicago. Sick at leaving Mama Jean, Jimmy nevertheless joins Crab on a cross-country trek that ultimately takes them to Marion, Tennessee, where Crab grew up. Along the way, Jimmy gradually learns more about his father: that he is dying of kidney failure, that he is not on parole but, rather, broke out of prison to meet his son again before he dies. Crab wants desperately to convince Jimmy that he is innocent of the killings for which he was convicted and jailed. Jimmy wants desperately to forge some bond with the stranger who claims to be his father. They have only started to rebuild their relationship when Crab is re-arrested and dies shortly afterward, handcuffed to a hospital bed. Jimmy returns to New York changed, vowing to be an honest, compassionate father to his own future children.
    Somewhere in the Darkness' greatest strength is its characters, particularly the contradictory Crab—in turn, desperate for his son's respect and the meaning it will bestow on his life and then seemingly preoccupied by unrealistic dreams of easy money and easy relationships. Jimmy's confusion about his father is very realistic—his longing for closeness alternating with anger at his earlier abandonment and confusion over the rapid changes sweeping through his life. The entire story occurs over the course of just four days.

Although I have few specific criticisms of *Somewhere in the Darkness*, it does not have the power of some of Walter Dean Myers' other novels, such as *Fallen Angels* or *Motown and Didi*. On the other hand, it is a precise snapshot of a troubled father-son relationship and the painful process of trying to re-establish a relationship that has been missing for so long. The novel plays into the stereotypical dead mother/irresponsible, criminal father model so common in African American young adult fiction, though Myers does attempt to transform Crab a little with a dying wish to gain his son's respect. Mama Jean's character is strong and positive. But this book is really about the men. For that reason, boys will enjoy it more than girls. The reading level is appropriate for seventh to eleventh graders. The straightforward writing style and basic vocabulary make the book accessible for middle-school readers, while the complex characters and relationships will hold older readers' interest.

Myers, Walter Dean. See also the *18 Pine St.* series, listed under Stacie Johnson: written by Stacie Johnson, "created" by Walter Dean Myers

121. Petry, Ann. *Harriet Tubman: Conductor on the Underground Railroad*. New York: Pocket Books, 1971. 227 pages. ****

Minta or Minty Ross, born in 1820, in Cambridge, Maryland, became a legend in her own time: Harriet Tubman. Ann Petry vividly portrays Harriet Tubman the girl and woman—how she lived over the years, her physical features, clothing, speaking voice, and manner of carrying herself. The author details Harriet Tubman's joy in family and nature, the momentary delights of holidays, good news and the end of the work day, as well as her omnipresent fear of being sold away from her family. Petry recounts the repeated hiring-outs and abuses Harriet Tubman suffered in her childhood and the ongoing, tortuous debate within herself over whether to run away. The reader hears, along with the slaves, the rumors and news reports of slave uprisings and escapes and the slave masters' responses to them.

Although the book is about Harriet Tubman, its scope and setting are multidimensional and broader, telling the story of Harriet Tubman, her family, and other people within their orbit, plus legendary figures contemporary with, but far removed from Tubman. Each chapter ends with an italicized passage that relates anti-slavery advocates and incidents of which Harriet was, at the time, unaware, but which set in motion the bigger movement of which she was to become a part. The narrative shows how, as an adult, she grows in stature through her work as a conductor on the Underground Railroad, a speaker on the antislavery society circuit, a scout and nurse for the Union Army during the Civil War, and a campaigner for women's rights and poor people after the official abolition of slavery by the Thirteenth Amendment.

With the gripping ups and downs of adventure and the brilliant plotting of a suspense thriller, *Harriet Tubman: Conductor on the Underground Railroad* is a superb work of historical fiction, accessible and thoroughly appealing to middle-school and high-school readers. Ann Petry writes as if she were there, in a unique blend of intimate journal entries and newspaper articles. Throughout the narrative, the author relies on conversations, dreams, metaphors, prayers, premonitions, and songs to capture her protagonist's emotional and spiritual essence, her indomitable spirit and unshakable faith in God, as well as to elicit an emotional response in the reader. Though told in the third person, the stories Harriet Tubman tells the runaways to instill confidence, keep faith, and assuage fear have the immediacy and personality of a first-person voice.

Frequently, Tubman expresses awe for the white abolitionists; Ann Petry emphasizes the heroism of white abolitionists in the purely historical passages with which she concludes each chapter. While it is important for readers to know that not all white people were slave masters or their allies, it does not seem necessary for the author to go to such great lengths to pay homage to white people, primarily white men, in a book honoring a black woman.

Family is a central concern in the novel: it elaborates on the characters' powerlessness to protect loved ones and the pain of separation from family more than on their physical abuse and exploitation—an excellent choice, for it is guaranteed to pull on readers' heartstrings and facilitate their identifying with the story. The narrative strives to develop the characters of Harriet Tubman's concerned and caring parents, Old Rit and Ben Ross, and, reciprocally, the character of Harriet Tubman as the devoted daughter keeping her parents foremost in her mind until their rescue and death. Family has a negative side, too. Harriet Tubman's betrayal by her husband, John Tubman, whom she loves all of her lonely life, is wrenching. The legendary hero compensates by thereafter broadening her purpose to serve strangers instead of just family. In retrospect Harriet Tubman's triumphs seem bittersweet in light of her sacrifices. *Harriet Tubman: Conductor on the Underground Railroad* is not guts-and-glory history but superb storytelling which gives an accurate picture of slavery and of Harriet Tubman, an extraordinary, all too human person.

122. Petry, Ann. *Tituba of Salem Village*. New York: Harper Trophy, 1991. 254 pages. ****

Tituba of Salem Village is fascinating historical fiction based on the life of Tituba Indian, the only slave to be arrested during the Salem witch trials. Tituba and her husband John are sold from warm Barbados to freezing Massachusetts to pay off their mistress' gambling debts. Tituba finds herself in charge of the stern, mean-spirited Reverend Parris' household, including his bed-ridden wife, frail daughter Betsey, and resentful orphaned niece Abigail. Although her new life in the colonies of 1692 is dreary, filled with long winters and hard work, Tituba finds small pleasures in learning to weave, in Betsey's love, in John's stories by the fire, and in her ability to heal people by using herbal medicines and caring.

Soon, though, the furor of the witch hunt sweeps Salem Village, fueled by the mad fits and accusations of Abigail and other orphaned nieces and bound girls, misfits all. Abigail, resentful of Tituba's tenderness toward her younger cousin Betsey, has Tituba arrested. With other hapless Salem women, Tituba stands trial for witchcraft and is imprisoned under the harshest conditions. While some are hanged, Tituba's magic thunderstone reassures her that she will survive. Survive she does, to make a new life for herself and her husband with a kindly Boston weaver who has believed in Tituba all along and ultimately redeems her from prison.

Tituba of Salem Village is the only young adult story which treats the Salem witch hunt from a black perspective. Tituba's disenfranchisement as a slave and a black woman enables her to see the power which other disenfranchised females—orphans and poor bound girls—gain by their accusations of witchcraft. Her biggest mistake is in not taking the accusations seriously and in assuming that other adults will see through them as easily as she does. Once she is charged, however, Tituba saves her husband with cleverness and herself with endurance.

Teenagers will enjoy this book, with its absorbing plot and its setting in a grotesquely fascinating chapter in American history. Ann Petry evokes colonial America exquisitely and adds the historical correction of a slave perspective to an era that is often falsely portrayed as only Puritan and white. Since most of the characters are women and girls, female readers may identify with the story slightly more than males, although there are a number of strong male characters as well. The book's vocabulary is not particularly difficult, but its length will limit its readership to seventh to eleventh graders.

The protagonist, Tituba, is portrayed as a strong African-Caribbean woman bound by her times, first by slavery and then by imprisonment. Petry emphasizes both her protagonist's strengths and the limits—Tituba's insight and her supportive marriage to John help her survive, but like any slave, she does not emerge unscathed. This is an honest but not depressing book and an important contribution to young adult literature and historical fiction in general. Young adult readers will be lucky to discover it.

123. Prather, Ray. *Fish and Bones*. New York: Harper Collins Publishers, 1992. 255 pages. **

School Library Journal Best Books for Children and Young Adults, 1992

Sun City is normally a quiet, hot Florida town. But the summer of Bones' thirteenth year, somebody robs the Bank of Sun City, and a one thousand dollar reward is offered to whoever solves the crime. Toad Man, the lazy, smelly assistant to Bones' garbage-collecting father, convinces Bones to help him find the culprit. Soon, stolen money from the bank starts turning up in odd places: in the pockets of local punks, on the floor of Skip Goodweather's car during his wedding ceremony, and even in Reverend Black's possession. Bones and Toad Man follow one clue after another, eliminating suspects until they zero in on the probable thief.

Meanwhile, Bones becomes closer to Fish Baker and his older brother, Mose, just back from the Marines. Since Fish suffered brain damage in a prank accident, many townspeople have made fun of him or taken advantage of his gullible willingness to do anything they asked. But not Bones, who has always been nice to Fish. Mose, fiercely protective of his younger brother, rewards Bones' kindness by spending time with the younger boy. As the summer progresses, Bones learns the horrible truth about the lynching of Mose and Fish's father, and their certainty that many prominent white men in town participated in the killing. This knowledge helps Bones solve the bank robbery—as the stolen bills always turn up to embarrass people Mose suspects of lynching his father or ridiculing his brother. Before Bones can uncover the stolen money, however, Fish and Mose both die in a dramatic climax which has black and white townspeople working desperately to try to save them from a rushing river.

Fish and Bones is a strange book, entertaining as a mystery with quirky, small-town characters but interspersing strains of morbid seriousness. The growing "big-brother" relationship between Bones and Mose is developed nicely, as is Bones' struggle to come to terms with the deadly racism of foolish but seemingly innocuous white townspeople. However, the crashing climax simply does not work. Serious treatment of a lynching stretches the reach of what is otherwise a lighthearted mystery, but it almost works in the context of Bones' finding out more about his neighbors through investigating the robbery. Killing off two of the three main characters abruptly shifts the tone of the novel to no apparent purpose. Scant attention is paid to Bones' reaction to the deaths, and, frankly, I can't understand why Ray Prather decided to kill these characters unless it was the simplest (if most unsatisfying) way to solve the mystery without any character facing judgment. Until this essential flaw, *Fish and Bones* offers fun reading.

Although the book's characters are almost exclusively male, girls and boys can enjoy the humor and the fanciful adventures of Bones. Because of the book's length, its reading level is appropriate for seventh- to tenth-grade readers. I hope that Prather will write more mystery adventures of Bones in Sun City, foregoing overly dramatic and somber plot resolutions in favor of lighter solutions more consistent with the entertaining mystery genre.

124. Robinet, Harriette Gillem. *Children of the Fire*. New York: Atheneum, 1991. 134 pages. ***

In 1871, eleven-year-old Hallelujah witnesses the Great Chicago Fire. Hallelujah is an orphan whose mother, before she died, transported her family from southern slavery to Chicago on the Underground Railroad. Although Hallelujah and her older sister live with loving African American foster parents, she nevertheless feels inferior being an orphan. The Great Fire changes all that. Alone on the street, Hallelujah first approaches the Fire as a festive spectacle, entertainment on a dry summer's night. In the confusion, she meets and talks to people from whom she would normally be separated by race, class, and age: a Jewish immigrant girl, poorer even than Hallelujah; Hope, a graceful older lady whose outlook matches her name; a German worker going crazy because he has lost his shop and his family in the Fire; and most importantly, a wealthy white girl, Elizabeth, whose preoccupation with life's meaning matches Hallelujah's own. As the Fire turns deadly, Hallelujah and Elizabeth join forces, moving towards the river and trying to help people as they go. Meanwhile, together they try to understand the societal forces that have kept them apart.

Hallelujah inadvertently becomes a hero by rescuing a huge bag of money from the local bank. The money is used to start rebuilding Chicago, giving Hallelujah's poor but proud immigrant neighbors work for the first time in years. Meanwhile, Hallelujah's foster mother provides food and shelter to black and white folks left homeless by the fire. When Elizabeth's parents finally locate her at Hallelujah's house, they whisk her away, but she and Hallelujah promise not to let society's walls come up between them. Thanks to her experiences in the Fire, Hallelujah grows to understand that her worth as a person is internal, not dependent on her status as a poor child, or an orphan, or an African American.

With an eleven-year-old protagonist and at just 134 pages, *Children of the Fire* is geared toward younger readers, grades four to six. However, Hallelujah's self-awareness and her articulate musings about her self-worth would be more realistic in an older character, even making adjustments for the nineteenth century setting. This is my only criticism of the book, though. In all other ways, *Children of the Fire* is a delight, impassioned, thought-provoking, and engrossing. The Fire itself makes for a compelling plot, and the stream of characters Hallelujah encounters are entertaining and believable. With the exception previously noted, Hallelujah's own character is a fine example of a young adolescent struggling for identity and self-worth, expressing herself alternately in rebellion and cooperation, thoughtfulness and impulsivity.

Harriette Robinet does a great job exploring the issues of class in a northern industrial city. The Sullivans next door, proud of their status as "workingmen," are too ashamed to acknowledge the hot soup Hallelujah leaves by their door each night to feed them during their father's unemployment. Hallelujah's foster father is a self-employed shoemaker, giving him a level of autonomy and financial security unknown to most blacks and allowing his family to help those less fortunate. And just when Hallelujah sees Chicago mansions and realizes how much richer some white folks are, so does she see the Fire destroying homes of rich and poor equally, reinforcing the lesson that only who she is inside determines her value.

Although all of the main characters are female, Hallelujah is still in the largely androgynous stage of early adolescence, and little of her character depends on being a girl. This, combined with the fast-paced adventurous plot, gives the story appeal for boys as well as girls at an intermediate reading level. The historical setting reads authentically but will not interfere with contemporary readers seeing themselves in Hallelujah's shoes. *Children of the Fire*, equal parts adventure story and morality tale, will entertain and educate.

125. Shepard, Ray Anthony. *Conjure Tales*. New York: E.P. Dutton and Co., 1973. 99 pages. ****

In *Conjure Tales*, Ray Shepard reworks six classic stories originally written and published by Charles Chesnutt in 1899. Set in pre-Civil War North Carolina and narrated by a former slave named Uncle Julius, the stories "reveal much about slavery, in a way that a tired old history book can never do [and] make for good reading," which is why the author resurrected and revised them for contemporary readers.

Sandy, the enslaved protagonist of "Poor Sandy," panics when Master Marlboro plans to hire him out to a plantation far from his wife, Tenie. So Tenie uses her conjure powers to keep Sandy with her: she turns him into a tree and spends her nights sleeping by him. But greedy Master Marlboro devises multiple uses for the big pine tree, ultimately chopping it down for wood to build himself a new kitchen. Tenie, powerless to intervene, goes to the sawmill to bid good-bye to Sandy. Thereafter she spends her time on the kitchen steps, talking to Sandy's spirit. No one else will go near the kitchen, including Master Marlboro, for it seems haunted, "moaning and groaning, hollering and squeaking like it was in great pain and suffering."

In "The Conjurer's Revenge," Primus, a clubfooted slave, claims a stray pig which, unbeknownst to him, belongs to a conjure man. The conjure man converts Primus into a mule and sells the mule to Primus' Master McGee. The slaves notice "queer things" about the mule: he munches on the tobacco crop, slops in the wine press, and attacks Dan, his wife's new love interest. Meanwhile, the conjure man "gets religion" and decides to undo the harm he caused Primus. Unfortunately, the conjure man dies before he completes his reversion of Primus, and Primus returns to Master McGee's plantation with one mule foot, an appropriate symbol of his stubbornness and wildness.

Dan, a slave, in "The Gray Wolf's Haint," kills a conjurer's son for flirting with his girlfriend, Mahaly. Knowing that it is only a matter of time before the conjurer seeks revenge, Dan acquires a life-charm from conjurer Aunt Peggy. However, the conjure man cleverly locates and destroys Dan's life-charm, then begins to slowly torture Dan mentally and physically. Eventually, he deceives Dan into attributing his troubles to a black cat. The conjure man transforms Mahaly into a black cat and Dan into a wolf, so that Dan as a wolf unknowingly slaughters Mahaly. Thereafter, Dan howls by her grave for eternity.

Master James McLean of "Master James' Nightmare" is an intensely cruel slave master. Spurned by Miss Libbie of a nearby plantation, he punishes a slave couple for their romantic bliss by whipping the man and selling away the woman. The man, Solomon, seeks help from conjure woman Aunt Peggy to help him reunite with his lover. Aunt Peggy creates a spell and Master McLean rapidly undergoes a metamorphosis: he fires the wicked overseer, moderates the slaves' workload, grants them more social functions, and, eventually, allows Solomon to "fetch" his lover. In the end, Miss Libbie changes her mind about Master McLean and renews their courtship.

Wine maker Master Dugal hires Aunt Peggy to conjure his grapevines so that the slaves will stop consuming his livelihood in "The Goophered Grapevine." A new hand, Henry, unwittingly feasts on the grapes and falls prey to the hex. Aunt Peggy advises him to protect himself from the conjure by smearing on his scalp the oozing sap from the vines that he prunes; the sap revitalizes Henry so dramatically that Master Dugal hires him out for a stupendous profit. The conjure triumphs, however, in the form of a Yankee who persuades Master Dugal to try a different farming method which will increase his harvest and, thus, his profits. But the method causes the grapes to die and, without their sap, Henry dies, too.

In "Hot-Foot Hannibal," Master Dugal grooms Hannibal to become his house slave and the husband of his wife's house slave, Chloe. Chloe prefers field slave Jeff. So she and Jeff obtain a conjure doll from Aunt Peggy that burns Hannibal's mind and feet, driving him to work so distractedly and clumsily that Master Dugal returns Hannibal to the field and auditions Jeff for the job. In the field, the conjure wears off, Hannibal untangles the mystery of his troubles and avenges them by tricking Chloe into believing that Jeff has another lover. Chloe, driven by hurt and jealousy, betrays Jeff and Master Dugal sells him away. When Chloe learns of Hannibal's cunning and Jeff's suicide, she dies of grief, her spirit waiting by the willow tree for Jeff's return.

Conjure Tales ends on a happy note. Colonel Penleton of "Sister Becky's Child" trades Sister Becky for a horse he fancies, separating her from her beloved son, Mose. Aunt Peggy reunites mother and son by making the horse and Sister Becky sick, so both parties want a refund. Sister Becky returns to Colonel Penleton's plantation where she and Mose thrive. When Mose grows up, he buys their freedom.

Ray Shepard creates the impression of a folk storyteller who puts the reader under the narrator's spell with authentic-sounding syntax and colloquialisms woven seamlessly into the prose. The end result is especially accessible, graceful storytelling. The stories are at once poignantly horrifying and humorous, with their commentary on slavery running immediately below the surface. The use of conjure obviously symbolizes the slaves' utmost desire: freedom; through conjure, the slaves manage a modicum of resistance. The stories' minor subplots further testify to the slaves' other strategies of resistance, such as deceit, fawning, sabotaging work productivity, and running away. It is no coincidence that all of the conjurers are free blacks.

Ray Shepard's spotlight on resistance provides a moving and suspenseful antidote to typical stories about slavery. Another corrective to the generally inadequate history of slavery is the appearance of free black characters in every story, a reminder that the pre-Civil War African American experience includes much more than the experience of slavery. Through the presence of poor white characters, regarded as "trash" by slave masters and slaves alike, the author rightfully complicates the dichotomy between black and white, inserting class as well as race into the dynamics of slavery. And the inclusion of house slaves versus field slaves adds another dimension to the hierarchies and antagonisms on the plantation.

Although the stories' plots rely on the supernatural, their themes concern the human realm. They emphasize the slaves' humanity—primarily their intense emotionality and strong bonds of love—in stark contrast to the inhumanity of the slave masters, who arrange and destroy the slaves' relationships thoughtlessly, to make a profit.

Young adults will pick up the book simply for its stated subject matter, conjure, i.e., hoodoo or voodoo. In every story, a conjure doctor creates a goopher mixture which transforms people to save or punish them. Although only two of the stories feature women as the key protagonists, women are a strong presence in this collection as powerful conjurers, mates, and mothers, and the equality of the sexes when it comes to possessing supernatural powers is refreshing. *Conjure Tales* will appeal to middle-school and high-school students of both sexes, and it will slyly educate as it entertains. Although its illustrations suggest a young readership, the book is wholly appropriate for older readers, too.

126. Shepard, Ray Anthony. *Sneakers.* New York: E.P. Dutton and Co., 1973. 103 pages. ***

Thirteen-year-old Chuck lives with his mother in public housing in Roxbury, a black section of Boston. It is the early 1970s and Chuck is one of the first black students to be bused out to Lexington, a predominantly white, wealthy Boston suburb. But Chuck doesn't feel lucky about the opportunity. He hates the long bus ride and the feeling of being on exhibit. Chuck is bored in school, but classes are peripheral anyway. Being the star of the eighth grade football team is Chuck's raison d'être, and each game gives him a chance to prove himself. This year's team has some exceptional talent, but co-captains Chuck and Craig, who's white, finish every practice fighting. Incapable of changing Craig, Chuck focuses on another problem that he can fix, getting a new pair of cleats to replace the raggedy, tread-worn sneakers he has. With new sneakers, he will be able to magically compensate for the team's weaknesses in their big game against the ninth graders. Chuck dreams of long-term, long-shot possibilities from this game— being seen by high school coaches from all over the city, becoming a high-school football star, then a college all-American, and eventually a pro.

However, Chuck's mother doesn't have money for anything that's not absolutely necessary. Each discussion between mother and son leaves both feeling misunderstood and hurt, until his mother finally promises to juggle bills and buy him the new sneakers if the welfare check arrives in time for the game. The welfare check arrives, but it's the wrong amount, and Chuck's mother can't buy him new sneakers. He wants them so badly that he steals money his mother had set aside for groceries and buys the cleats. In the end, though, the new cleats are either stolen or misplaced before the game, and Chuck ends up playing in his cruddy sneakers after all. However, Craig and Chuck get beyond their power struggle and work as a team; Chuck scores the winning touchdown and realizes "the magic was in *him*," not the sneakers. After the game, the janitor finds Chuck's new sneakers, and Chuck vows to find work to repay his mother.

Sneakers is easy to read, with short chapters that focus generally on only one occurrence. Although the references to hairstyles, sneaker models, and popular music date the book, its essential message is timeless. It's disturbing that a book written roughly twenty years ago should be even more appropriate today; the fixation of many of today's youth on designer athletic gear, especially fancy sneakers, would put Chuck, with his basic bargain-sale cleats, to shame.

Since almost half the book is about boys and football, girls will probably not care as much for the story as boys will. However, the only adolescent female character, Thelma, will be easy for female readers to identify with. She's bright, scrappy, attractive, and comfortable with herself—and puts Chuck in his place when he displays irresponsibility and immaturity. Ray Shepard does a good job of delineating the developmental differences between young adolescent boys and girls through his description of Chuck and Thelma's friendship. Meanwhile, Chuck's male friends, who ride the bus with him from Roxbury, make the point that material possessions matter much less than integrity, community, and talent.

As for Chuck's mother, the author works her into the story skillfully to help get his message across about personal responsibility and self-honesty. Almost everything Chuck's mother tries to teach him goes right over his head: "He knew he didn't want to hear any lectures. He figured maybe that's the way parents are. Give you something, then want to lecture you about it until they feel you've paid for it." But this attitude is part of what makes the story so realistic and Chuck so easy to identify with. Yet, through occasional passages of terse dialogue, Chuck's mother emerges as a very real, loving, pragmatic, and moral woman who has her son's best interests in mind. She's not intentionally harsh and she's not passive, although she is relatively powerless in the face of the mega-bureaucracy of public assistance. It is to the author's credit that the arguments between mother and son will draw in young readers rather than turn them off. *Sneakers* is an upbeat story that offers action and a moral message in a most enjoyable manner.

127. Smothers, Ethel Footman. *Down in the Piney Woods*. New York: Alfred A. Knopf, 1992. 151 pages. ***

Ten-year-old Annie Rye Footman narrates the major and mundane events of one fateful summer in the 1950s, when her half-sisters come to the Footmans' sharecropping farm in rural Climax, Georgia, to stay forever. Prior to the half-sisters' arrival, Annie Rye displayed the typical oldest child behaviors of self-possession and precocity, bossing around her younger brother and hogging her parents' attention. Annie Rye will not allow herself to be forced to assume middle child status, to share her family, her bed, her chair at the table, and her chores without a fight. She behaves deviously, selfishly, and sometimes cruelly, despite her half-sisters' overtures of friendship.

Finally, the children become a family as they scrape together enough money to buy a baseball uniform as a surprise for Daddy (the star pitcher in a recreational league). The collective effort teaches Annie Rye that she can do almost anything when she sets her mind to it, including becoming "a family."

Altercations with new white supremacist neighbors, the sharecropping Lampkin family, also pit the Footman siblings together as a team. Lampkin is fired from his job at the sugarcane mill following a cross burning in front of the Footmans' house, which serves to further stoke the white family's hatred of the Footmans. In the tense climax of the story, Daddy saves baby Sissy Lampkin out of a well right after the senior Lampkin tries to stab him with a pitchfork.

Unlike Mama, who prefers to tolerate trouble hoping it will go away of its own accord, Daddy seizes opportunities to tackle problems head on. He demands respectful treatment from the few white folks with whom he has to interact—the boss at the sugarcane factory, the doctor, and Lampkin—and he stands friendly but steadfast in these encounters.

Although the trouble with Lampkin is certainly far more serious than Annie Rye's trouble with her siblings, the author indulges it only sporadically and the white world otherwise seems a planet away from the Footmans' remote enclave "down in the piney woods." The children's sheltered life emerges as the dominant theme, not their poverty or hardships. Annie Rye's narrative mainly dwells on the daily routine of farm chores, housecleaning and chasing wayward pigs; the diversions of fishing, making grass dolls and buying penny candy from the "rolling store"; and special problems such as Brother's double pneumonia, the death of Miz Soota, the prize breeding pig, and snakes invading the house.

Ethel Smothers indicates that this work is a fictionalized recollection of her childhood. Her personal connection to the novel's characters and plots and her solid storytelling ability join forces to produce a very good book. She allows the reader to see and share Annie Rye's slow maturation. The protagonist's storytelling style is matter of fact more often than dramatic. At times wise beyond her years—but believably so—Annie Rye draws out lessons from the natural world and from her Granddaddy's poetic folklore. In the tradition of Zora Neale Hurston, Smothers seamlessly weaves folklore and music into the story. Furthermore, she renders the characters' language effectively, and she keeps the story flowing with their lively dialogues.

For young readers who require a lot of stimulation, *Down in the Piney Woods* will be too slow. Temporary suspensions of the plot, unfamiliar expressions, and the transliteration of the dialogue may present challenges. Overall, however, this is a clear and engaging narrative that brings alive a way of life that will be alien to most readers. Readers who enjoy historical fiction and who don't require a city setting will enjoy this novel. Because the novel's perspective and protagonist belong to a ten-year-old girl, preteen readers will best appreciate her story. Fifth- to seventh-grade girls are the best candidates for this book's readership, but its lessons and the sense of time and place it evokes don't rule it out for older readers.

128. Steptoe, John. *Marcia*. New York: Puffin Books, 1976. 69 pages. **

Marcia is a fifteen-year-old smart-talking girl from Brooklyn. This novel focuses on her relationship with her boyfriend Dan—their growing closeness and their decision (well, mostly his pushing and her submitting) to have sex. Marcia agonizes for some time over the decision, resisting at first, talking to her mother and her friend Millie about it, and then deciding to "let it happen."

Sex is a vitally important theme for young adult readers, but few African American young adult authors deal with it. *Marcia* deals honestly with a young woman's feelings and confusion about sex and also offers a glimpse of a teenage boy's perspective. The novel is so short that it tends to skim over many aspects of its theme, but at least it acknowledges the jumble of mixed motivations that goes into teenagers' sexual decision-making.

Marcia is outspoken and opinionated, a typical adolescent. Her mother is strong and supportive—a rare depiction of a positive single mother—and as the voice of reality, I wish she had played a bigger part in the novel. One strength of *Marcia* is its lack of didacticism. It skillfully represents typical adolescent views on relationships, sex, birth control, and the overconfidence of youth (for instance, Marcia insists that if she did get pregnant, she could handle raising a child and supporting herself and still go to college, no problem!). However, this wholly adolescent perspective is also a potential problem—young readers may find confirmation of their own misconceptions in Marcia's voice (e.g., teenage sex is "inevitable," the diaphragm is disgusting, fifteen-year-olds can handle pregnancy and childrearing responsibilities).

Despite its strengths, it's not clear what age is right for this book. Its short length, large print, and simplified plot are appropriate for fourth to sixth graders, but its theme applies more to junior and senior high school students. The dialogue—street talk and sexual precociousness—will be most relevant to urban readers. However, readers will be disappointed with the ending: a cutesy rhyming poem informs us that Marcia "let 'it' happen," but the book offers no information about the experience toward which the narrative has been leading (and which is probably one of the key reasons readers would choose this book) or Marcia's feelings about it. Sex and sexual decision-making could have and should have been explored much more fully for a young adult audience.

129. Strickland, Dorothy, ed. *Listen, Children: An Anthology of Black Literature.* New York: Bantam Books, 1982. 132 pages.
****

Here is an eclectic and thoughtful anthology of twentieth-century writings by African Americans from Verna Aardema's "Ol-Ambu and He-of-the-Long-Sleeping-Place" (1905) and Langston Hughes' "My People" (1926) to Wilma Rudolph's *Wilma* (1977) and Eloise Greenfield's "Way Down in the Music" (1978). The anthology's forty selections are organized thematically into four sections—"Feeling the Joy of Being Me," "Feelings About My Roots: Folktales and Folkways," "Feeling the Pain and Pride of Struggle," and "Feelings About Who I Am and What I Want to Be"—to represent the developmental stages of young people's progressing self-awareness and sociopolitical consciousness. Strickland selected predominantly positive reflections on being African American and young in the United States, "a celebration of growing up Black," and pieces which testify to the omnipresence and power of love in African American families and communities.

From a literary standpoint, *Listen, Children: An Anthology of Black Literature* offers young people an unusually accessible introduction to renowned American writers and activists: for example, autobiographical and biographical sketches of Maya Angelou and Rosa Parks; a play by Alice Childress about Harriett Tubman; poetry by Gwendolyn Brooks, Lucille Clifton, Langston Hughes, Dudley Randall, Sonia Sanchez, and Margaret Walker; a speech by Martin Luther King, Jr.; and stories by Virginia Hamilton and Kristin Hunter. Stylistically, the poetry and prose are simple and the literal sense is clear, yet these pieces can be read on a deeper level for the more sophisticated student. Some of the pieces' language and allusions are dated. Although the publisher labeled the book a "young adult anthology," the use of "children" in the book's title and the representation of elementary-school children in two of the three pictures on the book's cover may turn off high-school readers. Furthermore, the anthology's large print, occasional drawings, and basic reading level suggest it would be most appropriate for sixth to eighth graders.

For a young person yearning for writing by African Americans about African Americans, this book provides a smorgasbord of material. Best of all, it is that rare book that is guaranteed to make readers feel good about themselves as readers and thinkers, as African Americans, and as young people.

130. Tate, Eleanora E. *Just an Overnight Guest*. New York: Dial Press, 1980. 182 pages. ***

The setting is present day Nutbrush, Missouri, a small town where the pace is slow and the gossip steady. Here live the Carsons, a close-knit, middle-class black family. Daddy's a truck driver for a moving company; he's a gigantic teddy bear, very affectionate toward his daughters. Mommy's the only black teacher in the town's high school; she's a twenty-four-hour-a-day teacher, straining to inculcate her brand of unconditional kindness and stiff propriety into her unwilling daughters. Thirteen-year-old Alberta channels her raging hormones into softball and sneaky rendezvous with a boyfriend she's not supposed to have until she turns sixteen. The baby of the family, and the main character of this novel, is nine-year-old Margie.

Momma Carson offers to take care of four-year-old Ethel Hardisen while Ethel's mother goes to St. Louis. Margie protests; she sees Ethel, biracial and impoverished, through her neighbors' eyes as a "trashy little kid." Ethel lives in a filthy trailer in Hickory Sticks, the "white-trash" part of Nutbrush. Ethel's single parent, Mary, drinks heavily, beats Ethel out of frustration and ignorance, and locks her alone in the trailer or drops her off at the Children's Home when drunkenness and wanderlust call. Mary fulfills the townspeople's perceptions of her; ever the unfit mother, she delivers Ethel to the Carsons for, supposedly, just an overnight stay, and then never returns to Nutbrush. Ethel initially throws her trademark tantrums and terrorizes the Carson household. However, surrounded by this loving, gentle, and generous family, she gradually reforms.

Margie must adjust to some significant changes quickly. Previously the baby of the family, she becomes a middle child, whose infantile tantrums and selfishness will not be tolerated by her parents. She needs to share a bed, her clothes, her toys, her friends, and, most difficult of all, her parents. The interesting twist in the story comes at its end when Daddy explains to Margie that Ethel will be joining the family permanently. He explains that Ethel is Margie's cousin, and Ethel's father is Momma's brother, Uncle Jake, who lives in St. Louis. This revelation throws Margie off center but ultimately delivers enough power to shape up her attitude toward Ethel.

All of the events within *Just an Overnight Guest* occur within three weeks in June. The major activities in Nutbrush are softball, fishing, church, and detours to the Dairy Queen. And although these activities are not especially exciting, the story moves along quickly. The reader gets a good feel for small-town life and antsy prepubescents and adolescents.

Margie's obsessive anger and fear about Ethel are developed in depth without making the narrative seem monotonous. Eleanora Tate's descriptions and dialogues render realistically the volatile relations among family members. Despite occasional negative actions, all of the Carsons create a favorable impression, perhaps because they are all too human. Margie, in particular, is easy to sympathize with—a testament to Tate's strong character development skills.

The divisive power of rumor and stereotyping is subtly condemned. Tate expresses, through Margie and her nosy neighbors, the prevailing prejudice against poor people, against unmarried mothers, and against people who cross racial lines for love. Likewise, Momma looks down on Alberta's boyfriend, Billy Ray Morgan, because he's not from an upwardly mobile family. And Momma and Alberta are considered pretty because they're thin and light-skinned, while Daddy and Margie are not because they're heavy and dark-skinned. The classism and racism are givens in this setting. But Tate only mentions these problems; she doesn't explore or debunk them. Of course, presenting the story from the perspective of a nine-year-old doesn't provide an easy way to challenge such complex issues.

The lessons that Margie learns—that a family always has room to take in kin, that there is plenty of love to go around, that kindness can make a difference, that life is not always fair but it's her duty to try to do the right thing, that she has to deal with what life dishes out—are made obvious. Margie's growing ability to empathize with Ethel is rendered believably. This novel also provides solid coverage of sibling rivalry, especially between adopted and biological children. One weakness is that the reader learns little about how Ethel feels, particularly about being abandoned by her mother.

This novel portrays a strong and positive father and a family with strict rules about sex. Daddy's handling of Alberta's secretive relationship with her boyfriend is funny and right on the mark. He offers to chaperone them to the movies and to sit behind them. He lovingly teases Alberta, and it's clear that he cares about her reaching a level of maturity that will lead to her making healthy decisions for herself in her dealings with men.

Although Margie is nine, her behavior is not out of the realm of possibility for older children. Margie is a character with whom some middle-school students may identify. Alberta, at thirteen, provides another pull for middle-school readers. *Just an Overnight Guest* is simple to read, and its issues are primal. Because a lot of attention is paid to the close relationship between Daddy and Margie, girls will have an easier time getting into this novel than will boys.

131. Tate, Eleanora E. *The Secret of Gumbo Grove*. New York: Bantam Books, 1988. 199 pages. **

Parents' Choice Award, 1987

Gumbo Grove prides itself on being South Carolina's most famous seaside resort town. For Raisin Stackhouse's family and the other black families in town, that means jobs as maids and cooks in the hotels, restaurants, and shops catering to rich tourists. During summer vacation, Raisin helps her mother clean condos at night and by day helps her father sell fruit, vegetables, and crabs from the back of his truck. But eleven-year-old Raisin is dissatisfied with her life in Gumbo Grove. Determined to be a history teacher when she grows up, Raisin wonders why she never learns local black history in her school. When her teacher insists that no local blacks have ever done anything worth talking about, Raisin is determined to prove her wrong. She longs for African American heroes and sets out to find them.

Then old Miss Effie Pfluggins asks Raisin to help her clean up the old cemetery at the New Africa No. 1 Missionary Baptist Church. As they work, Miss Effie tells her about the people buried there. She tells about Gussie Ann Vereen, a slave girl who died of a broken heart after her father ran to freedom and never returned for her. She tells about Sarvis Exile, Raisin's own great uncle, who owned much of the land in Gumbo Grove until his house was burned down, with him in it, by the Ku Klux Klan. And she drops hints about Alexander Morgan Grove Dickson, the African American senator who founded Gumbo Grove. Raisin is thrilled with her newly discovered heroes but soon learns that others, both black and white, would rather deny the past.

When powerful members of the New Africa Church want to tear down the old church building and move the cemetery, Raisin despairs of losing the town's most important piece of black history. With Miss Effie's help, she organizes her neighbors to uncover Alexander Dickson's grave and publicize his identity as the town's founder. In the process, she teaches her town about the importance of claiming its history, both painful and triumphant.

The Secret of Gumbo Grove is based on an interesting premise, but the story itself is not that interesting. Much of the plot revolves around Raisin's parents' resistance to her efforts to uncover local black history, and it gets tired fast. Although they finally come around to her point of view, their approach to her is so authoritarian that she never really gets to plead her case. Furthermore, the story is somewhat didactic about the importance of black history, repeatedly stating its importance rather than simply demonstrating it through the increasing pride of local African Americans. Raisin's consuming interest in black history despite discouragement from her friends and punishment from her parents is somewhat unbelievable.

Among the book's strengths are Miss Effie's stories about the town's African American ancestors; I wish more space had been devoted to these stories. In addition, Eleanora Tate does a good job of exploring the reasons for adults' ambivalence at digging up black history, from snooty Miss Aussie's denial of descending from slaves to others' worries of how whites will react to their publicizing an African American town founder. Still, these strengths do not overcome the book's weaknesses, and I suspect *The Secret of Gumbo Grove* will be hard pressed to hold young adult readers' attention. Also, a subplot which involves the county's Miss Ebony Pageant rewards the African American girls who can raise the most money, buy the prettiest clothes beyond what they can afford, and show poise while parading around a runway. While this may be a realistic reflection of southern, small town culture, it reinforces sexist values. Only as an afterthought, and with less impact, is Raisin's award for community service tacked on. The real prize goes to beauty, materialism, and salesmanship.

It's hard to discern an appropriate audience for *The Secret of Gumbo Grove*. Although its protagonist and her concerns are fairly young, speaking to the ten- to thirteen-year-old crowd, the book is too long for these readers. Older teenage readers are likely to be bored by the slow pace. On the other hand, the novel should appeal equally to girls and boys; despite an almost all-female cast, the characters could be any sex (except those in the Miss Ebony Pageant). Finally, the book did win a Parents' Choice Award, suggesting that other readers found it more absorbing than this reviewer.

132. Tate, Eleanora E. *Thank You, Dr. Martin Luther King, Jr.!* New York: Bantam Books, 1992. 237 pages. **

Nine-year-old Mary Elouise, of Gumbo Grove, South Carolina, does not like herself or her skin color very much. Every time someone gives her a black doll, she loses it. Every time a teacher talks about African American history or Africa in school, she wishes she were invisible. She is desperate to become friends with Brandy, the whitest, blondest girl in her class, although Brandy is not very nice and has made it clear that she doesn't care about Mary Elouise. The last straw is when Mary Elouise gets the part of the narrator in the black history portion of the school play and tries to bribe other students to get out of her part.

Mary Elouise's world is peopled by adults almost as confused as she is. Her teacher is patronizingly racist, focusing on the "glorious" history of the old South, and portraying black history as a history of African savages, happy slaves, and impoverished freed blacks. Mary Elouise's mother can't understand why her daughter is "color struck," although she herself, in a moment of anger, calls her daughter a "stupid little ole ugly Black thing." On the positive side, her grandmother lectures Mary Elouise about the importance of loving and believing in herself and cautions her to judge others by their characters rather than their appearance, skin color, or possessions. Her principal, Miz Thomas, tries mightily to instill a sense of black pride and history in her students. And two African American storytellers awaken in Mary Elouise her first glimpse of her own history as something prouder and more powerful than slavery alone.

The story's plot limps along, going into far too much detail about Mary Elouise's schooldays, plots of the TV shows she likes, and purposeless exchanges with her siblings that do nothing to advance the theme. The plot's strengths include Mary Elouise's close relationship with her grandmother, from whom she learns the most about loving herself, her interactions with the storytellers who serve as role models, and her growing pride in the black history play, which parallels her changing self-image. Mary Elouise and her grandmother are developed reasonably well, but there are far too many other minor characters to keep straight. Her teacher is a stock type, unbelievable in her excessive, naive racism.

Thank You, Dr. Martin Luther King, Jr.! has an admirable message about loving oneself and respecting African American history and identity. Mary Elouise's growing self-esteem is touching and instructive. However, the author is so heavy handed as to annoy even readers who agree with her message. Even younger readers will feel like they've been repeatedly hit over the head with the message.

With a tighter, more focused plot, the story could have accomplished its goals in about half the length and thus remained accessible for younger middle-school readers. At 237 pages, it is likely to be too difficult for fourth- through sixth-grade readers, who are the only ones who might be able to identify with the young characters and their concerns. Older readers will find the story silly and tedious. Within *Thank You, Dr. Martin Luther King, Jr.!* there is a core of a fine novel, but it is hidden beneath the multitude of characters, overly detailed plot, and didactic tone.

133. Tate, Eleanora E. *Front Porch Stories at the One-Room School*. New York: Dell Publishing Co., 1992. 98 pages. *

One hot summer night, when there's nothing to do in Nutbrush, Missouri, but watch reruns on television, Matthew Carson creates alternative entertainment for his daughter, twelve-year-old Margie, and his niece, seven-year-old Ethel. Matthew sets the girls on the steps of Douglass School, the one-room school which he attended as a boy, and tells them stories. *Front Porch Stories at the One-Room School* contains ten chapters that contain, within each, sequences and fragments of stories. Each story is prompted by questions from the spunky, cynical girls and is resolved by their responses to it. Author Eleanora Tate uses an interesting narrative technique here: Matthew tells the stories, but Margie narrates the book.

In most of the stories, Matthew paints a romantic picture of bygone days filled with childish pranks and eccentric neighbors and relatives. Three of the best tales are ghost stories. "The Shadow" describes how a monster threatens Aunt Daisy while she is doing her laundry under a full moon on a Sunday, which is considered bad luck; she exorcises her attacker by locking herself, Bible in hand, in a closet all night. "The Light" is the best ghost story. In it, Grampa Wally comes back from the dead to haunt his children. During his lifetime, nobody slept on his couch without permission, but after his death, his children take over the couch without his permission! "Ghosts Galore," describes how the ghosts of slaves drowned while trying to raft across the Mississippi River to freedom helped subsequent slaves to escape. The other top story in this collection is "The President's Wife," which describes how Matthew met Eleanor Roosevelt when she visited a local college; the characterization is full and the dialogue quick and funny.

Eleanora Tate has created some fun characters but not fun stories. Matthew's nostalgia hinders his storytelling. He rambles anecdotally rather than develops, tells rather than shows, and ironically devotes most of his time to stream-of-consciousness reflection. This book has structure but little substance. There is little action and even less suspense— surprising, since the book is billed as a collection of ghost stories! The author fails to recreate for her readers the enchantment that, according to the narrative, Matthew elicits in his audience.

At the end of the book, the author reveals that her hometown and her elementary school served as models for the fictional Douglass School in Nutbrush, Missouri. She also provides notes on the inspirations for the stories. Unfortunately, this interesting chapter does not redeem the flat body of the collection.

Front Porch Stories at the One-Room School is really on the level of its youngest character, seven-year-old Ethel. So maybe the readership ought to come from elementary-school ranks. Its short chapters and numerous illustrations make it accessible for elementary-school readers, but its meandering style demands an older reader, fifth through eighth grade, with the patience for a slice-of-life story. But rare will be the reader of any age who'll find this collection engrossing.

134. Taylor, Mildred D. *Roll of Thunder, Hear My Cry*. New York: Bantam Books, 1976. 210 pages. *****

American Library Association Notable Books for Children and Young Adults, 1976; Coretta Scott King Honor Book, 1977; Jane Addams Honor Book, 1977; John Newbery Medal Award, 1977; New York Times Best Books for Children and Young Adults, 1976

Roll of Thunder, Hear My Cry describes a year in the life of the Logans, a strong and loving African American family living in rural Mississippi in 1933. It is a tale about African American children's loss of innocence and a family pulling together to resist racism. The family includes Cassie, her three brothers, her parents, grandmother, uncle, and Mr. Morrison, the giant who comes to live with them after he loses his job on the railroad.

In the course of the year, Cassie learns about racism both through white insults to her sense of self-worth and through violence against African Americans in her town. When her parents organize a boycott against the white store owners who set fire to three black men, Mama Logan loses her school teaching job, white men attack Papa, and the bank tries to foreclose on the Logan's farm. Through these and other incidents, Cassie's parents teach her the difficult task of balancing self-preservation and self-respect in an environment that demands black subservience as the price of survival.

This is a fantastic book. Mildred Taylor offers an abundance of strong African American role models, both male and female, as well as several white characters who stand up against injustice. She also offers complexity in her characters and plot. Although racist incidents pervade the plot, they are set in the context of the Logan's full lives, which are about farming, going to school, growing up, negotiating friendships, and caring for each other. *Roll of Thunder, Hear My Cry* avoids easy answers in its unflinching focus on racism and the story's ending is therefore bittersweet, but overall the book is empowering. The characters inspire, the plot illuminates, and the ultimate message is one of human love and resistance in the face of dehumanizing conditions. Because of its rich detail, languid pace, and explicit descriptions of anti-black violence, this novel is most appropriate for older readers, ninth through twelfth graders. Although ostensibly told in fourth-grader Cassie's voice, the story's insight and wisdom are fully adult.

135. Taylor, Mildred D. *Song of the Trees*. New York: Bantam Books, 1976. 52 pages. ****

Coretta Scott King Honor Book, 1976; Council on Interracial Books for Children Award, 1973; Jane Addams Honor Book, 1976

Cassie Logan lives on a Mississippi farm with her grandmother, her mother, and her brothers, Stacey, Christopher-John, and Little Man. Her Papa is down in Louisiana laying tracks on the railroad, trying to scrape up money to send home to his family during the Great Depression. But someone steals the ten-dollar bill from Papa's letter one week, and the family can't afford to buy Mama's medicine nor to replace the flour and sugar that are nearly gone.

Then, Mr. Andersen, a white man, offers Cassie's grandmother sixty-five dollars to chop down the trees on her land. The money doesn't convince her, but his threats that Papa might have an "accident" unless she agrees to his "offer" force her to go along. Cassie is dismayed, for the trees are her friends and she listens for their song each morning. Cassie's Mama, determined to stop Mr. Andersen, sends Stacey off on horseback to fetch Papa home from Louisiana. How Papa stops Mr. Andersen, protects his family's forest, and preserves his own dignity is summed up by his challenge: "One thing you can't seem to understand, Andersen, is that a Black man's always gotta be ready to die. And it don't make any difference if I die today or tomorrow. Just as long as I die right."

Song of the Trees is a beautiful novella. Beautifully illustrated, this book introduces the young reader to the Logan family of *Roll of Thunder, Hear My Cry* and their powerful example of standing up for their rights and dignity in a time when it sometimes cost African Americans their lives to do so. Cassie and her brothers learn from their parents' example how to be proud, self-respecting African Americans.

Because *Song of the Trees* is short and its tone gentle, it is appropriate for readers in grades four to six. Strong male and female role models abound in both adult and child characters.

Further, the story describes a black family whose members take care of each other through whatever adversities life presents. Their model of love and courage is a welcome addition to the body of African American young adult literature.

136. Taylor, Mildred D. *Let the Circle Be Unbroken.* New York: Bantam Books, 1981. 339 pages. ****

American Library Association Notable Books for Children and Young Adults, 1981; Coretta Scott King Award, 1982; Jane Addams Honor Book, 1982

Let the Circle Be Unbroken, the sequel to *Roll of Thunder, Hear My Cry,* continues the Logan family's story, told in fifth-grader Cassie Logan's voice. The Logans struggle to hold on to their four-hundred-acre farm in Mississippi in the midst of the Depression, while sharecropping families all around them are put off their land. Like its predecessor, this book chronicles the intensity of southern racism in the 1930s through descriptions of a young black boy's trial for murder, a black grandmother's attempt to register to vote, and fourteen-year-old Stacey Logan's exploitation on a sugar cane plantation. The Logan's mixed-race cousin Suzella comes to live with them during this time, and Cassie's ambivalent reactions to her and her changing relationship with her brother Stacey presage her approaching adolescence.

This is another strong novel from Mildred Taylor, replete with complex characters and realistic, if disturbing, plot. As in *Roll of Thunder, Hear My Cry,* Taylor offers models of African American resistance without understating the risks and potential costs to resisters. For instance, when black and white sharecroppers try to form a union, one man is killed and several are beaten up. When a sixty-five-year-old African American sharecropper goes to register to vote, she is thrown off her land.

Let the Circle Be Unbroken addresses the economics of racism in more detail than *Roll of Thunder, Hear My Cry* did, particularly with the devastating descriptions of Stacey's experience on the sugar cane plantation. Overall, though, I found *Roll of Thunder, Hear My Cry* to be the stronger book (the characters of the entire Logan family are more finely drawn), while *Let the Circle Be Unbroken* gets somewhat mired in Cassie's jealousy toward Suzella. Nevertheless, it is an absorbing book with a powerful vision of the African American family and its history of resistance to racism.

137. Taylor, Mildred D. *The Friendship and the Gold Cadillac.* New York: Bantam Books, 1989. 87 pages. ****

American Library Association Notable Books for Children and Young Adults, 1989; Boston Globe-Horn Book Magazine Honor List, 1989; Christopher Award, 1989; Coretta Scott King Award, 1988; New York Times Best Books for Children and Young Adults, 1987

Cassie Logan, the young Mississippi girl who narrated *Roll of Thunder, Hear My Cry*, also narrates the forty-two-page story, "The Friendship." Cassie and her three brothers visit the Wallace Store, despite dire warnings from their parents to stay away from the dangerously racist Wallace men. While there, they witness an astounding drama—old Mr. Tom Bee, a black man, insists on calling white John Wallace by his first name. Mr. Tom Bee saved John Wallace's life several times when they were younger, and John Wallace said that they were like family and would always be on a first-name basis. John Wallace changes his mind after ridicule from other white men, but Tom Bee refuses to call him "Mister," especially since no whites call black men "Mister." Finally, John Wallace shoots Tom Bee in the thigh "to teach him respect," but as Tom

Bee drags himself away, he still shouts defiantly, "John! John!"

"The Gold Cadillac," a thirty-four-page story set in Toledo, Ohio, is narrated by another young girl, 'lois. One day, her father buys a gold Cadillac, surprising and delighting the whole family, except for 'lois' mother, who would have preferred to buy a new house in a better neighborhood. 'lois' mother refuses to ride in the Cadillac at all until 'lois' father announces his plans to drive it down to Mississippi to visit his parents. All of the relatives try to talk him out of it, recognizing the danger of a black man flaunting his success in the South, but he insists. Sure enough, just over the Mississippi line, the police arrest him. Although he is released with just a speeding ticket, the family is badly scared and borrows a cousin's Chevy for the rest of the trip. When they return to Toledo, 'lois' father trades the Cadillac in for a Ford, deciding that keeping the family together, safe and harmonious, is more important than having a showy car.

Mildred Taylor brings her outstanding storytelling talent to both of these stories, creating interesting characters and arresting plots. As with all of her fiction, she examines the effects of racism on good African Americans and chronicles the courage of their responses to it. The characters in "The Friendship" and in "The Gold Cadillac" display caring and dignity common to all of Taylor's protagonists, and "The Gold Cadillac" offers a role model of an upright, intact African American family. At the same time, the characters are not perfect; both male protagonists make brave but foolhardy decisions over issues that are important only as symbols—using first names and driving a fancy car. Still, Taylor makes the reader understand how such symbols become vital to people who live under an intensely racist system that seeks to rob them of respect and dignity.

The length of this book and the relative simplicity of the stories suggest a fifth- to sixth-grade reading level. The child narrators' befuddled viewpoint in each story makes it more accessible and less threatening for young readers and shows up the absurdity of certain racist practices. At the same time, both stories contain plenty of depth to interest readers up through high-school age. However, the violence in "The Friendship" may well disturb younger readers, so discretion is recommended. The book should also interest girls and boys, offering male protagonists and female narrators in both cases. Finally, the stories offer an excellent starting point for a guided discussion on the history of racism in the United States and the many ways it affected and still affects people's lives and self-images.

138. Taylor, Mildred D. *The Road to Memphis*. New York: Dial Books, 1990. 290 pages. ****

American Library Association Notable Books for Children and Young Adults, 1990; Coretta Scott King Award, 1991

Cassie Logan, a junior in high school in 1941 in Jackson, Mississippi, finds herself caught up in two serious racial incidents. In the first, she goes out hunting with her brothers and several friends. She and Harris, her fat and gentle neighbor, get separated from the rest of their group and run into several white men who decide to hunt Harris instead of raccoons. Although both survive the terrifying incident, Harris ends up with a severely fractured leg, broken ribs, and dog bites. In the second incident, Cassie's friend Moe is taunted by the same white men until he snaps, attacking them with a tire iron. Cassie, her brother Stacey, and their friends Clarence and Little Willie try to save Moe by spiriting him out of town and up North. The bulk of the novel describes their sobering adventures trying to reach the train station in Memphis without being caught. Along the way, they face fear, racist violence, and Clarence's death from illness. And in the end, Moe's rescue depends on Jeremy, a white neighbor boy who earns his family's hatred by saving the black boy. Woven throughout the novel are subplots about falling in love and the ongoing threat of World War II.

  The Road to Memphis contains the same strong writing and character development as Taylor's previous novels and the same unflinching focus on racism. Unfortunately, Cassie's parents and grandmother are barely in this story and the absence of their powerful characters leaves a gap. Also, this third novel about the Logans focuses more exclusively on racist humiliation and violence than the first two novels did. While racism was an integral and inescapable part of those other stories, it was set within the full context of the Logans' lives. The complete focus on racism in the third novel is certainly legitimate, but I prefer the fullness of the earlier stories and their implication that African American's lives are about a lot more than racism alone.

  Still, *The Road to Memphis* is a strong book with content and reading level appropriate for tenth through twelfth graders. The novel offers a compelling plot and important theme, and , as always, Taylor provides plenty of strong role models, including both black and white characters who stand up against racism even at great personal cost.

139. Taylor, Mildred D. *Mississippi Bridge*. New York: Bantam Books, 1992. 62 pages. ****

Christopher Award, 1992; Jane Addams Honor Book, 1992

  Mississippi Bridge is another choice book from Mildred Taylor. Actually, it's more of a single story, comparable to one chapter of her longer novels, but Taylor's superb storytelling abilities are in full force. The narrator is Jeremy Simms, a poor white Mississippi boy with an unusual yearning for justice in the Jim Crow South. He watches in shame as the white storekeeper gives preferential treatment to white customers, and as his own rabidly racist father humiliates black Josias for having a job lead while the Depression keeps scores of white men unemployed. Jeremy, lonely in his compassion, hungers for friends among his black neighbors. He cannot understand why Stacey Logan, of *Roll of Thunder, Hear My Cry*, keeps a cool distance from him, regardless of his overtures.

Jeremy watches one Jim Crow charade play itself out in front of the general store. Stacey's grandmother comes to catch the bus to go tend her sick sister, while Josias buys a ticket to travel to his new job. But they, along with all of the African American riders on the bus, are forced off in the pouring rain when a large white family of latecomers wants their seats. Just outside of town, though, the bridge washes out, sweeping the bus and all of its white passengers into the river. Josias is the first one in to try to save them, without success. As Jeremy helps pull the drowned victims onto shore, he wonders whether they were punished for their racism. But among the victims are his beloved old schoolteacher and her four-year-old granddaughter, so Jeremy realizes that the reason for the tragedy is nothing so simple.

As with Taylor's other books, vivid characters, elegant plots, and a strong moral mark *Mississippi Bridge*. Taylor has an ear for southern dialogue that brings the characters right into the reader's room. Her depiction of Jeremy as a lonely white boy trapped between his empathy for his black neighbors and the uncompromising racist demands of his own white South is heartbreaking. Josias' character, meanwhile, provides a perspective of just how damaging that same racism was for African Americans. As always, Taylor incorporates a lesson in black history and survival into her story without ever becoming didactic. True to real life, the story is a seamless mix of powerful moral incidents and seemingly arbitrary acts of nature, all mixed up in one young boy's experience.

Although *Mississippi Bridge* features a white narrator/protagonist, it is included in this bibliography because it features strong African American characters from Taylor's other novels and because its topic is race. Jeremy's understanding that racism is inherently wrong provides a valuable model for young white readers and a challenge to young African American readers to not oversimplify race issues. At the same time, Taylor provides strong black characters in Stacey, whom Jeremy admires, and Josias, who overlooks his own mistreatment to try to save people's lives.

This book's short length and the youth of its characters make it accessible to fifth through seventh graders though high-school readers will also enjoy it. Adults should be prepared to have a discussion with younger readers after they finish the book, particularly about the serious racial incidents and the deaths in this story. However, all are handled in an honest but sensitive way that should not bar young readers. Most of the characters are male, but since Taylor avoids any sex role stereotyping, girls as well as boys will be able to identify with the characters.

140. Thomas, Joyce Carol. *Marked by Fire*. New York: Avon Books, 1982. 172 pages. ****

American Book Award, 1983

Abyssinia, born to Patience and Strong Jackson in an Oklahoma cotton field, grows up among tornadoes and floods, church fairs and school assemblies. All the women of the town consider Abby their own child, including Patience's sisters, who try to steal her, and Mother Barker, who teaches her to heal with roots and herbs. Her father dotes on her until a tornado destroys his barbershop, causing him to flee town and to abandon his family. Then, Abby is raped by a trusted uncle, robbing her of her youthful openness and her beautiful singing voice. As she recovers slowly, with the love and help of the women around her, Abby grows into the strong healer that her community needs to replace aging Mother Barker. In her turn, Abby saves herself and her friend's children from a deranged neighbor to continue the cycle of love that keeps her community alive.

Marked by Fire is a lyrical, understated novel which can be read on many levels. Abyssinia's life from birth to early adulthood is presented in a series of vignettes, strong in details of daily life but weak on plot development. For instance, the chapter after Abby's father's departure is not devoted to her coming to terms with the abandonment but instead moves right on to the next event. Such understatement of the emotional consequences of losing a father may bewilder readers.

It is difficult to judge an appropriate reader age for this novel. The short chapters, quick-moving plot, and straightforward sentence structure make it accessible to sixth- through eighth-grade readers, but its topics of child rape, wife abuse, and metaphysical healing may be too mature for them. On the other hand, Joyce Carol Thomas treats these topics sensitively and allegorically, avoiding gory physical detail, and manages to paint Abby's world as stable and loving despite periodic cataclysmic events. At the same time, the book may well appeal to high-school age and adult readers, who can appreciate Thomas' beautiful poetic imagery and the powerful message of physical and spiritual healing woven throughout *Marked by Fire*.

Girls will feel especially affirmed by this novel, with its female protagonist and the circle of loving women who help her to grow to adulthood. Male readers will find fewer characters to get into, though Abby's father is the light of her early life and is portrayed as a caring man, even when he abandons her temporarily. Overall, *Marked by Fire*'s poetic voice, engrossing plot, and positive message strongly recommend it. However, young readers in particular should be given an opportunity to discuss and come to terms with its more disturbing themes.

141. Thomas, Joyce Carol. *Bright Shadow.* New York: Avon Books, 1983. 125 pages. ****

Coretta Scott King Honor Book, 1984

Bright Shadow continues the sagas of families from two of Joyce Carol Thomas' other novels, the Jacksons of *Marked by Fire* and the Jeffersons of *The Golden Pasture.* In *Bright Shadow*, Abyssinia Jackson and Carl Lee Jefferson are now, respectively, pre-med and pre-law students at Langston University in Ponca City, Oklahoma. More important to this novel's plot, however, they are in love.

"Father problems" put a strain on Abby and Carl Lee's relationship. Abby's father, Strong, is overprotective of his daughter and wants to keep her away from the opposite sex. By the novel's end, Strong comes to terms with his daughter's womanhood and her desires, and finally supports her relationship with Carl Lee. Carl Lee's father, Samuel, bullies his son past the point of repair. To punish him for not performing excessive chores to perfection, Samuel tries to force Carl Lee to eat a pile of salt and rat stew. Samuel wields a shotgun to bolster his authority, but Carl Lee walks away— with the gun aimed at his back—from his father forever.

After Carl Lee leaves, Samuel, an alcoholic with severe liver disease, indulges himself until he dies. During his final drunken stupor, he confesses his love for and pride in Carl Lee to everyone in town except Carl Lee himself. Strong helps the drunk and despairing Samuel cope with his uncontainable rage at the unfairness of life. Confronting Samuel's anger and frustration softens some of Strong's hard edges and reconfirms Strong's commitment to his family, to whom he's recently returned (after abandoning them when a tornado destroyed his barbershop in *Marked by Fire*). Carl Lee feels guilty because his shame about his father prevented him from understanding Samuel's behavior well enough to try to mend their father-son relationship.

Guilt and grief also affect Abby and Carl Lee's relationship. Abby withdraws when she mourns the loss of her

Aunt Serena. She projects guilt—about her taking time away from her aunt to spend with her boyfriend—onto Carl Lee. By the end of the novel, the couple have conquered their grief. Their relationship has helped them to grow emotionally and spiritually, and, conversely, their individual challenges have strengthened their relationship.

The story balances the histories of African Americans and Native Americans in Oklahoma, along with the mystical spirituality possessed by both peoples. Joyce Carol Thomas manages to incorporate the spiritual element without it seeming clichéd or stereotyped.

Joyce Carol Thomas writes beautifully. In the best tradition of contemporary African American women's writing, she combines the metaphysical mysticism of Toni Morrison and Gloria Naylor with the natural metaphors of Alice Walker to tell a poignant story. Through the voice of Abby's mother, Patience, the author expresses wisdom about love and loss, about marriage and family. Through Abby's vivid dreams and nightmares and her mother's interpretations of them, the author adds another level of action to the narrative and encourages a multilayered reading of it.

Older readers will appreciate the quality of the writing as well as the story. Younger readers can enjoy the story on a simpler level. Some of the sappy tone and flowery language used to represent Abby and Carl Lee's romantic and sexual feelings may make some readers laugh. Although Abby doesn't dominate the story, this novel will appeal more to high-school girls than to boys of any age.

Readers of all ages may find it hard to suspend disbelief during the mystical moments in the story. The phrase "bright shadow" appears in connection with Abby's receiving Serena's superb singing voice after her aunt dies and with Carl Lee's deceased Native American mother leading Abby and Carl Lee to a place in the woods where she ceremonially buried Samuel. Whether the reader reads these events literally or figuratively, s/he may get thrown by the suddenness with which they drop into the story.

Additionally, the reader may be disturbed by the details surrounding Aunt Serena's death, particularly because the author doesn't fully explore or explain Serena's murderer's motivations and means. Joyce Carol Thomas makes it clear, in fact, that her refusal to explain away every event in the story is precisely the point of this story. The novel's title refers to the message that Aunt Serena sends Abby in a nightmare: "We are all taken from the same source: pain and beauty. One is the chrysalis that gives to the other some gift that even in death creates a new dimension in life. . . . [I]f you could catch us in the palm of your hand and hold us up to the light as you would jewels, you would see the flickering of a bright shadow. A bright shadow cast by one jewel on the other." Good and evil, joy and pain, anger and forgiveness, coexist in this world; one cannot understand why, but each encounter with these couplings can bring strength and change—that is *Bright Shadow's* message.

142.   Thomas, Joyce Carol. *The Golden Pasture*. New York: Scholastic, Inc., 1986. 136 pages. **

Twelve-year-old Carl Lee is the son of a Cherokee mother, who died giving birth to him, and an African American father, who is jealous and distant. Carl Lee leaves his father Samuel to live with his grandfather, Gray, on his horse ranch in Oklahoma. During the summers, Carl Lee not only gets grandfatherly adoration and respect from Gray but also gets to express his own love for horses, riding from morning 'til night. He dreams of performing in the annual rodeo although he is too young.

Then one night, Carl Lee discovers a beautiful, injured Appaloosa in one of Gray's distant fields. Nursing the horse back to health, Carl Lee forms a magical bond with him. He teaches the horse to overcome its great fear of fire to perform a trick that is sure to win Carl Lee entrance to the rodeo.

However, he soon learns that this horse has a past as Thunderfoot, the untamable rodeo horse that no one could ride. Carl Lee's father saved the horse from certain death many years ago, but ever since, Thunderfoot has been stalked by Hellhound, a bitter cowboy sworn to kill the horse for besting him at a rodeo. The rodeo offers Carl Lee a chance to bond with his father over a horse they both love, but it also exposes Thunderfoot to Hellhound's wrath. The events that follow help Carl Lee to see his father as the hero he once was.

James Baldwin rated *The Golden Pasture* as one of his two favorite books. Far be it for me to dispute the opinion of such an exquisite writer, but the plot of *The Golden Pasture* simply did not hold my interest. The book is, above all, a horse story; readers who love horses will love this book. As always, Joyce Carol Thomas' writing is beautifully lyrical and descriptive, but the story line depends on the reader having a keen interest in horses and being able to identify strongly with a rural setting. Although Carl Lee's relationship with his father ostensibly is the linchpin of the plot, the exploration of this relationship is too insubstantial. On the other hand, Carl Lee's relationship with his grandfather is depicted nicely, with the grandfather stepping out of traditional male roles to nurture (and cook for) Carl Lee.

The Golden Pasture is entirely male. The one female character, Carl Lee's mother, dies during his birth in Chapter One and plays no further part in the story. Carl Lee's motherless state apparently does not bother him, which seems unrealistic. The story will speak to boys more than girls though female horse-lovers may be able to overcome the lack of female characters. Readers of either sex with little experience of rural life may have trouble enjoying the plot. The reading level is appropriate for fifth through ninth graders.

143. Thomas, Joyce Carol. *Water Girl.* New York: Avon Books, 1986. 119 pages. ***

Fifteen-year-old Amber Westbrook lives in a beautiful California community with her parents, grandfather, and twelve-year-old twin brothers. Although they experience the usual sibling rivalry, Amber loves her brothers and her kind, understanding parents. Her boyfriend, Wade, also seems too good to be true—gentle, compassionate, handsome, and completely in love with Amber. They all accept Amber's eccentricities—her love of solitude, her magical flute playing, her obsession with books, and her brooding about injustices done to any group of people. As she learns more about various oppressions of African Americans, Native Americans, Chicanos, Jews, and Japanese Americans, Amber becomes more and more upset.

Then one day Amber discovers a secret about her own past hidden in an attic trunk. As a baby, Amber's biological parents gave her up to be raised by the family she has always considered her own. In her horror, she runs away, spending several days in the forest grieving and seeking to reconcile these new facts about herself. Amber fears that she doesn't belong anywhere, but eventually the river and her flute speak to her, helping her to understand that love creates belonging far stronger than any accident of birth.

Water Girl's mystical style follows the pattern of Joyce Carol Thomas' other novels. Human characters learn lessons from the natural world—from animals, rivers, and earthquakes—and music. The characters in *Water Girl* and their idyllic relationships are not particularly realistic, but they're not meant to be, since this is a fairy tale. Amber's obsession with one historical oppression after another is somewhat didactic, particularly since she resolves her feelings about each and moves onto the next so facilely. However, Thomas writes a lovely fairy tale, poetically describing the natural world with its mystical lessons for humans. Thomas' clear, simple prose is a pleasure to read, and her moral is both grounding and important.

The short chapters, short overall length, and simple prose make this novel accessible to readers as young as the sixth grade, but certainly high-school readers can enjoy reading more deeply into the text's symbolism. Although the protagonist is female, her vision and experiences are not gender based, so boys and girls both should find the novel interesting. Like Thomas' other novels, *Water Girl* will appeal most to readers who enjoy mild fantasy.

144. Thomas, Joyce Carol. *Journey*. New York: Scholastic, Inc., 1988. 153 pages. ***

As an infant, Maggie Alexander giggles at the stories of a friendly tarantula and watches her weave light into her web. As a teenager, Maggie again meets up with tarantulas as she attempts to solve the murders of several teenagers in her Oklahoma hometown. Her sleuthing eventually draws her boyfriend, Matthew, and herself into deadly danger, as they uncover the horrifying motive for the murders.

Journey cannot decide whether to be a straightforward murder mystery or a lyrical account of a teenager coming to terms with evil. Either story would work well alone, but together they are discordant, with neither one fully developed. This is especially unfortunate because the early chapters of the book, before the mystery begins, are exceptional in their imagery and wisdom. Strong character development and sharp dialogue balance a few overly didactic scenes which have absolutely no relation to the remainder of the book. The mystery portion, once it begins, is fun and fast paced. It unsuccessfully tries to build both horror and suspense but succeeds mainly as a mystery with a likable teenage sleuth.

Despite its discordance, *Journey* is an absorbing book which may hook students who normally don't like to read. Its reading level and content are suitable for seventh- to tenth-grade readers. It offers an outspoken female protagonist, positive female and male adult role models in Maggie's parents, and an action-oriented plot that should appeal to all readers. Explicitly African American content is incorporated clumsily into clichéd conflicts between black students and a white teacher, but the author needn't try so hard to highlight African American themes; the rhythm and mysticism of the first part of *Journey* and the dialogue throughout the novel clearly place the work and its characters in an African American literary tradition.

145. Thomas, Joyce Carol. *When the Nightingale Sings.* New York: Harper Collins Publishers, 1992. 148 pages. ****

The star of *When the Nightingale Sings* is a fourteen-year-old orphan named Marigold. She lives in a ramshackle cottage by the swamp in south Sweet Earth, a rural enclave somewhere in the southeastern United States. Marigold toils every waking moment for her adoptive mother, Cousin Ruby, and "sisters," Ruby's twin daughters. The family abuses Marigold in myriad ways: they daily tell her that she looks and sounds awful; they force her to create songs and costumes for the twins, unattractive croakers whose mother has made them believe that they are perfect, and who compete in singing competitions as, ironically, the Twins of Harmony; and they tell her that her own mother rejected her at birth and abandoned her by the swamp. To add insult to injury, Ruby hires Marigold out to sing at weddings, funerals, and baptisms, then whisks the girl away before the audience can thank her and praise her talents, before they can let her know that her singing is a blessing from God.

Fortunately, Marigold has only partially internalized the abuse. She strains to get in touch with her deepest creative powers and dreams of becoming the lead singer—the "nightingale"—in the Rose of Sharon Baptist Church. Marigold accompanies her sisters to the church's Great Gospel

Convention, where Anthony, the church's handsome minister of music, hopes to find a new nightingale to replace Letty, the retiring Queen Mother Rhythm. When Marigold sings from behind a curtain to help her sisters win, the entire congregation immediately recognizes Marigold as its new nightingale.

The singing and preaching put the entire congregation under a sanctified "spell." Ruby and Letty stand with Marigold between them on the podium, and the mystery at the heart of the book unfolds. The reader learns that Ruby and Letty are sisters, and that Marigold is their sister Melissa's daughter. At the original gospel sing-off a generation before, the sisters were split apart by Jimmy, the M.C. and promoter of their act, "The Nightingale Sisters." Although Jimmy was married to Ruby, he took Melissa up North to make her a star and his lover. After the sisters won the contest, a fight broke out backstage— Ruby cursed Melissa and Letty, the former to always be alone and the latter to always be barren. Melissa died giving birth to Marigold, her only child; Letty promised to raise Marigold, but Ruby kidnapped her and revengefully raised her instead. The family testifies how Marigold bore the brunt of the old feud, and they end it in total forgiveness. The story ends on a Cinderella-like note. Marigold gets the spotlight and Anthony as a boyfriend. Letty gets a husband, Reverend Honeywell. The twins get to sing the background harmony for Marigold. And Ruby gets her family and a clean conscience.

Joyce Carol Thomas' poetic writing, her allegory for a young girl's coming into her own, realizing her potential as an individual and part of a community, works very well here. The themes of unity and love are powerful. The lessons of how rivalries and hatred are perpetuated cross-generationally to inflict wounds on the innocent and render the larger community dysfunctional are made evident. The author has crafted a story that is almost flawless. Of course, if the reader only appreciates gritty realism, s/he will not appreciate Joyce Carol Thomas, for reading her novels requires one to suspend disbelief and engage with the protagonist's fanciful, romantic visions. Being a fairy tale, *When the Nightingale Sings* represents characters symbolically as either angelic or evil figures until its final scene of reconciliation.

Because this book can be read on several levels, it will appeal to seventh to twelfth graders. Since it is centered around a young woman's struggles and longings, most male readers will probably not enjoy it the way female readers will.

My only reservation about this novel is that a major ingredient of its happy ending is romance. Part of what propels Marigold toward the gospel convention is her desire to see Anthony; realizing her potential as a person and an artist is inextricably linked to coupling with a man. Yet the author makes it clear that Anthony likewise needs love to fulfill his life. It would be refreshing to find a fairy tale that didn't have to hammer home the marriage imperative as the heart of its happy-ending formula. For a fairy tale where the underdog triumphs over abuses and disadvantages to realize her dreams, however, *When the Nightingale Sings* is an outstanding choice.

146.   Thurmon, Ralph Cheo. *The Future and Other Stories.* Chicago: Third World Press, 1991. 132 pages. *****

The collection's title story concerns a sixteen-year-old young man named The Future, who lives for the moment, day by day. Rejecting his disciplined grandparents' plea for him to stay with them instead of returning to the city where they foresee his death, he disappears on a train whose conductors treat passengers as anonymous strangers. An unnamed eighteen-year-old narrates "City Life Ethos," explaining how his father's death and his attending college in Mississippi make him more serious. When he returns to Chicago for summer break, he feels stung by the alcohol, drugs, incarceration, murder, unwanted pregnancy, and violence that define the lives of his family, friends, and neighbors. In "Son of Obatala," an African elder passes on his walking stick, designed with symbols of a young man's ancestral legacy, and upon holding it, a young man gains pride and wisdom. "The Birth of Memory" relates how Thomas leaves Christine, his white wife, after a revelatory experience in a jazz club. In "Corner Brothers," a pool-hall game between young Marlon and Moon escalates into a showdown to defend their respective reputations until Moon experiences an epiphany of peace and love and defuses the confrontation. "Ain't No Barbeque in Heaven" describes a father who radically changes his family's diet after hearing Malcolm X speak. After the father predicts that "Black people gone be actin like pigs, without manners, always fighting," his son witnesses the approximate realization of that nightmare at a family reunion barbecue, after which only one family member survives "to warn future generations to not love this life their ancestors lived." "One Rose" follows Olu through his rationalizations for extramarital affairs and unclaimed children to his eventual resolution to be faithful to his wife and a true friend to the women he meets.

Other stories feature girls and young women as their central protagonists. Fourteen-year-old Velma of "Kissin in the Dark" shocks her churchified parents when she confesses that she got pregnant at a revival, until it is revealed that she misunderstood how conception occurs and could not possibly be pregnant. In "When Death Casts a Shadow," Lena takes over her parents' funeral home when they die, her loss balanced by gaining their energy and wisdom when their spirits inhabit her. "What Is Born from Pain?" describes the troubles of sixteen-year-old Ora. When she gets pregnant, her first boyfriend leaves and she miscarries; when she gives birth to her first child, her second boyfriend leaves because he wants a boy, not a girl. In "Rashida," the seven-year-old title character avoids a fight with classmates and, in the process, wins their respect and builds unity. Mrs. Peaches of the story of the same name stops a pimp from seducing her daughter into prostitution, then talks him out of being a pimp by sharing her devastating girlhood experience as a whore and asking, "You wouldn't want nobody misusing yo' mama, would you?"

As Margaret Walker aptly writes in her introduction,
"These are stories taken from the Past, the Present and the
Future of Black people. . . . Thurmon's language, message and
orientation come from the folk. . . . [T]he bottom line is African
American feeling and tone, whether in language, religion,
music, and all in graphic detail." Every story in *The Future and
Other Stories* is masterfully executed. Ralph Thurmon's points
are understated, sometimes expressed through characters'
cryptic comments but most often through exquisite allegory.
Through dialogue the author develops characterization and
plot, and the result is a startlingly immediate brand of
storytelling that will absorb readers and leave them awestruck
by its power and craft. The author keeps description and
exposition to a minimum, which makes this collection
particularly accessible and appealing to young adult readers.
The stories' settings are not pristine, another drawing card for
young readers: alcohol, drugs, sex, and violence abound, though
never gratuitously. An abundance of love and compassion helps
balance the negative elements.

A unifying element in this collection is the use of the
supernatural. The author relies on magic realism to portray
characters' rebirths and their fantasies of "lifting Black
people from this city and placing them into a saner place."
Oftentimes, the supernatural component is disgusting or
horrifying because it conveys past atrocities or present demons,
real or imagined. The author incorporates supernatural
elements into his stories so well that readers will find it easy
to suspend disbelief. Because these stories can be read on
several levels, with multiple interpretations, they demand a
high-school readership.

Thurmon's typical approach to his characters is
striking. The young men are not stoic; they are confused,
vulnerable, unpredictable, and awed by women. All of the
female characters, regardless of age, are strong and inherently
righteous. Young women will be affirmed by Ralph Thurmon's
distinctively reverent treatment of women in this collection;
young men will be encouraged by the struggles and radical

departures in thinking and feeling of the collections' male characters.

Ralph Thurmon has written a gem, offering unusual approaches to relevant and complex issues, predominantly from the perspective of young people. Like the writing itself, the messages in this collection are both down to earth and fantastic, obvious and mysterious, ordinary and radical. Less didactic than most young adult writers, Ralph Thurmon nevertheless transmits lessons necessary for the future of African America.

147. Walter, Mildred Pitts. *Because We Are*. New York: Lothrop, Lee and Shepard Books, 1980. 192 pages. **

Coretta Scott King Honor Book, 1981; Parents' Choice Award, 1980

High-school senior Emma Walsh attends Marlborough High, a prestigious, mostly white, public school attended by a few select middle-class black students. Emma dreams of becoming a doctor like her father, maintains perfect grades, dates the handsome basketball star, and worries incessantly about being chosen as a Golden Slipper debutante. Although her life has all of the trappings of success, she feels torn between two worlds at Marlborough—lured by whites offering success and misunderstanding, alternately ridiculed and supported by African Americans who want her undivided allegiance. Pushed to the breaking point, Emma snaps one day and curses a teacher. The next day she is expelled and banished across town to all-black Manning High.

At Manning, Emma once again feels like an outsider, facing African American peers who accuse her of not being black enough. Her parents, deeply disappointed, don't understand Emma's dilemma. Only her new friend, Allan, understands despite the vast class differences that divide them. When the

Golden Slippers pass Emma by, she is devastated. But with Allan's help, she goes to work on injustices that she *can* affect and begins to develop pride in her own unique identity as a smart African American girl on the verge of adulthood.

Because We Are tackles important issues of class prejudice, racism, and black identity "tests." Emma's parents also provide fertile ground for exploring the issues of divorce and racial intermarriage. Unfortunately, Mildred Pitts Walter does justice to none of these issues. Emma's character, with her supposed sensitivity and seriousness of purpose, is profoundly trivialized by her obsession with becoming a debutante. The class assumptions and conflicts hinted at throughout the book are never explored nor resolved. And Emma's inability to cope with real life problems, such as bullying by girls at school or hostility from a teacher, is baffling.

On the other hand, Walter does an excellent job of depicting Emma's feeling of constantly being an outsider. Similarly, Allan's character is well developed and he nicely articulates one path for successfully negotiating conflicting demands of society, peers, parents, and self. The latter third of the novel finally becomes substantive and thus interesting as Emma organizes a protest against a racist teacher and begins to define her own identity in the process. If Walter had started the novel with this segment and developed the story and characters from there, *Because We Are* would have had much more to say.

Length and vocabulary make this novel suitable for ninth- through twelfth-grade readers, though older readers may become impatient with Emma's character. Boys will be turned off by Emma's focus on female social dilemmas as will serious female readers. The most appreciative audience for *Because We Are* will be fourteen- to sixteen-year-old girls for whom social standing and middle-class social events are primary concerns. Unfortunately, those issues overshadow the book's important themes.

148. Walter, Mildred Pitts. *The Girl on the Outside*. New York: Lothrop, Lee and Shepard Books, 1982. 149 pages. ***

The Girl on the Outside features two protagonists, Eva and Sophia, who don't meet until the very end of the book. Eva, a high-school sophomore, will be one of nine African Americans hoping to desegregate Chatman High School in Mossville, Alabama, in the coming school year. Sophia, a white senior, feels confusion and resentment at the thought of African American students "invading" her school and ruining her senior year. Both girls stand within the whirlwind of fears and opinions of their families and communities. Eva's father is proud of her; her mother fears for her safety and happiness; and her boyfriend Cecil worries that she'll become "too white." Eva herself is, by turns, proud, excited, and fearful, especially after her family receives bomb threats. On the other side of town, Sophia makes a pact with her friends to ignore the "darkies" and to ostracize anyone who befriends them. But she grows angry and more confused as her brother and her boyfriend challenge her racist assumptions and as she starts to see black people around her—her family's maid and her horse's groom— with new eyes.

The Girl on the Outside covers just three days leading up to Chatman High School's opening day. As tension builds within the girls and within Mossville, racists come from the surrounding states to fight the desegregation. When last-minute legal appeals fail to block desegregation, the National Guard is sent in. The nine African American students, with help from the local N.A.A.C.P. representative, strategize ways to support each other to survive the first traumatic days and weeks of school. They decide on a buddy system, and on the appointed day, Eva boards the bus to meet up with her buddy, Bobbie. Unbeknownst to Eva, however, the other black students have been told to stay home at least one more day, and she arrives at Chatman to face an angry white mob all alone. Placing her hopes in the National Guard, Eva approaches the door, only to have the Guard turn against her and force her back into the mob. As she races back to the relative safety of the bus stop, Eva is spit on and threatened by the mob. Only one person comes to her rescue, Sophia, who braves the fury of her community to try to shield Eva from some of the racism which she herself so recently espoused.

The Girl on the Outside has an interesting structure, exploring the thoughts, feelings, and actions of two very different girls leading parallel lives in the same southern town. This structure dramatizes the different conditions under which black and white citizens lived, worked, and learned in 1957. Mildred Pitts Walter avoids making either girl a caricature but, rather, shows the positive and negative influences that have shaped the character of each. Walter portrays each community with evenhandedness, describing courageous and fearful African Americans, racist and anti-racist whites. Ultimately, this is a very hopeful and somewhat idealistic tale that underscores the power of adolescents to create social change, the courage of African American youth to fight for equal rights, and the ability of white youth to change themselves and their communities.

A fictionalized account of the 1957 integration of Central High School in Little Rock, Arkansas, *The Girl on the Outside* offers insight into that historical moment. Unfortunately, Walter spends so much time exploring the girls' feelings in anticipation of desegregation that the slow plot may not hold young adult readers' attention until the last few chapters, when Eva actually attempts to enter Chatman. I wish that Walter had moved this event up to the middle of the book and then devoted the succeeding chapters to the African Americans' experiences once they started attending classes regularly. As it is, the book climaxes with Eva's brave but unsuccessful approach to school and Sophia's change of heart. But these events are the beginning, not the end, of the actual struggle.

Walter portrays a strong, intact black family in Eva's family, with its supportive parents. The book features girls and women in leadership roles, including Eva, Sophia, most of the integrating students, and the N.A.A.C.P. representative. This is a nice corrective to the traditionally male-centered accounts of the Civil Rights struggle. Two strong male characters also offer positive role models—Eva's father, who gives her courage to take a stand, and Sophia's brother, who argues the evils of racism with everyone who'll listen. This novel is accessible to eighth- through eleventh-grade readers, girls and boys.

149. Walter, Mildred Pitts. *Trouble's Child.* New York: Lothrop, Lee and Shepard Books, 1985. 157 pages. ****

Coretta Scott King Honor Book, 1986

Martha lives with her grandmother Titay, a midwife and healer, on Blue Isle in the Gulf of Mexico. The island houses a close-knit, superstitious community where the girls marry by fourteen and fishermen frequently drown in Gulf storms. Blue Isle's school only goes up to the eighth grade, but nobody leaves the island to attend high school or for any other reason. However, fourteen-year-old Martha desperately wants to leave, to see the outside world, and to complete high school. Her grandmother wants her to stay and marry and then to learn Titay's healing knowledge so the old woman can retire. Martha is not sure she wants to take over as healer, and she knows she's not ready to marry! Even when a handsome outsider washes up on shore and is nursed back to health by Martha and Titay, Martha asks him only to help her get to the mainland.

Meanwhile, island folks are calling Martha conceited for wanting to leave and for refusing to marry. Cora, a bilious hoodoo practitioner jealous of Titay's healing power, begins spreading rumors about Martha and turning the island against Titay as well. Martha feels terribly torn between the expectations of her community and the dreams of her own heart. Events come to a head when Martha's former friend Ocie dies in childbirth, attended only by Cora. Martha realizes then that she must become the island's healer and midwife but only after arming herself with all the knowledge the mainland schools can offer. Titay reluctantly agrees to let her go, knowing that Martha must learn for herself that Titay's traditional wisdom is more valuable than any foreign teachings.

Trouble's Child is a fascinating, engaging book about a young girl's struggle to blend tradition with modernity in an isolated culture. It made me very curious about whether Mildred Pitts Walter based Blue Isle on any existing island culture. In any event, the story explores the common, though usually less dramatic, teenage task of evaluating one's familial and cultural values to decide what to keep and what to reject. Teenage readers will easily identify with Martha's confusion in trying to balance her own needs with community expectations. On the other hand, urban readers and any modern reader with limited imagination may have trouble identifying with the particulars of Martha's dilemma—marrying at fourteen, attending births, and digging herbs when she would rather be finishing high school. Similarly, for male readers, *Trouble's Child* will be even more like visiting a foreign world as its concerns are particularly female.

The female focus of the book is also a strength, though. It insists that girls' decisions and lives are important and that even in a traditional culture, females can claim their power. *Trouble's Child* additionally affirms the value of traditional, non-literate knowledge, even as it distinguishes it from harmful superstition. This, too, is a vital message for teenage readers growing up in a culture that devalues traditional, intuitive and non-Western knowledge in favor of the dominant, white-controlled, "objective" knowledge. The vividness of *Trouble's Child* is another strength as are the all-too-real petty jealousies which spring up in any small community.

Although I thoroughly enjoyed this book, I fear its audience will be limited to twelve- to sixteen-year-old girls who either live in rural areas or who enjoy fanciful, imaginative novel settings. The realities of Martha's life may simply be too different from most African American readers' lives to grab their interest. However, fans of Walter's other young adult books may be willing to give this fine novel the chance it deserves.

150. Wesley, Valerie Wilson. *Where Do I Go from Here?* New York: Scholastic, Inc., 1993. 138 pages. *****

As one of only ten African American students at Endicott Academy, an elite, wealthy prep school, fifteen-year-old Nia Jones feels like an outsider. She looks up to junior Marcus Garvey Williams, who manages both to be himself and to fit in—in fact, he is the most popular student at school . . . until he mysteriously disappears. Shortly afterward, Nia gets suspended for two weeks following a fist fight with a white student, Lucinda Spinotta, who attacks Nia for speaking out against the institution's racism. Lucinda, a closet scholarship student, works hard to hide her own humble Newark, New Jersey, origins.

During her suspension, Nia returns home to Newark to escape the stress at Endicott. However, she feels uneasy with her former friends and is pained to notice how her Endicott experience is influencing her world view and values. She soon learns that her Newark friends' lives are going nowhere. Malika toils like Sisyphus in a greasy fast-food establishment to save money for college, fully aware that her inferior high school undermines her chance for acceptance, let alone a scholarship. Debra, who desperately wants to be somebody, hangs on to her druglord boyfriend Snake, who buys her extravagant gifts and promises to make her a video star. Both Malika and Debra are distracted by violence in school and deterred by the school's mediocrity.

Nia tracks Marcus down in New York City and is shocked to learn that he left school to raise his son—the product of a semester-break affair—after the baby's mother abandoned him to Social Services. Marcus never recovered from the loss of his own father, who left his family when Marcus was twelve and died when Marcus was fifteen. So he defies his mother's pleas to put fatherhood on hold long enough to complete Endicott and moves in with his grandmother to care for his baby son. He works full time and finagles the credit he needs to get his high school diploma through a nontraditional route. Talking with Marcus brings Nia to the conclusion that she has a responsibility to take full advantage of the opportunities at Endicott. On the train returning to school, Nia and Lucinda apologize and confess their mutual feelings of alienation at Endicott and now at home. Nia realizes that leaving home does not have to mean losing herself.

Where Do I Go from Here? is noteworthy for its diverse and well-developed African American teenage characters. Opinionated, funny, and rebellious, Nia is an entertaining and perceptive narrator. She makes palpable the paradoxical feeling she has at Endicott of being rendered simultaneously invisible and on display as well as the dehumanizing and exhausting experience of being objectified and stereotyped, her individuality inconceivable to the white students who see only her color and class. Nia makes the reader feel what she feels, being surrounded by wealthy classmates who take luxuries like prep school for granted while she aches not to have to worry about every dollar for tuition and the ride home.

Nia's condemnation of Endicott is thrown brilliantly into relief by her Aunt Odessa's and Malika's enthrallment with the opportunities it represents. One of *Where Do I Go from Here?*'s most effective qualities is that, despite the bias—albeit realistic and legitimate—of its first-person narrator, it is not a diatribe; it is an open forum. The author does not dichotomize the characters as types but instead presents African Americans and whites who are poor and rich, in favor of prep school and opposed to it. The novel is a candid, constructive, and ultimately hopeful exposé of the prep school experience for African Americans, particularly when it centers on Marcus. He copes with his classmates' racism and classism by being better than everyone, academically and athletically. He defuses racial tensions and turns tokenism to his advantage by noting commonalities with his classmates as well as differences. And he teaches Nia to pick her battles instead of getting mad all the time. Similarly, Aunt Odessa, who works double shifts as a licensed practical nurse to put Nia through Endicott, lectures her: "You can't lose it every time somebody says something dumb. . . . What if Sojourner Truth had reacted to every dumb comment somebody made about her? Or Frederick

Douglass? What if they had been set off their course by nonsense? Where would we be? What about Dr. King . . . ? Now I know that you didn't have to face anything like Dr. King faced, did you?" Because Odessa and Marcus are undeniably "Black and proud," their advice cannot be taken as assimilationist or compromising, but as empowering.

Without belaboring the point, Valerie Wilson Wesley counters the stereotypes to which Nia and Marcus are subjected at Endicott. Their being on scholarship does not mean that their families sponge off welfare; on the contrary, their families sacrifice their health working hard to put their children through school. And instead of leaving Endicott for the selfish and deadly purpose of dealing drugs, Marcus leaves out of responsibility and affirmation of life. His assuming the duties of fatherhood with conviction and grace implicitly contradicts the stereotype of the irresponsible, promiscuous young African American male. On the other hand, the author points out that even the brightest, most responsible young men often do not use any protection against pregnancy or sexually transmitted disease. Nevertheless, Marcus' future still seems promising, suggesting that there are many ways to go after a dream.

Even the minor characters are well developed, a remarkable achievement for the animated and rapid-fire narrative. Even the jerks and villains are extraordinarily humanized and three dimensional. Valerie Wilson Wesley does justice to class and race issues as separate and intertwined entities and as they affect African Americans and European Americans in unprecedented and unsurpassed style. Readers who identify with Nia or Marcus will derive confirmation and comfort from the novel, while readers who are strangers to the characters and their circumstances will find them equally irresistible and thought provoking. *Where Do I Go from Here?* is highly recommended for middle-school and high-school students.

151. Wilkinson, Brenda. *Ludell*. New York: Bantam Books, 1975. 168 pages. **

School Library Journal Best Books for Children and Young Adults, 1975

Ludell Wilson is an eleven-year-old African American girl growing up in Waycross, Georgia in 1955. She lives alone with her grandmother, next door to her best friend Ruthie Mae Johnson and the whole Johnson crowd of brothers and sisters. *Ludell* is about being a child in an all-black, poor southern town. Ludell's greatest worries are whether she'll get blue jeans for Christmas and how to keep her classmates from making fun of the time she peed in her pants in school. Her grandmother and the Johnsons are somewhat more concerned about money but never so much that it seriously intrudes on Ludell's consciousness. This is not a book about racism or even about coming of age—it's more a slice of childhood story in the vein of *Little House on the Prairie*.

Although *Ludell* is well written, both its protagonist and its concerns are too young to hold the interest of most young adult readers. It is appropriate for fourth to sixth graders, who can best identify with Ludell's first kiss, her giddy conversations with Ruthie Mae, and her preoccupation with hot dog day at school. The book is relatively long and the Black English dialogue may be difficult for some younger readers, but the writing style is otherwise accessible. *Ludell* is interesting in its own way, but only to younger readers.

152. Wilkinson, Brenda. *Ludell and Willie*. New York: Harper and Row Publishers, 1977. 181 pages. ***

American Library Association Notable Books for Children and Young Adults, 1977; School Library Journal Best Books for Children and Young Adults, 1977

Ludell and Willie continues the chronicles of Ludell Wilson's girlhood in Waycross, Georgia, during the era of the early Civil Rights Movement. Now Ludell is in her last year of high school, living with her grandmother, whom she calls Mama. The novel documents the numerous ways racism and classism affect one young African American girl and her community. The oppression is particularized in descriptions of Ludell's daily routine—walking miles to the decrepit, non-accredited, all-black Central High School, then working after school cleaning the Seaman family's bathroom for fifty cents an hour, to help Mama keep the lights on and the water running. Ludell suffers not only the rudeness of her white employer but also of the white boys who taunt her on her walk to school. Otherwise, she lives in an all-black world and likes the segregation, but she wants equal resources and opportunities.

All that said, however, *Ludell and Willie* is essentially a love story. The dominant plot is the intense romance between Ludell and her longtime neighbor and friend, Willie Johnson. Their kinfolk have a cynical view of young love which has been reinforced by the experiences of both families. Ludell doesn't know who her father was, and her mother, Dessa, left Ludell with Mama to go to New York. Willie hasn't seen his father since he was four, when he left in search of work. Willie's oldest sister, Mattie, barely finished school before she left her five-year-old son in her mother's care to follow another man to Florida. Even Reverend Copeland is notorious for "[g]oing wit everything in a skirt." So Mama keeps Ludell practically imprisoned in the house, and Ludell has to devise clever means of sneaking out to be with Willie. She succeeds often enough for most of the plot to revolve around her and Willie's sweet talk and furtive kissing.

Only six weeks before graduation, Mama's health deteriorates and she dies. The author delineates Mama's deterioration and its impact on Ludell graphically but not morbidly, with action more than description—a few vignettes aptly convey the changes Mama and Ludell go through during the dying process. What seems unrealistic, however, is that Dessa insists on coming down to bring Ludell back to New York, even though local kinfolk offer to take care of her. Ludell doesn't consider Dessa her real mother and, understandably, treats her with insolence. Going to New York only means hurt for Ludell, with graduation so near and with Willie and other loved ones all down in Georgia. A little more insight into Dessa would have been helpful. But this story is told from Ludell's point of view, and Ludell, being an adolescent, naturally vilifies her bad mother.

In New York, Ludell indulges in romantic longings—mostly, to be with Willie forever, but also longings to go to college and to see the world outside of Waycross. She and Willie plan to marry right after graduation. The end of the book suggests that their separation will only delay, not destroy, their plans. *Ludell and Willie* ends with the emphasis on romance, with the pain of separation, waiting and uncertainty. This "up in the air" ending works well, leaving readers eager for a sequel.

Ludell and Willie raises issues tied to racism, but they take a back seat to the book's primary concern: love. Wilkinson nevertheless does a fine job of working thoughtful subplots into the story, giving sophisticated readers much to reflect on. Wilkinson offers excellent historical detail and savvy analysis of how racism can affect an African American's identity. The story also offers delicate treatment of other forms of oppression, including internalized racism, classism, and poverty. In Waycross, light-skinned black people are "color-struck." The cheerleaders and club leaders at the high school are middle-class blacks, either light skinned or bleached. These "cross-town" kids hold attitudes of superiority over Ludell, Willie and their neighbors. Similarly, the author's brush-stroke development of Ludell's relationship with her gay English teacher, Mr. Tyson, accomplishes much economically: "Ludell left the room regretting that she hadn't gotten to know Mr. Tyson better earlier in the year. . . . Often she'd wanted to speak to him, show him some of her private work, but she'd avoided it because of what everybody said about him being so funny. How ironic it was, she thought . . . that she'd stood there talking about her hatred for Negroes discriminating against other Negroes, when in essence she had been that way with him."

Ludell and Willie have serious plans for a couple of teenagers, though no one takes their commitment seriously. Adults worry because they assume that only their level of sexual activity is serious. In fact, Ludell and Willie are passionate, kissing and groping whenever possible, but they do nothing more. Willie never pressures Ludell for even a kiss, and Ludell's lust for Willie seems to be satisfied just by being in his company often and by being physically close. The difference between Willie and the "typical" man suggested throughout the story is striking. It's nice to have such negative stereotypes of male sexuality contradicted. And it's nice, if somewhat unreal, that there's no double standard in Ludell and Willie's relationship. Wilkinson gives some explanation for Willie's uncharacteristically gentlemanliness and tenderness; he identifies with his mother's struggle to raise her six children after her husband abandoned the family. Willie's frustration about not being able to provide for his mother and siblings is convincingly drawn.

Ludell and Willie leaves no doubt that, for African Americans, living in the 1950s and 1960s in the segregated South was extremely trying. A hard heart was almost inevitable for those who lived this hard life. The incredible affection, warmth and nurturing that Ludell and Willie share with each other stands in dramatic contrast to the generally depressing environment in which they live. This puts the reader right into the heads and hearts of the couple. Most significantly, it affirms the power of young people, through simple acts of love, to enable each other to do more than survive during hard times.

Sometimes the novel's dialogue is slow, and the printed dialect may be hard for some younger readers to figure out at first. The book will appeal most to female readers, in middle or high school, who are die-hard romantics. Even the most romantic boys will probably not enjoy the book much because the power struggle between Ludell and her grandmother and mother is distinctly female. Some readers may find the restrictions which Mama imposes on Ludell unbelievably extreme and may not believe Ludell and Willie's carefully self-controlled sexual activity. Overall, though, *Ludell and Willie* is a well written book with strongly defined characters and situations.

153. Wilkinson, Brenda. *Ludell's New York Time*. New York: Harper and Row Publishers, 1980. 184 pages. *

This third and final book in the series follows Ludell to New York City, where she lives with her mother Dessa after her grandmother dies. In New York, Ludell sleeps on a cot in the living room of the subsidized apartment which her mother shares with her alcoholic boyfriend Jimmy. Dessa forces Ludell to register at Harlem High School although she was only one month from graduating from her Waycross, Georgia, high school. Ludell finds Harlem High School big, ugly, and intimidating, with nasty, disrespectful students. Her mother pressures her to learn a trade and find a job, although Ludell dreams of going to college. Through a series of vignettes, *Ludell's New York Time* presents Ludell's naive discoveries of the wonders and horrors of big city life in 1963—the widest selection of clothing she's ever seen and her first taste of pizza contrasting with crowded buses, rathole public housing, sleazy men, and irresponsible teenagers.

Dessa tries to remake Ludell to fit in with fast city life, urging her to become friends with her own friends' teenage daughter, Regina. Regina's parents allow her to smoke and drink alongside them, and permit her to skip school and party with whomever she wants. Every time Ludell goes out with her, she gets stuck in an awkward situation of drinking and sex. Premarital sex is a recurrent theme in the novel—nearly everybody is having sex and worrying constantly about becoming pregnant, without taking any active precautions to prevent it. Everyone, from the former valedictorian at Ludell's

Georgia high school to local churchwomen, becomes pregnant and finds unplanned pregnancy a disaster. Meanwhile, Ludell abstains, dreaming obsessively about her boyfriend Willie back in Waycross, with whom she exchanges sappy love letters constantly. Willie's plans to join Ludell in New York are postponed by a series of family disasters, until he is drafted for the Vietnam War. At the last moment, he and Ludell have a quickie marriage, and she vows to try to follow him wherever the army sends him.

Ludell's New York Time is an insipid book not worth the paper it's printed on. Between Ludell's obsessing over her squabbles with her mother and missing Willie, she grows tiresome very fast. It's hard to believe that any modern girl could be as naive as Ludell, so her astonishment with New York seems overblown. Similarly overblown is her mother Dessa's evil character—if Dessa is not forcing her daughter out to work, she's pushing her to be more like the totally unsuitable Regina. She never stops ridiculing Waycross or Ludell's marriage plans, and tries to shatter her dream of attending college as well. Ludell's love for Willie takes a sexist turn in this third novel, when she is subsumed in becoming his wife. By the story's end she has a job and attends college at night after many fights with her mother, but then gives up college to follow Willie around.

The only positive African American role models offered are two older churchwomen, one a traditional woman whose identity is totally wrapped up in her husband, the other a newly radicalized activist who organizes northern blacks to work in the South for civil rights. Balancing out these characters is a host of boozing, no-count black adults and irresponsible, partying teens. In addition, the novel portrays Puerto Ricans as sleazy, high-strung foreigners who need to learn English, and Jews as unattractive, materialistic neurotics. Because of these many faults, and because Ludell's character is so foolish that few readers of any age or sex will find the book engaging, *Ludell's New York Time* is better skipped.

154.   Wilkinson, Brenda. *Not Separate, Not Equal.* New York: Harper and Row Publishers, 1987. 152 pages. *

Not Separate, Not Equal chronicles a few days in the life of fictional Malene Freeman, a seventeen-year-old Georgian who integrates all-white Pineridge High School in 1965 along with five other black students. Malene is even more of an outsider than the other black students, who all come from Pineridge's "Black elite." Malene comes from a poor sharecropping family and has only recently been adopted by the wealthy Freemans after losing her family in a fire. At school, however, the black students stick together despite conflicts over class, assimilation, militancy, and pride. Together and separately, they face police dogs, snubbings, attacks, kidnappings, and finally, more militant activists accuse them of being Uncle Toms.

Early public school integration efforts offer promising subject matter for a young adult novel, both because of the subject's historical importance in civil rights struggles and because of its immediate relevance to high-school age students. The opportunity to creatively reconstruct the students' experiences should draw many young adult authors, but I hope that future books will explore this topic better than *Not Separate, Not Equal.* Aside from a few fantastic plot twists, the story is almost entirely dialogue—dialogue that alternates between the silly and the didactic, spoken by characters who never develop beyond caricatures of different points of view. I admire Wilkinson's attention to class issues and her attempt to portray the complexity of blacks' and whites' responses to desegregation, but her novel just does not work. The plot climax, which has the students locked in a barn by a foolish, drunken, old white man, trivializes the very real danger which the first black student desegregationists faced. Furthermore, the students in this story behave like ten-year-olds, despite the fact that they are supposed to be high school juniors and seniors. Ultimately, the characters are too flat and the plot too contrived to evoke either the reader's identification with the students or a sense of the intensity of the times.

Not Separate, Not Equal has a reading level suitable for upper-elementary and middle-school students, but even young readers deserve a more serious treatment of this significant topic.

155.   Wilkinson, Brenda. *Definitely Cool.* New York: Scholastic, Inc., 1993. 167 pages. ****

Definitely Cool traces three months in the life of twelve-year-old Roxanne Williams as she enters junior high school. In anecdotal fashion, the story presents one mini-drama and lesson after another. Brenda Wilkinson takes the reader through a roller coaster ride of expectations and bittersweet disappointments, the crises and the lesser problems that are easily blown up to monumental disasters by junior-high-school students—from figuring out a new class schedule and building plan to finding someone to sit with in the cafeteria, from arguing with a parent over wearing makeup to talking on the phone with a boyfriend. There are also the serious problems which a parent cannot fix—racist white teachers belittle African American students in subtle but insidious ways, and the students themselves perpetuate de facto segregation.

Roxanne lives in a public housing project with her mother. She speaks with her father on the telephone every day, and on the weekends they get together to shop or see a movie. Her parents are strict but sensible, explaining to Roxanne the rationale behind their every rule. As Roxanne enters adolescence, though, she and her mother have predictable power struggles—over having company in the apartment when mom's at work, over wearing makeup and showy jewelry, over wearing miniskirts and ratty jeans, over using jargon instead of "proper English," etc.

At her new school in an affluent section of the Bronx, Roxanne desperately wants to make new friends. She treats her oldest friends, Maxine and Rolland, the way she treats her parents. On the one hand, she wants to break out on her own, to grow and change. On the other hand, she reluctantly recognizes that the familiar relationships and shared history enable her to maintain her sense of self. As she makes new friends, she struggles to stay true to herself and her values. When she manages to resist peer pressure urging her to skip school, get a boyfriend, or sneak around her parents, she finds that what her parents and teachers call silly or inappropriate or dangerous or unattractive really is—not only in her opinion, but in the view of those peers whom she comes to appreciate as real friends. This coming of age story makes the point that what's inside counts more than cool poses.

Brenda Wilkinson has written a very readable book that should appeal to middle-school students and perhaps to high-school students undergoing a transition or challenge similar to Roxanne's. Any student who knows firsthand the power struggle between parent and teen, the dilemma of conforming to peer pressure, or the pain of cliques and outsider status   will   readily   identify   with   the   protagonist's experiences. Roxanne's parents are attractive characters with strengths and weaknesses.

Roxanne herself is a realistic character, a little stronger and wiser than the average adolescent, but not perfect. Her friend Maxine is bossy, but in a delightful way. Her friend Rolland is sweet and silly, trying to grow up and to shift from being Roxanne's friend to being her boyfriend. Rolland and Marcus, Roxanne's lukewarm love interest, are the only male characters. While they are decently developed and not simply idealized or debased, they are still not full enough figures in the story to make male readers feel entirely invited into the action. This is really a book for girls.

Readers who identify with Roxanne will find confirmation of their own concerns and values in the story. The big message craftily woven throughout the novel, which Roxanne matter-of-factly sums up at the book's end, is this: "Each of them had fronted in one way or another. Now everything was in the open. No one in their group had it all together, but then who *did* in seventh grade?" Roxanne learns that Kenya and Pat live in foster homes and welfare motels. Margarita and N.E., who skip school to attend Raheem's party that they confess turned out to be foolish, get caught and punished and gain a reality check on what's important. Roxanne learns to think for herself: that's what's really cool.

Readers will appreciate Roxanne's interior monologues, long enough to make a point but short enough for readers with limited attention spans. Readers will also enjoy Wilkinson's rendering of the latest colloquialisms, although a few years from now some of this dialogue will unfortunately date the book.

156. Williams-Garcia, Rita. *Blue Tights*. New York: Lodestar Books, 1988. 138 pages. ***

In Jamaica, New York, fifteen-year-old Joyce Collins dreams of being a dancer like her mother and of being accepted by the cool crowd at school. But Ms. Sobel, her ballet teacher, picks on Joyce incessantly and announces that Joyce's butt is too big for ballet. Meanwhile, Cindi and Jay-Jay, who are cooler, richer, and more popular than Joyce, cruelly ridicule her friendly overtures. Joyce also has to contend with her fast reputation, although in reality she has never had a boyfriend before Sam. Sam, a middle-aged man, pressures Joyce for sex in exchange for attention and ten-dollar bills; when she finally refuses angrily, she loses him.

Then Joyce gets involved in the Kuji Je Tea Ujama Dance Ensemble, an African American troupe rehearsing African dances for a Kwanza performance. There, with the drumming beat and the freer, more expressive dance, Joyce finds her place. Chosen for the lead part, she learns discipline and perseverance from Hasan, the director, while coping with the jealous rivalry of the other dancers.

She falls in love with J'had, the Muslim drummer, and wrestles with her sexual attraction to him. When she finally starts to make love with him, he makes her feel lovable, refuting all of the people who never touched her lovingly—her father, whom she never knew; her mother, who left her as a baby to dance; and her Aunt Em, who raised her but never touched her. But J'had, overwhelmed by guilt at breaking the Muslim taboo against premarital sexual contact, flees Joyce and forsakes Muslim practice completely.

Devastated, Joyce can barely force herself to go through with the Kwanza performance. However, the audience loves her, catapulting her to local fame and popularity and increasing her self-confidence immensely. As Joyce respects herself more, she approaches dance, her relationships, and her future more maturely.

Blue Tights starts out slowly, with a cast of disagreeable characters. Joyce's initial concerns are annoyingly immature, and it's hard to care about her desperate bids for popularity and approval. Almost the whole first half of the book describes how disappointing Joyce's life is in every area: school, family, friends, and dance.

Presumably, this serves to set the stage for the major transformations after Joyce joins the African American dance ensemble, at which point *Blue Tights* becomes much more engrossing. The plot picks up as Joyce becomes more challenged to define her commitment to dance and to the important people in her life: her mother, J'had, and her new friend, Tamu. The second half of the book is quite good, despite J'had's uncountered religious sexism and the suggestion that Joyce's sexuality is single-handedly to blame for his default to street life. Nevertheless, Joyce's self-discovery is inspiring, offering a believable role model for teenage readers struggling with issues of sexuality, self-worth, and popularity in their own lives.

Eighth- to eleventh-grade readers, girls more than boys, will identify with *Blue Tights*.

157.   Williams-Garcia, Rita. *Fast Talk on a Slow Track*. New York: Bantam Books, 1991. 182 pages. ****

American Library Association Notable Books for Children and Young Adults, 1991

Denzel Watson was valedictorian and president of the senior class at his Queens, New York, high school, and he scored higher on the SAT than anyone else in the school. So when he gets invited to a Princeton University program for minority students from "under-enriched educational backgrounds," he's confident that he can fly through with his usual mix of brains, fast talk, and *Cliff Notes*. Instead, the professors demand that he work hard and think hard, which he has never had to do before. Afraid of failing, Denzel rebels, insisting that he doesn't need a college education and never wanted to go to Princeton anyway.

In the weeks between Princeton's summer program and the beginning of school, Denzel returns home to his summer job of hustling candy and cookies door to door. He excels at this job and enjoys the competition with co-worker Carmello, an illiterate Puerto Rican teenager. At the same time, Denzel rationalizes his decision not to return to Princeton and tries to tell his parents. In the end, though, a brutal falling-out with Carmello drives Denzel back to Princeton, where he faces his fear of failure only to find out that he enjoys the challenge of learning.

Fast Talk on a Slow Track is an excellent book about a hot topic. Rita Williams-Garcia captures perfectly the self-doubt, excuses, and fast talk of a teenage boy faced with the scariest challenge of his life—going to a demanding, competitive college and risking failure. The novel is never didactic, but manages to expose every self-deceptive rationalization that African American boys use to explain their failure to make the most of their talents.

Denzel's character is completely believable, as are his relationships with his family, friends, and co-workers. Because the book is written in Denzel's own voice, readers will easily identify with him. His parents' personalities are somewhat caricatured—his father an overblown black activist and his mother an apologetic church-going woman who loves to brag about her son's accomplishments; however, these caricatures are Denzel's own adolescent perspectives of his parents, exaggerations which will undoubtedly absorb adolescent readers.

The only small problem with this novel is that it spends too much time describing Denzel's summer workdays and not enough time describing his transformation at Princeton. In the last chapter, Denzel learns that he can compete as a thinker, that, in fact, he loves to use his mind. I wanted to know more about this metamorphosis and to follow him through more of it. On the other hand, one sign of a great book is that the reader hates to say good-bye to the characters at the end; *Fast Talk on a Slow Track* is such a book. Anyone who is considering college should read it.

The novel's reading level and length make it best suited for ninth to twelfth graders. Boys will enjoy the protagonist, while girls will enjoy the book because it lovingly pokes fun at teenage boys. In addition, any teenager will benefit from reading the story because it addresses fear of failure, a topic vital to every teenager, but rarely addressed in African American young adult fiction.

158.   Wilson, Johnniece Marshall. *Oh, Brother*. New York: Scholastic, Inc., 1988. 121 pages. ***

Alex shares a bedroom with his resentful older brother, Andrew, since the arrival of their baby sister, Bonnie. The two brothers differ dramatically. Considerate and responsible Alex obeys his parents, lavishes his sister with attention, tends to his lonely elderly neighbor, Mrs. Pettaway, and excels in school. Andrew does the opposite with a vengeance and gets away with it. What he does most consistently is play in a nearby lot with his cronies who, like him, get held back in school or take Alex's bike without permission and return it too late for Alex to use it to deliver the newspapers on his route. Andrew's friends bully and taunt Alex, and his parents offer no help.

Because of Andrew's carelessness, Alex's bike is stolen; on top of that injustice, Andrew takes some of Alex's stashed-away paper route money—which Alex is saving to buy himself a fancy new bike—to spend on fooling around with his friends. Even though their parents seem determined to make Andrew reform, Alex doubts that Andrew will compensate him for the stolen bike or money. After Alex learns that Andrew borrowed the bike for a secret prescription delivery job and after Andrew gets beaten by the gang that stole the bike, Alex sees another side to his brother. Then Alex rescues Mrs. Pettaway from a fire in her home and beats up Andrew's friend, Mungo, for harassing him; Andrew, with difficulty, admits that he admires Alex for his heroism, hard work, and dedication to school.

Oh, Brother is an aptly titled book focusing on sibling abuses and annoyances. Alex is not perfect; he succumbs to anger and frustration and fights back frequently. The motivation for Andrew's behavior is explained, but nonetheless remains an extreme manifestation of jealousy and resentment of his younger siblings. Still, what explains the jolting disparity between these brothers in a seemingly "together" suburban family headed by a teacher? Is the way that Andrew treats Alex acceptable? And is Andrew's self-destructive behavior acceptable? The author, through the moral authority figures of the parents and Mrs. Pettaway, practically excuses it.

Mrs. Pettaway is the principal teacher in the novel. She explains to Alex that Andrew's behavior is part of his growing up and wanting to be more in charge. Mrs. Pettaway's points are solid but within the context of the story seem to legitimate a damaging sibling dynamic. On the other hand, her other key lesson is uncompromised: that difficulty helps to build character.

Instruction from Alex's parents comes in the concrete form of daily rituals that teach responsibility, from expecting the brothers to baby-sit Bonnie to scheduling them to rotate chores like washing dishes and maintaining the yard. In addition to its hearty emphasis on sharing household responsibilities as a given, the narrative also stresses another healthy concept: that young people should work hard to save for the extras they want, regardless of what their parents can provide. Alex's old bike, at twelve dollars, and his new bike, at three hundred and fifty dollars, are "luxuries" for which it's appropriate and character-building to work and save.

Although the central characters are boys, their essential circumstances will lure in any reader who can identify with sibling rivalry and chores or jobs. Not a lot happens in *Oh, Brother*, and, although it's not a boring novel, it seems overweighted with descriptions of daily routines at home and in school and with nearly identical arguments and fight scenes. Because the protagonists are in elementary school, and the author has accurately captured their young mind-set, primarily upper elementary-school readers will appreciate it, though some middle-school readers plagued by sibling problems and in need of catharsis may enjoy it, too.

159. Wilson, Johnniece Marshall. *Robin on His Own*. New York: Scholastic, Inc., 1990. 154 pages. ***

Robin on His Own is a warm, tender story about a boy coming to terms with his mother's death and the changes that follow in his own life. Robin lives with his musician father, his Aunt Belle, a cat named Watusi, and a singing parakeet. Although he has many neighborhood friends, he has been lonely since his mother's death, unable to talk about his feelings with his preoccupied father and unable to sing in the church choir because of the emptiness he feels inside. In addition, new changes threaten his already shaky equilibrium: Aunt Belle marries and moves to West Virginia, and Robin's father announces that they must sell the house and move into an apartment in a new neighborhood. When the new baby-sitter hired to replace Aunt Belle leaves Robin alone in the middle of the night, he leaves home to find Aunt Belle in West Virginia. Along the way, he is trapped in an abandoned house and wakes up in the hospital, surrounded by the strength and stability of his family and friends.

Robin on His Own is a book for fourth to seventh graders. Although author Johnniece Marshall Wilson never specifies Robin's age, his preoccupation with kickball and Saturday morning cartoons suggests a boy of ten or eleven. The writing is not heavy handed even though it deals with the themes of loss and change through the daily events in a young boy's life—getting a new pet, returning to the church choir, feeling separate from his friends. However, the pace of the plot is too slow for older readers; the entire book spans less than two weeks, and each chapter contains only one event, often something as simple as a conversation or preparing dinner.

The characters are likable and realistic, including a father who protects himself from his own grief by burying himself in his music and distancing himself from his son. Robin's Aunt Belle offers a loving ear, but she, too, "abandons" him to go on with her own life. And Robin himself must finally break through his sense of isolation to share his feelings with his father so that they can begin to build a home together. Unlike many other African American young adult books whose young characters are forced to raise themselves in the absence of parents, *Robin on His Own* offers a father who simply needs jarring to return to his nurturing role. This, too, makes the novel reassuring for younger readers. Overall, this is a nice book, somewhat simple at times, but it deals thoughtfully with the topic of loss and may be particularly helpful to initiate a conversation with any young person coping with death or another kind of loss.

160.   Wilson, Johnniece Marshall. *Poor Girl, Rich Girl*. New York: Scholastic, Inc., 1992. 179 pages. ***

Poor Girl, Rich Girl is an entertaining and edifying tale, recounted in the voice of fourteen-year-old Miranda Moses. Hating the heaviness of her eyeglass frames and the gross distortion of her eyes that the glasses' lenses cause—and being a typically self-conscious teenager—Miranda sets her sights on getting contact lenses. However, she faces two challenges. First, her parents adamantly state that they cannot afford to buy her contact lenses. The Moseses are a hard-working, upwardly-mobile but pragmatic middle-class family who are recent first-time homeowners. Michael's earnings at his own repair shop and Justine's wages as a hospital dietitian go primarily towards their mortgage. Miranda finds her parents maddening when they flatly rebuff her begging, but she also appreciates them for being loving and principled. Clearly, they have raised their only child well, for she works toward her goal of getting contact lenses with the same determination that enabled her parents to buy their home.

Miranda plans to buy the contact lenses herself, but jobs are scarce for young people under sixteen. Miranda is ambitious and resourceful, however, and she manages to fill her summer schedule with assorted jobs: baby-sitting, camp counseling, grocery clerking, and dog walking. Along the way, she learns the value of hard-earned money.

In a cute subplot, Miranda shares responsibility with her mother for cooking dinner. As she teaches herself to cook, she grows gracefully into accepting her responsibility and doing a good job of it.

Woven into the story of Miranda's working all summer are episodes with her closest friend, fellow ninth-grade classmate Teena, and with her archenemy, Catriona. During the school year, Miranda envied Catriona's full figure and stylish clothes but tried to avoid her. During the summer, she realizes that Catriona is lonely and she reaches out to her gradually. Catriona's pretense of being "together" keeps her separate from her more "mundane" peers and alienates her even from herself, unwilling to admit to family struggles. Catriona's wardrobe and her mother's Cadillac suggest wealth, but in reality, her family is struggling like every other family to make ends meet. Hence the novel's title: substance counts, and in that, Miranda recognizes she's wealthy, and she stops measuring everything in material terms.

Miranda Moses makes for an endearing protagonist. She's brainy yet down to earth, funny but not cruelly so at another's expense. Her family is solid. *Poor Girl, Rich Girl*'s messages about money and work are refreshingly realistic and much needed in America's ever-more materialistic society, especially since youth are intensely targeted as consumers. *Poor Girl, Rich Girl* is not exactly an exciting story, though many junior high-school students, particularly girls—as well as sixteen-year-olds new to the working world—will see their own power struggles and values struggles between adult and youth culture reflected authentically here.

My only reservation about this superb novel is that Miranda's mother wants her to become a competent cook now so that she will be able to cook and cook well for a husband in the future. This is a surprisingly sexist glitch in a story where her parents' main thrust in expecting her to assume more responsibilities as she matures is to help her become an independent and competent person, not a servant to a husband.

161. Woodson, Jacqueline. *Last Summer with Maizon*. New York: Delacorte Press, 1990. 105 pages. ****

Margaret and Maizon are best friends, almost sisters, in Brooklyn until the summer between sixth and seventh grade. That summer, Margaret's father dies of a heart attack and her mother cries every day. That summer, Mrs. Dell, Margaret's downstairs neighbor with the "sight," warns her that she'll have to learn to be strong. That summer, Maizon applies for a scholarship to Blue Hill School in Connecticut, threatening to leave Margaret behind and alone.

Come fall, Maizon does leave for Connecticut, and Margaret worries that they will grow apart, especially when months pass with no word from her friend. Meanwhile, the empty sadness Margaret continues to feel about her father's death distracts her from her own schoolwork. Her teacher urges her to write her feelings out, so Margaret starts writing poetry and keeping a diary. When her poetry wins an award, Margaret realizes that Maizon's absence frees her to try new things. With the help of her teacher, her mother, and wise neighbor women, Margaret starts to come to terms with the changes in her life. Then, Maizon, devastated by the cold treatment she received from white girls at school, leaves Blue Hill to return to Brooklyn. She wants to pick up her friendship with Margaret where they left off. Both girls have changed, but they realize that their love for each other can weather their differences and their growth.

Last Summer with Maizon is a fine book, simple and understated, with the profound message of facing and growing through life's difficulties. Jacqueline Woodson handles the death of Margaret's father honestly and sensitively, depicting Margaret's sadness and sense of confusion over her loss. Woodson is equally honest in exploring the loss of a friend through distance and new experiences, portraying both Margaret's hurt and her new freedom to make other friends and to develop new talents.

Both Margaret and Maizon are likable characters. The older women who people the book give the girls a sense of comfort and security, while helping them to understand their lives. This sense of adult support distinguishes *Last Summer with Maizon* from many other African American young adult novels where teen friendships help kids survive the absence of any substantive parenting. This makes *Last Summer with Maizon* a more comforting book for younger teens (and, interestingly, the author works with homeless children and runaways, an audience crying out for such comfort). The age of the protagonist and the reading level of this novel also make it appropriate for younger teens, grades five to nine.

Because it is a very female-centered book, girls may find themselves reflected in the story in more ways than boys will. However, there are no negative messages about males—a largely female world is simply a fact of life for these characters. Similarly, there are no strong externalized statements about race in this book—an African American environment is also a fact of life for the characters, at least until Maizon goes to Connecticut. Even then, the story suggests that Maizon's mistreatment at Blue Hill results partly from racism and partly from Maizon's own self-protective cockiness. *Last Summer with Maizon* offers realistic characters and a sensitive story relevant to any young adult struggling with the difficult task of growing up.

162. Woodson, Jacqueline. *The Dear One*. New York: Delacorte Press, 1991. 145 pages. ***

Feni is a loner, a twelve-year-old only child living with her mother in an upper-middle-class black suburb in Pennsylvania. Feni has built a protective wall around herself ever since her mother became an alcoholic, her father moved out and became a stranger, and her beloved grandmother died in a horrible accident. So when Feni's mother announces that her college friend's pregnant daughter, Rebecca, will be coming to live with them until she has her baby, Feni rebels. Despite Feni's protests, Rebecca does come, and the two girls clash immediately. Fifteen-year-old Rebecca feels intimidated by Feni's wealth and the sheltered suburb she calls home. Feni resents Rebecca's intrusion and feels threatened by her worldly toughness, learned on the streets of Harlem. Eventually, the girls overcome their mutual mistrust to become friends, though, and Rebecca even names her baby after Feni.

Interesting adults people the story as well. Feni's mother, a recovering alcoholic, struggles to balance her career with raising her daughter alone. Her best friend, Marion, is Feni's adopted aunt and shows by example that lesbians are just as tender, strong, funny, and dependable as everyone else. Rebecca's mother, struggling to recover from a nervous breakdown, is portrayed as a warm and generous woman overwhelmed by her circumstances. Jacqueline Woodson casts an unfailingly compassionate eye on her adult characters, depicting them as loving and always struggling to do their best despite their significant parenting faults. One of Woodson's great strengths is her dual empathy for children growing up under difficult circumstances and for adults being less than perfect parents.

Another strength is the authenticity of her voice. She is an author who clearly knows young teenage girls, knows their quirks and dreams, their fears and wonder. She knows and describes the way they explain their lives to themselves, especially the things they can't control, like an alcoholic mother, changing bodies, and poverty. She writes about girls in early adolescence whose attention is still focused on female friendships and self-discovery before boys take over their emotional lives. *The Dear One* is strongly female and will interest girls much more than boys. Seventh- to ninth-grade readers will find its themes and style inviting and accessible.

The Dear One tackles important issues of class differences and conflicts among African Americans, homosexuality, teenage pregnancy, giving a baby up for adoption, alcoholism, and divorce. Woodson's treatment of Marion is the most positive, destigmatizing treatment I've seen of lesbians in any young adult book and the only one I've seen in an African American young adult book. Unfortunately, the plot doesn't quite keep up with the book's other strengths: the central conflict between Rebecca and Feni resolves itself without explanation—almost as if several chapters had fallen out of the center of the novel—and this weakens the story considerably. Despite its plot failings, *The Dear One* is well worth reading. The prologue, with its breathtaking honesty, reminds me of some of James Baldwin's most beautiful fiction. Woodson is a writer of great promise—look for her future books.

163. Woodson, Jacqueline. *Maizon at Blue Hill.* New York: Delacorte Press, 1992. 131 pages. ****

American Library Association Notable Books for Children and Young Adults, 1992

Maizon at Blue Hill continues the story of Maizon Singh, first introduced in *Last Summer with Maizon.* In this story, Maizon reluctantly leaves her grandmother and her best friend, Margaret, in Brooklyn to attend elite Blue Hill preparatory school in Connecticut. Entering the seventh grade, Maizon learns that she is one of only five African American students at Blue Hill, and one of even fewer scholarship students. Maizon has never been outside of Brooklyn before and she is used to an all-black environment, so initially she feels relieved to be welcomed into the clique of black students at Blue Hill. But the black girls demand her undivided loyalty, insisting that she eat, socialize, and play only with them. Maizon soon finds their demands constricting and falls out of their favor entirely when she looks into the all-white Debate Club and insists on her right to make white friends.

At the same time, Maizon feels confused by her interactions with the white students at Blue Hill. Some are as ignorant as she expects, but others surprise her. In her English class, for example, white students understand Toni Morrison's novel, *The Bluest Eye*, with insight that astounds Maizon. Maizon rebukes her white roommate Sandy's attempts to be friendly until she learns that Sandy is also on scholarship, which destroys some of Maizon's assumptions about all whites being rich. Still, Maizon feels that she doesn't fit in anywhere at Blue Hill, and she's afraid that her experiences there have changed her so that she will not fit in in Brooklyn anymore either. She tries to hide her unhappiness from her Brooklyn family and friends, but finally, Maizon decides that, despite her shame of returning home as a "failure," she must go home to Brooklyn to carve out a place to belong.

Maizon at Blue Hill continues author Jacqueline Woodson's elegant evocation of the internal life of twelve-year-old girls. Maizon struggles valiantly to define herself in a world that does not reward smart black girls from poor families. Her sadness at realizing that she may never completely belong is poignant and believable. And her hard-won solution—to look inward for her own strength and outward for support from people who may only be able to understand part of her—is a mark of growing up.

The novel's plot moves quickly, and its protagonist is sympathetic. Woodson finds a perfect balance in exploring complex issues of race and class, self-definition, individualism, and community, with a simplicity that makes the analysis accessible to young readers. Her characters are primarily young adolescent girls, but where adults appear, they tend to be understanding and supportive. Although the novel's characters are almost exclusively female, the perspective offered is not overwhelmingly female, so boys as well as girls will be able to connect with the situations presented. *Maizon at Blue Hill* is enjoyable, high-quality literature for fifth- to seventh-grade readers.

164. Woodson, Jacqueline. *Between Madison and Palmetto.* New York: Delacorte Press, 1993. 112 pages. ****

Brooklyn eighth graders Maizon and Margaret have been best friends for many years through the death of Margaret's father and Maizon's aborted attempt to attend a predominantly-white boarding school. Now they are both back on Madison Street attending Pace Academy in the city. But still everything seems to be changing. Gentrification is coming to the old neighborhood, with whites moving in, rents going up, and the old neighbors worrying they'll be pushed out. Maizon grows close to Caroline, a white student whose parents moved into the city so that she could grow up around all sorts of people. Meanwhile, Margaret alternates between jealousy and a desire to be alone. She doesn't like her developing body and becomes bulimic in an attempt to stay thin. At the same time, Maizon's father suddenly appears after having abandoned her to her grandmother as a baby. Maizon, who has always dreamed of his return, finds herself furious at him for thinking he can waltz back into her life after twelve years. As they gradually grow closer, though, Maizon decides to give him another chance.

Throughout these changes, Margaret and Maizon swing back and forth between closeness and estrangement. With the help of caring adults around them, they grow in acceptance of themselves and the inevitable changes in their lives. In the end they realize that their friendship is strong enough to survive change and to grow along with them.

All of Jacqueline Woodson's novels display the sensitivity of an author who still remembers clearly what it was like to be young. The third book in the Maizon and Margaret trilogy, *Between Madison and Palmetto* tackles difficult issues in the lives of young teenage girls and addresses them with honesty and simplicity. In the midst of Maizon's and Margaret's all-too-common growing pains, Woodson also weaves through the themes of loss and forgiveness, change, and black self-esteem. Through the characters of Maizon's father Cooper and her friend Bo, Woodson also explores the special hatred and fear which African American males face and the damage it can do to their psyches. Both of these male characters find their own healing answers, Cooper through long years of personal reflection, and Bo through an all-male, all-black school which emphasizes self-love, self-awareness and self-esteem. The girls' struggles are primary in the story, however, and ring true at every point.

This short, fast-reading book chronicles Margaret's and Maizon's development via brief incidents over the course of a winter and spring. Although the story works as it is, I wish Woodson had gone into more depth in her plot because her characters are so appealing that I wanted to spend more time with them, and her insight into the issues deserves greater elucidation. For instance, *Between Madison and Palmetto* is the first young adult book I've seen to address bulimia in an African American teen, and a beautiful dialogue between Margaret and her mother exposes the underlying issues which drive girls to vomiting and crash diets. However, Woodson does not go far enough, resolving the issue too facilely with a brief parental infusion of love and concern. She has the characters and the insight to explore these issues as few other young adult authors can, and I hope in her development as an author we will see novels with ever-increasing depth and beauty.

Between Madison and Palmetto avoids the silliness of some stories of girls' friendships, while remaining true to central young adult concerns of changing bodies and identities. Its reading level and size make it accessible to younger or weaker readers, and its fast pace will keep them engrossed. Like the other Maizon and Margaret novels, *Between Madison and Palmetto* features a reassuring cast of caring adult characters to help guide the girls, but acknowledges that much of the work of growing up must be done independently. This novel will definitely be a hit with female readers ages ten to fifteen, while young male readers may also find it an interesting exploration of girls' experience.

165. Wright, Richard. *Rite of Passage*. New York: Harper Collins Publishers, 1993. 114 pages. ***

One day fifteen-year-old Johnny Gibbs is feeling wonderful, a report card full of A's in his pocket and an invitation to a free movie on his mind. But disaster awaits him at his Harlem apartment. He is a foster child, taken in at six months of age by the people he considers Ma and Pa. Now the social service authorities have determined that Johnny must move to a new family for no reason whatsoever. When Ma breaks the news to him, Johnny is devastated. Feeling rejected by the only family he has ever known, although they too are devastated, he rejects them in return by running away.

On the street, Johnny quickly falls in with a small gang of street boys, all of them fugitives from foster care. Before Johnny is accepted, he must prove himself by fighting Baldy, the gang's leader. When Johnny thoroughly defeats Baldy, the gang inducts him as their new leader. The boys support themselves by mugging people in Morningside Park. Johnny's first experience with mugging turns his stomach, and he longs for a mother to rescue him from street life. Despite his sensitivity and intelligence, however, he realizes that only hardness will help him survive. The novella closes with Johnny lying in a temporary bed, mourning the knowledge that "he was alone and had to go on alone to make a life for himself by trying to reassemble the shattered fragments of his lonely heart."

Richard Wright began writing *Rite of Passage* in 1945, but it was not published until 1993. The moving transformation of a well-loved and sensitive African American boy into a gang leader and criminal is as relevant today as it was in the 1940s. Unfortunately, many other aspects of the novella are dated, limiting its appeal for modern young adult readers. For instance, the mugging in which Johnny participates is so much less violent than the violence urban teenagers see all around them today that the impact of his "degeneration" may be lost on many modern readers. Similarly, modern readers intimately familiar with extreme poverty, parental abandonment, or worse may feel that Johnny overreacts to the trauma of learning that he is a foster child and being wrenched from his family to live with a new family around the corner. Finally, modern teens may be alienated by the dated language and the teenage characters' sexual naiveté. ("Say, Johnny, do people have babies when they get drunk?" one fifteen-year-old character asks.)

On the other hand, *Rite of Passage* packs the same punch as Wright's other classics, with an immediacy of emotion that pulls the reader in. It is impossible not to sympathize with the protagonist's palpable confusion and despair and, in the process, to start to understand the conditions that draw him into reluctant violence. Most moving is Johnny's vacillation between childhood and adulthood, longing for the safety of a stern, loving mother one instant and hiding his fear to lead his gang the next. The plot is simple and fast moving, spanning only one day and night, with a lifetime of disillusionment packed into twenty-four hours. The story also opens discussion on why this group of African American boys starts breaking the law and what internal processes accompany the transformation from innocence to delinquency. Wright identifies despair, separation from stable families, and a feeling of impotence as primary contributing factors. *Rite of Passage* offers teens, particularly teens in urban settings, an important opportunity to voice their own reflections on the modern reasons for gang participation, youth violence, and illegal activities.

Rite of Passage is accessible to seventh- to eleventh-grade readers. The story may appeal more to boys than girls, since all the main characters are male and their response to the conditions of their lives is singularly male. However, for both girls and boys, this novella is easier to read than Wright's adult novels, both in reading difficulty and in the intensity of the plot. The violence and emotional devastation of *Rite of Passage* is not quite as complete as in *Black Boy* or *Native Son*. Yet because the writing is just as powerful, it offers an excellent young adult introduction to Wright's work.

166. Yarbrough, Camille. *The Shimmershine Queens*. New York: Random House, 1990. 142 pages. ***

Parents' Choice Award, 1990

Separated parents too depressed to pay attention to her and cruel classmates who call her stupid and ugly are destroying ten-year-old Angie Peterson's self-esteem. Angie's mother, Amanda, overwhelmed by the responsibility of caring for an infant and toddler in an uncertain marriage, sometimes cannot even get out of bed. Luckily, ninety-year-old Great Cousin Seatta, visiting New York from Atlanta, penetrates Angie's worries. She gives Angie a mini-psychohistory of African and African American strategies for surviving and thriving under the harshest conditions, including slavery. She explains how some African Americans internalize racism and project their self-hatred onto others. Most importantly, Seatta teaches Angie about the African legacy of the "get-up gift," a dreaming technique to maintain courage and determination and to gain heightened self-respect—the "shimmershine" glow.

With the support of her best friend Michelle, Angie resolves to try to understand people's motivation for mistreating her and to speak up for herself instead of reacting passively. She also vows to "glory in learning" now that she has an appreciation for education's historically special meaning for African Americans. When bully Charlene pushes Angie past her breaking point, Angie shocks everyone by fighting back, and Charlene never again threatens her physically. The other turning point in Angie's developing confidence is her being cast as the storyteller for the new Afrocentric drama and dance troupe at school. The new program, which makes Angie thoroughly excited about school, introduces the meaning and origins of African dances and African American dramas to enhance the students' pride in their heritage.

Despite gains in school, it is not within Angie's power to bring her father back, although she misses him dearly. When it seems he'll miss her major performance, she temporarily quits the troupe and steals makeup from a department store. But her mother, her teacher Ms. Collier, and Michelle straighten her out, warning, "It's hard, but when you feel hurt and rejected, that's the time you have to stand up and show what you made of. You can't go crazy just because somebody hurt you.

. . . I thought you was a shimmershine queen." The pep talk works, and Angie wins everyone's respect with her guts and her performance.

Camille Yarbrough develops a rich and diverse cast of characters in *The Shimmershine Queens*. The impact that parents, teachers, and peers have, deliberately or more often inadvertently, on a young person's self-esteem is depicted with complexity and sensitivity in the character of Angie. The story takes the reader along for Angie's spiritual transformation through slight breakthroughs and assorted setbacks, all of which take place at a believable pace. Angie's empowerment, coupled with her wonderful friend Michelle's self-assurance and vibrancy, will touch young readers to the core.

Angie's parents are, paradoxically, a presence in their absence. Both parents are sympathetically portrayed without diminishing the appropriateness and intensity of Angie's upset with them. Frayed emotionally but clearly devoted to her children and doing the best she can under the circumstances, Amanda wants to protect Angie but also wants Angie to protect herself. Although Kenny, Angie's father, never speaks in the narrative, the reader learns indirectly that his feelings of inadequacy about not providing enough for his family led to flight and defensive anger to protect his delicate ego.

Seatta and Ms. Collier's lessons, which help Angie appreciate her African features and heritage, are articulated in concrete examples and metaphors that make their heartfelt messages immediately accessible to young readers. Their lessons are interrupted by Angie's questions and responses. Angie's engagement with the lessons and her reflection on their messages assist the reader in doing the same. These stylistic devices mask what might come across as preachy and boring if written by a less skilled writer.

The Shimmershine Queens dramatizes the importance of balancing the abuses with the triumphs when educating young people about the past. Initially, the students are resistant to hearing about slavery, eager to sever ancestral ties to slaves, for in learning only about the slaves' exploitation, poverty, and miseducation, the students fear that identifying with slaves will reflect on their abilities and achievements. But by focusing on the slaves' retention of African values and cultural practices and their resistance to being enslaved, Ms. Collier eases the students into connecting with the slaves' experience which, in turn, provides them with positive roots and boosts their self-esteem.

The novel also spotlights the blessings of extended family, good friends, and good neighbors. Camille Yarbrough approaches the taboo topic of internalized self-hatred within the context of safe and secure discussions among family and friends, a narrative strategy that breaks down the reader's potential resistance to the topic.

Regrettably, although *The Shimmershine Queens* focuses on topics relevant to all young adult readers, its protagonist is obviously in elementary school. The novel's analyses of social and political issues will give middle-school and high-school readers much to ponder, but only third-through sixth-grade girls will be able to identify with Angie.

Appendix A:
Publishing Chronology of African American Young Adult Fiction Issued 1968-1993

1951
Boy at the Window. Owen Dodson. Republished in 1970.

1955
Harriet Tubman, Conductor on the Underground Railroad. Ann Petry. Republished in 1971.

1958
South Town. Lorenz Graham.

1964
Tituba of Salem Village. Ann Petry. Republished in 1991.

1965
North Town. Lorenz Graham.

1968
The House of Dies Drear. Virginia Hamilton.
The Soul Brothers and Sister Lou. Kristin Hunter.
Tessie. Jesse Jackson.
To Be a Slave. Julius Lester.

1969
That Ruby. Margery W. Brown.
Whose Town? Lorenz Graham.

1970

Black Folktales. Julius Lester.
Brooklyn Story. Sharon Bell Mathis.
Daddy Was a Number Runner. Louise Meriwether. Republished
     in 1986.
On To Freedom. Mary Kennedy Carter.

1971

His Own Where. June Jordan.
Journey All Alone. Joyce Hansen.
The Planet of Junior Brown. Virginia Hamilton.
The Sickest Don't Always Die the Quickest. Jesse Jackson.

1972

The Fourteenth Cadillac. Jesse Jackson.
Long Journey Home. Julius Lester.
Teacup Full of Roses. Sharon Bell Mathis.
Two Love Stories. Julius Lester.

1973

Conjure Tales. Ray Anthony Shepard.
The Friends. Rosa Guy.
Guests in the Promised Land. Kristin Hunter.
A Hero Ain't Nothin' but a Sandwich. Alice Childress.
Sneakers. Ray Anthony Shepard.
Spirits in the Street. Alexis DeVeaux.

1974

If Beale Street Could Talk. James Baldwin.
Listen for the Fig Tree. Sharon Bell Mathis.
M.C. Higgins, the Great. Virginia Hamilton.
Peaches. Dindga McCannon.
The Second Stone. Margery W. Brown.
Sister. Eloise Greenfield.

1975

Fast Sam, Cool Clyde, and Stuff. Walter Dean Myers.
Ludell. Brenda Wilkinson.
The Survivors. Kristin Hunter.

1976

Arilla Sun Down. Virginia Hamilton.
Marcia. John Steptoe.
Return to South Town. Lorenz Graham.
Roll of Thunder, Hear My Cry. Mildred Taylor.
Ruby. Rosa Guy.
Song of the Trees. Mildred Taylor.

1977

Cartwheels. Sharon Bell Mathis.
Come Home Early, Child. Owen Dodson.
Growin'. Nikki Grimes.
Ludell and Willie. Brenda Wilkinson.
Marvin and Tige. Frankcina Glass.
Mojo and the Russians. Walter Dean Myers.
Phoebe and the General. Judith Berry Griffin.

1978

Edith Jackson. Rosa Guy.
It Ain't All for Nothin'. Walter Dean Myers.
Justice and Her Brothers. Virginia Hamilton.

1979

The Disappearance. Rosa Guy.
The Young Landlords. Walter Dean Myers.

1980

Because We Are. Mildred Pitts Walter.
Don't Explain: A Song for Billie Holiday. Alexis DeVeaux.
Dustland. Virginia Hamilton.
The Gift-Giver. Joyce Hansen.
Just an Overnight Guest. Eleanora E. Tate.

1980 (con't.)

Ludell's New York Time. Brenda Wilkinson.
Something to Count On. Emily Moore.
Squarehead and Me. Henry Louis Haynes.

1981

The Gathering. Virginia Hamilton.
Hoops. Walter Dean Myers.
The Legend of Tarik. Walter Dean Myers.
Let the Circle Be Unbroken. Mildred Taylor.
Lou in the Limelight. Kristin Hunter.
Rainbow Jordan. Alice Childress.
This Strange New Feeling. Julius Lester.
Wilhelmina Jones, Future Star. Dindga McCannon.

1982

A Girl Called Bob and a Horse Called Yoki. Barbara
     Campbell.
The Girl on the Outside. Mildred Pitts Walter.
Home Boy. Joyce Hansen.
Listen, Children: An Anthology of Black Literature. Dorothy
     Strickland.
Marked by Fire. Joyce Carol Thomas.
Sweet Whispers, Brother Rush. Virginia Hamilton.
Won't Know Till I Get There. Walter Dean Myers.

1983

Bright Shadow. Joyce Carol Thomas.
The Magical Adventures of Pretty Pearl. Virginia Hamilton.
New Guys Around the Block. Rosa Guy.
Willie Bea and the Time the Martians Landed. Virginia
     Hamilton.

1984

Circle of Gold. Candy Dawson Boyd.
A Little Love. Virginia Hamilton.
Motown and Didi. Walter Dean Myers.

1984 (con't.)

The Outside Shot. Walter Dean Myers.
Paris, Pee Wee, and Big Dog. Rosa Guy.

1985

Breadsticks and Blessing Places. Candy Dawson Boyd.
Junius Over Far. Virginia Hamilton.
The People Could Fly: American Black Folktales. Virginia
    Hamilton.
Trouble's Child. Mildred Pitts Walter.

1986

The Golden Pasture. Joyce Carol Thomas.
Water Girl. Joyce Carol Thomas.
Which Way Freedom? Joyce Hansen.
Yellow Bird and Me. Joyce Hansen.

1987

And I Heard a Bird Sing. Rosa Guy.
Charlie Pippin. Candy Dawson Boyd.
Crystal. Walter Dean Myers.
The Mystery of Drear House. Virginia Hamilton.
Not Separate, Not Equal. Brenda Wilkinson.
Sweet Illusions. Walter Dean Myers.
A White Romance. Virginia Hamilton.

1988

Anthony Burns: The Defeat and Triumph of a Fugitive Slave.
    Virginia Hamilton.
Blue Tights. Rita Williams-Garcia.
Fallen Angels. Walter Dean Myers.
Journey. Joyce Carol Thomas.
Me, Mop, and the Moondance Kid. Walter Dean Myers.
Oh, Brother. Johnniece Marshall Wilson.
Scorpions. Walter Dean Myers.
The Secret of Gumbo Grove. Eleanora E. Tate.
Whose Side Are You On? Emily Moore.

1989

The Bells of Christmas. Virginia Hamilton.
The Friendship and the Gold Cadillac. Mildred Taylor.
The Girls of Summer. Anita Cornwell.
The Shimmershine Queens. Camille Yarbrough.
The Ups and Downs of Carl Davis III. Rosa Guy.
Willy's Summer Dream. Kay Brown.

1990

Abdul and the Designer Tennis Shoes. William McDaniels.
Cousins. Virginia Hamilton.
Freedom Songs. Yvette Moore.
Last Summer with Maizon. Jacqueline Woodson.
The Mouse Rap. Walter Dean Myers.
The Road to Memphis. Mildred Taylor.
Robin on His Own. Johnniece Marshall Wilson.
Thank You, Dr. Martin Luther King, Jr.! Eleanora E. Tate.

1991

Children of the Fire. Harriette Gillem Robinet.
The Dear One. Jacqueline Woodson.
Fast Talk on a Slow Track. Rita Williams-Garcia.
The Future and Other Stories. Ralph Cheo Thurmon.
Just My Luck. Emily Moore.

1992

The Dark Thirty: Southern Tales of the Supernatural. Patricia
    C. McKissack.
Down in the Piney Woods. Ethel Footman Smothers.
18 Pine St. #1: Sort of Sisters. Stacie Johnson.
18 Pine St. #2: The Party. Stacie Johnson.
18 Pine St. #3: The Prince. Stacie Johnson.
18 Pine St. #4: The Test. Stacie Johnson.
Fish and Bones. Ray Prather.
Front Porch Stories at the One-Room School. Eleanora E. Tate.
Just Like Martin. Ossie Davis.
Koya Delaney and the Good Girl Blues. Eloise Greenfield.

1992 (con't.)

Maizon at Blue Hill. Jacqueline Woodson.
Mama, I Want to Sing. Vy Higginsen.
Mississippi Bridge. Mildred Taylor.
Mop, Moondance, and the Nagasaki Knights. Walter Dean
      Myers.
The Music of Summer. Rosa Guy.
NEATE To the Rescue!: Together Forever. Debbi Chocolate.
Poor Girl, Rich Girl. Johnniece Marshall Wilson.
The Righteous Revenge of Artemis Bonner. Walter Dean Myers.
Somewhere in the Darkness. Walter Dean Myers.
When the Nightingale Sings. Joyce Carol Thomas.

1993

Between Madison and Palmetto. Jacqueline Woodson.
Chevrolet Saturdays. Candy Dawson Boyd.
Definitely Cool. Brenda Wilkinson.
18 Pine St. #5: Sky Man. Stacie Johnson.
18 Pine St. #6: Fashion by Tasha. Stacie Johnson.
18 Pine St. #7: Intensive Care. Stacie Johnson.
18 Pine St. #8: Dangerous Games. Stacie Johnson.
18 Pine St. #9: Cindy's Baby. Stacie Johnson.
*Many Thousand Gone: African Americans from Slavery to
      Freedom.* Virginia Hamilton.
Plain City. Virginia Hamilton.
Rite of Passage. Richard Wright.
The Sweetest Berry on the Bush. Nubia Kai.
Toning the Sweep. Angela Johnson.
Where Do I Go From Here? Valerie Wilson Wesley.

Appendix B:
Award-Winning Authors in This Bibliography

"Other" indicates that the author won an award for the text of a children's or nonfiction young adult book which did not fit the requirements for inclusion in this bibliography.

Baldwin, James
American Library Association Notable Books for Children and Young Adults: *If Beale Street Could Talk,* 1974

Boyd, Candy Dawson
Coretta Scott King Honor Book: *Circle of Gold,* 1985

Childress, Alice
American Library Association Notable Books for Children and Young Adults: *A Hero Ain't Nothin' but a Sandwich,* 1973; *Rainbow Jordan,* 1981
Coretta Scott King Honor Book: *A Hero Ain't Nothin' but a Sandwich,* 1974; *Rainbow Jordan,* 1982
Jane Addams Honor Book: *A Hero Ain't Nothin' but a Sandwich,* 1974
Lewis Carroll Shelf Award: *A Hero Ain't Nothin' but a Sandwich,* 1975
School Library Journal Best Books for Children and Young Adults: *A Hero Ain't Nothin' but A Sandwich,* 1973; *Rainbow Jordan,* 1981

Chocolate, Debbi
Parents' Choice Award: other, 1992

Davis, Ossie
American Library Association Notable Books for Children and
    Young Adults: other,1978
Coretta Scott King Award: other, 1979
Jane Addams Honor Book: other, 1979

DeVeaux, Alexis
American Library Association Notable Books for Children and
    Young Adults: other, 1987
Coretta Scott King Honor Book: *Don't Explain: A Song of Billie
    Holiday*, 1981; other, 1988

Glass, Frankcina
American Library Association Notable Books for Children and
    Young Adults: *Marvin and Tige*, 1978
Coretta Scott King Honor Book: *Marvin and Tige*, 1978

Graham, Lorenz
American Library Association Notable Books for Children and
    Young Adults: other, 1975
Boston Globe-Horn Book Magazine Honor List: others, 1971,
    1976
Coretta Scott King Honor Book: other, 1971

Greenfield, Eloise
American Library Association Notable Books for Children and
    Young Adults: other, 1975, 1978, 1981, 1988, 1989, 1991,
    1992
Boston Globe-Horn Book Magazine Honor List: other, 1975,
    1980, 1991
Carter G. Woodson Book Award: other, 1974
Coretta Scott King Award: other, 1978

Greenfield, Eloise (con't.)

Coretta Scott King Honor Book: other, 1976, 1978, 1980, 1981, 1982, 1990, 1992

Jane Addams Book Award: other, 1976

New York Times Best Books for Children and Young Adults: other, 1978, 1989

School Library Journal Best Books for Children and Young Adults: other, 1988

Grimes, Nikki

Coretta Scott King Honor Book: other, 1979

New York Times Best Books for Children and Young Adults: other, 1978

Guy, Rosa

American Library Association Notable Books for Children and Young Adults: *The Friends*, 1973; *Ruby*, 1976; *Edith Jackson*, 1978; *The Disappearance*, 1979; other, 1981; *The Music of Summer*, 1993

Parents' Choice Award: *New Guys Around the Block*, 1983

School Library Journal Best Books for Children and Young Adults: *The Friends*, 1973

Hamilton, Virginia

American Library Association Notable Books for Children and Young Adults: *M.C. Higgins, the Great*, 1974; *Arilla Sun Down*, 1976; *The Gathering*, 1981; *Sweet Whispers, Brother Rush*, 1982; *The Magical Adventures of Pretty Pearl*, 1983; *Willie Bea and the Time the Martians Landed*, 1983; *The People Could Fly: American Black Folktales*, 1985; *Anthony Burns: The Defeat and Triumph of a Fugitive Slave*, 1988; other, 1988; *The Bells of Christmas*, 1989; *Cousins*, 1991; *Many Thousand Gone: African Americans from Slavery to Freedom*, 1993; *Plain City*, 1993

Boston Globe-Horn Book Magazine Award: *M.C. Higgins, the Great*, 1974; *Sweet Whispers, Brother Rush*, 1982

Hamilton, Virginia (con't.)

Boston Globe-Horn Book Magazine Honor List: *A Little Love*, 1984; *The People Could Fly: American Black Folktales*, 1986; *Anthony Burns: The Defeat and Triumph of a Fugitive Slave*, 1988; other, 1989; *Cousins*, 1991

Coretta Scott King Award: *Sweet Whispers, Brother Rush*, 1983;*The People Could Fly: American Black Folktales*, 1986; *Many Thousand Gone: African Americans from Slavery to Freedom*, 1993

Coretta Scott King Honor Book: *Justice and Her Brothers*, 1979; *The Magical Adventures of Pretty Pearl*, 1984; *A Little Love*, 1985; *Junius Over Far*, 1986; *Anthony Burns: The Defeat and Triumph of a Fugitive Slave*, 1989; *The Bells of Christmas*, 1990

E.A. Poe Award: *The House of Dies Drear*, 1968

International Board on Books for Young People Honor List: *Sweet Whispers, Brother Rush*, 1984; *The People Could Fly: American Black Folktales*, 1986

International Reading Association Hans Christian Andersen Award: 1992

Jane Addams Book Award: *Anthony Burns: The Defeat and Triumph of a Fugitive Slave*, 1989

John Newbery Medal Award: *M.C. Higgins, the Great*, 1975

John Newbery Honor Book: *The Planet of Junior Brown*, 1972; *Sweet Whispers, Brother Rush*, 1983; other, 1989

Lewis Carroll Shelf Award: *The Planet of Junior Brown*, 1972; *M.C. Higgins, the Great*, 1975

National Book Award: *M.C. Higgins, the Great*, 1975

New York Times Best Books for Children and Young Adults: *The House of Dies Drear*, 1968; *M.C. Higgins, the Great*, 1974; *Sweet Whispers, Brother Rush*, 1982; *The Magical Adventures of Pretty Pearl*, 1983; *Willie Bea and the Time the Martians Landed*, 1983; *The People Could Fly: American Black Folktales*, 1985; *Anthony Burns: The Defeat and Triumph of a Fugitive Slave*, 1988; other, 1988; *Cousins*, 1990

Parents' Choice Award: *The Magical Adventures of Pretty Pearl*, 1983

Hamilton, Virginia (con't.)

Regina Medal: 1990

School Library Journal Best Books for Children and Young Adults: *The Planet of Junior Brown*, 1971; other, 1974; *Arilla Sun Down*, 1976; *Sweet Whispers, Brother Rush*, 1982; *The People Could Fly*, 1985; *Anthony Burns: The Defeat and Triumph of a Fugitive Slave*, 1988; *Many Thousand Gone: African Americans from Slavery to Freedom*, 1993

Hansen, Joyce

American Library Association Notable Books for Children and Young Adults: *Which Way Freedom?*, 1986; *Out From This Place*, 1988

Coretta Scott King Honor Book: *Which Way Freedom?*, 1987

Parents' Choice Award: *Yellow Bird and Me*, 1986

Hunter, Kristin

American Library Association Notable Books for Children and Young Adults: *The Survivors*, 1975

Christopher Award: *Guests in the Promised Land*, 1974

Coretta Scott King Honor Book: *Guests in the Promised Land*, 1974; *Lou in the Limelight*, 1982

Lewis Carroll Shelf Award: *The Soul Brothers and Sister Lou*, 1971

Jackson, Jesse

Carter G. Woodson Award: other, 1975

Johnson, Angela

American Library Association Notable Books for Children and Young Adults: other, 1990; *Toning the Sweep*, 1993; other, 1993

Coretta Scott King Award: *Toning the Sweep*, 1993

Coretta Scott King Honor Book: other, 1991

New York Times Best Books for Children and Young Adults: other, 1989

Johnson, Angela (con't.)

Parents' Choice Award: other, 1989
School Library Journal Best Books for Children and Young
Adults: other, 1989;*Toning the Sweep*, 1993

Jordan, June

American Library Association Notable Books for Children and
Young Adults: other, 1975
Coretta Scott King Honor Book: other, 1971
School Library Journal Best Books for Children and Young
Adults: *His Own Where*, 1971

Lester, Julius

American Library Association Notable Books for Children and
Young Adults: other, 1987, 1988, 1989, 1990
Boston Globe-Horn Book Magazine Honor List: other, 1988, 1989
Coretta Scott King Honor Book: *This Strange New Feeling*,
1982; other, 1988
John Newbery Honor Book: *To Be a Slave*, 1969
Lewis Carroll Shelf Award: other, 1970; *Long Journey Home*,
1972; other, 1973
New York Times Best Books for Children and Young Adults: *To
Be a Slave*, 1968; other, 1972, 1987
Parents' Choice Award: *This Strange New Feeling*, 1981; other,
1987, 1990
School Library Journal Best Books for Children and Young
Adults: *To Be A Slave*, 1968; other, 1972; *Long Journey
Home*, 1972; other, 1976, 1988

Mathis, Sharon Bell

American Library Association Notable Books for Children and
Young Adults: *Listen for the Fig Tree*, 1974; other, 1975
Boston Globe-Horn Book Magazine Honor List: other, 1975
Coretta Scott King Award: other, 1974
Council on Interracial Books for Children Award: other, 1969
John Newbery Honor Book: other, 1976

Mathis, Sharon Bell (con't.)
School Library Journal Best Books for Children and Young Adults: other, 1975

McKissack, Patricia
American Library Association Notable Books for Children and Young Adults: other, 1988, 1989, 1992; *The Dark Thirty: Southern Tales of the Supernatural*, 1992
Boston Globe-Horn Book Magazine Honor List: other, 1987, 1993
Carter G. Woodson Book Award: other, 1989
Coretta Scott King Award: other, 1990; *The Dark Thirty: Southern Tales of the Supernatural*, 1993
Coretta Scott King Honor Book: other, 1993
Jane Addams Award: other, 1990
New York Times Best Books for Children and Young Adults: other, 1986, 1988
Parents' Choice Award: other, 1989, 1992, 1993
Randolph Caldecott Honor Book: other, 1989
School Library Journal Best Books for Children and Young Adults: other, 1986; *The Dark Thirty: Southern Tales of the Supernatural*, 1992

Meriwether, Louise
School Library Journal Best Books for Children and Young Adults: *Daddy Was A Number Runner*, 1970

Myers, Walter Dean
American Library Association Notable Books for Children and Young Adults: *Fast Sam, Cool Clyde, and Stuff*, 1975; *It Ain't All for Nothin'*, 1978; *The Young Landlords*, 1979; *Hoops*, 1981; *Scorpions*, 1988; *The Mouse Rap*, 1990; *The Righteous Revenge of Artemis Bonner*, 1992; *Somewhere in the Darkness*, 1992; other, 1992; 1993
Boston Globe-Horn Book Magazine Honor List: *Fallen Angels*, 1988; other, 1991; *Somewhere in the Darkness*, 1992
Coretta Scott King Award: *The Young Landlords*, 1980; *Motown and Didi*, 1985; *Fallen Angels*, 1989; other, 1992

Myers, Walter Dean (con't.)

Coretta Scott King Honor Book: *Fast Sam, Cool Clyde, and Stuff*, 1976; *Somewhere in the Darkness*, 1993; other, 1993

Golden Kite Award: other, 1991

Jane Addams Honor Book: other, 1992

John Newbery Honor Book: *Scorpions*, 1989

Margaret A. Edwards Award: 1993

New York Times Best Books for Children and Young Adults: *Motown and Didi*, 1984; *Scorpions*, 1988

Parents' Choice Award: *Won't Know Till I Get There*, 1982; *The Outside Shot*, 1984; other, 1985;*Crystal*, 1987; *Fallen Angels*, 1988; *The Mouse Rap*, 1990; *The Righteous Revenge of Artemis Bonner*, 1992

School Library Journal Best Books for Children and Young Adults: *Fallen Angels*, 1988; *Somewhere in the Darkness*, 1992

Prather, Ray

School Library Journal Best Books for Children and Young Adults: *Fish and Bones*, 1992

Steptoe, John

American Library Association Notable Books for Children and Young Adults: other, 1987

Boston Globe-Horn Book Magazine Honor List: other, 1987

Lewis Carroll Shelf Award: other, 1978

New York Times Best Books for Children and Young Adults, 1969, 1984: other, 1987

Randolph Caldecott Medal: other, 1984

Randolph Caldecott Honor Book: other, 1985, 1987

School Library Journal Best Books for Children and Young Adults: other, 1987

Tate, Eleanora

Parents' Choice Award: *The Secret of Gumbo Grove*, 1987

Taylor, Mildred

American Library Association Notable Books for Children and Young Adults: *Roll of Thunder, Hear My Cry*, 1976; *Let the Circle Be Unbroken*, 1981; *The Friendship and the Gold Cadillac*, 1989; *The Road to Memphis*, 1990

Boston Globe-Horn Book Magazine Award: *The Friendship and the Gold Cadillac*, 1989

Children's Book Council Honor Program Award, 1988

Christopher Award: *The Friendship*, 1989; *Mississippi Bridge*, 1992

Coretta Scott King Award: *Let the Circle Be Unbroken*, 1982; *The Friendship and the Gold Cadillac*, 1988; *The Road to Memphis*, 1991

Coretta Scott King Honor Book: *Song of the Trees*, 1976; *Roll of Thunder, Hear My Cry*, 1977

Council on Interracial Books for Children Award: *Song of the Trees*, 1973

Jane Addams Honor Book: *Song of the Trees*, 1976; *Roll of Thunder, Hear My Cry*, 1977; *Let the Circle Be Unbroken*, 1982; *Mississippi Bridge*, 1992

John Newbery Medal Award: *Roll of Thunder, Hear My Cry*, 1977

New York Times Best Books for Children and Young Adults: *Roll of Thunder, Hear My Cry*, 1976; *The Friendship and the Gold Cadillac*, 1987

Thomas, Joyce Carol

American Book Award: *Marked By Fire*, 1983

Coretta Scott King Honor Book: *Bright Shadow*, 1984, other, 1993

Walter, Mildred Pitts

Christopher Award: other, 1993

Coretta Scott King Award: other, 1987

Coretta Scott King Honor Book: *Because We Are*, 1981; *Trouble's Child*, 1986; other, 1993

Walter, Mildred Pitts (con't.)

New York Times Best Books for Children and Young Adults:
  other, 1979, 1983
Parents' Choice Award: *Because We Are*, 1980; other, 1985

Wilkinson, Brenda

American Library Association Notable Books for Children and
  Young Adults: *Ludell and Willie*, 1977
School Library Journal Best Books for Children and Young
  Adults: *Ludell*, 1975; *Ludell and Willie*, 1977

Williams-Garcia, Rita

American Library Association Notable Books for Children and
  Young Adults: *Fast Talk on a Slow Track*, 1991

Woodson, Jacqueline

American Library Association Notable Books for Children and
  Young Adults: *Maizon at Blue Hill*, 1992

Yarbrough, Camille

Parents' Choice Award: *The Shimmershine Queens*, 1990

Appendix C:
Award-Winning Books in This Bibliography

Anthony Burns: The Defeat and Triumph of a Fugitive Slave

American Library Association Notable Books for Children and Young Adults, 1988; Boston Globe-Horn Book Magazine Honor List, 1988; Coretta Scott King Honor Book, 1989; Jane Addams Book Award, 1989; New York Times Best Books for Children and Young Adults, 1988; School Library Journal Best Books for Children and Young Adults, 1988

Arilla Sun Down

American Library Association Notable Books for Children and Young Adults, 1976; School Library Journal Best Books for Children and Young Adults, 1976

Because We Are

Coretta Scott King Honor Book, 1981; Parents' Choice Award, 1980

The Bells of Christmas

American Library Association Notable Books for Children and Young Adults, 1989; Coretta Scott King Honor Book, 1990

Bright Shadow

Coretta Scott King Honor Book, 1984

Circle of Gold
Coretta Scott King Honor Book, 1985

Cousins
American Library Association Notable Books for Children and Young Adults, 1991; Boston Globe-Horn Book Magazine Honor List, 1991; New York Times Best Books for Children and Young Adults, 1990

Crystal
Parents' Choice Award, 1987

Daddy Was a Number Runner
School Library Journal Best Books for Children and Young Adults, 1970

The Dark Thirty: Southern Tales of the Supernatural
American Library Association Notable Books for Children and Young Adults, 1992; Coretta Scott King Award, 1993; School Library Journal Best Books for Children and Young Adults, 1992

The Disappearance
American Library Association Notable Books for Children and Young Adults, 1979

Don't Explain: A Song of Billie Holiday
Coretta Scott King Honor Book, 1981

Edith Jackson
American Library Association Notable Books for Children and Young Adults, 1978

Fallen Angels

Boston Globe-Horn Book Magazine Honor List, 1988; Coretta Scott King Award, 1989; Parents' Choice Award, 1988; School Library Journal Best Books for Children and Young Adults, 1988

Fast Sam, Cool Clyde, and Stuff

American Library Association Notable Books for Children and Young Adults, 1975; Coretta Scott King Honor Book, 1976

Fast Talk on a Slow Track

American Library Association Notable Books for Children and Young Adults, 1991

Fish and Bones

School Library Journal Best Books for Children and Young Adults, 1992

The Friends

American Library Association Notable Books for Children and Young Adults, 1973; School Library Journal Best Books for Children and Young Adults, 1973

The Friendship and the Gold Cadillac

American Library Association Notable Books for Children and Young Adults, 1989; Boston Globe-Horn Book Magazine Honor List, 1989; Christopher Award, 1989; Coretta Scott King Award, 1988; New York Times Best Books for Children and Young Adults, 1987

The Gathering

American Library Association Notable Books for Children and Young Adults, 1981

Guests in the Promised Land

Christopher Award, 1974; Coretta Scott King Honor Book, 1974

A Hero Ain't Nothin' but a Sandwich

American Library Association Notable Books for Children and Young Adults, 1973; Coretta Scott King Honor Book, 1974; Jane Addams Honor Book, 1974; Lewis Carroll Shelf Award, 1975; School Library Journal Best Books for Children and Young Adults, 1973

His Own Where

School Library Journal Best Books for Children and Young Adults, 1971

Hoops

American Library Association Notable Books for Children and Young Adults, 1981

The House of Dies Drear

E.A. Poe Award, 1968; New York Times Best Books for Children and Young Adults, 1968

If Beale Street Could Talk

American Library Association Notable Books for Children and Young Adults, 1974

It Ain't All for Nothin'

American Library Association Notable Books for Children and Young Adults, 1978

Junius Over Far

Coretta Scott King Honor Book, 1986

Justice and Her Brothers

Coretta Scott King Honor Book, 1979

Let the Circle Be Unbroken

American Library Association Notable Books for Children and Young Adults, 1981; Coretta Scott King Award, 1982; Jane Addams Honor Book, 1982

Listen for the Fig Tree

American Library Association Notable Books for Children and Young Adults, 1974

A Little Love

Boston Globe-Horn Book Magazine Honor List, 1984; Coretta Scott King Honor Book, 1985

Long Journey Home

Lewis Carroll Shelf Award, 1972; School Library Journal Best Books for Children and Young Adults, 1972

Lou in the Limelight

Coretta Scott King Honor Book, 1982

Ludell

School Library Journal Best Books for Children and Young Adults, 1975

Ludell and Willie

American Library Association Notable Books for Children and Young Adults, 1977; School Library Journal Best Books for Children and Young Adults, 1977

The Magical Adventures of Pretty Pearl

American Library Association Notable Books for Children and Young Adults, 1983; Coretta Scott King Honor Book, 1984; New York Times Best Books for Children and Young Adults, 1983; Parents' Choice Award, 1983

Maizon at Blue Hill

American Library Association Notable Books for Children and Young Adults, 1992

Many Thousand Gone: African Americans from Slavery to Freedom

American Library Association Notable Books for Children and Young Adults, 1993; Coretta Scott King Award, 1993; School Library Journal Best Books for Children and Young Adults, 1993

Marked by Fire

American Book Award, 1983

Marvin and Tige

American Library Association Notable Books for Children and Young Adults, 1978; Coretta Scott King Honor Book, 1978

M.C. Higgins, the Great

American Library Association Notable Books for Children and Young Adults, 1974; Boston Globe-Horn Book Magazine Award, 1974; John Newbery Medal Award, 1975; Lewis Carroll Shelf Award, 1975; National Book Award, 1975; New York Times Best Books for Children and Young Adults, 1974

Mississippi Bridge

Christopher Award, 1992; Jane Addams Honor Book, 1992

Motown and Didi

Coretta Scott King Award, 1985; New York Times Best Books for Children and Young Adults, 1984

The Mouse Rap

American Library Association Notable Books for Children and Young Adults, 1990; Parents' Choice Award, 1990

The Music of Summer
American Library Association Notable Books for Children and Young Adults, 1993

New Guys Around the Block
Parents' Choice Award, 1983

Out From This Place
American Library Association Notable Books for Children and Young Adults, 1988

The Outside Shot
Parents' Choice Award, 1984

The People Could Fly: American Black Folktales
American Library Association Notable Books for Children and Young Adults, 1985; Boston Globe-Horn Book Magazine Honor List, 1985; Coretta Scott King Award, 1986; International Board on Books for Young People Honor List, 1986; New York Times Best Books for Children and Young Adults, 1985; School Library Journal Best Books for Children and Young Adults, 1985

Plain City
American Library Association Notable Books for Children and Young Adults, 1993

The Planet of Junior Brown
John Newbery Honor Book, 1972; Lewis Carroll Shelf Award, 1972; School Library Journal Best Books for Children and Young Adults, 1971

Rainbow Jordan
American Library Association Notable Books for Children and Young Adults, 1981; Coretta Scott King Honor Book, 1982; School Library Journal Best Books for Children and Young Adults, 1981

The Righteous Revenge of Artemis Bonner

American Library Association Notable Books for Children and Young Adults, 1992; Parents' Choice Award, 1992

The Road to Memphis

American Library Association Notable Books for Children and Young Adults, 1990; Coretta Scott King Award, 1991

Roll of Thunder, Hear My Cry

American Library Association Notable Books for Children and Young Adults, 1976; Coretta Scott King Honor Book, 1977; Jane Addams Honor Book, 1977; John Newbery Medal Award, 1977; New York Times Best Books for Children and Young Adults, 1976

Ruby

American Library Association Notable Books for Children and Young Adults, 1976

Scorpions

American Library Association Notable Books for Children and Young Adults, 1988; John Newbery Honor Book, 1989; New York Times Best Books for Children and Young Adults, 1988

The Secret of Gumbo Grove

Parents' Choice Award, 1987

The Shimmershine Queens

Parents' Choice Award, 1990

Somewhere in the Darkness

American Library Association Notable Books for Children and Young Adults, 1992; Boston Globe-Horn Book Magazine Honor List, 1992; Coretta Scott King Honor Book, 1993; School Library Journal Best Books for Children and Young Adults, 1992

Song of the Trees
Coretta Scott King Honor Book, 1976; Council on Interracial Books for Children Award, 1973; Jane Addams Honor Book, 1976

The Soul Brothers and Sister Lou
Lewis Carroll Shelf Award, 1971

The Survivors
American Library Association Notable Books for Children and Young Adults, 1975

Sweet Whispers, Brother Rush
American Library Association Notable Books for Children and Young Adults, 1982; Boston Globe-Horn Book Magazine Award, 1982; Coretta Scott King Award, 1983; International Board on Books for Young People Honor List, 1983; John Newbery Honor Book, 1983; New York Times Best Books for Children and Young Adults, 1982; School Library Journal Best Books for Children and Young Adults, 1982

This Strange New Feeling
Coretta Scott King Honor Book, 1982; Parents' Choice Award, 1981

To Be a Slave
John Newbery Honor Book, 1969; New York Times Best Books for Children and Young Adults, 1968; School Library Journal Best Books for Children and Young Adults, 1968

Toning the Sweep
American Library Association Notable Books for Children and Young Adults, 1993; Coretta Scott King Honor Book, 1993; School Library Journal Best Books for Children and Young Adults, 1993

Trouble's Child
Coretta Scott King Honor Book, 1986

Which Way Freedom?
American Library Association Notable Books for Children and Young Adults, 1986; Coretta Scott King Honor Book, 1987

Willie Bea and the Time the Martians Landed
American Library Association Notable Books for Children and Young Adults, 1983; New York Times Best Books for Children and Young Adults, 1983

Won't Know Till I Get There
Parents' Choice Award, 1982

Yellow Bird and Me
Parents' Choice Award, 1986

The Young Landlords
American Library Association Notable Books for Children and Young Adults, 1979; Coretta Scott King Award, 1980

Index of Authors by Book Number

Index of Book Titles by Book Number